Rival Queens

Rival Queens

*Actresses, Performance,
and the Eighteenth-Century
British Theater*

Felicity Nussbaum

PENN

UNIVERSITY OF PENNSYLVANIA PRESS

PHILADELPHIA • OXFORD

Copyright © 2010 University of Pennsylvania Press

All rights reserved. Except for brief quotations used for purposes of review or scholarly citation, none of this book may be reproduced in any form by any means without written permission from the publisher.

Published by
University of Pennsylvania Press
Philadelphia, Pennsylvania 19104-4112

Printed in the United States of America on acid-free paper
10 9 8 7 6 5 4 3 2 1

Library of Congress Cataloging-in-Publication Data

Nussbaum, Felicity.
 Rival queens : actresses, performance, and the eighteenth-century British theater / Felicity Nussbaum.
   p. cm.
  ISBN 978-0-8122-4233-1 (alk. paper)
  Includes bibliographical references and index.
  1. Women in the theater—Great Britain—History—18th century. 2. Theater and society—Great Britain—History—18th century. 3. Actresses—Great Britain—Biography.
  PN2582.W65 N87   2010
   792.02'8082094109033—dc22   2009029041

For my students

CONTENTS

Introduction: At Stage's Edge 1

CHAPTER 1
The Economics of Celebrity 31

CHAPTER 2
"Real, Beautiful Women": Rival Queens 61

Chapter 3
Actresses' Memoirs: Exceptional Virtue 92

CHAPTER 4
Actresses and Patrons: The Theatrical Contract 122

CHAPTER 5
The Actress and Performative Property: Catherine Clive 151

CHAPTER 6
The Actress, Travesty, and Nation: Margaret Woffington 189

CHAPTER 7
The Actress and Material Femininity: Frances Abington 226

EPILOGUE: CONTRACTED VIRTUE 265

NOTES 285
BIBLIOGRAPHY 339
INDEX 365
ACKNOWLEDGMENTS 381

ILLUSTRATIONS

1. *Critical Balance of the Performers at Drury-Lane Theatre*   2
2. "Scale of Tragedians"   4
3. "Scale of Comedians"   5
4. "David Garrick and Mrs. Pritchard in The Suspicious Husband"   7
5. "Mr. Smith in the Character of Alexander"   69
6. "Rival Queens of Covent Garden and Drury Lane"   77
7. Possibly Nell Gwyn   96
8. "Mrs. Oldfield the celebrated Comedian"   102
9. "Residence of the late Mrs. Clive at Twickenham"   154
10. "Mrs. Clive from the Picture at Strawberry Hill"   155
11. Mrs. Clive as the Fine Lady of *Lethe*   157
12. "Woffington's First Interview with Manager Rich"   190
13. "Mrs. Margaret Woffington"   192
14. *The Female Volunteer*   209
15. "Mrs. Barry as Sir Harry Wildair"   211
16. "Frances Abington as Lady Bab Lardoon"   232
17. "Mrs. Abington in the Character of Aurelia"   243
18. "Mrs. Abington as Estifania"   251
19. "Miss Younge, Epilogue to *The Runaway*"   253
20. "Mrs. Wilson, Prologue to *Polly Honeycombe*"   254
21. "Mrs. Yates, Epilogue to *The Earl of Warwick*"   255
22. "Mrs. Abington, Epilogue to the *Tragedy of Zingis*"   256
23. "Mrs. Abington as Miss Prue"   262
24. "David Garrick"   263
25. "Miss Younge in the Character of Hermione"   267
26. "Mrs. Yates in the Character of Calista"   268
27. "Miss Younge in the Character of Artemis[i]a"   269
28. "Mrs. Lessingham in the Character of Oriana"   270
29. "Portraits in the Character of the Muses"   275

Introduction: At Stage's Edge

> [Garrick's] jealousy and envy were unbounded; he hated Mrs Clive till she quitted the stage, and then cried her up to the skies to depress Mrs Abingdon. He did not love Mrs Pritchard, and with more reason, for there was more spirit and originality in her Beatrice than in his Benedict.
> —Correspondence from Horace Walpole to Lady Ossory, 1 February 1779

> Mrs. Pritchard was Garrick's rival in every scene [of *Much Ado About Nothing*]; which of them deserved the laurel most was never decided.
> —Arthur Murphy, *Life of Garrick* (1801)

IN THE HEYDAY of David Garrick's management of Drury-Lane Theatre (1747–76), numerically coded charts provided playgoers with comparative ratings of their favorite performers. The arithmetical scale offers a fascinating glimpse into the qualities that eighteenth-century theater audiences valued most highly in the actors of both sexes. *A Critical Balance of the Performers at Drury-Lane Theatre* (1765), a broadsheet costing a shilling, printed a table quantifying each actor's figure, grace, spirit and ease, sensibility, taste, dignity, manners, expression, pantomime, low and genteel humor, elocution, voice, dress, and "noise"[1] (Figure 1). No actor is assigned a total score, and the anonymous reviewer, leaving the tables blank in a few categories, apportions the numbers somewhat erratically. The actor Mr. Clough, for example, is granted 16 points for pantomime but allotted no points in any other category. Similarly, a solid 20 points damns Mrs. Bennet, who earns no other grades, for "noise." Mrs. Palmer, whose role as Statira in Nathaniel Lee's *The Rival Queens* is specifically mentioned, is awarded 8 points each for figure and dress. Most

Figure 1. *A Critical Balance of the Performers at Drury-Lane Theatre. For the last Season 1765.* London, 1765.

instructive in regard to the relative merits of actors and actresses is the fact that women players earned the highest rankings of the forty-one players across all the categories. While Mrs. Yates was awarded 20 points in each of seven categories, Mrs. Cibber and Mrs. Pritchard followed closely behind with six scores of 20 points each. Especially noteworthy regarding the centrality of women to the eighteenth-century theater's success, in spite of the limitations of a dramaturgy usually regarded as lackluster, is that the three highest *total* scores went to Mrs. Pritchard (188), Mrs.Yates (173), and Mrs. Cibber (172), who were trailed by the male actors Mr. Yates (162), Mr. King (161), and Mr. Powell (158). In other words, when the relative merits of thespians were set side by side in a dozen categories, several star actresses outranked *all* of the men. The women appear, then, to have been not only superior actors but more versatile in their performances. None of the tragic women players is assigned marks for "low humor" or "noise," obviously undesirable qualities when performing in that mournful genre, though Mrs. Pritchard is inexplicably awarded 20 points for "pantomime, dumb-shew."

Another intriguing set of grading scales, published in *The Theatrical Review* for the 1757–58 season, ranked tragedians and comedians separately, and reflects the Enlightenment urge toward quantification as a measure of personal value[2] (Figures 2,3). Although both tragic and comic players were measured "in this stage-mad age" (5) according to their genius and judgment in the alphabetically arranged chart, tragedians were distinguished for their proper use of expression, action, and voice, and comedians assessed on the basis of *vis comica* (comic power or talent) and variety. In tragedy Garrick stood supreme with a total of 88 points, but Susannah Cibber ran a close second with a tally of 82 points. Hester Thrale, a discriminating theater-goer, supplies a pertinent anecdote regarding Garrick's rivalry with a fellow actress: "I always thought [Hannah] Pritchard superior to Garrick; he felt her so in one Scene of Hamlet, one of Macbeth, & one of the Jealous Wife, when all the spontaneous Applause of the House ran to *her*."[3] George Anne Bellamy tells of Garrick's annoyance when the Earl of Mansfield showed favors to his star actress: "For more apprehensive of a rivalship in fame, than an eastern monarch of his power, he could not bear, *even a sister* near the throne."[4] James Boaden's early biography of Sarah Siddons offers similar evidence of Garrick's jealous guarding of his reputation, his professional insecurities, and his manipulating the repertory, especially in competition with the women in his troupe. He reports that "the great actor was extremely sensitive upon the subject of popular favour, and . . . he even practiced many arts as a manager, to secure to himself the most constant

The Scale of Tragedians.	Genius	Judgment	Expression	Action	Voice
Quin	15	17	14	15	17
Garrick	17	18	18	17	18
Barry	15	13	14	14	16
Mossop	14	14	14	15	16
Smith	10	9	10	12	12
Havard	12	14	12	14	12
Rofs	10	11	10	9	11
Berry	9	13	11	7	5
Holland	10	9	10	8	13
Sheridan	12	16	15	10	7
Sparks	9	12	11	8	8
Mrs. Cibber	16	15	17	16	18
Mrs. Bellamy	13	12	14	12	14
Mrs. Pritchard	12	13	12	8	13
Mifs Macklin	11	11	12	9	13
Mrs. Woffington	12	13	14	14	6

Figure 2. "The Scale of Tragedians." *The Theatrical Review: For the Year 1757, and Beginning of 1758*. London, 1758. 45.

pre-eminence." The theater manager-actor "anxiously" gauged "the comparative *value* of the male and female characters" when offered potential additions to the repertoire. Applying the observation explicitly to Mrs. Cibber's talent, Boaden continues, "The true secret of Mr. Garrick's *coldness* to [John Home's] *Douglas*, [Robert Dodsley's] *Cleone*, and [Arthur Murphy's] *Orphan of China*, was that in them the female interest predominated—Mrs. Cibber would have overwhelmed him."[5] After canvassing tragedies by Shakespeare and Otway, Boaden concludes that, unlike the aforementioned tragedies, none of them affords "a single instance of a great and transcendent female part to which the *male* character was strikingly inferior" (1: 158). Boaden clearly believed that Garrick's fear of being upstaged and out-acted resulted not from flaws in the playscript but from his own failure of confidence in displaying his talent as superior to the female costars. The relative merits of actors and actresses were the frequent subject of critical discussion in the eighteenth-century press, and

The Scale of COMEDIANS.	Genius.	Judgment.	Vis Comica.	Variety.
Quin	16	16	17	11
Theo. Cibber	12	8	13	10
Macklin	10	17	12	10
Garrick	18	16	18	18
Arthur	16	14	16	11
Woodward	15	12	13	13
Shuter	16	9	17	16
Yates	13	10	12	12
Berry	12	11	11	10
Palmer	12	13	9	11
Smith	11	10	9	10
Dyer	11	12	11	10
Taswell	12	15	12	11
Mrs. Clive	17	16	17	15
Mrs. Pritchard	15	14	10	13
Miss Macklin	12	13	11	12
Mrs. Green	14	10	12	13
Mrs. Pitt	13	12	12	13
Mrs. Woffington	16	15	12	15
* Mr. Foote				

* This gentleman's talents are so much out of the common road, that I cannot at present settle what his excellence is in each particular, and will therefore leave every reader to rate his merit according to his own feeling.

Figure 3. "The Scale of Comedians." *The Theatrical Review: For the Year 1757, and Beginning of 1758.* London, 1758. 46.

David Garrick's worry that the women in his company would overpower his talent was a common subject of theater gossip (Figure 4).

These broad-ranging scoring systems provided an early equivalent to theatrical reviews, for they supplied finely calibrated measures of actors' relative commercial drawing power. To return to the actor rating tables in *The Theatrical Review*, we find that among the tragedians James Quin (78), Spranger Barry (72), and Henry Mossup (71) placed next after Garrick and Mrs. Cibber, followed closely by George Anne Bellamy (65), whose more consistent scores allowed her to outrank Sheridan (60). Peg Woffington and Hannah Pritchard also inched up on Sheridan with 59 and 58 points respectively. Given that tragedy held precedence over comedy in the prevailing genre hierarchy, it is somewhat surprising that the women, more prolific in comedy, scored as well as they did. In the comic scale 80 points was the highest number possible to be awarded. There Kitty Clive with a total of 65 points exceeded *all* of the men except Garrick, who scored 70 points. These figures shed considerable light on Garrick's jealousy of Clive, for she was represented by this calculation to be gaining ground as his nearest rival. Woffington, narrowly beaten out by Quin (60) ranked a close second to the men, scoring in all a total of 58 points. The tallies in these tables and the minute distinctions made among them reflect intense rivalries among actors of both sexes and their fiercely competitive battles to remain high in these kinds of published ratings. Most significantly, these tabulations demonstrate the enormous popularity of eighteenth-century actresses and their ability to rival male actors for the audience's highest regard.

"It has been said again and again," Allardyce Nicoll reminds us, "that the eighteenth century was an age, not of the author, but of the actor."[6] The eighteenth century might be labeled more accurately, I suggest, the age of *women* in the theater and especially the age of the *actress*. Several generations of theater historians have maintained that Thomas Betterton, John Rich, David Garrick, and Richard Sheridan dominated theater history and criticism as actors, managers, and playwrights. It is unfortunate that the actresses who played alongside of them have not yet been given their due, even though women's roles stand firmly at the center of eighteenth-century dramatic forms including genteel comedy, she-tragedy, ballad opera, and bourgeois sentimental drama. Scholarship over the past few decades has emphasized the economic achievements of women writers but slighted those of actresses, an equally powerful and influential group. After the Restoration the growing celebrity of women players, still regarded as something of a novelty, accompanied and sometimes exceeded the celebrity of actors that had begun in the Renaissance with Will Kemp

Figure 4. "David Garrick and Mrs. Pritchard in Benjamin Hoadley's *The Suspicious Husband*." Francis Hayman (1747), oil on canvas. Paul Mellon Collection, Yale Center for British Art.

(Shakespeare's clown), Edward Alleyn, and Richard Burbage, but awaited the explosion of print culture to reach its fuller realization.[7] Actresses—urban, newly moneyed, and thoroughly engaged with the world—were among the first of their sex to achieve social mobility, cultural authority, and financial independence by virtue of their own efforts. For the first time in history, a privileged but anomalous group of actresses could actually earn a living wage by crafting a theatrical career.

Continental women had preceded Englishwomen on the stage. French actresses, who pioneered public performances as early as the fifteenth century, like their successors stemmed mostly from humble origins; they were probably attracted to the stage by the promise that their pay could potentially equal that of modestly paid professional men.[8] Traveling French and Italian companies included women who sang and danced; and as early as the 1630s, the debate over female performance as actors and singers was fully in process in England. Sophie Tomlinson remarks that "records of amateur theatricals both before and during the Interregnum confirm that female participation in drama was common and widespread."[9] During the English Civil War women wrote, read, and sang in unsanctioned dramas performed in private and academic venues. Following closely upon Sir William D'Avenant's return from France, where he had perhaps witnessed the talents of French actresses, "Enter Ianthe, Veil'd" was staged in September 1656 at Rutland House in Aldergate Street in which an actress sang and performed. This was soon followed by the first stage performance with an actress, probably Margaret Hughes, playing Desdemona when Killigrew's company performed Shakespeare's *Othello*, 8 December 1660. Tomlinson contends that bringing women to the Restoration stage in Charles II's court was actually long overdue rather than avant-garde (156). Whether a belated or timely response, flesh-and-blood women on the stage provided hefty competition for the audience's attention and unquestionably helped propelled the success of the increasingly commercial eighteenth-century theater.

With very few exceptions, women had not been seen acting publicly in dramatic roles before the Restoration. Inserting their bodies into public space thoroughly eroticized them in a way that male actors were often able to evade. The sexually charged intimacy with women on stage underscored the uneven power relations that pertained to actresses prevalent in the theater and its audience. The antitheatrical pamphlet *The Playhouse Pocket-Companion, or Theatrical Vade Medum* (1779) testifies to the legendary difference that the sex of the dramatic speaker was believed to have made:

> An obscene jest, or a double entendre, which would have lost half its poignancy out of the mouth of a young man, or boy in petticoats, was highly relished when spoken by a beautiful woman. A female, gay, loose, and wanton, represented by a beardless youth, would have been a character not likely to be well received, but when filled by a young and handsome woman, desiring and desirable herself (it may be too, the very original from whence the poet in the warmth of his fancy, perhaps a little heated by love, drew the glowing picture) the odiousness of the representation was wiped off, vice was rendered amiable, and she herself became the object of impure desires. Thus we find that *Charles* was so irresistibly charmed on seeing Mrs. *Ellen Gwyn* in some such character, that he carried her off, like *Jove* the mighty ravisher of *Olympus*, in her stage-clothes.[10]

Women's very presence on stage justified illicit desire, and actresses had to fend off unwanted suitors who ignored the boundary between audience and stage in hot pursuit of them. Moral judgments regarding actresses' alleged lack of virtue persisted well into the twentieth century. To take only one example, when theater historian John Harold Wilson determined whether actresses' entrance onto the Restoration stage resulted in a positive or negative influence, he ruled against the theatrical feminine. "Regretfully," he lamented, "we must admit that [their performance] was as good or as bad as the private character of the actress. The fact is that, in the small intimate theatrical world, it was difficult for an audience to separate the stage character of an actress from her real character."[11] For Wilson, as had been the case in *The Playhouse Pocket-Companion* and a raft of commentaries up to the present day, sexual behavior could contaminate an actress's performance and determine her success.

This book attempts to extricate the discussion of the actress from the restrictions that the familiar proper lady/prostitute opposition imposes upon women players to situate them within other more productive frames of reference.[12] Unquestionably actresses peddled their talents, sexual and otherwise, in order to follow their passions and ambitions, or simply survive; but these parameters have largely blinded scholars to other approaches.[13] In the pages that follow I consider only the most celebrated women players and their principal roles in the British theater from the early eighteenth century until the 1780s when the star system, developing throughout these decades was firmly established. I analyze here the ways that the eighteenth-century stage reflected, shaped, and performed British womanhood on the porous boundary between the theater and the larger society to which it was central. Much-admired actresses such as Anne Oldfield (1683–1730), Catherine Clive (1711–85), Margaret Woffington (1720?–60), Frances Abington (1737–1815), Susannah Cibber (1714–66), and George Anne Bellamy (c. 1731–88) are among those who animated theatrical concerns vital to the period—including especially patronage, property, national identity, and fashion—in the context of their dramatic performances. This book focuses on the exceptional actresses who changed the course of theater history and afforded unprecedented models of public display as they confronted the social and theatrical strictures that traditional femininity imposed.

My book does not provide a comprehensive survey of female performers in the London theater, nor the kinds of roles written for them, nor their function in the theaters. Instead it considers exceptional women as exemplary of critical issues raised by their unprecedented incursion into public spaces.

Though I make considerable use of theater history, I seek to enliven its empirical bent and step outside its strictures to make larger claims. The chapters that follow analyze the fictions that circulated around actresses' lives as they meshed with the particular roles that made them famous, and with the tribulations of the theater companies in which they participated. I am not attempting to write biography here, although life histories are significantly interwoven with their dramatic performances. While factual documentation remains central to this study, I cautiously piece together evidence from anecdote and innuendo in order to counter the low estimate of theatrical women and to reassess their crucial functions in the eighteenth-century theater. The great majority of actresses—such as those players in non-patent and provincial theaters who were poorly paid, doomed to minor parts, or who performed only irregularly with lesser troupes—never became celebrities, and they richly deserve separate study. I have limited my focus here to the London theaters, with some attention to the frequent exchange of personnel and plays with the Dublin theaters. I am seeking in this way to give articulation to the space between the archive and the repertoire, a gap Diane Taylor defines as located between "the *archive* of supposedly enduring materials (i.e., texts, documents, buildings, bones) and the so-called ephemeral *repertoire* of embodied practice/knowledge (i.e., spoken language, dance, sports, ritual)" (19). According to this narrative of theater practice, the repertoire provides an inventory that enables individual agency actively to produce embodied meaning (20).[14]

In this sense, then, actresses' special performative magic unquestionably transformed the single-sex stage into a complexly gendered space. The recent renewed attention to women's participation in the theatrical during the Stuart period provides a welcome addition to the record of actresses' entrance onto the legitimate stage. Katherine E. Maus early articulated the broad ideological shifts that women players signaled in coming to the stage; more recent studies of thespian women that focus on earlier periods include Gilli Bush-Bailey, *Treading the Bawds: Actresses and Playwrights on the Late-Stuart Stage* and Tomlinson's aforementioned *Women on Stage in Stuart Drama*.[15] Most relevant to our period are the achievements of women playwrights at the turn into the eighteenth century (such as Aphra Behn, Catherine Trotter, Mary Manley, and Mary Pix) that resonate with those of the actresses who played the roles they created, though the extraordinary productivity of women playwrights in the early period was not matched until the twentieth century. After Susanna Centlivre's relatively lonely forays into the theater in the first two decades of the eighteenth century (accompanied the sporadic productions of

Eliza Haywood, Charlotte Charke, and Elizabeth Cooper), a cluster of gifted women playwrights surfaced again, this time in the 1760s and 1770s, when Hannah Cowley, Elizabeth Griffith, and Frances Sheridan began to write.[16] In the interim of the lean mid-century years, actresses took up the slack to challenge and complicate conventional assumptions about women, and a few actresses such as Kitty Clive crafted plays, afterpieces, and paratexts themselves.

The eighteenth century has often been regarded as a period when dramatic standards crumbled because of the corrupting influences of sentimentalism, neoclassicism, Italian opera, and pantomime,[17] but women's stage presence, linked with the excitement of new genres and methods of acting, provides a counternarrative to the British theater's alleged degeneration. Here I unite the consideration of plays in performance with analysis of them as literary texts to build on a number of important studies. Kristina Straub's *Sexual Suspects: Eighteenth-Century Players and Sexual Ideology* offers a compact, scholarly, yet readable approach to the subject and remains an essential starting place for studies of gender and the theater in this period. Elizabeth Howe's *First English Actresses* alerted scholars to the inventive performances of the first generation of women in the English theaters. Her groundbreaking and still central work was followed shortly by that of Sandra Richards, *The Rise of the English Actress*, a broad-ranging historical study that devotes approximately one-third of the book to an astute overview of eighteenth-century actresses.[18] Lisa Freeman's *Character's Theater: Genre and Identity on the Eighteenth-Century English Stage* and Bridget Orr's *Empire on the English Stage, 1660–1714*, are among the most significant recent books on Restoration and eighteenth-century drama, and my book is in frequent dialogue with them.[19]

Rival Queens, then, combines an emphasis on celebrated actresses with close analyses of their performances in works by major playwrights, including Nathaniel Lee, George Farquhar, Nicholas Rowe, Colley Cibber, Arthur Murphy, David Garrick, Isaac Bickerstaff, and Richard Sheridan. In addition, I give considerable attention to the intermingling of actresses' lives and roles. My book deals primarily with the second and third generations of actresses on the English stage from 1700 until the 1780s who recognized the exchange value of their labor and their potential for self-commodification; they demanded remuneration commensurate with their talents. The scope of the book thus extends from accounts of actresses at the turn into the early eighteenth century until the full blossoming of celebrity in Sarah Siddons's masterful performances at century's end.

We are beginning to understand that the long history of femininity includes performances onstage and off, and that audiences, managers, and memoirists struggled to reconcile actresses' economic agency with feminine virtue. Later generations of women players differed from earlier ones because they were able to benefit from the mistakes of their talented predecessors, to develop new strategies for becoming respected professionals, and to serve as mentors for younger actresses. Unlike Elizabeth Barry, Anne Bracegirdle, and Anne Oldfield, the second generation of actresses faced the consequences of the 1737 Licensing Act. As is well known, the Act restricted the legitimate venues where actors could perform to two patent theaters (a monopoly that Charles Fleetwood at Drury Lane and John Rich at Covent Garden exploited), and curtailed the production of new plays. This period of retrenchment reined in theatrical creativity and stripped the drama of political innuendo, but celebrity women players may have actually profited from these reforms in offering a form of novelty. Still, the Act made conditions more difficult for many actresses of ordinary talent who were relegated to provincial theaters or traveling companies,[20] while star actresses in the patent theaters benefited from less competition. It meant that less work was available to underling actresses, thus foregrounding the talents of the fortunate few. Though actresses possessed both creative and organizational skills, they, unlike their fellow actors, were with few exceptions denied the opportunity to become participant sharers in theater management. Such conditions were part and parcel of the conditions under which star actresses' celebrity developed. Still, the few extraordinary actresses led the way, not only for other actresses but also for the nobility and gentry, bourgeois women, apprentices, and servants who found sanction in their preferences for previously unimaginable behaviors. They posed alternatives to the more respectable kinds of proper womanhood—aristocratic, professional, and middling women who have often been privileged in arguments concerning women's place in British culture in the eighteenth century. In short, celebrity actresses advanced women's emergence as modern subjects who possessed new consciousness of their ability to determine their identities and reflect upon them.

Stella Tillyard has helpfully described the eighteenth-century London theater as "the crucible of celebrity," though the word first appears in its modern usage only in 1849.[21] In the first half of the century, England witnessed an emergent cult of celebrity that reached well beyond private social circles. Celebrity rose to special prominence in the two decades following the Seven Years' War (1757–63), and began to take its recognizable modern shape across England and Europe. This shift may be attributed to at least three historical tendencies at the end of the seventeenth century: the loss of faith in monarchical divine right accompanied by increased parliamentary control, the lessening of the hold of the 1695 Licensing Act on printing, and an emergent public sphere. A free press accompanied by ineffective libel laws encouraged furious scandal-mongering at an unprecedented level and invaded individual privacy. The diminishing power of the aristocracy, along with the proliferation of print culture, the emergence of mercantilism, and an increase in leisure gave rise to a media apparatus that was essential to the construction of inordinately powerful and often enticingly mysterious public figures. Tillyard adds a crucial economic element to the cultural mixture to show that celebrity's inaugural moments were thoroughly entangled with the formation of a distinctly private sphere: "Celebrity was born at the moment private life became a tradeable public commodity" (25). Privacy, as some scholars have argued, rather than being valued principally because of its separation from the public sphere, paradoxically increased its value as a result of its exposure in the public realm.[22] "The privileging of the ordinary and the consciousness of man's ability to shape himself," as John Brewer remarks in his summary of eighteenth-century technologies of the self, "had the paradoxical effect both of enhancing a sense of privacy—especially of the corporeal and psychic self—and of providing the grounds on which it could be invaded, policed and remade."[23] The emergence of celebrity at the turn into the eighteenth century may be linked not only to privacy, I suggest, but also to the appearance of women on stage for the first time.

Tillyard's account of celebrity follows the line of reasoning in Jürgen Habermas's *Structural Transformation of the Public Sphere*, the impact of which persists in spite of intense critique, revision, and elaboration of his ideas.[24] While Habermas defined a bourgeois public sphere in which a consensus of opinion might be formed as typical of modern society, positioned between an intimate domestic sphere and the official domain of the state, others have refined his theories by describing the varied eighteenth-century publics that extend well beyond the state and the print culture that deliberated its actions.[25] It is in this context that feminist scholars have radically reevaluated women's position throughout the century vis-à-vis the public.

In the now very familiar argument, Habermas maintained that through a public culture of letters, private people formed a public sphere that prodded the state to become more responsive to civil society. The periodical press and the circulation of its products in public gathering places such as coffeehouses were vehicles of this transformation in which private people, a mingling of aristocrat and bourgeois but extending to apprentices and servants, congregated in public spaces for "rational-critical" debate. The public and private spheres were, of course, not nearly as distinct as Habermas painted them: multiple public and private spaces existed, not to speak of the many public-in-private and private-in-public assemblages. Scholars have convincingly argued that the public and private are shifting, fluid categories rather than sharp divisions.[26] John Barrell, for example, has demonstrated the political impact that private spaces within public venues such as the pub, the coffeehouse, and curtained theater boxes could wield.[27]

J. A. Downie has mounted a vigorous critique of Habermas's claim that a bourgeois revolution followed immediately after the Glorious Revolution; he questions whether the abolition of the 1695 Licensing Act in fact brought an end to state censorship of the press and therefore spurred greater freedom of expression through periodical publication. He cites as counterevidence that more pamphlets were published in the 1640s and between 1679 and 1685 than at the turn into the eighteenth century.[28] A full response to Downie's claims awaits another time and place, but several aspects of his argument that have bearing on women and performance in the British theater might be addressed here. Downie's dispute with Habermas derives in part from a disciplinary divide between historical and literary studies, and his questioning about the effectiveness of the republic of letters in shaping public consensus reveals a deep skepticism regarding the power of text to bring about social change. Most notably, he disparages Habermas' privileging of the periodical press and circulating libraries as enabling the citizenry to exert significant effects on governmental policies.

Downie contends that the formation of a unified *vox populi* speaking consensually is a fiction. Focusing on the silencing of the voices of women and servants, he seeks to refute Habermas's claim that "a public sphere from which specific groups would be *eo ipso* excluded was less than merely incomplete, it was not a public sphere at all" (Habermas 57). Downie (70) mocks the idea that the views of tradesmen, servants, and women would have been "accorded equal status with those of the nobility and gentry." The early eighteenth-century theater affords a partial rebuttal to this view, however, in attracting all ranks—including apprentices and servants of both sexes—to a public venue where critical opinion and taste began to materialize and a press developed that reviewed, and thus monitored, the theater. Even if Downie is accurate, for example, in claiming that "financial independence—the ability to pay one's way" determined "the price of admission to the political public sphere" (68), celebrity actresses (and certainly the manager-actors and star actors) who were born into social strata other than the nobility or gentry, were capable of exerting political influence. Is it the numbers of people who may be counted as bourgeois who matter, or is it relevant that some persons other than the elite—such as actors and actresses—were able to wield significant political power in the first and second decades of the eighteenth century? In addition, while it is accurate to assert that "there is very little evidence of the London theater around 1700 being patronized by a 'great' public of bourgeois origin" (67), it is precisely because the London patent theaters experienced financial troubles that they became steadily more populist in the early decades of the eighteenth century, appealing to more diverse audiences, bolstered by manager John Rich's brilliant strategy of incorporating pantomime, John Gay's stunningly successful *Beggar's Opera* (1728), and George Lillo's *London Merchant* (1731) with its direct appeal to apprentices. Further, Downie seriously underestimates the potential political threat of the theater signaled by the government's belief that the Licensing Act of 1737 was needed in order to mandate greater censorship.

The putatively distinct spheres exhibit remarkably unstable borders in constituting potential citizens within the coffeehouse, the pub, the salon, the theater, clubs and other assemblies. Fashionable assemblies, entertainments, and the urban space of the patent theaters were, as we are increasingly learning, important sites for the exercise of women's political and social influence. Although the legal restrictions on eighteenth-century women are irrefutable, women's alleged retreat into exclusively domestic settings has been much debated and contested over the past several decades.[29] The notion of women's isolation in the private domestic sphere versus men's debate in public venues and in print culture has been transformed by discussions of women's ability to own property (Susan Staves, Amy Erickson), to converse about books and news of the day in salons (Harriet Guest), to engage in charitable endeavors (Elizabeth Eger, Nicole Pohl), to publish their own works (Paula Backscheider, Ruth Perry, Betty Schellenberg), and to participate in political discussions at ostensibly private gatherings. The chapters that follow take up specific instances of the way that the theater, and women's performances in it, made possible imagining, if not always realizing, a normative ideal against which audience members, regardless of gender or social status, could judge their aesthetic as well as political opinions. Women's presence on the eighteenth-century stage and in the audience reinforced the fact that the theater offered one of the few public places where both sexes could freely congregate, where women's distinctive voices could be heard, and where women's critical opinions could be honed.

It is the argument of this book that actresses with loyal fans in tow participated significantly in this shifting of public/private boundaries. In the chapters that follow I show that the audience's imagined intimacy with the theatrical and social being of the celebrated actress flourished throughout the century and surpassed that which was accorded to male players. This effect is in part a result of the culture's regarding the feminine as more accessible than the masculine, and its exercise of a double standard in centering on the actress as a locus of cultural desires. The increased presence of women in the public sphere, giving celebrity a "feminine face," meant that sexual rumor advanced with greater fervency as these well-known figures became fair game for the growth and circulation of gossip.[30] Things theatrical have long been linked with the feminine and particularly with the stage's more pejorative connotations, and frequently associated with misogynous satire, including artifice, masquerade, dishonesty, and deviousness.[31] In spite of these negative associations, most celebrated actresses, as we shall see, had the opportunity to carve out a coherent personhood while projecting an accessible, layered interiority that traversed the boundaries between dramatic character and private self, between public display and personal revelation. If, as C. B. Macpherson wrote in his classic study, "the individual . . . is free inasmuch as he is proprietor of his person and his capacities," then star actresses seeking to make a property of their characteristic personalities became candidates for status as subjects under the law through self-commodification.[32] The kind of personhood they created was an enabling fiction of a knowable self, an effect of performance, but that personhood also took on an economic reality in the marketplace where it became a valuable commodity.

Early actresses manipulated anecdotes circulating about their private lives into an imagined offstage personality ("public intimacy," as Joseph Roach has termed this phenomenon)[33] that served as a theatrical substitute for authentic knowledge about them. In Roach's illuminating book *It*, he identifies actors' creating an illusion of availability, encouraging the audience's vicarious experience, and promoting the spellbinding effect that their charismatic personalities exerted as part of the deep structure of emergent celebrity. Spectators became enchanted with theatrical personae of both sexes in a way that had previously been reserved for monarchs and sacred personages, but actresses from the first possessed a magnetic allure that exceeded the sexual power that had always been accorded them. Actors of both sexes inspired theater audiences to engage in surrogation; patrons satisfied their erotic desires through consumption and pursuing exotic travel, imagined and otherwise. Roach's study of the material objects imaginatively constituting these vicarious experiences—including the actors' accessories, clothes, hair, skin, flesh, and bone—has considerably influenced the pages that follow. At the same time, however, Roach takes no special notice of women's introduction to the stage, though women dominate his examples of abnormally interesting people. Neither does he argue as I do here that celebrity flourished in large part because fascinating *women* gathered to themselves sexual powers exceeding those that were ascribed to men. Male actors unquestionably possessed stage magnetism, of course—Betterton, Rich, Garrick, and Sheridan notable among them—but as I show here, the discourse surrounding actresses involved a different sexual politics. While male actors shared significantly in celebrity, and satisfied audience needs by taking on the status of a charismatic other (attracting both heterosocial and homosocial desires), the mechanics of gossip depended upon identifying significant aspects of sexual difference, and women's compromised position in this regard fed the circulation of scandal.[34] The spectators' fantasies of intimacy with actresses' theatrical and social being were more intensely eroticized, even when one contemplates the compromised masculinity of eighteenth-century stage actors. This came about in part through their reiteration of consistent character traits in acting roles that became synonymous with their persons, but also especially in reciting epilogues, as I shall show throughout the case studies of particular actresses. Women players also inspired reactions, both negative and positive, to their very public enactment of new freedoms.

While *It* carries us forward energetically toward the contemporary obsession with celebrity, I seek to reinsert celebrity firmly within its inaugural moments. Modernity, according to Carla Hesse, is characterized by the individual's "consciousness of oneself as self-creating," of the possibility to shape and mold a "self," and eighteenth-century celebrity actresses figured as spectacular examples of women capable of autonomous action.[35] Actresses, I argue, were among those who constituted the first female subjects in the public arena. They were self-reflexive economic agents who actively shaped their identities to make celebrated properties of themselves in a historical period marked by increasing privatization of property and identity, even as identity increased its circulation and commodification. Unlike the female author who, according to Catherine Gallagher, acted as a "nobody" who represented a "definitive lack of property," star actresses gained cultural authority because they took possession of their own persons and encouraged the assignment of a particular value to them.[36] The fictional nobodies that Catherine Gallagher found in the novel became theatrical somebodies when they mounted the stage as dramatic characters; actresses trading on their acting reputations represented quite the opposite of the disembodied female author who often veiled her public identity, appearing as a nameless, anonymous being. Actresses, however, learned to overcome the challenges to the possibility of female self-representation that plagued early women authors from Aphra Behn on.[37] Thus, these celebrity actresses may be counted among the first modern women, heralding new possibilities for women, in their ability to fashion a complex yet recognizable personality that projected a combination of public display and personal revelation, and united dramatic character and a private "self" in a manner that we usually associate with the eighteenth-century novel rather than the drama.

My interest here, then, is primarily in *performance* as a practice of the self rather than *reading* as a practice of the self. The novel has been regarded as the preeminent form for imagining interiority and internalizing value.[38] Such views of the novel often limit the enormously varied forms of fiction to the domestic novel and thus assume that it occupies principally the private, interior space of reading. Actresses, on the other hand, in encouraging a dialectic between public and private, personified the crisis around determining the very notion of worth, and in locating where value was to be found. Deirdre Shauna Lynch has influentially argued that eighteenth-century readers used fictional character (incorporating character's double meaning as printed letters on a page) "to renegotiate social relations in their shared, commercialized world, to derive new kinds of pleasure from the changes, [and] to render their property truly private," a tendency toward "intense personal identification" that she finds realized circa 1770 (4, 79).[39] These functions of fictional character are anticipated, I am suggesting, in the enjoyment that eighteenth-century audiences experienced in imagining the inner lives of actors and actresses through their performances rather than through reading. Their theatricalized identity was thus imagined not as private property but as a mutual, consensual, interplay. Individuality and its objectification in the marketplace operated as a kind of currency with fluctuating worth in an emergent credit economy as inner life was projected onto the stage. When actresses such as Oldfield, Clive, and Woffington inserted their personalities into the otherwise impersonal space of the market, and created the impression that their interiority could be known, it enhanced their commercial value and mediated the distance between them and the aristocratic women and proper ladies in their audiences. While this performative interiority may seem to "exist independent of exchange relations," as Lynch believes that the "round characters" of late eighteenth-century fiction did, star actresses much earlier in the century were at pains to insist that the market value of that expression of interiority should accrue to them. In short, I am suggesting that what critics of the novel have found true for nineteenth-century characters—that they "became the imaginative resources on which readers drew to make themselves into individuals, to expand their own interior resources of sensibility" (Lynch, 126) and thus contributed to the formation of taste—found its early manifestation in eighteenth-century celebrity actresses.

In ways not previously acknowledged, star actresses even in the 1750s and 1760s became competitors to women of elevated standing, as well as rivals to the more decorous version of the modern bourgeois individual familiar from eighteenth-century novels such as Samuel Richardson's *Pamela* and *Clarissa*.[40] The most successful actresses, I suggest, recognized the necessity of creating an "interiority effect" which allowed the theater to compete with other nascent forms reflective of inwardness—such as the epistolary novel, the periodical, and autobiographical writing—in fostering and revealing a sense of individuality and intimacy. The emergence of celebrity actresses brought a newfound recognition that women's personalities exposed in public could be translated into profit, but also could redefine feminine virtue.

In her illuminating study of eighteenth-century drama, Lisa Freeman has claimed that character was largely determined by generic conventions, that plays were more formulaic than realist novels, and that this difference in expectations meant that the dramatis personae on stage resulted in "only public space and public displays," and thus excluded a "public/private split" (*Character's Theater*, 27). Freeman focuses on the concept of character to challenge the dominance of the novel's subject as the primary structure for shaping modern identity. The drama then was the "site of resistance to the rise of the subject" forwarded in the realist novel, and the drama's snapshot presentation of personhood is incompatible with "the growth of individual consciousness across time" (1). The character's consciousness as imagined by the audience derived from drama's generic formulaic conventions, though she adds, "The fictional persona created by a playwright often had to compete with the persona or public reputation of the actor or actress taking that part. In this very basic sense, the 'character' presented to an audience was neither singular nor unitary, but rather manifold and incongruous" (18). She believes that "the discourse of 'the subject' fails and, in fact, is conceptually inappropriate as a paradigm to figure or assess the representation of identity in the drama of this period" (7). Deflecting the pursuit of subjectivity, the drama substitutes a reliance on protean surfaces that mirror the theatrical bent of the larger culture. Freeman is right to reinstate the theater as affording a confluence of powerful forces in shaping modern identity, and our approaches are parallel in finding the theater's formulation of a contingent "character" to be an alternative model to the novel's development of a deep and ever unfolding bourgeois interiority.

Freeman finds, then, that genre conventions provided characters with codes that at times simulated an interiority, but "character" affords a more appropriate paradigm than "subjectivity" when speaking of performative identity. While I agree that the particular aspect of "character" that gains priority in a given play may not be clear, and that the limitations of character certainly govern genre,[41] genre varies through time and is reflective of historical change even in the eighteenth century with its heritage of classical hierarchies.[42] It may indeed be the case, as Freeman suggests, that actors, instead of remaining in character, performed virtuoso set pieces, and that especially when playing tragic parts, they expressed their passions as highly conventional exterior signs rather than reflections of interior feeling. But a talented actress could affect a persona that carried far beyond the surface codings typical of a particular genre, sometimes mocking those codings with gesture or intonation. Actors—and especially star actresses—created, I suggest, an illusion of interiority that I have labeled an "interiority effect." Blending the actress's putative personality with the assigned character's emotions and thoughts, this simulation of interior depth is constructed and exposed alongside them. Rather than transcending one's private self, acting involved animation and sometimes exaggeration of an alleged personal identity. Each subsequent reiteration of a familiar role allowed an actress to revise and perfect her unique combination of personal elements along with genre expectations in a given character.

Talented star actresses affected to possess consistent personae in plays and especially in epilogues in order to create characters that displayed an apparent interiority to which celebrity could attach itself. This came about to some considerable degree, then, because of the interaction between actresses and their parts, their self-referential allusions, and the reciprocal relationship of mutual give-and-take realized between audience and stage. Their epilogues were critical as occasional pieces, topically relevant and often addressing specific segments of the audience such as apprentices, milliners, cits and beaux, and especially "the Ladies." Epilogues also frequently engaged the audience in a way that broke the barrier of the stage's edge; and failing physical access to actors through seating on the stage or entrance to backstage dressing rooms, the audience would have relied increasingly on imaginative access to them.[43] Women performing epilogues at stage's edge served as au courant intermediaries between the theater and the real world to ease the transition between the historical moment of the play and its actual performative occasion, to update classical or heroic plays and translate one culture or period to another. Speaking an epilogue allowed the actress more directly to survey the audience, equalizing the relationship, though a dissatisfied audience could interrupt the play to call for an epilogue before it was finished, setting pit and stage against each other in contentious exchange.[44] Written expressly for a specific occasion, an epilogue often begged the audience through an actress's plea for an extension of the play to a third night, reinforcing the commercial nature of actresses as procurers: "No Character from Fiction will I borrow, / But, if you please, I'll talk again to-morrow."[45] The precipice between stage and audience provided, as Robert Weimann has indicated, "a precariously built-up tension between both worlds, the one associated with the fiction of the text, the other associated with its *actual use in society*."[46] Sometimes disrupting or competing with the public image of the actress, the character's consciousness evolved in performance to meld together with it. In the eighteenth century's collaborative theater, this imagined "real" interiority competed with that of dramatic characters to reflect an ongoing, shifting, performative personality. The interplay between the two was critical in actively engaging the audience to speculate about which portion of the inner consciousness of the actress was shared with the character.

Brilliant actresses such as Oldfield, Clive, Woffington, and Abington prefigured a modern subjectivity, a commoditized version of the self that they offered to consumers as an *effect* of an interiority that encapsulated and ascribed a certain value to be exchanged in the theatrical marketplace. That "interiority effect" is not transparent but rather a provisional, multitiered, and situational interiority bolstered by the circulation of celebrity news and gossip, and one that, reduced to a fetishized version of itself, comes to substitute for the living, evolving person that is the actress herself. The actress's imagined interiority is a kind of property subject to market conditions, one that produces value and puts into circulation a kind of commoditization distinct from the women of varying social classes who admire it.

The dramatic characters that these star actresses represented were indeed governed by genre conventions and patterns, but also by rumor and knowledge about these living subjects poised at stage's edge. Neither the character on stage nor the person assumed to inhabit that character were fixed and "real" but rather virtual identities locked together in the imagination, rather than probing an actual interior consciousness. The staged character assumed a value that produced an illusion of credibility directed toward an approximation of a "real" person whose identifiable worth varied according to the vicissitudes of the market. Actresses exploited the fact that the "I" they were impersonating, even in self-referential epilogues, was distinct from the "I" who was performing. In 1770 James Boswell, a lawyer who engaged in daily theatrics, described this phenomenon in his treatise, "On the Profession of a Player": "A player is the character he represents only *in a certain degree*." An actor maintains "a kind of double feeling" while remaining conscious of his own views and feelings.[47] Boswell here voices ideas resembling those forwarded by Denis Diderot in *Paradoxe sur le comédien* (written in 1769 but published posthumously) in which he argued that an actor's self-possession and detachment from a dramatic character's emotion made him superior to one who surrenders his judgment to the imagined sentiment.[48] Actresses found space to maneuver within this double consciousness.

Star actresses such as Oldfield, Clive, Woffington, and Abington also served as intermediaries between older modes of production and emergent speculative properties that were less easily assigned a certain value.[49] In a time of expanding print culture women authors, like actresses, were active participants in the ongoing transition to a commercial theater from a patronage system. With the increase in the potential commercial value of women writers in the early years of the century, especially the 1720s, female authorship provided an appropriate occupation for a respectable woman whose works could be successfully marketed to the reading public.[50] Booksellers, banding together to protect their profits, sought good investments and, perhaps surprisingly, found them in women writers. Forwarding a model of the proper lady as a writer was also an effective means of distracting readers from the commercial nature of their publishing ventures.[51] Linking these two kinds of markets, actresses made highly visible their cultural function as the loci of residual values and as the much maligned—and much desired—harbingers of the new.

Restoration and eighteenth-century women, especially those from the working and middling classes, seldom had access to possessing property in their own persons. John Locke's argument implicitly excludes women from possessing a modern "self"; and in stating that "Every Man has a *Property* in his own *Person*," he underscored their difficulty in maintaining legal and political sovereignty over themselves, as Carole Pateman definitively demonstrated in *The Sexual Contract*.[52] I show throughout the book, and especially in the chapter dealing with Kitty Clive, that star actresses gained unprecedented access to contractual negotiations through making themselves into "performative properties," as I term them. The most successful actresses exploited the difference between their performative identities and their autonomous private selves as they shrewdly cultivated a recognizable public personhood. This performative identity was mutually constructed along with the audience but fully possessed by the actress. It is not that the performative self usurped the self-governing individual, but rather that the interplay of these versions of identity afforded ambitious women new professional prospects. Clive, for example, cleverly manipulated the relationship between performer and private person in the afterpieces she authored by inventing characters that audiences recognized resembled the actress herself. Although male actors attempted to take exclusive possession of roles identified with their own persons in order to acquire these kinds of lucrative properties, for actresses the opportunity to exercise power over their economic futures was truly unprecedented. The number of such celebrity actresses is of course relatively small, but the very fact of their exceptional existence in the eighteenth century made such an option spectacularly visible.

Performance studies has increasingly moved beyond circumscribed settings to encompass more radically the quotidian by spotlighting, as Diana Taylor, has written, "a series of practices, conventions, presentations of self, and the aesthetics of everyday life" as performance.[53] Taylor points out that performance refers to "a set of rehearsed and codified behaviors (dance, theater performance, a music recital, sports events, rituals, and so on) with conventions, beginnings, and ends, taking place in a bracketed space and time separated from daily life." Expanding the object of study from theatrical events to more broadly defined performances in the eighteenth-century world would be a worthy pursuit, but it is not the goal of this study, for it would tend to erase important distinctions between the theater and the larger world: by this definition, nearly every kind of quotidian activity could be defined as performance.[54] Still, as Gillian Russell has convincingly demonstrated in her study of social interactions among the female aristocracy and upper gentry in the later eighteenth century, the theater pervaded the larger social world, which in turn intruded into the theater's spaces.[55]

In her lucid summary of the feminist debates that arose in the 1970s in the aftermath of deconstructive theories, Shannon Jackson demonstrates that sexual difference, especially as it relates to theater and performance, exceeds any simple binary division between men and women and depends upon relational and situational factors.[56] In drawing together the different lineages of gender theory and performance theory, Jackson helpfully explicates the controversies that erupted as a reaction to poststructuralist quarrels over the relationship between corporeal reality and its representation. These discussions have centered especially on questions of embodiment, presence, experience, and intention—all issues that relate to the material world. As the corporeal focus of ideological conflict then and now, eighteenth-century actresses present an appropriate and interesting test case for attempting to resolve the controversies that performance studies and gender theories have aroused.[57] Embodiment is unique to the theater, yet the person of the actress is not present on stage in any fixed, essential, or transhistorical way. According to Elin Diamond, the body of the actor "is not just 'there,' a live unmediated presence" but is inevitably responsive to the contingencies of time and place (1997, 52). Theatricality, in serving both as a "metaphor for representation" and "as an anti-representational ground for the authentic," as Jackson argues, "functions ubiquitously and contradictorily because of its "flexible essentialism.'"[58] Theatricality's suppleness, Jackson contends, "allowed feminism to have it both ways"—as a radically contingent but viable political project dependent upon a knowing subject (199). While gender in the culture may be "a system of regulatory norms which the subject cites" (Diamond, 1997, 46), the subject may also attempt to maneuver creatively into unfamiliar combinations of norms, mimicking them, or holding them up to ridicule rather than merely citing or repeating them. Faced with the instability of the subject, and with the shifting and heterogeneous differences bundled together in the concept of "woman," how then is it possible to maintain a viable feminist project (Jackson, 191)? Is gender ruled by cultural expectations or by something inherent within? As Judith Butler succinctly described the conundrum, "To be a 'woman,' is to have *become* a woman, to compel the body to conform to an historical idea of 'woman,' to induce the body to become a cultural sign, to materialize oneself in obedience to an historically determined possibility, and to do this as a sustained and repeated corporeal project."[59] To study eighteenth-century star actresses offers, then, a fertile ground for understanding women's agency as actual persons without reducing them to a fixed and unitary subject, on the one hand, or constructing them as merely a free-floating mass of discursive contradictions on the other.

Feminist critics have developed a way of talking about agency even as they have at the same time elaborated upon the ways that gendered conventions can be engaged, teased, and resisted. Since Judith Butler's still fundamental yet much-critiqued *Gender Trouble*, gender has often been regarded as a series of performative acts, while cross-dressing is perceived as parodic. Refining and adjusting her position in *Bodies That Matter*, Butler emphasized the importance of the corporeal but argued that the body was contingent and not fully known: "The body is always *posited* or *signified* as prior . . . . If the body signified as prior to signification is an effect of signification, then the mimetic or representational status of language, which claims that signs follow bodies as their necessary mirrors, is not mimetic at all. On the contrary, it is productive, constitutive, one might even argue *performative*, inasmuch as this signifying act delimits and contours the body that it then claims to find prior to any and all signification."[60] It is this provisional element of the body in performance that star actresses in the early period learned to employ to their advantage.

Eighteenth-century actresses, making use of the moving target of the feminine as a posture from which they could depart and improvise, spoke as the embodied and delimited women they were, but they also exploited the ways that femininity could be perceived as enigmatic and indecipherable. For them, identity is engaged as an effect produced through multiple performative iterations. While the ownership that we take in the assumed character of the actress is partial and fragmentary, the interiority effect allows audiences to assume that they possess that personhood through the embodied character rather than through character in text. Among the salient questions, then, is in what ways were eighteenth-century actresses' bodies mediated by specific moments and occasions, and what elements of independence and creativity were they able to exercise when assigned specific roles and scripts to play? How, for example, did extemporization, gesture, and personal reputation counter or elaborate upon the words they were given to speak? In the chapters that follow I address these questions as they might be framed within the careers of individual actresses.

This book, then, offers case histories of extraordinarily talented actresses as a means of describing the unprecedented phenomenon of women's entrance onto the stage. The women I discuss are, of course, unusual because their remarkable skills were combined with magnetic appeal and public notoriety, and subject to serendipity. This book, as should be obvious, purposely veers away from familiar narratives of the actress as prostitute, even though many actresses were mistresses to wealthy patrons and others led unorthodox lives, while some remained chaste and others were unhappily married or separated;

unquestionably, the London and Dublin theater districts were erotically charged zones. As I demonstrate in Chapter 1, the concepts of "woman" and "actor" often clashed in this formative period, encouraging their ready association with sex work because the early players were among the first mercenary professionals. A woman player thus negotiated between a stable identity that allowed her to fix a salary and working conditions, and a more mutable one that was responsive to the fluctuations of the emergent credit economy and the changing definitions of the feminine.

As is well known, eighteenth-century star actresses were accused of being *queans* because their labor, sometimes assumed to be sexual, was liberally rewarded; but more significantly, they were rival *queens* as celebrities who assumed positions formerly reserved for the royal court and other elite personages. Central to my thesis is the concept that performing women entered a competitive economy as rivals to each other, as well as to managers and other actors, and also to prevailing ideas about women. They were fearless competitors with other talented actresses, and worthy rivals to male actors and managers in commanding the highest salaries, the most liberal benefits, and the best parts. They also competed with fashionable ladies in amassing cultural cachet and with polite middling women in embodying new definitions of virtue. As aging actresses, they even found themselves competing with earlier performances and younger versions of themselves.

By inventing new definitions of womanhood at stage's edge (including their recitation of epilogues in propria persona), these early celebrities exploited the permeable boundaries of the stage and found innovative ways to mold a recognizable, though exotic, femininity in a public space. Chapter 2 offers an extended example of the ways that canny actresses heightened their commercial appeal by catapulting their rivalries to center stage. Nathaniel Lee's heroic tragedy, *The Rival Queens*, first produced in 1677 but popular in various versions throughout the entire century to follow, is typical of the heated competitions between female characters, and female players, that theatergoers came to expect. Public quarrels staged between actresses, though touted as catfights enacted for an audience hungry for celebrity fodder, were instrumental in increasing attendance and receipts on benefit nights. Reflective of the cultural and social struggles in their updated reenactments of Renaissance and Restoration plays, star actresses in tragic reenactments embodied both a reassuring historical consciousness and an exhilarating sense that history was beginning anew. These tragedies interestingly yoked traditional classical themes drawing on the past together with light, topical epilogues reflective of Enlightenment optimism regarding the future.

In Chapter 3 I turn to actresses' memoirs, some of which are now exceedingly rare, to show that their biographies and other life-writings demonstrate considerable cultural ambivalence regarding women's virtue. A breach of chastity was not, actress-manager and dramatist Elizabeth Griffith maintained, "the highest crime, that a woman can be guilty of";[61] and virtue more broadly defined, which I describe as "exceptional virtue," could survive an unfortunate sexual slip or even a very public affair, as Anne Oldfield's biographers made clear. These biographical texts ultimately redefined the idea of public virtue and its performance on stage to accommodate actresses as commercial subjects who were in some instances buried in Westminster Abbey, along with the monarchs and divines they superseded in the public imagination, in spite of having conducted unorthodox private lives.

Becoming a celebrated actress depended not only on natural talent but also on flattering patrons in the audience to cultivate the women as well as the men. The spectator/spectacle model has dominated recent criticism of the period, and Chapter 4 suggests an alternative view of the early and mid-eighteenth-century theaters as vitally alive with active exchanges between actors and their audiences. A survey of London stage records, correspondence, and theatrical memoirs reveals that elite women, "Ladies of Quality," patronized celebrity actresses and exerted considerable influence on the kinds of plays that were commissioned throughout the century. Actresses and female playwrights encouraged women spectators to develop critical opinions but also exerted an influence on shaping their ideas of womanhood. Elite women helped shape aesthetic taste through patronage and sometimes through imitating the actresses' audacious dress: even female apprentices became adoring fans. George Anne Bellamy's *Apology* (1785) figures importantly in demonstrating these tendencies toward an interactive theater. Rather than assuming that the audience policed the actors into particular forms of sexual difference, I argue that audience and actress often jockeyed for control of the theatrical space as they furthered its increasingly democratized tenor. The actors also addressed audiences directly in prologues and epilogues, improvising and sometimes breaking character, and unruly audiences on many occasions interrupted the action. In short, actors and audience were thoroughly entangled with one another inside and outside the theater.

A number of actresses managed to gain influence through an extraordinary level of financial independence that had been heretofore unknown except for upper-class women. Successful actresses could become consumers themselves rather than settling for being mere objects of possession and acquisition, for they legitimately earned their wages, even as they portrayed abject female characters onstage. Their careers reflect these tensions between being victims and agents.[62] Chapter 5 describes Kitty Clive's demands for improved working conditions for actors. In the process Clive transformed herself into "performative property," as she made use of her power in the theater to expand women's ability to "own" themselves, their talents, and their roles. This is a remarkable feat in a period when, under the gendered structure of property law, women were seldom able to possess property or to sign contracts in their own names. Singer and actress Clive also straddled the boundaries between opera and theater, and between the Dublin and London theaters. In her dramatic afterpieces, Clive revealed her own particular brand of Irish patriotism on the English stage that differed markedly from her contemporaries, Irish actors and playwrights Charles Macklin and Thomas Sheridan.

In contrast to the singing chambermaid Clive, the Irish Peg Woffington, appearing in dozens of plays and comic epilogues, curiously became a cross-dressed symbol for English patriotism during the years following the 1745 Jacobite rebellion. In many roles and epilogues written expressly for her, she adopted a political voice and helped shape the narratives and performances of a nation. As I show in Chapter 6, Woffington in breeches as Silvia, Wildair, Lothario, or female volunteer soldier embodied a gender ambiguity and displayed an erotic aggression that fused her personal life with her onstage roles to expose the nation's contradictory impulses. Though mercantile capitalism may have strengthened traditional gender divisions at this time, as Laura Brown has persuasively argued, the most public and popular star actresses threatened these facile distinctions to emphasize their constructed nature.[63] Woffington's female libertine characterizations in comedy, tragedy, and patriotic epilogues displayed the transgressive desires of eighteenth-century actresses, but without the redeeming trait of exceptional virtue.

Throughout the eighteenth century, women players were literally commodified in portraits, fans, playing cards, chess sets, chinaware, and screens emblazoned with the likenesses of popular actresses such as Lavinia Fenton as Polly in Gay's *Beggar's Opera*, or Kitty Clive, holding a pug dog, transformed into a porcelain figurine as Mrs. Riot in the afterpiece *Lethe*. In Chapter 7 I describe how Frances Abington parlayed her fashion flair into an early trademark, the "Abington cap," and supplemented her stage income as a well-paid advisor for elegant social events. Women of rank sometimes donated their clothing to actresses who in turn reciprocated by offering their costumes to noblewomen. The sought-after actresses were linchpins between the polite culture of the salons and the public sphere of belles lettres on the one hand, and the theater and popular entertainments on the other. Celebrity circulated via these costumes from stage to court and town, and back again into the theater. In this chapter I discuss the public identity of this "priestess of fashion" in her dramatic roles as Lady Bab, Widow Bellmour, Roxalana, and the Capricious Lady, bound up as they were with things for sale. I treat not only her spectacular display of modish variations on classical or historical costumes, but also her surprisingly consistent persona as a free-spirited embodiment of women's rights on the eve of the French Revolution. Her outspokenness was shared with other actresses in the 1770s who helped reshape notions of public womanhood.

Finally, a short epilogue describes the way that at century's end, a canon of plays emerges, accompanied by a surge in writing by women playwrights, and testifies to the powerful influence of star actresses' roles in determining the repertoire. This final chapter gestures briefly toward the actresses who, in the last two decades of the century, offered fuller accounts of their lives than earlier actresses had done—some in first-person, others in letters and memoirs— including Sophia Baddeley (1742–86), Mary Robinson (1758–1800), and Dorothy Jordan (1761–1816), in striking contrast to the moral exemplar Sarah Siddons who debuted at Drury Lane in 1782–83. "The Siddons" (the article added to her proper name as was the practice for opera divas), became a charismatic reflection of the qualities Britons believed to be characteristic of their nation. That stellar actress's public and private performance of maternal virtue, at one point parading her children onstage, signals that the theater, after having relaxed the tensions between the proper lady and the actress that I trace throughout the book, redraws that division but somewhat differently at the end of the century. It is the argument of this book that Siddons, though unprecedentedly brilliant, was not completely sui generis, in the sense that her career was built on those of earlier celebrity actresses. At the same time Siddons came to embody a tragic grandeur that had never before been witnessed: she carried her public persona, combined as it was with domestic respectability, into her private life rather than drawing the personal into the public.

In short, celebrated actresses revealed the performative nature of femininity even as they helped redefine its margins and tentatively, if significantly, advanced professional opportunities to offer bold, highly visible models for women. Eighteenth-century actresses and the characters they played, long overshadowed by our attention to actor-managers Betterton, Garrick, and Sheridan, reshaped the dramatic repertoire to exert an indelible but now largely forgotten effect on theater history. Pivotal in effecting and reflecting social change, these celebrated public women when taken together, though relatively few in number, possessed sufficient sway to cause us to reassess the importance of the actress during a most vital period of the British theater.

CHAPTER 1

The Economics of Celebrity

> I am the Famous She, Whose moving Arts
> Give Life to Poetry, to Poets Fame:
> I Charm Spectators Eyes, and chain their Hearts,
> 'Till their Applause and Love are but the same.
> —Thomas Otway, "Under Mrs. B—[arry]'s Picture" (1689)

THE LONDON THEATER stood at the center of urban life in Restoration and eighteenth-century England. Women were vital participants in its success as actresses, playwrights, patrons, orange girls and pawnbrokers, costume makers and vendors. Star players such as Elizabeth Barry, the subject of Otway's poetic lines, linked public fame to audience affection through the magnetic theatrical appeal of their palpable feminine presence. Barry and other actresses openly violated the conventional injunction aimed at ambitious women during this historical period: "Your sex's glory," enjoined Edward Young in *Love of Fame* (1725–28), "'tis, to shine unknown; / Of all applause be fondest of your own."[1] Ranging in reputation from prostitutes to socially respectable ladies, early actresses afford a dynamic cultural site for examining unequivocally public women in a period that ostensibly fostered domesticity as an ideal. Social and economic forces encouraged lively social exchange and a thriving print culture that was crucial to the construction of celebrity. Actors' worth in the theatrical marketplace fluctuated depending upon public demand throughout a period that witnessed the change from a powerful aristocracy's dominance to an increasingly urban landscape of merchants and traders. Women's emergence as celebrities culminated at century's end in the staggering popularity of Sarah Siddons whose ardent fans breakfasted near the playhouse to claim much-coveted tickets. Yet the concepts of "woman" and "actor" were often at odds in this formative time that balanced a long-standing patronage system together with an emergent market economy. At first women who engaged in theatrical activities seem to have been regarded as curiosities in the same aberrant category as the exotics who peopled fairs and other popular entertainments—the hog-faced woman, hairy wench, or baboons—exhibited in public for commercial return in the seventeenth century. By what definition were these first actresses who displayed an unprecedented public femininity to be regarded as women? How could one reconcile "the rarity and beauty of their talents" with "the discredit of employing them"?[2] How were the passionate feelings aroused in both sexes in the audience to be channeled into higher profits? The economic realities of the theater, I argue here, disrupted any simple staging of femininity.

Throughout the earlier seventeenth century and even during the Interregnum, women participated sporadically in court entertainments, public theatricality, popular festival rituals, and guild performances, but no women appeared in London's legitimate theaters until the Restoration in 1660. Male actors had earlier interpreted the roles of Cleopatra and Desdemona, Kate and Ophelia, in the often eroticized parts Shakespeare created with the expectation that boys would play them. Partly as a response to the shortage of experienced boy actors caused by the closing of the theaters in 1642 for nearly two decades, the restriction against women's performing was lifted upon the restoration of Charles II, although Edward Kynaston of Duke's Company (whom Samuel Pepys called "the loveliest lady that ever I saw in my life")[3], as well as James Nokes and Charles Hart of King's Company continued to perform occasionally as women. Pepys, an inveterate theatergoer, reported that he witnessed Kynaston playing both male and female roles in Ben Jonson's *The Silent Woman* (7 January 1661). James Nokes also played a woman when he acted as Lady Beardly and spoke in female character the epilogue to Thomas D'Urfey's *The Virtuous Wife; or Good Luck at Last* in character in September 1679.[4] More than a century later Sarah Siddons' early biographer, Thomas Campbell, attributed actresses' assumption of women's roles to Puritan fears that men's dressing in female attire contradicted Levitical law in the Book of Deuteronomy, a concern he dismisses, for the fact that actresses would have had to utter licentious language was more likely to have been a legitimate concern.[5] The itinerant nature of the early English touring companies contributed to making women's participation unacceptable because of their being suspected to be prostitutes, and the establishment of patent theaters provided a stable, potentially more reputable, location. The hoped-for effect of actresses coming to the stage to usurp the gender-bending place of Renaissance boys and supplant men in "skirts roles" did not rid the stage of effeminacy; but as dramatic roles for real women were for the first time invented and then expanded, the Restoration theater, and the new plays that were written for it, became more fully rooted in the female body.

It seems likely that the most compelling reason that women had been prevented from appearing on stage was that actors feared the economic competition which actresses would bring to the commercial theater.[6] Memoirists, managers, fellow actors, and audience members consistently understated the cultural—and economic—power that actresses might wield. In addition, female dramatists after the turn of the century (most significantly Susanna Centlivre, Susannah Cibber, and later Hannah Cowley, Frances Burney, Elizabeth Griffith, and Elizabeth Inchbald) were attracted to the burgeoning business of writing for the newly feminized stage. In short, women's indispensability to the success of the commercial theater was firmly, if sometimes grudgingly, established over the course of eighteenth century.

Though professional female players did not mount the legitimate stage until the Restoration in England, some craft guilds in earlier periods may have allowed young women, in addition to the occasional itinerant female stroller, to act in the French and English plays they produced. Medieval convents would have staged same-sex performances in which the nuns participated (Shapiro, 178), and women occasionally appeared in Tudor pageants and popular entertainments. In the fifteenth and sixteenth centuries French, Italian, and Spanish women had been permitted to perform as professionals, though permission was at times rescinded.[7] These early actresses were also forbidden to cross-dress in order to keep sexual difference clearly defined. Performing commedia dell'arte in 1564, the Italian actress Lucrezia Senese was probably the first European professional woman player, followed later by the Roman Flaminia and Isabella Andreini of Padua, although the Papal States decree required that castrati should substitute for women until the late eighteenth century. Italian companies traveling in France began to encourage the cultivation of homegrown actresses first in Bordeaux and then in Paris. Actresses also appeared in Spain, performing with an Italian troupe in 1587, though they were again outlawed in Spain from 1596 to 1600, at which time only married women could act in public. Abbé Hedelin cautioned that no single woman should act unless her mother or father was a member of the company, and that widows must marry with a year and half if they were to perform.[8] While such rules are commonly assumed to have been designed to protect actresses' chastity, restricting their marital status would also have controlled their access to their earnings. In the Restoration and eighteenth century, married couples who were both actors were often listed as earning a single shared wage, even when the wife commanded the superior salary.

Happenstance or luck is often an important part of the prevailing narrative as to why women were recruited into the theater, but it also seems possible that placing themselves within listening range of well-known playwrights, managers, or other actors may well have been, rather than an accident, a clever young woman's taking an opportunity to audition for a potentially lucrative position in order to support herself and incidentally to regain the status that her family had lost. A considerable number of actresses were "discovered" in relatively public places. Charles Taylor insisted that George Farquhar was totally responsible for Oldfield's becoming an actress rather than attributing it to her initiative after her eloquent dramatic reading at Mitre Tavern in St. James's Market led the playwright to become her patron.[9] Peg Woffington, the daughter of a journeyman bricklayer and washerwoman in Dublin, was apprenticed at age twelve to Mademoiselle Violante after the Italian gymnast and equilibrist noticed her natural talent. Kitty Clive's fortuitously singing within hearing of the Beef-steak Club at Bell Tavern may have led to her promotion to the stage by Club members Mr. Beard and Mr. Dunstall—though William Chetwood insists instead that he and Theophilus Cibber recommended her to Colley Cibber upon hearing her lilting voice.[10] Perhaps Woffington, Oldfield, and Clive firmly planted themselves within close proximity to influential men to expedite their ascent to the stage.

It is not known whether women were apprenticed to master actors after they began appearing on the stage in 1660, and it is beyond the scope of this study to provide a full history of thespian education. Renaissance practices would not have included women, of course, and not a great deal is known about actors' training before or after 1660. It is clear, however, that early modern apprentices in the craft of acting were usually tutored by individual masters to whom they were bound, rather than being instructed within the larger theater troupe, and many boys continued with their training for the requisite seven years. The boys acted in adult roles when they reached majority, though adult men also took on skirts roles after 1642. Indentured workers, some of whom may have been young adults, may have played female roles under duress because a stigma of effeminacy was attached to them.[11] The "play-boys" taking the roles of women characters in the Renaissance were often apprentices to grocer or weaver guilds and most likely occupied a lower social standing than the adult male actors who lived in the homes of their masters (Shapiro, 183).[12] As manufacturing, service, and construction industries declined, there was less need to train new workers, who turned instead to the newly developing trades.[13]

Tutors assumed a proprietary role over trained apprentices and could lease or even sell them to theater companies. Corrupt and abusive practices evolved from the expectation that masters sometimes adopted the role of moral guide and disciplinarian.[14] Female performers introduced into this situation suffered special difficulties and could easily have been sexually compromised. As Michael Shapiro rightly pointed out, "It is hard to imagine many literate girls or young women whose families would have allowed them to become apprentices (which would have meant leaving home and moving into the master's house) at an age probably even earlier . . . than for . . . domestic service" (188), but unexpected financial strains might have induced families to indenture their daughters if, for example, they could be apprenticed into the relative safety of a widow's home. Women were sometimes taken into a noble family and treated as one of their own, as in the case of Elizabeth Barry who became part of Sir William and Lady Davenant's household, or Anne Bracegirdle who lived with the acting family of the Bettertons.[15] John Harold Wilson maintains that the theater companies would have relied for potential actresses on "genteel poor" women who merely assumed an air of refinement, but this argument rests on the questionable assumption that performing the roles of Restoration heroines required less labor, skill, and talent than acting demanded of men.[16] Another avenue to the theater would have been as tradeswomen such as seamstresses, dressers, milliners, and spinsters who were subsidiary to the theater but absolutely essential to it. Male apprentices were bound not to marry during their indenture, but female apprentices, constrained until age twenty-one, may well have sought to wed in order to be freed from any obligation to their masters.[17]

The historical relationship between apprentices to the theater and actresses is not simple, though they were in fact very closely intertwined. For example, the prologue to George Farquhar's *The Constant Couple* (1699) implies a petty criminal relationship of boy actors to their masters, one that is also explored later in George Lillo's bourgeois tragedy, *The London Merchant* (1731):

> And now the modish Prentice he implores,
> Who with his Master's Cash stol'n out of Doors,
> Imploys it on a brace of—Honourable Whores.

Because actor boys often played whores and may have been objects of sexual desire for the adult male actors, the assumption that actresses could also be treated as erotic playthings may suggest a continuation rather than a break with the practices of predatory actors before the Interregnum. For example, in 1688 apprentice boys attacked bawdy houses and rioted against prostitutes, but the boys, provoked by their fear of sexual and economic competition from whores, may have wanted to protest more generally the low wages and poor conditions of laborers.[18] The violence against female prostitutes may have erupted because they, like actresses, posed a special challenge to masculine prerogative of various sorts. The fledgling actors, Katherine Romack persuasively argues, may also have been attempting to preserve the homosocial situation that pertained before women professionals came to the stage. We might conclude from the evidence available that actresses, like the whores with whom they were so closely aligned, were poised to become both sexual *and* economic rivals to boy actors and apprentices. The line between female apprentices and sex workers was thus very finely drawn from the Restoration on. Prostitution was sometimes used as a paradigmatic catch-all term for female labor of any sort, as revealed in the mid-century burlesque pamphlet that purports to be actress Ann Catley's biography: "The word *Prostitute* does not always Mean a W-- but is used also, to signify any Person that does any Thing for *Hire*."[19] Similarly, a treatise entitled *Chiron: or, the mental optician*, jests at the too refined sensibilities of the female apprentice who refused to carry linens to a young gentlemen's chambers for fear of being sexually compromised, because she recognized that her job was at stake, and that "her cruel mistress . . . would sell her at the market price."[20]

How then did women become trained actresses when there were so few formal opportunities to be tutored in their craft? Our knowledge of the training available to fledging actresses is relatively slim. The London nursery that Lady Davenant formed in 1671 had disappeared by the 1680s, but there is some evidence that nurseries for young actors persisted until the late nineteenth century. The two legitimate London companies in the Restoration shared a joint nursery, and another performance school was set up in Norwich. Training for Restoration actors also took place at the George Jolly Hatton Garden Nursery established by Thomas Killigrew. On 30 March 1664 Davenant and

Killigrew were authorized to set up a playhouse "for ye instructing of Boyes & Girles in ye Art of Acting . . . .in the nature of a nursery."[21]

Elizabeth Howe suggests that the coterie nature of the Restoration theater encouraged hothouse breeding for the few actresses determined to merit presentation at court: "The actresses apparently represent an exception to the general decline in professional opportunities for women after 1660."[22] But it seems most likely that aspiring women players participated in a more informal kind of apprentice system than that which obtained among the actors. Some actresses learned gestures, movement, and enunciation from the playwrights who wrote for them, or from the male actors who were their lovers or husbands, as in the case of Mary Saunderson and her husband Thomas Betterton. A woman housekeeper taught acting to girls while Betterton instructed the boys in his company (Freeburn, 152). The Bettertons schooled Anne Bracegirdle and Mary Porter, and Lady Davenant is believed to have tutored Elizabeth Barry for her role in *The Man of Mode*. Lord Rochester was long rumored to have also instructed Barry, albeit with differing motivations; and though the assertion lacks credibility because he was not residing in London on the appropriate dates, it does suggest that lovers may have served as tutors as well. Oldfield's biography maintains that her lover Maynwaring's training contributed heavily to her success as a player (Egerton, 4).

From the beginning, actresses would have been recruited primarily from among those who could read, or at least memorize easily by rote, requiring their possessing a certain basic quickness and education. A narrow time gap existed between performance and rehearsal with little time allotted for practice, and individual actresses also prepared lines on their own with occasional coaching from a fellow actor who might have greater experience.[23] In some companies a trial period of acting for three months without salary resembled a sort of apprenticeship that would have allowed inexperienced players to attend rehearsals and to attempt to learn parts from veteran members of the company.[24]

At the turn into the eighteenth century, however, training would still have been haphazard. As a second generation of actresses developed, they garnered skills and techniques from the seasoned senior players. Occasionally mothers or sisters of actresses imparted their understanding of specific dramatic parts. Kitty Clive protested that she coached a fellow actress at her own expense, and that she deserved greater remuneration for those services, especially when she compared her regular salary to the income of Susannah Cibber, who made about twice as much. Clive demanded that Garrick raise her salary to compensate for the expenses she had incurred while coaching the younger woman: "The year Mrs. Vincent Came on the Stage, it cost me above five Pound to go to and from London to rehears with her and teach her the Part of Polly, I coud not be calld on to do it, as it was long before the house oppend, it was to oblige Mr Garrick."[25] Mary Betterton was also a generous mentor: "When she quitted the Stage, several good Actresses were the better for her Instruction" (*Memoirs*, 1731).[26]

When schools of acting differed, such inbred tutoring could backfire. Garrick complains that Jane Cibber's training in tragedy by Colley Cibber was inadequate, and that "the Young Lady may have Genius for all I know, but if she has, it is so eclips'd by the Manner of speaking ye Laureat has taught her, that I am afraid it will not do—We differ greatly in our Notion of Acting (in Tragedy I mean) & If he is right I am & ever shall be in ye wrong road."[27] Charles Macklin's memoirs speak of Mrs. Dancer (who later became Mrs. Barry and Mrs. Crawford) whose skills were magnificently improved after "the *silver-toned* [Mr.] Barry" coached her. As is well-known, Sarah Siddons learned her craft on the provincial circuit, and Dublin also frequently served as a training ground for women players. Acting on the legitimate stage continued to be a sought-after means of earning a living, and star actresses regularly fielded appeals from young hopefuls. George Anne Bellamy remarks that while she played at the Edinburgh theater, "an incredible number" of letters came to her "from itinerant players applying to be engaged. . . . They generally wrote in such a style, as to shew they all thought themselves Garricks and Cibbers."[28]

Young apprentice workers in many trades were seduced by the attractions of celebrity and the hope that instant success would relieve the drudgery of their manual labor. Their plebeian idealization of acting as a plausible alternative serves as a material example of the appeal that stage models of identity could hold for the working-class imagination. Both men and women alike romanticized performative labor because it seemed to offer an alternative to lifelong drudgery with potential to yield an economic windfall and unprecedented class mobility. The threat was sufficient for Samuel Richardson to write *The Apprentice's Vade Mecum* (1734), which defends the statutory regulations against apprentices frequenting the theater, and the tract severely warns the young men about the stage's corrupting effect. Plays and other popular entertainments, Richardson cautions, pandered to low standards of taste and tempted lower tradespersons to avoid disciplined work and to affect high style. Though apprentices apparently accrued some discretionary income through legitimate means, their conspicuous consumption attracted the kind of envy and animosity usually aimed at upwardly mobile nabobs returning from travels abroad. The criticisms were especially directed at the finely dressed apprentices who thwarted sumptuary laws and dared to display confusing markers of social class. The Lord Mayor and Common Council had required apprentices to dress in the apparel their masters gave them as indicative of their station. They were to wear only woolen caps, the plainest of doublets sans ruffles, fancy pumps, or jewelry, and to carry no sword: "And 'tis now to be wish'd that some such good Law were thought of, to restrain the far more destructive Practices of our modern Apprentices, *viz.* those of Whore and Horse-keeping, frequenting Tavern Clubs and Playhouses, and their great excesses in Cloaths, Linen, Perriwigs, Gold and Silver Watches, &c."[29] For the worst offender against sumptuary regulations, the term of indenture could be extended beyond the agreed-upon time. As these young workers accrued capital, they threatened to abandon industrious application to their trades, the very means that had earned them the shillings necessary to purchase a theater ticket. Though these public directives were largely directed at male apprentices, women workers were equally attracted to the stage.

In 1729 the justices of the peace carped that Thomas Odell's theater in Ayliffe Street, like other London theaters, drew "Tradesmans Servants and others from their lawful Callings, and corrupt[ed] their Manners."[30] This was exacerbated because the six o'clock curtain time conflicted with business hours that typically extended until eight or nine at night for apprentice workers (*Vade Mecum*, vi). Plays were specifically designed to be performed for apprentices on work-free holidays, the best-known being of course Lillo's didactic tragedy, *The London Merchant*, produced for the first time three years before Richardson's manual. Warned against neglecting business, and against the addictive quality of theater, the frivolous nature of the entertainment, and the temptation to whore with lewd women in the theatrical environs, apprentices were enjoined to be modest and frugal, religious and affable, and obsequious to their masters. In a related example, the *Weekly Miscellany* (8 March 1735) made reference to the rowdiness of apprentices at the opening of a new playhouse.[31] The poorer apprentices sat in the upper gallery with the footmen, though those with a few more shillings to spend occupied the boxes and sideboxes.[32] Crowding into the mid-eighteenth-century theater, the notoriously ill-behaved apprentices sitting on the stage "three or four rows deep" interfered with productions. Tate Wilkinson describes the unruly scene: "A performer on a popular night could not step his foot with safety, lest he either should thereby hurt or offend, or be thrown down amongst scores of idle tipsy apprentices."³³ The theater, then, sorely tempted apprentices into engaging in immoral behavior and disrupting the social order from the bottom up.

Arthur Murphy's *The Apprentice*, the afterpiece to Southerne's *Oroonoko* performed on 2 January 1756, gives a specific instance of the special perils awaiting stage-struck plebeian women. It features Dick and Charlotte, apprentices who haunt the theater in hopes of learning the craft of acting. The publication in newspapers and monthlies of *The Apprentice*'s paratexts, David Garrick's prologue and Christopher Smart's epilogue written for Kitty Clive, heightened their importance in the popular imagination; they reinforced the advice to apprentices of both sexes to return to their shops. Both the prologue and epilogue dwell on the real labor of the actor and the many hangers-on who sought instant celebrity, just as earlier city comedies had cautioned apprentices not to assume that the labor of court life was easier than working as a craftsman.³⁴ In the prologue the playwright directly addresses the young men who do not recognize the genuine difficulties of an actor's life, while the epilogue "written by a Friend" speaks more specifically to women. In the play itself, Dick's ambition to become an actor threatens to diminish his manhood and to perpetuate his sycophantic relationship to his master, thus playing on the alleged effeminacy of the theater. Along with woolen drapers, tobacconists, and haberdashers, Dick attends a "spouting club" that serves as a nursery for hopeful actors three times a week. The scenes in the spouting club provide low comic dialogue as the upstart actors, including a Scotchman and an Irishman, garble lines because of the "impediments" of their Celtic accents. The farce, a variation on a rehearsal play, comically interweaves well-known passages from Shakespearean tragedies and popular eighteenth-century plays such as *The Fair Penitent, The Beaux Stratagem, Venice Preserv'd, Mourning Bride, The Suspicious Husband*, and *The Distrest Mother*. In the apprentices' naïve confusion between illusion and reality, they recite in ordinary conversations on London streets the lines they recall from these popular plays.

For Dick's mistress Charlotte, however, being tormented by a passion for acting has more serious consequences. When Charlotte catches "the infection" of wanting to be an actress, her desire to be a player is compared to contracting a venereal disease. The result for a young woman affected by this contagion is economic, social, and corporeal. When Gargle, Charlotte's father, threatens to withhold his daughter's dowry if the couple become actors, Dick decides they should instead become avid theatergoers who attend plays "a hundred times in a season at least."³⁵

Kitty Clive's epilogue, itself an elocutionary display, specifically addresses female apprentices.³⁶ As the character "Nobody," she speaks to the fascinated milliners' apprentices, largely women, who are oblivious to "the dreadful trials—actors undergo."³⁷ She begins by charging Murphy with professional jealousy over the success of her burlesque afterpiece, *The Rehearsal* (1750), which led him to exclude her from his play. His envy, Clive conjectures, is heightened because of her bold confidence in daring to produce a farce:

> Malice and envy to the last Degree!
> And why?—I wrote a Farce as well as He.
> And fairly ventur'd it,—without the Aid
> Of Prologue dress'd in black, and Face in Masquerade;
> O Pit—have Pity—see how I'm dismay'd!³⁸

Subsequent lines insist on the significance of *women* apprentices, including especially milliners, who aspire to popular tragic roles and deceive themselves into thinking they are celebrated queens:

> A spouting Junto of the Female Kind.
> There dwells a Milliner in yonder Row,
> Well-dress'd, full-voic'd, and nobly built for Shew,
> Who, when in Rage, she scolds at *Sue* and *Sarah*,
> Damn'd, Damn'd Dissembler!—thinks she's more than ZARA. (546)

In the epilogue Clive boasts that she can match every male apprentice with an equally star-struck would-be actress: "Oh! Little do those silly people know, / What dreadful Trials—Actors undergo" (546). Her daughter, a lacemaker, attempts the role of Ophelia, while her cousin with "squinting Eyes," "waddling Gait," and a "Voice like *London Cries*" attempts to act the part of Lady Townly (546). The apprentices are oxymoronic "Royal Milliners" and "apron'd Kings" (547). The epilogue warns men to return to their counting books, and women to give up their dreams for the stage and return to "A Shop with Virtue." Demonstrating the greater sexual and social-class dangers that actresses face, Clive's epilogue warns that female apprentices' unrealistic expectations will have greater consequences than for the male workers.

Contrasting to the stern warnings in both Richardson's *Vade Mecum* and Clive's epilogue, actor Theophilus Cibber envisioned apprentices less as misguided sycophants than as a lucrative potential market for teaching acting skills and supplementing his income from the patent theater. Cibber planned to set up a "Histrionic Academy" where he would "instruct (on very reasonable Terms) such young Persons of Genius as I can find, in the Arts of Action and Elocution, &c. so as to enable them to speak with Propriety in Publick, whatever Stations of Life they may be called to, whether the Stage, the Bar, the Pulpit, or the Senate; but more particularly in the Theatrical Way: Thus this Academy may become a Nursery of Actors and Actresses, for the future Entertainment of the Town, when any Casualty may deprive the Play-houses of those Proficients who now appear on the different Stages."[39] Cibber extended his plans for private instruction to public rehearsals to which he invited patentees in search of acting talent for their productions. His sister Charlotte Charke, Colley Cibber's infamous youngest daughter, intended to set up an acting school that would require attendance three days a week from ten in the morning until eight, "Where Ladies and Gentlemen shall be . . . instructed both in the Art of Speaking and Acting; that though they should never come upon the Stage, they shall be enabled even to read a Play more pleasingly to the Auditor, by a few necessary Hints."[40] Charles Macklin and Thomas Sheridan encouraged similar kinds of projects. In 1753 Macklin transformed a Covent Garden tavern into a venue for delivering public lectures when a drinking house scheme came to naught. Calling his new commercial project "The British Inquisition," he attracted an audience of almost eight hundred men and women for pedagogical lectures (some of which were delivered by former actors), debates, and concerts.[41] Whether women were included in these entrepreneurial ventures remains uncertain, although their payment for such instruction was probably equally welcome. Finding training to ascend to the stage was a risky and costly business for impressionable female apprentices who sought to become celebrated players through the fantastic imaginings made available every night of the season for the price of a theater ticket.

Seeming to be unmoored from the fathers and husbands who defined their status, the social rank of women players was, as I have been arguing, more complicated than it was for most men. Their uncertain class position brought into play the sign of the "actress-as-whore," if not the actuality of trading money for sex, though it is too simple to declare that "society assumed that a woman who displayed herself on the public stage was probably a whore."[42] The often indeterminate social class of the newly professionalized actresses, made opaque through the diverse roles they played and the clothes they wore, could also empower them. Laura Rosenthal has argued that the actress, as "an untitled and unmonied professional . . . theatricalized an emergent instability of class identity" and destabilized real gender relations because male audience members "forgot" that an actress playing an aristocratic lady was simply inhabiting a role and was not properly marriageable in her own person.[43] That actresses often wore the cast-off clothing of noblewomen may well have heightened their ability to attract libertine aristocrats, and actresses in turn sometimes bequeathed clothing, costumes, and jewels to their servants. Tate Wilkinson is among those who complained that the fancy dress of women servants on stage, including their elaborate headdresses and satin shoes, encouraged sartorial upstarts in the audience to affect elevated social standing: "I have seen Mrs. Woffington dressed in high taste for Mrs. Phillis, for then all ladies' companions or gentlewomen's gentlewomen, actually appeared in that style of dress; nay, even the comical Clive dressed her Chambermaids, Lappet, Lettice, & c. in the same manner, authorised from what custom had warranted when they were in their younger days" (*Memoirs*, 4: 89). Peg Woffington left to her servant "all my wearing apparel Laces Excepted."[44] The practice of ladies giving their discarded dresses to inferiors was not confined to actresses, of course: servants appeared on the street wearing the clothing of their superiors, and class instability came into consideration onstage and off. *The Servants Calling* (1725) urged employers to refrain from the common practice of giving fine clothes to their servants whose heads are "fill'd with Notions of their Advancement," cautioning them to avoid dressing above their degree, and to "act the Part that belongs to them."[45] Actresses violated these injunctions both as benefactors and as willing recipients of gifts of clothing from their patrons and admirers.

In life and on the stage, then, the star actress taught lesser beings—the common servant girl and the aspiring apprentice—the art of social emulation. Moving through the social classes in drama and in life while mastering the etiquette of nobility, actresses revealed the performative nature of social status to audiences consisting of tradespersons, citizens' wives, ladies of quality, and even queens.[46] The memoirs of actresses attempted to reconcile the fact that even though these women were *not* queens, they could convincingly impersonate the elite ranks and inspire the kind of adulation usually reserved for them; they represented the imagined possibilities that social change could bring.

Private Identity, Public Character

The economics of acting depended not only on players finding a means of seeking mentors and learning the business, but also on cultivating a theatrical version of a private persona. Though it is commonly recognized that Colley Cibber and Charles Macklin, among others, fashioned stage alter egos, this marketing strategy was especially effective for women. Audiences of both sexes recognized that the woman player acting on stage joined the virtual body of the character she represented with her actual body as a person.[47] These dual bodies were not easily separated. Creating this simulation of intimacy involved performing within the public realm with the express intent to expose private matters and to generate affect around one's own person in order to kindle celebrity.[48] Early actresses, sometimes seeming to perform a stylized version of their personal lives on stage, manipulated privacy into the construction of a partially fictive offstage personality that became a theatricalized substitute for authentic knowledge about the actress's life. The audience's illusion that they were privy to intimate understanding of the player could also obscure their recognition of women as working professionals who learned to be businesswomen in order to protect their own interests. The actress's theatrical genius, sometimes overshadowed by her reputation for sexual license, was often unequally compensated in comparison with male players, especially the lesser players. Star actress Elizabeth Barry, for example, slandered as "that mercenary Prostituted Dame," began at 50s. a week, while her co-star, Thomas Betterton, received £5, including a portion of the profits as a sharer in the company.[49] But actor-managers such as Betterton, John Rich, Colley Cibber, and David Garrick recognized the commercial potential in capitalizing on the tensions between public persona and private identity. From their first appearances, actresses raised the question of whether a woman's commercial value lay in her dramatic roles, in her character as a private person, or in some fusing of the two, especially when those identities were discontinuous.[50] Actresses' "virtue" was always at issue, unlike that of the male actors.

Celebrity could also result in disastrously negative effects, especially for female players. The gossipy biographical publications written about them, and the memoirs they composed for the first time, also created an expectation of the public's right to claim ownership of these women. Casting for new plays usually occurred *before* a new script was fully drafted, and Restoration and eighteenth-century playwrights created parts especially for particular popular actresses, as well as familiar "lines" of parts from play to play, so that celebrity adhered both to the person and the part. The actress's character onstage was confused with the woman herself when her name became virtually synonymous with her most famous role as in the case of Roxalana (Hester Davenport), Lady Betty Modish (Anne Oldfield), Polly (Lavinia Fenton), Sir Harry Wildair (Peg Woffington), Perdita (Mary Robinson), or Lady Teazle (Frances Abington). After Lord Mohun's scurrilous attempt to abduct Anne Bracegirdle, the actress's reputation was repaired when she portrayed Fulvia (in *The Richmond Heiress*), a character who, like Bracegirdle herself, triumphs over abduction attempts.

In short, the theater challenged the boundary between public and private, between the virtual and the real, as ordinarily clandestine domestic affairs and political intrigue spilled over into the larger public culture. The "interiority effect," the theatricalized intimacy that produced a simulacrum of complexity and depth, evolved into a commodity that actresses as businesswomen transacted with audiences and traded upon. By the end of the century this form of moveable property had been reduced to fetishized property, to the actress herself as a product, who turned that self-commodification into a position from which to mobilize her rights as a woman even before the 1790s.

In delivering timely prologues and especially epilogues at stage's edge, eighteenth-century actresses teased audiences with secret knowledge of their lives as a way of increasing their popularity or notoriety. The popular Jane Rogers, for example, played virtuous tragic heroines (such as Imoinda in Thomas Southerne's *Oroonoko*) while she engaged in a notorious affair with actor Robert Wilks. To defend herself from spiteful critics, she ventured out upon the stage's apron to protest her virtue as "herself," saying she would "*Study to live the Character I play*," thus attempting to make her person and her roles seem less discordant, but also to invite the invasion of her privacy.[51] Peg Woffington flirted from the stage, as did Kitty Clive who amused herself by breaking character and acknowledging patrons in the audience: "Mrs. Clive would suffer her eyes sometimes to wander from the stage into the boxes in search of her great acquaintance, and now and then give them a comedy nod or curtsy."[52] Personal patronage remained a common means of support for actors into the late century, and coquetry with audience members was an inventive way to solicit potential benefactors and augment receipts.

The highest praise for a star actress in eighteenth-century commentaries was to commend her ability to transform herself convincingly into the person she impersonated. Speaking of Anne Oldfield's contagious talent, Colley

Cibber described the reciprocal relationship between stage and life, causing ladies of quality on occasion to emulate the actress rather than the reverse: "I have often seen her in private Societies, where Women of the best Rank might have borrow'd some part of her Behaviour without the least Diminution of their Sense or Dignity" (*Apology*, ed. Lowe, 1: 309). Claiming unverifiable genteel origins on her maternal side, Oldfield was rumored to have flaunted her status by traveling to the theater in a hired sedan chair accompanied by liveried footmen. As an actress in the public light, she displayed the accoutrements of a woman of quality, and a catalogue of her belongings testifies to her accumulation of luxury goods including rich tapestries, japanned chests, gold snuff-boxes set with brilliant stones, French and English books, diamond and ruby necklaces, "Tables of *Marble, Agate*, and *Jasper*," and a "*French* Repeating Clock." Her will awarded £5000 and two-thirds of her considerable estate to her son Maynwaring, and the Grosvenor Street house to her son Churchill.[53] Other star actresses independently purchased country estates and left significant accumulations of valuables upon their death.[54]

Though Oldfield was vilified in Pope's *Epistle to a Lady* as Narcissa, she exemplified an actress who competed with and ultimately countered the more familiar label of prostitute. Oldfield and some of her fellow women players were described as possessing a natural elegance, an inherent affinity for imitating people of rank, or at least a capacity to learn it quickly. While Oldfield conducted illicit relations with the two men who fathered her sons, Charles Churchill (a supporter of Prime Minister Walpole) and the heavy-drinking spendthrift Arthur Maynwaring, she was reportedly welcomed into the homes of women of fashion and quality, as were Frances Abington and Kitty Clive. Access to actresses, sexual and otherwise, was often regarded as an aristocratic privilege. Elizabeth Barry under Davenant's patronage was invited into the best company where she became "soon Mistress of that Behaviour which sets off the well-bred Gentlewoman"; she was reputed to have powerfully influenced the countesses of Rutland and Nottingham and was friendly with Lady Lisburne, who may have been a patron.[55] Kitty Clive was on intimate terms with Viscount Nuneham, afterward Earl Harcourt and Lord Lieutenant of Ireland from 1772 to 1777, and his wife. George Anne Bellamy claimed that female patrons eagerly consulted her about fashion and borrowed theater costumes for masquerades in return for providing financial support for her benefit nights. She boasts, "And what was still more flattering to my pride, females of the first rank, and those, *exemplary patterns of rectitude*, admitted me to their intimacy. A *Powerscourt*, a *Dillon*, and a *Tyrawley*, honoured me with their friendship.

I visited occasionally those ladies, and, though I was not in a situation of life, even if I had been married, to hope for a return, they always returned my visits, and accepted my invitations" (*Apology*, 2: 219). She specifically mentions mentors and patrons Lady Anson who tutored her in natural philosophy, the Countess of Rochford who educated her in politics, and Lady Essex.

For the first time in history, celebrity created real as well as feigned social mobility for women and allowed them to defy the restrictions of rank. Actresses' alluring linkage between the aristocratic and the commonplace meant that celebrity competed with class in determining their social standing and revised the tenacious residue of the whore. A woman player who acted aristocratic roles could of course assume the position of a woman of quality by becoming the mistress of an admiring aristocrat, and even in rare cases, marrying him.[56] Pepys, visiting Nell Gwyn and Beck Marshall behind stage, remarked that actresses in the greenroom oozed with the self-assurance that accompanied social connection: "But, Lord, their confidence, and how many men do hover about them as soon as they come off the stage, and how confident they [are] in their talk. Here I did kiss the pretty woman newly come, called Pegg, that was Sir Ch. Sidly's mistress" (9 May 1668).

This easy entrée into women players' private lives may also have given actresses practice in fending off admirers, lewdly or otherwise, and toughened them to become the saucy women who could compete, even physically, with managers and with other female actors for the most coveted and lucrative parts. Lavinia Fenton, a stunning success as Polly in Gay's *Beggar's Opera*, lived with the Duke of Bolton for over two decades until she became the duchess upon the death of his wife. William Cooke writes of the event, "The last century has not produced, perhaps, a greater instance of the change of fortune in an individual, than in the character before us . . . *no body's daughter*, bred up, in the early part of her life, at the bar of a public coffee-house; afterwards introduced upon the stage; with a handsome person, and attractive accomplishments; and yet with all these links to seduction, conducting herself with that propriety and conduct, as to attain the first rank in the country, with the esteem and approbation of the public."[57] Similarly, Elizabeth Farren left Drury Lane in 1797 to marry the Earl of Derby. It is not the frequency which which these celebrated actresses managed to bypass traditional standards of chastity and class limitations that is remarkable, but the fact that it could ever be imagined as happening in real life that made the star actress both a curiosity and a formidable threat.

The earning power among star actresses was a primary factor in allowing them to disrupt the status quo. Dependent on the theater for a living wage, many were heads of households responsible for providing the family income. A husband could control his wife's money and claim at least half of it, making well-paid actresses attractive as prospective wives. Frances Abington's trumpeter husband gave her musical instruction, but they separated after he reportedly became jealous of her success; she agreed to pay him an annual sum from her earnings in return for his permanent withdrawal from her life. Susannah Cibber's substantial salary was purportedly the sole family income during the 1740s, though we should make allowance for the open hostility of the pamphleteer's account: "This Lady's Salary, I am credibly inform'd, is 600 Guineas for playing three times a Week only part of the Season with Mr. F——, besides a Benefit clear of Charges; and between 3 or 400*l.* more for singing about twenty times with Mr. *H--*; so that her Income, (without reckoning any Presents, or Gratuities, from any Particular Friends, for her Extraordinary Performances) may, by a moderate Computation, be reckon'd at 1200*l.* for less than six Months Labour; while her Husband (who made her an Actress) and his Daughters (her children in Law) have yearly—0*l*. 0*s*. 0*d*."[58] Theophilus Cibber, who orchestrated his wife's adultery and then subjected her to a criminal conversation trial, took the "clothes, linen, half her salary, and the £50" that Charles Fleetwood had given her after an enviably successful performance as Zara (Highfill et al., *Biographical Dictionary* 3: 267). Cibber's "fondness" for his wife Susannah seemed to increase with her success, and he brazenly sued her lover William Sloper for depriving him of his wife's income as an actress.[59] Dorothy Jordan, the long-term mistress to the Duke of Clarence and mother of his children, lent her lover £2400 in summer 1797. She was, according to her recent biographer, "both in public acclaim and in earning power . . . the man of the family."[60] Small wonder that many actresses attempted to keep their earnings free of patriarchal interference. Elizabeth Barry and Anne Bracegirdle never married, Clive and Abington early separated from their husbands, and Woffington, though a mistress to many lovers, remained single and was described as a "spinster" on her gravestone.[61] These great actresses established themselves as astute, profit-oriented women as they exploited the economic opportunities that the stage offered.

A variety of theatrical pamphlets registered the public's complaints against actors, and especially against women players, who believed that they should be substantially rewarded for their labors. One such tract, *Theatrical Correspondence in Death* (1743), complains about the domestic help that an actress's "high Salary enabled her to keep" and her insisting "upon an annual

Income superior to those of many private gentlemen, equal to those of some ennobled."[62] Women who became pregnant (though Anne Oldfield apparently worked until the birth of her son in 1713, George Anne Bellamy delivered her daughter on 28 February 1754, the day after a performance, and Susannah Cibber played at Drury Lane more than eight months pregnant and returned to work within four months) could suffer at least temporary dismissal from the stage. Added to that, they could be saddled with supporting a child in spite of its aristocratic parentage, or they could easily lose custody of the child to the father, as in the case of Elizabeth Barry and Lord Rochester. In addition, the actresses' entitlement to social privilege was often complicated by their true circumstances as the daughters of families of substantial means who had lost their fortunes.[63] Not only did Restoration and eighteenth-century actresses effectively impersonate quality, many actresses actually *were* women of quality attempting to repair the fortunes of their fallen families.

Earning Power: Salary and Benefit Performances

Though early actresses were underpaid and earned significantly less than men, it has not been recognized that the most celebrated women players in the eighteenth century could make more money from acting than many male thespians, more than men who labored in other trades, and—most significantly—more money than any other working women up to that point in history.[64] In the ladder system of the eighteenth-century theater, the budding star system encouraged large disparities between major and minor actresses.[65] The difference between the ordinary actor and the famous or infamous star only became more extreme during the century.[66] Women novelists with their erratic incomes generally earned less than well-placed actresses and could seldom reach even the middling ranks by writing fiction. Fees paid for fiction manuscripts ranged from about five guineas rising to ten guineas by the end of the century: "The average copyright fee from one novel was roughly equivalent to the annual wages of a laundry, scullery, or dairy maid, and therefore entirely inadequate for anyone attempting to maintain middle-class status."[67] To enter the middle ranks, one would have to bring in at least £50 per year, a sum that would require writing about ten novels.[68] Even the renowned Frances Burney was paid only £25 for *Evelina* (1778), though she commanded £250 for *Cecilia* (1782). When Charlotte Smith was able to earn £50 per volume, that was thought to be a significant sum. By the early nineteenth century Elizabeth

Inchbald eventually received an annual income of about £260 from her writing of novels and plays, though her earnings fluctuated wildly.

Playwrights earned profits from the third, sixth, and ninth night performances. These benefits on behalf of playwrights earned them an average of £43 pounds from 1714 to 1721, and an average of £154 pounds from 1721 to 28. Robert Hume speculates that only two of the 150 playwrights from 1700 to 1750 supported themselves from the takings. That amount would, then, have equaled the sum that a play earned through performance, but publication was a different matter. Susanna Centlivre, for example, earned £10 for her comedy, *The Busy Body* (1709). In the 1740s an author would have earned about £30–40, divided with the publisher, which would have afforded a living wage for a year; but that amount is significantly less than a celebrity actor or opera singer would have made.[69] Still, the most celebrated actresses were paid considerably more than women writers and many male writers. This includes women playwrights who could not survive on their earnings until a new compensation system, no longer based on benefit nights, was initiated in 1794, after which time Elizabeth Inchbald made more as a playwright from one benefit night than from a year's salary as an actress.[70] Judging from the few records extant for plays written by women before 1760, it seems that none could gain a sufficient income until late in the century. After 1760 there was a meteoric rise of women playwrights to prominence when they wrote one in five of the new plays produced for the London stage.[71] The average fee earned by a woman playwright in 1776–94 was £74, though eventually Inchbald, Hannah Cowley, Frances Sheridan, and Elizabeth Griffith were able to garner substantial sums from their writing.[72] Writing a novel required a considerable investment of time, however, while writing a play might constitute a week's work. Inchbald favorably compares playwriting to novel writing in a letter to Godwin: "I have frequently obtained more [pecuniary?] advantage by ten days labour in the Dramatic way than by the labour of this ten months."[73]

The combination of salary, benefit nights, and gratuities for actresses exceeded the advantages of patronage, subscription, and direct sale of copyright available to novelists. In fact, then, the most talented and savvy actresses could compete with eminent actors in the theatrical economy. Many relatively well-known actresses were, then, wealthier than the middle classes but lacked the social cachet of the propertied elite, occupying a status somewhat equivalent to a female nabob—*nouveau riche* and slightly déclassé. While it is beyond the scope of this book to offer a complete tracking of actresses' salaries, Anne Oldfield, for example, beginning with a weekly salary of 15s., soon earned as much as two or three times the annual salary required for sustaining a modest but comfortable living.[74] In the 1708–9 season when Oldfield's benefit brought in £62, the guineas or gratuities she collected amounted to £120 for a total benefit package of £182, though she disputed the house charges that Rich had deducted before paying her remainder. Oldfield was reportedly invited to become a joint-sharer at Drury Lane in 1710, but management reneged and instead raised her salary to £200 rising to 300 guineas, along with the promise of a benefit free of deductions which, according to Cibber, amounted on average to an astounding sum of 600 guineas during her tenure at Drury Lane (*Apology*, ed. Lowe, 2: 70–71). In 1703 Oldfield's estimated earnings of £70 to £80 per annum put her in the midrange of actresses in the company, and in 1706 she earned £120 a year at the Haymarket, advancing to well over £500 in 1728–29.[75] This sum would have exceeded the income expected for a "Gentleman," while the income of a merchant or artisan family would have ranged around £200 (Hume, "Economics of Culture in London," 495). An army officer would have earned well under £100, while Jane Rogers was promised a guaranteed salary of £100 in 1711–12. In 1707 Anne Bracegirdle was sufficiently wealthy to retire with a good living, supplemented by gifts and bequests from admirers such as the Earl of Scarsdale, William Congreve, and Edward Porter. Such money is not completely untainted, but a considerable portion of her capital was actually earned.

The actresses who were in greatest demand could accumulate substantial wealth and influence. To cite a few other telling examples, Kitty Clive is believed to have bested Charles Macklin in the 1742–43 season by about £40; and Peg Woffington topped the men by earning £800 at Smock Alley House in 1752 after increasing the theater's receipts to £4,000 in the previous season.[76] In 1774 Mrs. Yates earned £700 plus £50 for costumes, and David Garrick was reputed to have given Hannah Pritchard £500, or £200 more than John Rich, in a dispute between the theater companies in 1747.[77] Later in the century Dora Jordan earned the same fee as John Philip Kemble, £31 10s. a week, while Sarah Siddons was paid an equivalent sum *per night* for a season of about thirty weeks.[78] With their discretionary income actresses became patrons of the arts, subscribers to book publication, philanthropists, or benefactors to their relatives and heirs; they loaned money, made wagers and investments, extended credit, borrowed substantial funds, and even entertained the possibility of purchasing a theater patent.[79] They cunningly and adeptly negotiated contracts, and several rose to become managers or co-managers. The notorious Charlotte Charke made history as a female manager of several

London troupes in the mid-1730s and at the St. James's Street playhouse in 1742–43.[80]

During the first decade when actresses appeared on the Restoration stage, the women in the troupe were allowed an annual collective benefit performance. Women were equal sharers in the profits when Elizabeth Barry, Anne Bracegirdle, Mrs. Bowman, and Mrs. Leigh were shareholders in Betterton's company in 1695, but the privilege was soon exchanged for establishing the risky but potentially lucrative practice of benefit nights.[81] Benefits could serve as the means to transform an unreasonable manager's point of view into an appeal to the public. James Boaden writes in his biography of Dorothy Jordan, "The benefit play of an actress is, at least, an opportunity of putting the town in possession of her own opinion of herself, and is, therefore, commonly seized for the purpose of extending the performer's claims. She can then invade the line of a rival, and correct the, perhaps, obstinate prejudice of a manager."[82] Mrs. Sterling played Polly Peachum with such skill that the House demanded that she should have a benefit night for which she received £105. 14s., along with about £30 thrown onto the stage.[83] Because actors sold many of their own tickets, the benefit often amounted to a popularity contest that relied heavily on social connections. Apparently benefit tickets could be returned without penalty, thus increasing uncertainty about the exact amount of guaranteed receipts. Ann Catley's biographer describes her attending a masquerade dressed as an orange girl to sell several dozen box tickets for a benefit at a considerable profit which she then donated to an impoverished family.[84] Yet actresses, especially the best actresses, often complained about managers who slighted their contractual obligations or allowed their salaries to fall into arrears. While women players such as Oldfield, Barry, Clive, and Woffington were sometimes chided for their headstrong or greedy nature, one wonders if these epithets are in fact unfairly applied, and that the women were simply unrelenting in their demands for equity and their just deserts for hard work. In short, trading on celebrity, many actresses managed to gain power and influence through shaping the repertory, generally elevating the status of women in the public arena, and exploiting the economy of celebrity.

The power of the benefit in establishing star power and increasing an actress's salary cannot be overestimated.[85] For the most favored players, a benefit allowed an actor to garner the profits from her chosen program on a single night, less the overhead expenses. Attaining sufficient professional status to command a benefit night was a critical turning point in an actress's career after which she could capitalize on her loyal following. The salary scale for the

United Company, for example, began at 12s. per week, moving up through 25s., 40s., 50s., and 60s. (Hume and Milhous, "Account Books," 200–241). These sums would have been rather paltry, barely sufficient to provide a living wage. But once an actress merited a benefit night, she could enlarge her salary not only by gaining public acclaim but also by reaping personal rewards from her private efforts at cultivating celebrity. Elizabeth Barry had broken new ground in 1708 when, according to Colley Cibber, she was the first woman to negotiate such an opportunity. The coveted "clear benefit" free of house charges was an unmistakable sign of stardom; the rarified status of favorites such as Woffington, Siddons, and Garrick merited two clear benefits a season.

In addition to offering an alternative means to support a commercial theater, from the end of the seventeenth century, actors' benefits also added the need to sell tickets to actor's responsibilities: "To appreciate the struggle to attract an audience, any audience, one must read the newspaper advertisements."[86] The theaters grew from a seating capacity of 800 spectators in the 1670s to 3,000 in the 1780s. Drury Lane, built in 1674 and enlarged in 1747, seated about 1,000 spectators. Covent Garden, constructed in 1732 to accommodate 1,335, was enlarged in 1782 to nearly 3,000. In 1741–42, Covent Garden held 218 seats in the boxes, 498 in the pit, and 222 in the first gallery, while the upper gallery held about 39 spectators. Boxes cost 4s. until the 1740s when they were raised a shilling.[87] *The Prompter* (no. 47, Tuesday, 22 April 1735) remarks that only "one-tenth part" of the audience were "true judges" of a play because the playwright relied on his friends to fill the seats, and the pay given to actor-shareholders would have fluctuated according to the earnings of the house.[88]

The exact amount of the house charges was often subject to dispute, and theater managers could adjust their books to benefit an impoverished performer, a favored one, or the whole company. The reduction or loss of a benefit could be used to discipline actors, and rumors of the manager's favoritism often circulated regarding the timing or terms of benefits. The most celebrated and highest salaried actors were granted preferred place to perform in benefits earliest in the season, though they sometimes were asked to make up the shortfall when the house did not fill. Bargaining and trading of benefits occurred when, for example, George Anne Bellamy relieved Rich's pleas of insufficient receipts to pay her salary by accepting one of *his* benefit nights instead (*Apology*, 1: 67–68). Frances Abington became incensed when she found that her scheduled benefit conflicted with an opera night that inevitably competed for the elite patrons who engaged the costly boxes, and David Garrick appeased her by trading benefit nights. Contests over being favored for a particular night erupted when Kitty Clive refused to play on 17 March, the date set for her benefit, because Mrs. Dancer's benefit had occurred earlier, and because St. Patrick's Day celebrations threatened to distract theatergoers. Actors also aimed for benefit nights that corresponded with an influx of potential theater customers, including the landing of naval fleets near London. George Anne Bellamy probably earned the largest proceeds, in excess of £1100, from a benefit when the usual take would ordinarily have been nearer to £200, after it was enhanced by the attendance of the military to ingratiate themselves by purchasing a side or upper box near Bellamy's lover, Foreign Secretary Charles James Fox.[89]

Actors sought patronage from sales of advance tickets that were supplemented by the coveted "gold tickets," or "guineas" and gold or silver plate that served as tips offered in advance for an announced performance. While guineas varied in their value, "gold tickets" were apparently issued in multiples of £50 (Troubridge, 105–6). Actresses personally sold reservations and tickets from their homes, often collecting substantial gratuities from generous benefactors. Bellamy, for example, records her disappointment that for her performance as Juliet she received *only* one hundred gold tickets from Lord Holderness and fifty apiece from four other gentlemen (4: 114). Actresses were especially susceptible to the advantages and drawbacks of benefit performances, for they encouraged the servile relationship of actor to audience, though York theater manager Tate Wilkinson restricted beggarly practices such as those undertaken by the actor Frodsham, "bred as a gentleman with fine natural talents and esteemed in York as a Garrick, the Hamlet of the age, running after, or stopping a gentleman on horseback to deliver his benefit bill and beg a half a crown" (Wilkinson, *Memoirs*, 4: 67). The identical supplicating behavior by a woman would have made her seem to be no better than a whore.

Because actresses cultivated the patronage of the aristocracy they emulated on stage and off, the line between actress and itinerant panhandler could become tenuous. Actresses would have been vulnerable to sexual and social compromise in making house calls to theater patrons in the hope of selling tickets, though they also received in their own homes the messengers or servants who were sent to buy the attractively designed benefit tickets. Though coffeehouses served as agencies for distributing tickets, it would have been very unlikely that women—even women servants—would frequent those venues, and it is much more probable that ladies—and perhaps occasionally gentlemen—received actresses in their homes in order to purchase box seats, thus affording another opportunity for sociable connection. Acting a particular part at a patron's instigation might also become a means of barter for an enterprising actress. George Anne Bellamy notes that "in return for Mrs. Sparks's great attention to me during my illness, I not only consented to play the 'Mourning Bride' for [Mr. Sparks's] benefit, but I disposed of near two hundred gold tickets for him" (*Apology*, 3: 161). Though Bellamy immodestly claims that her benefit in Voltaire's tragedy *Alzira* (translated by Aaron Hill) was "as usual, very brilliant; and lucrative to an excess" (3: 51), she frequently found herself penniless. Actresses peddled their tickets to various public institutions, clubs, and societies as a means of selling out the playhouse, but such a means of distribution might also have proved an embarrassment. At Bath Sarah Siddons instituted the more dignified and impersonal practice of placing a registry at the theater lobby box office where ladies and gentlemen could subscribe to a particular benefit, a practice that eventually made its way to Drury Lane (Troubridge, 111).

For the most famous, salary and benefits were regularly supplemented by barter, bribes, favors, gifts, loans, and offers of living accommodation from wealthy male and female playgoers. A few other specific examples will clarify the importance of the benefit, and the peculiar circumstances preventing actresses from sharing fully in its advantages. From the 1720s to the 1760s, three Drury Lane actresses—Catherine Clive, Susannah Cibber, and Hannah Pritchard—earned from one-third to one-half of their annual incomes on benefit nights, and each cultivated a devoted following. The most celebrated stars could bargain for acting in their drama of choice, and each of these actresses further improved the theater's receipts by cleverly asking David Garrick to co-star with them. Increased popularity meant that their fans and friends would turn out for the benefit night, boosting the night's profits. Mrs. Cibber, for example, earned £100 during the 1734–35 season, doubling her salary in the next two seasons, tripling her benefit earnings by 1747–48, and doubling them yet again to make a total of £700 in the 1755–56 season.[90] Elizabeth Barry earned £100 annually and the profits from a benefit even after her 1710 retirement (Highfill et al., *Biographical Dictionary*, 1: 323). Though Barry's salary figure may not be completely reliable, it is clear that benefit nights could be enormously profitable and their success depended heavily upon sustaining a public intimacy that contributed to a visible celebrity and popularity.

Playbills for benefits announced the whole evening's entertainment, and gave specific mention to the seating arrangements, the ticket-selling locations, and the patrons who supported the benefit in advance. Securing the patronage and promised attendance of public officials, of nobility or royalty in the boxes, also meant that tickets to regularly scheduled plays or benefits would sell more easily. There is frequent mention in memoirs and theater histories of ladies of quality who furthered the careers of celebrated actresses in particular roles with their patronage, and these women also wielded influence over the plays that the actresses chose. George Anne Bellamy was especially popular with the Duchess of Queensberry who, accompanied by her entourage of aristocratic ladies, purchased on occasion 250 tickets for the actress's benefit (1: 73), and the duchess rewarded Bellamy with an additional 150 guineas. Lady Spencer gave Sarah Siddons 90 guineas for a side box at her benefit, and Lady Aylesbury provided a £50 bank note for an upper box (Troubridge, 107). In short, selling tickets for a benefit allowed patrons a legitimate means of contributing to the actress's income, but it was also a means of trading favors, engaging in bribery, seeking beneficence or sexual favors, or even subjecting oneself to abjection. When actress Mrs. Long paraded her eight children dressed in scarlet jackets as playbill distributors, she succeeded in attracting an overflow house to her performance.[91]

The prevailing resentment over the fact that actresses occasionally appeared to be women of means was sometimes justified by recounting their charitable and philanthropic acts (as I will discuss in more detail in Chapter 3). Mrs. Oldfield, writes William Chetwood, was "made up of benevolent Charity, affable and good-natur'd to all that deserv'd it" (Chetwood, *General History*, 202). The "celebrated virgin" Anne Bracegirdle granted alms to the poor unemployed basket women in Clare Market "so that she could not pass . . . without the thankful Acclamations of People of all Degrees." Lavinia Fenton contributed a regular maintenance to her stepfather, and her biography touts her "*Humanity* to the *Distressed.*"[92] Peg Woffington not only settled a pension on her mother but also a bequest to support her sister Mary (Polly) Cholmondeley consisting of stage jewels that originally belonged to Queen Margaret. She generously endowed almshouses near her estate at Teddington (Highfill et al., *Biographical Dictionary*, 16: 207). Elizabeth Inchbald supported her destitute sisters. In "An Epistle to Mrs. Clive" Henry Fielding hints at the bitterness that Kitty Clive's financial success aroused when he details her kindnesses to family and fellow actors as a means of excusing her ambition, a theme reiterated in the memoirs of other actresses:

> But as great a Favourite as you at present are with the Audience, you would be much more so, were they acquainted with your private

Character; cou'd they see you laying out great part of the Profits which arise from entertaining them so well, in the Support of an aged Father; did they see you who can charm them on the Stage with personating the foolish and vicious Characters of your Sex, acting in real Life the Part of the best Wife, the best Daughter, the best Sister, and the best Friend.[93]

Clive, protesting against low salaries, also supported her fellow actors when they were caught in the dispute between players and patentees after Theophilus Cibber absconded to the Haymarket with part of the Drury Lane company: "You have been so far from endeavouring to exact an exorbitant Reward from Persons little able to afford it, that I have known you offer to act for nothing, rather than the Patentees should be injur'd by the Dismission of the Audience" (Fielding, "Epistle,"4). These accounts of private charitable behavior insert the actress within conventional expectations directed at women of quality, while seeking to define the parameters of an acceptable public femininity that depended upon the aesthetic performance of genuine sensibility and natural generosity.

Women players were literally commodified as admirers eagerly bought up trinkets and memorabilia imprinted with star actresses dressed as their favorite characters.[94] Colley Cibber openly acknowledged the way that actresses resembled commodities when he compared them to "Bawbles" for purchase in a "Toy-shop" (*Apology*, ed. Lowe, 2: 223). Anne Oldfield's memoirs described her as a visual treat to be consumed by the playgoers: "How have I seen the crouded Audience . . . devour her with their Eyes, whenever She appear'd!"[95] An engraving of the older Kitty Clive as Mrs. Riot in *Lethe* holding a pet pug dog (1750) appeared in Bow and Chelsea porcelain; the image of Peg Woffington as a sphinx from a painting by Pond became a china statue; Mary Ann Yates was immortalized on Delftware tile, as was Susannah Cibber as Monimia. Staffordshire figurines of Mrs. Siddons represented her as Lady Macbeth, and 130 Wedgewood chess sets featuring Siddons as the queen sold between 1785 and 1795.[96] Such representations of actresses' faces, bodies, and characteristic clothing both defined and amplified their celebrity.

Actresses too served as arbiters of fashion and displayed, especially after mid-century, their own modish variations on classical or historical costumes.[97] Singer-actress Ann Catley's playful fan-like haircut, "Catlified hair," became all the rage and persisted among "the lower classes of those ladies who strole the streets" late in the century.[98] Frances Abington transformed her fashion sense into trademark accessories. Dressing in high vogue on the stage set clothing styles, and actresses served as fashion icons to women of rank, who sometimes donated their dresses to women players—who were known to reciprocate in turn by offering their costumes to noblewomen. Celebrity attached itself to clothing and costume and thus could be transplanted from one rank to another, and from the theater to the town. For example, Maria Beatrice of Modena (second wife of James II) famously loaned Elizabeth Barry her wedding suit and coronation robes, while Sarah Siddons mentions in her correspondence that Lady B. borrowed her Lady Macbeth banquet dress for a masquerade where "many of these beauties will appear in my stage finery."[99]

Actresses' battles throughout the eighteenth century erupted over ownership of a leading role, profits, and reputation as well as lovers. Recognizing that other women in the troupe were her principal economic competitors, George Anne Bellamy, upon learning that Barry had given Peg Woffington 500 pounds, insisted on getting 500 guineas, "a larger salary than any other female performer at that theatre" (3: 12). An oft-repeated but specious anecdote recounts a quarrel supposed to have erupted between Oldfield and Bracegirdle in 1707 concerning who was the superior actress in Thomas Betterton's *The Amorous Widow; or, The Wanton Wife* (1670). Legend has it (although a check of *The London Stage* reveals that these competing performances probably never occurred) that when each acted the part in turn, Oldfield outshone Bracegirdle, thus shaming her into retirement. A similar anecdote is told regarding the competition between Anne Oldfield and Jane Rogers for the part of Lady Lurewell in *The Constant Couple* when Wilks allegedly urged them to resolve the quarrel by performing on succeeding nights. Oldfield's trial was a smashing success, and Rogers gave up her claim to the role by default.[100] Whether true or not, these kinds of rumors of rival actresses' querulous nature circulated widely and were preserved for posterity.

In another very public quarrel, Susannah Cibber competed with Kitty Clive in 1736 for the coveted part of Polly in *Beggar's Opera*.[101] Fleetwood, the new manager of Drury Lane, assigned Clive the inferior role of Lucy and awarded Polly to Cibber. Both actresses engaged the press, including *Fog's Journal*, *The Grub-Street Journal*, *The Daily Journal*, and *The Town*, and the media attention competed with the play itself. The paper wars that circulated within the coffeehouse culture of the 1730s created the equivalent of modern tabloid rumor and innuendo in the periodical press. A character speaking in the person of "Theo" Cibber complained, "I find that by our theatrical squabbles and altercations we make as much amusement to the town in a morning as by our performance in an evening."[102] The public disagreement reached mock-epic proportion in a ballad in *The Beggar's Pantomime* in which dueling prima donnas named Madam Squall and Madam Squeak, scratching and tearing at each other's clothes, were anything but silent, as the lyric composed on the occasion conveys:

> Cibber, the Syren of the Stage,
> A Vow to Heav'n did make,
> Full Twenty Nights in Polly's Part,
> She'd make the Play-house shake.
> When as these Tidings came to Clive,
> Fierce Amazonian Dame;
> Who is it thus, in Rage she cries,
> Dares rob me of my Claim.[103]

The end result of the heightened gossip was increased receipts. In a purported dialogue with Clive regarding the theater dispute, the attorney Dash protested that the manager "certainly encreased Kitty's salary so extravagantly as made it much above any Woman's now upon the Stage," though she still protested that her pay was in arrears.[104] When the stormy public fight continued for three months, the flinty Kitty Clive, as Letitia Cross had attempted to do before her, insisted that dramatic parts should become the legitimate property of the person accustomed to playing them.[105] The irate actress indicated that she feared a larger conspiracy was afoot to steal her principal parts in order "to make me so little useful to the Stage, as not to deserve the Sallary I now have, which is much inferior to that of several other Performers" (Chetwood, *Dramatic Congress*, 22). Clive and other eighteenth-century actresses like her, rather than being merely annoying harridans, were indefatigable advocates for the rights of actors and campaigners for their own equitable treatment as professionals; her activities were aimed squarely at engaging audience and press to protect her income and her reputation.

In sum, celebrity for the first and second generation of actresses in the British theater was not merely an accident of circumstance, and women players struggled to achieve equity in training, compensation, choice of roles, benefits, and theater management. Economic advancement for these very public women was curiously enhanced by their constructing an allegedly private space intentionally invaded, sometimes at the actress's own instigation, by an emergent media apparatus and bound up with public reputation. An actress's private passions added luster to her theatrical identity or sometimes contaminated it, but her hard-won entrepreneurial ability to advance her interests improved her commercial appeal, her earnings, and her celebrity. The star woman actor, excessively sexualized in the eighteenth century and by later commentators, invented a public, performative femininity compatible with wealth, authority, and fame, while seeming to remain intimately accessible to her devotees. Fame *and* infamy increased the possibility of class mobility, enchanted patrons and lovers, improved the theater's take, and made possible the accumulation of unprecedented cultural capital. On the negative side, however, public intimacy sometimes distracted the audience from recognizing the intense labor and expertise involved in acting.

The boundary between these women's public and private identities was violated, exploited, and ultimately reconfigured during the eighteenth century. Unlike their fellow male actors, women players were sexually vulnerable; subject to the double moral standard and to pervasive misogyny in spite of and because of their income and talents, they met the challenges of inequality in theater practices and under the law. In response they defied class strictures, assumed a position compatible with women of rank, accumulated wealth, supported themselves and their dependents, acted as agents of their own celebrity, and came to exemplify an exceptional kind of personhood. Complicating their propensity to act up, the most celebrated of them began to lay claim to status as tough negotiators on their own terms: in other words, they became legitimate professionals.

CHAPTER 2

"Real, Beautiful Women": Rival Queens

> Theatrical revolutions are as frequent, and owe their rise to the same principles, as those in the political world.—Pique, resentment, ambition, or interest, which ever motive happens to preponderate, brings them about.
> —*An Apology for the Life of George Anne Bellamy* (1786)

THE EIGHTEENTH-CENTURY LONDON stage was haunted by the performance of older plays recycled from earlier periods, many of which centered on pairs of historical or classical female characters. The new phenomenon of actresses—real, beautiful women—catapulted the antiquated roles into an eighteenth-century present. "Before the Restoration," wrote theater manager, actor, and playwright Colley Cibber in his *Apology*, "no Actresses had ever been seen upon the *English* Stage. The Characters of Women, in former Theatres were perform'd by Boys, or young Men of the most effeminate Aspect," but after their appearance as players there was a radical shift, for "the additional Objects then of real, beautiful Women, could not but draw a Proportion of new Admirers to the Theatre."[1] The success of the innovation depended upon the erotic impact of live female bodies, but also, less obviously, as illustrated in the previous chapter, upon the women's genuine entrepreneurial skill and increasing economic authority. Actual women engaged in rivalries kept heroic tragedies such as Nathaniel Lee's *The Rival Queens* (1677), and other plays resembling it, viable. The characteristic scene of two women locked in combat remained a staple of the genre in, for example, *The Mourning Bride* (Zara-Almeria), *All for Love* (Octavia-Cleopatra), *The Indian Emperour* (Almeria-Cydaria) and *Jane Shore* (Jane-Alice), and the confrontation scene contributed to the popularity of the anachronistic plays for generations of theatergoers. In their sensational reenactments the tragedies were transformed into what prompter John Downes once called a "living play," featuring living, breathing actress-characters who, as embodied forms of cultural memory, repeated, appropriated, and transformed past performances to lend them currency.[2] Audiences anticipated certain formulaic structures, but the performances were also tantalizingly alive with potential for innovative parody.[3]

In spite of eighteenth-century genre hierarchies that privileged tragedy over comedy, new tragedy has never been regarded as the favored eighteenth-century mode. Susan Staves has argued that the preference for new comedy over new tragedy was an effect of the development of an optimistic Enlightenment narrative compatible with its hopes for progress.[4] Comedy, especially sentimental comedy, fulfilled that promise by demonstrating that moral efforts felicitously applied and providentially realized would bring economic and social rewards. But in spite of the apparent failure of new tragic dramaturgy in the period, with the exception perhaps of she-tragedies and domestic tragedies, the performance of older serious dramas found a ready audience in eighteenth-century theaters, in part because of the expertise of brilliant tragic actresses such as Susannah Cibber, Hannah Pritchard, and Sarah Siddons. By considering ongoing productions of Nathaniel Lee's popular Restoration tragedy *The Rival Queens*, I argue in this chapter that it was principally actresses who drew the eighteenth-century theater into its contemporary moment by resetting and realigning the audience's relationship to time.[5]

Relevant to my argument here is Jean-Christophe Agnew's influential book, *Worlds Apart: The Market and the Theater in Anglo-American Thought, 1550–1750*, which posited that the separation between market and theater had fully emerged by the middle part of the eighteenth century. Agnew, along with David Marshall and Richard Sennett, early provided the most sophisticated descriptions of the period's development of theatrical kinds of personhood, though none of them focused on its performative history.[6] Agnew defines commercialism and theatricality as "abstracted properties" and argues that a more fluid market, with its timeless and fleeting elements, comes to replace an actual theater situated within specific material practices (xiii). As Natasha Korda succinctly frames the issue, Agnew, "in defining the 'situated phenomena' of the marketplace as residual, and the 'placeless and timeless' [Agnew, x] market process as emergent (and ultimately dominant), privileges the latter."[7] This increasing abstraction of the market is represented in part for Agnew by the socially mobile actor for whom identity and class position were as unstable and unfixed as the emerging economy. But the concept of liquidity does not, as Korda points out, fully dominate the theater until the end of the eighteenth century and thus should not be applied to the earlier periods. Korda astutely analyzes how the material practices of the theater economy, instead of "the placeless market," intersected with the larger culture. Uncovering diverse networks of commerce, production, and exchange, she shows how women apprentices and workers in guilds, trades, and the informal commerce of pawnbroking and millinery, for example, permeated Renaissance theater walls to blend the theater into the larger culture, even at this early juncture (195–96).

Both Agnew and Korda largely exclude actresses from their consideration—in Agnew's case because he thinks of the actor as the "Protean *man*" (my emphasis) and consequently ignores the ways that a *woman's* situation differs vis-à-vis the market and the theater. Korda, on the other hand, is interested in the theater prior to the Restoration, and because the Renaissance stage included no women players, she focuses on tradeswomen's economic activities as they intermesh with theater productions. Here I will argue that between 1700 and 1780, women, especially pairs of celebrated actresses, through their often invisible labor, were intermediaries between residual forms of production and these newly emergent abstract and liquid practices. I join the several voices who have argued that "the modern individual was first and foremost a woman," as Nancy Armstrong described the bourgeois subjectivity of the domestic novel heroine. But rather than turning to fictional heroines who exemplify interiorized virtue, sentiment, and moral ascendancy in their characters, I am suggesting here that actresses as real persons crafted a public performative identity, in tandem with creating an effect of intimacy, that developed another kind of exchange value in the culture.[8] Combining social status with a new kind of worth, they might be considered powerful competitors—rival queens—to the more decorous version of the modern individual; as such they are embodied, rather than textual, signs of modernity who, along with aristocratic and professional women, moved into public realms as the century progressed. Manipulating and disentangling the pervasive association of actress with prostitute, Elizabeth Barry, Bracegirdle, Oldfield, Clive, Woffington, Bellamy, and Abington are among those who invented a new kind of labor and alternative identities for women. As we have seen, they often served as managers of their own careers in manipulating their conditions of employment, salaries and benefits, sales of tickets, assignment of roles, and costuming. In the first century of women's legitimate public performance, these women—"real, beautiful Women"—and their physical presence on the stage were commercial magnets that connected past and present, and drew the situated and the placeless into contiguity. Restoration and eighteenth-century actresses, giving the lie to the separation of public and private spheres, exemplified "public intimacy"—the private-in-the-public—in adapting to, and exploiting, modern commercial society.

Star actresses—much more than their counterpart male actors, I am suggesting—were the sentient site of negotiations regarding gender and genre, negotiations arising from specific practices and performances. I am of course speaking principally of celebrity actresses: women who, projecting an aura of mystery and appeal, attracted audiences quick both to praise and abuse them, and who commanded public attention and high salaries between their inaugural appearances in the Restoration and the rise of "the Siddons" in the 1780s.

As Peggy Phelan comments, the magic of performance "approaches the Real through *resisting* the metaphorical reduction of the two [representation and real] into one" (my emphasis).[9] The actress resists the reduction of her "self" and the character she impersonates into a unified identity, but she also plays with that elision as a means of creating agency. In fictional representations of the actress, Frances Burney's heroine Evelina (1778) is predictably appalled at being mistaken for a thespian when libertines trap the unsuspecting ingénue in the London streets: "'No,—no,—no,—' I *panted* out, 'I am no actress,—pray let me go, —pray let me pass—,'" while Eliza Haywood's Fantomina (1725), the ingenious heroine who sustains her lover Beauplaisir's interest by mischievously pretending to be several women in seriatim, embraces the actress's power to seduce.[10] There are also actress-characters who resist unifying representation with reality in order to teach women that they need to perform to protect their private subjectivities that may be at odds with cultural expectations. In Charlotte Lennox's *Female Quixote* (1752), Arabella, the deluded heroine, inhabits a world of romance that threatens to overwhelm her contact with the "real" world. When Arabella's imaginings begin to lead to dire consequences—potential drownings and a suitor's near-mortal wounding—Sir George hires an actress to impersonate Cynecia, a princess of Gaul, in an attempt to jolt the heroine out of madness through performance. The actress playing Cynecia, ensnaring Arabella into a trap, leads her to believe that they are both being pursued by the same suitor, Ariamenes (actually Glanville, Arabella's beloved). The actress pretends to be a wandering princess in Twickenham who ventured from her fictional romance home in the Pyrenees to London: in this way she serves as an intermediary between Arabella's textually based romance world and the "real" world that she refuses to enter. The figure of the actress, combining the romance world with a purported reality, represents both illusion and history while offering Arabella a corporeal bridge from past to present, and from elsewhere to here. When Arabella madly and futilely pursues her through Richmond Park, the elusive Cynecia disappears, as if into thin air. Abandoned, Arabella ultimately leaps into the Thames to escape imagined ravishers but finds herself baptized instead into the real, cold modern world of which she must learn to be a part. An untimely interloper into Arabella's world of fantasy, the actress is both a modern woman and a sympathetic reversion to an older paradigm—romance history—that the heroine learns is incompatible with the current times.

The actress-character in *The Female Quixote* offered a moral compass to Arabella and a potential resolution to her dilemma. Taking tutelage from her, and later from the Countess and the Doctor, Arabella learns to acknowledge publicly that her romance world exists only in books, though at first she stands firm and refuses to accept the actress's lesson as her own, a lesson that would enable her to resist the metaphorical reduction of representation and reality into one. Learning to perform, to pretend to be sincere, would have enabled her to act both as a "real" person satisfying social conventions, *and* as a virtual creation, a fictional romance heroine possessed of the sovereignty she craves.[11] I begin with this episode in order to show that eighteenth-century actresses provide a key to understanding the relations between representation and reality but also between genres, sexualities, historical moments, and shifting modes of production. Actresses as signs of modernity drove the economy of the playhouse and acted as agents of their own commodification: they signaled the emergence of a culture in which the "self"—creating the effect of a private interior depth combined with a very real physical presence— produces itself as a fluid commodity to be advertised and exchanged. I want to turn now to examine *The Rival Queens*, focusing on the importance of these first modern women, to argue that they, and the characters they played, were in large part responsible for this tragedy's anachronistic success throughout the period.

The Rival Queens

Many of the heroic characters in *The Female Quixote* derive from the same source as those in Nathaniel Lee's *The Rival Queens*—that is, the seventeenth-century romances of Madeleine de Scudéry and La Calprenède. In *The Rival Queens*, Lee transforms Calprenède's original romance tale in which Statira and Roxana become friends, in spite of their shared love for Oroondates, the Prince of Scythia, into a feverish competition for the emperor Alexander, who is poisoned by the treasonous Cassander and Polyperchon. How can we account for the lasting popularity of Nathaniel Lee's play, and for the audience's participation in the actresses' private aspirations? We are accustomed to think of tragedies such as Lee's bombastic *Rival Queens*, first produced in 1677, as relics of a genre that, mercifully, came and went quickly, and that soon attracted ridicule. Yet the performance history of that play tells us a great deal about the eighteenth-century theater's investment in novelty as it encouraged an ever-increasing audience to purchase an evening's ephemeral entertainment at Drury Lane or Covent Garden.

When critics speculate about the reasons for the public's failing interest in heroic plays in the last two decades of the seventeenth century, they neglect to consider the frequent restaging of Restoration plays throughout the period. After the union of the two theater houses in 1682, it became more difficult to launch *new* plays on the London stage, which meant that older plays were frequently revived and adapted to the taste of new audiences.[12] *The Rival Queens* was the most popular of Nathaniel Lee's plays, and it is arguably the only vestige of its kind in the eighteenth-century repertory. It was regularly produced throughout the Restoration and eighteenth century, reaching about 250 performances.[13] The heroic tragedy in its eighteenth-century incarnation responded to the constant demand for novelty while gesturing back toward an earlier time. The steady demand for the play may be attributed, I am suggesting, to its competing actresses who, in becoming spectacularly theatrical in staging their rivalries, adjusted to the changing demands of eighteenth-century audiences. Real, palpable women, professional actresses rather than boys, signal the modern and set up a dynamic disjunction between present and past. *The Rival Queens* occupies the unusual position of being both the most celebrated and most reviled of the heroic tragedies. According to Colley Cibber, "there was no one Tragedy, for many Years, more in favour with the Town" in spite of—or perhaps because of— the fact that it was, as the theatrical review *The Prompter* characterized the 1735 version, "a mad play wrote by a mad poet, . . . revived by a mad manager, to introduce a mad actor to a mad town" (*Apology* 1: 106).¹⁴ This eccentricity in its many productions made the play an exotic curiosity that from the early eighteenth century on made it an object for burlesque and the subject of numerous anecdotes—most of which were probably exaggerated or apocryphal, a matter to which I will return. So frequently performed was the play that one can imagine the audience mouthing the words as the actors spoke them, as they reportedly did for *The Beggar's Opera*, an impossibly popular play that also featured two rival actresses as Polly Peachum and Lucy Lockit. So beloved was *The Rival Queens* that specific lines were regularly parodied in other plays without the need to name the original source.¹⁵ Audiences obviously enjoyed the recycling of familiar dialogue and scenes of "twice-behaved behavior," as Richard Schechner has cogently described theater's reiteration of cultural memories.¹⁶

The Rival Queens, of course, focuses on Alexander, emphasizing his single-minded monarchical rule, his despotic claims to divine right, and his resemblance to the almighty Jove, but also his failed ambition. The play lingers over issues of political patriarchy in the king's assertions of authority over his subjects and his family; it reminds the audience of debates over patriarchal rights sparked by Robert Filmer's *Patriarcha* (1680); and it raises timely issues concerning women's liberty in the face of traditional masculine restraints upon the sex. Alexander's blatant violation of his subjects' rights hearkened back to the Jacobite threat and encouraged later eighteenth-century audiences to celebrate the end of arbitrary monarchical power through the play's reenactment.¹⁷ In addition, his apparent bigamy unfavorably contrasts an exotic polygamous East (Persian, Greek, and Macedonian) with a monogamous Christian England. Thus, the content of the play draws the classical past into contemporary concerns that remained urgent throughout much of the eighteenth century. For example, it may well have reflected a nation's discomfort with the Jacobite monarchy and the final abandonment of it after the 1745 resurgence was quelled. If, as Joseph Roach argues, "the key element of monarchical government . . . is the public visibility of its sacred head,"¹⁸ then the frequently reiterated visibility of Alexander the Great through Lee's *Rival Queens* may have come to substitute for that missing sacred head of the Jacobite kings, as the celebrity of actors and actresses assumed the cultural authority previously accorded royalty and priests.

Although *The Rival Queens, or the Death of Alexander the Great* gives twin billing to hero and heroines, the rival actresses were, I think, more instrumental than the lead actors to the play's success. Over thirty editions of *The Rival Queens* were published in the eighteenth and nineteenth centuries, including a well-known revision in 1756 and a more substantial alteration in 1770. In its revamped splendor, the heroic tragedy lent itself to engaging an increasingly class-diverse audience that welcomed bourgeois tragedy and opera, but also demanded farce and burlesque. Like other popular forms developed in the later eighteenth century, including the pantomime and the Gothic novel, the spoofs of heroic tragedy might be said to "reanimate . . . an extinct historical style for the purposes of mass entertainment."[19] The periodical *The Prompter* lambasted the play's "ill-chosen fable" and its lack of moral fiber in presenting a ridiculous, arrogant, drunken, debauched, and effeminate Alexander, and seemed to call for the restoration of a strong masculine ruler[20] (Figure 5). But Thomas Davies attributed its surprising longevity to the many celebrated players beginning with Charles Hart and Thomas Betterton who excelled in the role of Alexander, and to the play's ability to appeal across social class divisions: "As long as the stage will be able to furnish good actors for his Alexander, it will draw together all ranks of people, from the heroic lover, and the lady of high rank, to the lowest of the people."[21]

For some recent readers of the play the confrontation between the two paired women simply sidetracks the audience from the main plot, which focuses on Alexander's failed political ambition that makes him the central object of pathos. P. F. Vernon's introduction to the Regents Restoration Drama Series edition insists that the main action of the play is Alexander's decline rather than the queens' rivalry (xxiv–xxv). Similarly Robert Hume, in his otherwise illuminating analysis of the play, observes that the queens are merely "distracting,"[22] but I would argue that the eighteenth-century audience, witnessing over two hundred performances, found them absolutely critical to the play's success. Attesting to its popularity with female spectators, *The Rival Queens* was frequently performed at the desire of ladies of quality, as when, for example, in the 5 April 1709 production, Mrs. Porter acted Roxana for her benefit opposite Mrs. Bradshaw as Statira.[23] The tragedy was a favorite choice of actresses for benefit performances, almost certainly because it provided a theatrical vehicle for displaying a wide emotional range. Thus in spite of Alexander's prominence, the presence of actresses powerfully influenced the choice of plays on the eighteenth-century stage, and ultimately the formation of the dramatic canon.

The Rival Queens, of course, animated the metaphor of women's theatrical rivalries and alluded to the pejorative meaning of *queen*. Women's parts

Figure 5. "Mr. Smith in the Character of Alexander." Frontispiece to Nathaniel Lee, *Alexander the Great, with Alteration*. [John Bell, ed.], *Bell's British Theatre: Consisting of the most esteemed English plays*, 21 vols. London, 1776–81., vol. 7.

were from their inception a scarcer commodity than men's, and actresses were forced to quarrel over billing, salary, and ownership of roles in what Colley Cibber describes as a "Female Scramble" (*Apology*, 1: 306). Rivalries between Restoration actresses, as Elizabeth Howe has definitively demonstrated, pitted virtuous women characters against devious ones.[24] While a full performance history would be too tedious to rehearse, suffice it to say that Kitty Clive, Susannah Cibber, Margaret Woffington, George Anne Bellamy, Esther Hamilton, Maria Nossiter, and Sarah Ward (Mrs. West Digges) were among those acting as the rival queens. George Anne Bellamy as Statira and Peg Woffington as Roxana, for example, inaugurated a popular new production of *The Rival Queens* on 15 January 1756 that ran through sixteen performances in the season. A spectacular "Triumphal Entry of Alexander into Babylon" was added to the second act. Productions were mounted nearly every year, sometimes more than once a year, from the 1760s through to the 1790s with new songs, entrances, and epilogues. In other words, *The Rival Queens* resonated with an entire century's audience, and the vital issues it raised indicate the timeliness of a supposedly untimely play.

The exaggerated language and excessive emotion also made *The Rival Queens* a natural target for metatheatrical references pointed at the heroic drama's ridiculous extremes. More than half a dozen entertainments burlesqued the play, especially a parody in drag, *The Rival Queans* (1727), in which plot and characters revert absurdly to the all-male cast typical of the Renaissance. In its fullest and most dazzling productions it rivaled the fashionable forms of opera and pantomime. Indeed, some of the performances crossed over from the opera house where Lee's play afforded rich opportunities for military display, singing apparitions, dancing, trumpets and drums. An opera entitled *Alexander the Great*, perhaps inspired by Cibber's spoof, was presented as an afterpiece at Lincoln's Inn Fields on 26 April 1715. The 1733–34 season saw eleven performances of the tragedy, all of which included "A Pyrrhic Dance after the Manner of the Antients" that prefigured the pageantry of some of the later seasons.

The longest lull in performance occurred during the 1740s and early 1750s, but the play was then revitalized through the ambitious addition of Alexander's triumphal procession previously mentioned. The tragic hero's larger-than-life entrance eventually came to be a set piece that evolved into an ever more spectacular scene. In addition, *The Rival Queens* was often performed during the 1750s and 1760s in Ireland as a pantomime, where Spranger Barry as Alexander was drawn onto the stage by soldiers in a chariot that brilliantly, and probably comically, broke down into parts that doubled as weapons.[25] By 1777 as abolitionist debates began, black slaves added an exotic touch to Alexander's triumphal entrance. Even at century's end the play was still produced when a lavish 1795–96 revival in London boasted twelve performances, the second largest number in a season, and included John Philip Kemble's additions of new battle scenes, fresh costumes, elaborate decorative props, and complicated machinery. An Orientalist afterpiece by James Harvey D'Egville presented a fantastic pantomime on 12 February 1795 with elephants, horses, and splendidly dressed Macedonian and Persian soldiers. Similarly, in November 1795, a revival involved the onstage appearance of Alexander's magnificent horse, Bucephalus, along with the requisite banquet, Amazons, elephants, and battles (*Rival Queens*, xvi). Alexander's magnificent procession reinstated his power, paralleled England's imperial ambitions at the end of the century, and forecast an Orientalism in boasting a display of military trophies from Europe, Asia, and Africa.

Women at the Center

I now want to consider more specifically how actresses, though characters central to an antiquated play, raised various contradictions as they embodied fashionable and unsettling aspects of modernity. An earlier tradition of female heroism prefigured the play's heroines, emerging in women's early appearances in seventeenth-century court masques and private theater performances. To provide one important example here, Sir William Davenant's *The Siege of Rhodes* (1656) included the role of Ianthe, a virtuous woman who derived from the tradition of the Caroline queen as an Amazonian martial woman, that became, according to Sophie Tomlinson, "the first serious, heroic part scripted for a woman."[26] Ianthe is a *femme forte* who, though captive to the Turkish emperor, refuses his command to unveil. This antecedent to *The Rival Queens*, also an Oriental she-tragedy, features another vigorous heroine, the jealous Turkish empress Roxalana, and similarly locates women firmly at its center. Offering two coveted parts for actresses, *The Rival Queens* is perhaps the first she-tragedy on the English stage, though Thomas Otway's *The Orphan* and John Banks's plays have also been afforded that status.[27] The reason for the disappearance of she-tragedy and its female victim has been variously attributed to the retirement of Anne Bracegirdle in 1707 and of Elizabeth Barry in 1710, or, alternatively, to the more realistic portrayal of the emergent epistolary novel's pathetic heroine. But *The Orphan*, *The Fair Penitent*, and *Jane Shore*, like *The Rival Queens*, remained among the most popular plays presented throughout the century, especially for the ladies of quality, revealing that the pathetic heroine disappeared only from the *new* plays staged in London at mid-century.

In a now classic essay Laura Brown describes the context of economic change in which the transitions from Restoration to eighteenth-century forms are embedded: "The pathetic drama which [the tragic heroine] dominates represents the formal mediation between an aristocratic tragedy of social status and a bourgeois tragedy of moral worth."[28] She-tragedy, the tragedy of pathos, makes women characters key but reinforces the passivity typical of the women within the increasingly hegemonic cult of domesticity. Brown believes that the prototypical passive heroines, so crucial to aristocratic tragedy, are "economically impotent but dramatically vital" to the genre (443). Arguing from a somewhat different vantage point, Lisa Freeman contends that eighteenth-century tragedy promotes a version of national masculinity that pushes femininity to the margins. Freeman finds that male characters acted "as the exclusive and impregnable agents of tragedy and its ideological projects."[29]

Both of these prominent critics' arguments regarding the tragic heroine's marginalization omit the fact that actual women (as opposed to Renaissance boy actresses) with star standing possessed considerable cultural influence on the stage; and even as they played pathetic heroines or politically powerful queens, the women players were exchanging their labor for steadily mounting returns stimulated by their performances to generate real rather than fictional economies of agency and identity. *The Rival Queens*, through its paratexts and adaptations, as well as the anecdotes surrounding it, shifts from endorsing the chivalric and royalist ideals that appealed to its early audiences, to emphasize the newly popular motif of pathetic female victims. The celebrated actresses who played these roles represented hard-won professional achievement and significant economic power: *real women*, albeit women impersonating characters, shaped these forms of female subjectivity beyond mere suffering heroines. Even as they embodied negative aspects of theatricality, actresses represented attractive opportunities for patronage, emulation, and surrogation for women spectators. The opposition between male heroism and female victimhood also appears less definitive if we consider, for example, the daunting strength of actresses such as Susannah Cibber and Hannah Pritchard in the tragic roles of Zara, Calista, Juliet, Desdemona, and Sigismunda. In short, star actresses playing these central characters, rather than seeming merely to be "empty vessels" with "no social status, no inherent valuation" (Brown, "Defenseless Woman," 442–43), overflowed with social meanings far in excess of their roles. Unlike their fictional sisters, their material value to the theater was constantly being renegotiated, and the paratexts and redactions in which they acted were the vehicles of those negotiations.

The plot of *The Rival Queens* progresses, I suggest, from Alexander to the queens, and also from the past to the present. Though most of the play is in blank verse, the scenes in which the two queens compete for Alexander revert to the rhymed couplet characteristic of heroic tragedy. This makes the scenes between the rival women especially evocative of the past, in effect pulling it into contact with the present moment of performance. How exactly do repetitions and reiterations of *The Rival Queens* draw on cultural memory and combine the original play with demands for fresh interpretations? In fact, these down-and-dirty combat scenes between actresses are crucial to keeping not only *The Rival Queens* but other tragedies, such as *All for Love* and *The Mourning Bride*, alive on stage even as they increasingly lent themselves to parody. The paired would-be royals, in this case the clinging vine versus the sensual man-woman, may well represent between them the contest over a more certain past and the ephemeral nature of the future. If the prologue focuses on the classical hero Alexander, the comic epilogue puts the spotlight on the actress's dual identities—her character and person—that speak fully to the contemporary occasion of the play, and the epilogue, spoken by a woman, leavens the morose tragedy of the main plot.[30] The epilogue is, as Pierre Danchin painstakingly documented, an appealing form spoken frequently on the bonding between stage and audience by actresses in propria persona, a "new type of stage literature" that participates in the systematic "quest for novelty and originality" required for an increasingly commercial theater.[31] It attests to the centrality of the rival queens and sheer force of their presence as contributing to the audience's enjoyment of the play.

Each celebrated actress's debut as Roxana would have provided an occasion for presenting a new comic epilogue at tragedy's end. Even in the original epilogue the speaker compares the play's faults to a modern woman's beauty patch designed to cover her fatal moral defect for, as Alexander Pope would have it, woman's very name is defect. Yet, resonating with the anecdotes that emanate from the play, the epilogue ultimately sympathizes with the actresses who are acknowledged to be the prey of male audience members. Focusing on actresses' bodies, the speaker chastises the male spectators who, enthralled by the women's "panting breasts, white hands and little feet" (Epilogue, line

22), entice them into abandoning the stage to become their mistresses, only to exhaust them and return them to the theater "worn and stale" (Epilogue, lines 32–33). The epilogue threatens that, if the practice of stealing actresses, trained at the company's expense, does not cease, the company will revert to the Renaissance practice of allowing cross-dressed boy actors to take over women's roles: even women in breeches will be acted by boys.[32]

Though the first epilogue was probably delivered by Lysimachus, the speaker of choice became the forsaken Roxana who could thus transform the denouement—Statira's murder, Alexander's poisoning, and Roxana's escaping with her life—into an occasion for reflection on her victimization as the pregnant and deserted second wife. Thus Roxana's epilogue evolved into a kind of comic send-up of a she-tragic sufferer and a mockery of that popular form. It is not surprising, then, that Peg Woffington, more renowned for her comic than her tragic roles, played Roxana sixteen times from January to April in the 1755–56 season and spoke the epilogue.[33]

Roxana's comic epilogue delivered after the 1772 adaptation, *Alexander the Great, A Tragedy; with Alterations*, may in its ludic bravado be taken as representative of the epilogues, many of which are now lost, from productions of eighteenth-century versions of Lee's play. The inconsistency between the apparent message and the medium of its delivery, the actress, would have heightened the irony and the pleasure the audience took in the epilogue. In low comic language Roxana demands acquittal for murdering her rival Statira:

> But e'er you pass my sentence, hear my story.
> What passive woman, were she in my place,
> Cou'd brook such usage? Horrible disgrace!
> To kiss the saucy minx before my face;
> Hang on her neck, and sigh, and sweat, and bellow—
> Oh, I've not patience with the filthy fellow.

Speaking directly to the ladies in the audience, she appeals to their shared desire to keep their husbands faithful: "Each wrong'd wife's Roxana in her heart." And she plays on the audience's Christian morality in demanding monogamy in contrast to "Eastern" customs and memorably turns Alexander's "two wives" into a lilting refrain as she retreats from an Oriental alterity:

> Methinks I hear each wedded fair-one cry,
> Well done, Roxana—she deserv'd to die.

> What Christian wife cou'd bear such double dealing?
> And sure your heathen women have their feeling.
> Two wives! 'Tis matrimonial fornication:
> Pray Heav'n avert such customs from this nation!
> By such let Eastern wives be bubbled still.
> Two wives! For shame, two husbands if you will.[34]

The comedy rests on the audience's recognizing that adultery, if not bigamy, is common to England as well as the harem, and thus draws parallels between European and Oriental women. The meeting of Roxana and Statira may have reminded the audience of Charles II's introducing his mistress, Lady Castlemaine, to Queen Catherine, but later in the century the play's production would, of course, have resonated with the very public bigamy trial of the Duchess of Kingston in 1776.[35] And it would certainly have called to mind the public debates on the efficacy of polygamy aimed at resolving the problems of destitute women in the streets of London.

In other words, eighteenth-century actresses mediated between comedy and tragedy, past and present, performance and real life. Mary Beth Rose similarly described the mixed genre of Renaissance tragicomedy as offering "an alternative conception of heroism that connects public and private life . . . and is associated with the future."[36] *The Rival Queens* overturns traditional gender distinctions and challenges sexual stereotypes. For example, the tyrannical but effeminate Alexander, "rash, of hasty humour" (2.1.261), is "unmanned" (2.1.53) by love's madness: "Two wives he takes, two rival queens disturb / The court; and while each hand does beauty hold, / Where is there room for glory?" (1.1.65–67). Clytus also accuses him of being womanly in battle at Oxydrace (4.2.154–75). And in contrast to the weakened, feminine Alexander, Roxana is portrayed as an Amazonian Thalestris (an epithet commonly applied to actresses) who lured her "she-companions" (3.1.78) to abandon their domestic responsibilities and "to ride and chase/Wild beasts in deserts, and to master men" (3.1.82–83). Yet she also represents the spoils of the Indies and of Persia that Alexander has conquered, as she, along with fifty virgins, is displayed in all her luxurious decadence. These oppositions are even more prominently revealed in Colley Cibber's cross-dressed parody, *The Rival Queans*; but even in the original *Rival Queens* with its strong erotic charge, the parts convey significant possibilities for gender ambiguity in performance from the start.[37] Charles Hart who first played Alexander had been trained as a boy actress apprentice at old Blackfriars Theatre. Edward Kynaston, legendary for being among the most beautiful of the boy actresses, took the role of Cassander who remarks of Alexander, "He's a man, his flesh as soft and penetrable as a girl's" (1.1.263–65). And more than one woman played Alexander, further emphasizing his effeminacy. We learn from a perhaps apocryphal story that "in the performance of 'Alexander the Great' in 1706 at Windsor Susanna Carroll [the actress who would become playwright Susanna Centlivre] in breeches played Alexander and won the heart of Mr. Cent Livre, the Queen's cook."[38] A girls' boarding school performance of *The Rival Queens* in which "Even our *Alexander* is a Maid" apparently adapted itself well to having all the parts played by young women.[39] And in an entry to *The Daily Advertiser*, an admirer writes that he hopes to cajole Kitty Clive into cross-dressing as Alexander the Great for her benefit performance. The entry reads, "The enterprising Spirit which so conspicuously shines in all your Actions, makes me, the Slave of your just Merit, entreat you, if 'tis not yet too late, to act for your Benefit this Night the Part of Alexander the Great; and then, my Charmer, you have no more to do, than, with that renown'd Warrior, to weep there are no more Parts to conquer."[40]

While comic actresses regularly called attention to their curvaceous bodies in breeches roles and through bawdy references, tragic actresses used similar devices to remind audiences of their physical presence. It is worth stressing the extraordinary attention given to actresses' bodies in the revisions and parodies of *The Rival Queens*. Roxana in particular embodies the seductive yet compromised femininity of the actress who plays her, infinitely desirable yet scorned. We are provided some clue to the titillating, ribald nature of the 1735 production in *The Prompter*'s remarking on Alexander's "curling round Statira, and touching her like a god, [for he] created as crimson a blush as his moulding with his hands Roxana's rich globes" (Hill and Popple [1966], 121). The two actresses competed in the coarsest fashion to describe Alexander's amorous activities: "The Rival Queens who seemed, like *Fig's Champions*, to mount the Stage, in order to have a fair Trial of Skill, who could best describe the *actual Chamber Feats* of the Hero, in the Lewdest Manner" (Hill and Popple [1735], n.p.). The paired women excited so vulgar a sensuality that younger spectators were cautioned to resist actively its lascivious lines. The Prompter reports archly that he has "observed with pleasure in the countenance of the fair and young part of the audience an impression of disgust at the warmth of the descriptions of the rival queens"[41] (Figure 6).

The heroines' sensual response to each other and to Alexander also reminds the audience of the identities of the actual actresses. Elizabeth Barry in her performance as Roxana reportedly oozed from "her hot, bleeding heart

"Real, Beautiful Women": Rival Queens   77

Figure 6. "The Rival Queens of Covent Garden and Drury Lane Theatres, at a Gymnastic Rehearsal" (1782). *Catalogue of Political and Personal Satires . . . in the British Museum* (no. 6126). Courtesy of the British Museum.

[that] / Splits with the rack" (3.1.53–54) with a feverish sexual passion that seemed to emanate from her actual person. Curll (impersonating Betterton) writes, "Mrs. *Barry* when she talked of her *hot bleeding Heart*, seemed to feel a Fever within, which by Debate and Reason she would quench."[42] The torrid zone evoked by the play is overtly sexual as *Rival Queens* makes steamy erotic references to the actresses' body parts: heaving snowy breasts, bare necks and shoulders, melting or starry eyes, and wild loose hair. Statira, who had nursed Alexander's wounds after his Persian warfare, is somewhat sanitized through nurturing and maternal language—"all softness, / All melting, mild, and calm as a rocked infant," while Roxana's round breasts, the site of imperial power, are "rich worlds" superior even to "the globes of heav'n and earth" (3.1.111–12). The heated quarrels heighten the sensuality between the pair in acts 3 and 5, and the chemistry between the two actresses would probably have been spectacularly obvious. Statira claims that she could actually feel the traces of Roxana's kisses on Alexander's lips, and Roxana, who stalks Alexander and threatens

to set him afire, haunts her rival with visions of their passionate embraces imprinted on Roxana's body: "Do I not bear his image in my womb? / Which, while I meditate and roll revenge, / Starts in my body like a fatal pulse, / And strikes compassion through my bleeding bowels" (4.1.139–42). She hangs upon Alexander's every word and gesture: "Thy tongue will make me wanton as thy wishes; / And while I feel thy hand, my body glows" (3.1.335). Inflamed by jealousy for the pregnant Roxana, Statira, possessing "Diana's soul cast in the flesh of Venus," curses her and prophesies her own madness: "I will have remedy, I will, I will / Or go distracted; madness may throw off / The mighty load, and drown the flaming passion" (1.2.69–71).

The final act, in which the passions between the women again erupt, thrilled audiences with its bloody battle of wits when Roxana dramatically stabs Statira. The scene takes place within the bower of Semiramis, who was the Queen of Babylon and mythical empress of Ninevah in the Assyrian empire, and who represents both female sovereignty and tarnished femininity. This combination of female power and sexual looseness again exemplifies the *actress's* contradictions. Though powerful, Semiramis is also a contaminated woman, a brothel keeper, and Nimrod's paramour. The pathetic Statira finally expires, but her magnanimous forgiveness of Roxana allows her to triumph over her rival in death.[43] Roxana is spared, however, because she carries Alexander's baby in her womb. The rival queens preserve the performance of heroic tragedy even as they, real live actresses engaged in commercial rivalries made violently palpable, mock its awful assumptions.

Anecdotal Accounts

The anecdotes evoked by *The Rival Queens* also insert the reality of the actual actresses into the play's illusion and reflect a pervasive uneasiness about women's presence on stage. What, we might ask, is the larger cultural narrative of which these anecdotes evolving over the century are a part, and do they undermine or reinforce reigning cultural values? The gossipy anecdotes engage in reinterpreting the archive of documents and other materials surrounding the play over time.[44] One function of the biographical *bon mot* is, I think, to emphasize the actress's vulnerability and conflate her person with the character she plays. The peculiar propensity of Lee's *The Rival Queens* to produce lurid tidbits throughout the century arose because the acting paralleled the real-life situations of the actresses. For example, Lee's play spawned stories of ardent libertine admirers ignoring the boundary between audience and stage to pursue the actress queens. Aubrey de Vere, earl of Oxford, much enamored of the tall fiery brunette Rebecca Marshall who played Roxana, attacked her sedan chair in the streets in an attempt to abduct her forcibly. The shrewd actress engaged the king's guards to protect her and fended him off, but eventually he succeeded in seizing her and bringing about a false marriage that brought her considerable misery.[45] In another example, in December 1692 William Mountfort, who played Alexander opposite Mrs. Bracegirdle's Statira, was run through by Captain Hill who, along with Charles Lord Mohun, impassioned by her performances, allegedly attempted to kidnap the actress. After Mountfort's murder, the play's having been, according to Colley Cibber, "too frequently acted" and "worn out," the part fell to Thomas Betterton who "reviv'd [it] with so new a Lustre that for three Days together it fill'd the House."[46] The play filled with "furious Fustian and turgid Rants" succeeded, Cibber claimed, only because of Betterton's magnificent elocution that overcame the considerable defects of the play.

The folklore surrounding the play focused on the women and the stage properties that were associated with passionate feeling; props metamorphosed into real weapons in the battle between the sexes and between the rival queens. According to one account, when Elizabeth Barry assumed the role of Roxana, she engaged with Elizabeth Boutell's Statira in a supposed quarrel over a coveted bit of costume, the exotic veil that may have covered Roxana's face. Just as the Town had buzzed with stories about Rebecca Marshall's amorous affairs spilling over into her stage roles, they warmed to rumors that the real cause of the dispute was Mrs. Barry's reported jealousy of Mrs. Boutell's entanglement with Lord Rochester, though the timing of the incident makes this impossible. Heightening the melodrama in the final act, Barry as Roxana wounded Boutell as Statira to the fascinated audience's macabre delight: "*Statira* on hearing the King was nigh, *begs the Gods to help her for that Moment*; on which *Roxana* hastening the designed Blow, struck with such Force, that tho' the Point of the Dagger was blunted, it made way through Mrs. *Boutel's* Stayes, and entered about a Quarter of an Inch in the Flesh" while Roxana uttered "Die, soreceress, die! And all my wrongs die with thee."[47] As Edmund Curll under the pseudonym of Thomas Betterton recounts the sensational episode, Mrs. Boutell had been given the veil "by the Partiality of the Property-Man" (19–20). Curll teasingly mentions the gossip only to squelch it: it was the veil, not the man, that had raised Barry's fury. Barry's bizarre stabbing incident replays, in an example of what Herbert Blau calls "ghosting," a familiar dramatic pattern, while at the same time moving from representation to reality to destroy its theatricality.[48] The paired actresses locked in spectacular mortal combat destroy the play's illusion and substitute real, bleeding bodies. Thomas Davies similarly interrupts the fantasy when he insists on the women's failed chastity: "As it was well known these ladies were not vestals, it was reported jealousy gave force to the blow" (*Dramatic Miscellanies*, 3: 298).

The considerable force of the incident apparently lodged in the mind of principal actresses as part of its echoing history. When George Anne Bellamy retells the anecdote decades later, retaining many of the touchstones, she too describes the veil as having been loaned "by the contrivance or interest of the wardrobe-keeper," thus suggesting that Mrs. Boutell's sexual favors may have been liberally bestowed behind the scenes.[49] The veil, a disputed theatrical property that the actress claims as her exclusive possession, takes on an identity of its own. It thus becomes redolent with erotic associations, and the line between character and actress, between public and private, becomes blurred. The incident reveals the way that actresses' bleeding bodies and their affairs of the heart carry a personality onto the stage that traverses the stage's edge and, through its attachment to female bodies, far exceeds that of actors. Bellamy also attributes the confusion over the ownership of the veil to the theater companies' 1682 union rather than simply to an actress's misguided jealousy over a man's favoritism. Bellamy, then, would seem to speak as a professional who understands the commercial challenges her fellow actresses face. Whether fighting over a man or a costuming prop, the women players are perceived simultaneously to be both the dramatic characters and themselves, and any theatrical action is rife with personal meanings. Still, the incident allows the actresses to escape the tragedy of the play and its lessons, and to rise again for another performance.

Protesting that her anecdotes "though perhaps erroneous in point of time, are real facts" (6: 42), Bellamy adapts the often-told anecdote to her own performance as Statira: it seems entirely likely that she may have provoked her own sensational stabbing at the hand of Peg Woffington, or at least the rumor of it, when the theater manager John Rich obtained for Woffington the Princess Dowager of Wales's cast-off dress that "seemed to be a dirty white, by candle-light" (2: 217). Supposedly driven to a jealous rage by Bellamy's richly colored gown and mantua, Woffington demanded that the rival actress change her costume. In recounting the anecdote, Bellamy juxtaposes the actress with her role, and the envy over costuming with jealousy over the *character* of Alexander: "The sight of my pompous attire created more real envy in the heart of the actress, than it was possible the real *Roxana* could feel for the loss of the Macedonian hero" (2: 220).

The quarrel continued on the following night's performance, and Bellamy, wearing another splendid Parisian gown, reports that Woffington "drove me off the carpet, and gave me the *coup de grace* almost behind the scenes" (2: 221).[50] These infamous ruptures reveal not only the allegedly fierce tempers of the actresses but also the high stakes involved in their negotiations regarding maintaining celebrated status, including salary, benefit nights, and clothing allowance. These recurrent "scenarios," as Diana Taylor has defined repeated dramatic scenes, become "meaning-making paradigms," that make "visible, yet again, what is already there in cultural memory: the ghosts, the images, the stereotypes" (*Archive and Repertoire*, 28). The properties on stage seem to simultaneously possess a past and a present, as well as a public and a private life.

In short, the freakishness of Lee's original play paradoxically contributed to its long success with London audiences eager to remember but also to parody these tragic confrontations. It seems, then, that the topical relevance of anecdotes about these powerful, sexy Restoration and eighteenth-century actresses inserted a lighthearted disregard for history's repeated intrusions of the past's tragic lessons into the present, thus making tragedy more compatible with Enlightenment hopes to rewrite history in the interests of "progress." Thomas Davies lamented, "I am afraid we cannot read thirty lines together, even in Lee's best pieces, without encountering absurdity in sentiment and solecism in expression:—blunder and beauty as so blended together, you know not how to separate them" (*Dramatic Miscellanies*, 3: 272). The risible nature of the play's eighteenth-century performances extended as well to the disjunction conveyed through its costuming. In these anecdotes that kept theater gossip in perpetual circulation, the properties in the tragedy seem to mock the seriousness of the play by intruding their tawdry private existence onto the stage.

Comedy and Parody: The Rival Queans

The Rival Queens as it was produced during the eighteenth century often licensed audiences to laugh at their own absorption in the heroic tragedy when it called attention to the play's anachronistic popularity. *The Rival Queens* was especially susceptible to parodic reinterpretation—to a doubling of meaning as both tragic and comic—because of its spectacular excess, the comic epilogues attached to later versions, and the steady disruption and inversion of traditional gender roles. The conflict evident even at the play's inception between portraying Alexander as tyrannical conqueror and besotted lover points to the dissolution of the heroic ideal and lends itself to mockery. As a remnant of the Restoration drama, the tragedy's bluster aroused great hilarity; its hyperbolic lines were much parodied in other popular comedies of the period. Two significant burlesques of the play were Colley Cibber's cross-dressed *The Rival Queans* (performed 1710) mentioned earlier, in which the plot and characters are made more absurd because of its all-male cast; and George Alexander Stevens's *The Court of Alexander* (1770).[51] The productions at opposite ends of the century mock the original, for gender and genre ambiguities are reinforced by the central emphasis on women's bodies, although parody brings to the foreground the difficulty and occasional absurdity of attempting to transfer that interest back onto men's bodies.

Colley Cibber's response to Lee's tragedy had been to turn it into *The Rival Queans, with the Humours of Alexander the Great*, which first appeared in the late 1690s and was finally printed in 1729.[52] The burlesque may have been performed on 23 January 1710, at the desire of ladies of quality; but the first certain performance took place on 29 June 1710 at the Queen's Theatre Haymarket, and men in drag acted in the play that same year. When it was produced again on 29 June 1718, it was described as "a new Comi-Tragi-Heroick Farce," a term that might have inspired Henry Fielding's use of a similar term to describe the genre of *Joseph Andrews*, his novel that mocked Cibber's *Apology*.

The play's rhetorical repetition and heavy-handed passion easily lent themselves to an over-the-top operatic style. The title page of Cibber's parody includes a quatrain that laments Alexander's lost glory, but it is also almost certainly a comic elegy to the heroic tragedy:

> Once like a Vine I flourish'd; and was Young,
> Rich in my ripning Hopes that spoke me strong:
> But now a dry and wither'd Stock am grown,
> And all my Clusters and my Branches gone.[53]

Cibber's comical adaptation implies that the pathetic is portrayed at a substantial cost to masculinity, whether it is heroic or otherwise, for a man impersonating the victimized woman of she-tragedy would have visually reinforced the demise of a potent tragic heroism. I am suggesting here that forceful heroines in the person of star actresses who regularly contested the terms of their exclusion from such performances were not successfully excluded from the stage, in spite of efforts by Cibber and others.

In banning women and putting men in skirts roles, Colley Cibber's parody brings to realization the threat of the 1677 epilogue to *Rival Queens*. The notoriously foppish Cibber headed the travesty production as Alexander, and men, including Bullock Junior as Statira and Bullock Senior as Roxana, masqueraded as the royals. The joke would have been extended when *Mrs.* Bullock played Statira at least six times during the 1722–23 season at Lincoln's Inn Fields. Allusions throughout the play to the love of man for man heighten the homoerotic innuendos in the all-male production. The parody expected the audience to possess intimate knowledge of the play, often following the original play line-by-line. For example, Cassander's remark regarding the girlish appearance of Alexander's complexion would surely have inspired knowing laughter in the travestied performance that made the lines in the original tragedy embarrassingly literal: "Philip [Alexander's father] fought men, but Alexander women" (4.2.140–42). By transforming Statira and Roxana into transvestite objects of satire, Cibber's mocking comedy interrupted any sympathy that either woman might inspire. The parody continues as the dialogue between the two queans rapidly descends into Billingsgate language. Statira, a raging fishwife whom Alexander calls "Statty," screams at Roxana, "Wreak then thy bloody vengeance on me, / Wash in my blood, and swill thee in my gore, / Make puddings of my guts, minced meat / of my heart" (5.1). The language sinks even lower: Alexander sends Roxana, born a cook wench hailing from Bridewell, to the Rose tavern for pullet and eggs, beefsteaks, and sausages. Garlic rather than "fate" is on her breath.

The Rival Queans thus transforms the competition for Alexander into a homoerotic contest between silly, desiring men. When men turned women to sweep actresses off the stage they had recently mounted, the gesture toward the Renaissance past could be interpreted either as a threat or a wish fulfilled. In a century no longer accustomed to transvestite male actors, but not quite comfortable with women in breeches roles, the play would have more than hinted at a critique of normative heterosexuality. As Peter Stallybrass has written of the Renaissance stage, "Transvestite drama's emphasis on clothing and body parts suggest that gender itself is a fetish, the production of an identity through the fixation upon specific 'parts'."[54] If a passionate desire for women feminizes men, as heroic tragedies such as Dryden's *All for Love* and Lee's *Rival Queens* imply, then Cibber's foppish Alexander would have seemed strangely familiar as a failed prince and simpering momma's boy: "Why was I born a god, proclaimed a prince, / Yet never could arrive at common sense!" he whines to his cross-dressed mother/man (2: 1).

Cibber's parody also debases symbols of royalty and transforms them into ordinary theatrical properties: a throne becomes a joynt stool, goblets are downgraded to bumpers, drums and trumpets are metamorphosed into pots and pans. Occasionally the original heroic language descends into vulgar howlers as when Statira lunges at Roxana, who "doats" on Alexander's lips, "eats him with hungry kisses, / She gobbles him up, devours every inch of him" (1: 1). Cibber's Alexander openly whores with the boy Roxana, offering her "a guinea to be his[?] / Then talked, and kissed, and swore and lied" (3: 1). Scatological humor substitutes for the eroticism that women's bodies, missing from the production, would have aroused. Even the death scene is polluted with base humor when Alexander's last breath is compared to a fart.

In the climactic drinking scene between the two queens, Roxana labels Statira a "hatchet face" and an "abandon'd sow," and Cassander undermines Alexander's *vow* in giving it a porcine rhyme (3: 1). Roxana employs low feminine rhymes to satirize her rival: "Madam, I hope you'll think me not uncivil, / *Roxana* weeps to see *Statira* snivel" (3: 1). Statty bizarrely begs Alexander to squeeze him/her until s/he is black in the face. S/he finally accosts him and threatens unrelenting lust: "O thou dear teasing toad! / This night I will revenge me on thy body! / Thou shalt not sleep nor close thy eyes, / The idle hours shall all be joked away; / We'll play the fool all night, and do the same all day" (3: 1). In short, the parody is a thoroughly bathetic mockery of the *Rival Queens* characters, language, and plot made even more absurd because of its all-male cast. All-male performances were also staged in Dublin when *Rival Queans* was performed as an afterpiece to Cibber's *Love Makes a Man* (18 February 1737), and then at Drury Lane 17 May 1738.[55]

In response to Cibber's well-known spoof, a dialogue surfaced in which the ghosts of the two playwrights quarrel over theatrical taste in *Visits from the Shades: or, Dialogues Serious, Comical, and Political* (1704–5). Calling the parody "a Piece of Monstrosity" and damning Cibber as a monkey of a theater director, Lee's spirit complains about the younger playwright's bold mockery of the heroic play.[56] Lee poses a rhetorical question to Cibber: "Is it no Crime then to make my young *Ammon* a swaggering Bully, a town Rake, and ten times worse than a *Vinegar-yard* Captain? nor level *Statira* with one of your hungry Actresses, and render her an affectionate Lover of Beef-Stakes? Nor its no fault I warrant to draw the haughty *Roxana*, that Rag-gatherers, Cynderwomen, and Oyster Wenches wou'd disclaim her Acquaintance?" (21–22). Cibber is portrayed as seemingly unperturbed by the criticism because, he claims, both pit and boxes were heartily amused in spite of the ribald humor. Lee's ghost also acknowledges that popular songs (such as "Callia my Heart") from Cibber's parody are being sung in the London streets. Removing women's bodies from the *The Rival Queans* paradoxically reinforces actresses' importance by means of temporarily bringing into being a stage from which they are absent.

Rival Empires

The extraordinary variety of *The Rival Queens* throughout the eighteenth century extends to many other examples, but I will briefly discuss only two more sequels that reflect the ongoing campy treatments of the heroic tragic form. These sequels intersect tellingly with the play's arguably feminocentric perspective while incorporating foreign and domestic issues as well. How does the increasingly dominant conflict between the rival queens in later eighteenth-century corruptions relate to the staging of the Orient in Lee's play? These later versions incorporate anxieties about Britain's empire as much as national history and resist any comfortable retreat into a Manichean alterity. Emphasizing the Oriental aspects of the tragedy strengthens national identity while assimilating exotic difference within the court and the aristocracy, but later redactions of the play relate to England's taking up its role as an imperial state power.

In Lee's original play the Macedonian Clytus refuses to don Eastern fashions, the Persian robes associated with the French absolutist court that Alexander proudly wears. These robes would have reminded the audience of Charles II's having famously dressed in a "Persian" vest. Bridget Orr has argued that this kind of opposition between "us" and "them" in Restoration drama is gradually absorbed through England's recognition of its resemblance to foreign peoples;[57] but in later versions the epilogues to the *Rival Queens* very prominently depict the clash between bourgeois Christian values and Oriental ones as issues that played themselves out on women's bodies and in their lives. As Lady Mary Wortley Montagu famously wondered in her *Turkish Letters* (published posthumously in 1763), in which geographical region did women in fact possess greater freedoms? Alexander's popular entrance and procession point at once to the spectacular promise of empire and its tragic loss, but the women in opposition to each other represent the threat that illegitimate authority propelled by irrational forces poses to both of them. Theatrical pizzazz stands in for political power and relieves the cultural pressure represented by celebrated actresses to treat women as equals at home. While Roxana and, to a lesser extent, Statira, represent sexual license in their dramatic roles and in their persons as actresses, as a character in her epilogues Roxana reclaims her right to a proper English marriage—bourgeois, Protestant, and monogamous. Thus reassuringly domesticated in this fashion, Roxana (and on occasion the actress who plays her), though dressed as a seductive Oriental queen, resembles a proper modern Englishwoman.[58] In demanding a husband's fidelity the rival women, in spite of appearing to be exotic themselves, seem paradoxically to exemplify conventional Western values vis-à-vis Alexander's increasingly explicit Orientalization over the century, and thus they embody the limit case of the nation's conflict over its imperial aspirations. A woman's legitimate claim to monogamous marriage reassuringly draws the actress-characters back into English domesticity and strips them of their alienating alterity, confusingly identifying their exoticism with an actress's demand for star power.

Another variation on the play's connection to empire appears in a musical spoof of opera, *The Contre Temps; or, Rival Queans: A Small Farce* (1727). Based on Lee's play and drawing upon Cibber's burlesque, it, too, explores the close association between the theatrical world and the political domain in women's rivalry, on this occasion between two celebrated singers who represent imperial territory.[59] Though the lead characters are Italian, the disharmony between the singer actresses could easily be imagined as emblematic of any nation's discord, and the metaphor of imperial rivalry suited them perfectly. Lee's blank-verse heroic tragedy and its parodies readily lent themselves to opera's excesses and to the subordination of sense to sound. Colley Cibber's remark upon the original *Rival Queens* in his *Apology* could be fittingly applied to the production of *Contre Temps*: "When these flowing Numbers came from the Mouth of a *Betterton*, the Multitude no more desired Sense to them, than our musical *Connoisseurs* think it essential in the celebrate Airs of an *Italian* Opera."[60] The operatic vehicle mimics the political competition between the two internationally famous opera divas, Faustina Bordoni (1697–1781) and Francesca Cuzzoni (1696–1778), whose stage brawl announced their London careers and who were each immediately able to command salaries in the vicinity of £1500 per annum.[61] The comic excess of the opera reduces the representation of these powerful women to caricatures. The curtain opens to display a splendid altar within the Temple of Discord bedecked with crowns, globes, and scepters.

The chorus is arranged in two factions of "Under-Priests"—dukes, lords and "tupees," armed with catcalls, whistles, "serpents," cuckoos, and bells, supporting the two divas, and flanking either side of the crowded stage (*Contre Temps*, 373).[62] Speaking in heroic couplets, the character representing the impresario and producer Heidegger (1666–1749) seeks to heal the dispute between the female royals with flattery regarding their contrasting, but equally sublime, voices characterized as "falling Cataracts" and the sweet meanderings of "gentle Streams" (378). The audience took up the contest with such vehemence that the opera season was aborted.

The opera relies on an imperial conceit: winning the two queens becomes a metaphor for assuming power over coveted colonial territories: "Nor *Gibraltar* we seek, nor *Port-Mahon* [on the east coast of Minorca]; / Possessing you, makes all the World our own" (374). Faustina claims that women, denied the heroism that war produces for men, can only substitute theatrical spats for political triumph: "Pride rules our Female Souls; thus fir'd, we dare / Like Man all Dangers scorn; and thirst for War: / Our little Breasts will pant and heave for Fame, / Swell'd with th'Ambition of the foremost Name" (374–75). Her rousing speech is followed by a loud din from Cuzzoni's faction that is answered with a cacophony of pipe-tuning. The quarrel is staged as a war between states, and the symbols of royalty, crown, and scepter serve as battle weapons. Each woman reigns over an empire of fame, though her power is consistently denigrated as sexual rather than attributed to talent or to actual labor. Senesino, a neutered "Thing," urges the women to join forces to rule the world from "gilded Thrones" and in "triumphal Chariots" (374); but after Senesino's plea for a truce, the factions explode again in a disharmonious clamor of hisses and catcalls.

As the divas continue to hurl abuse, Faustina, contrasting her singing ability to Cuzzoni's canary-like chirp, boasts that her voice has thrilled crowds and enslaved princes. Cuzzoni, though born within a year of Faustina, attacks her as a "mouldy Virgin" and an impotent old bawd: "The judging Tupees on your Action doat, / Astonished at the Warble of that Throat, / And dwell with Raptures on your shaking Note: / While cunning you, the Want of Voice supply, / By Dint of wanton Hand, and rolling Eye" (377). The two divas mock each other's venereal complaints, and Cuzzoni responds in kind with a ribald allusion to the men's sexual organs ("pipes") that Faustina touches. Resorting to the conventions of antifeminist satire, Faustina describes women's capacious genitals to suggest that Madame Cuzzoni is, literally, full of holes: "That she's all over Pipe, from Side to Side; / Her Body looks as from the

Fairies stole, / Enough of Carcass to make one large Hole; / Where he in Love's wide Bay of *Biscay* tost, / Hard plys his Oar; but ne'er can touch the Coast" (379).

Cuzzoni's composer and harpsichordist husband, Pietro Giuseppe Sandoni (1685–1748), implores his "*petite Femme*" to cease and desist as she grabs Faustina's headdress, but when Faustina is equally brutal, Handel urges them to fight it out. Faustina complains that Cuzzoni tore her "*Mechlin* Pinner" (380), thus connecting the account to other reports of rival queens' disputes over props. The men at first resist joining in, but egged on by the unharmonious sounds emanating from the factions, they too pummel the queens. As in the anecdotes centering on the dagger in Lee's *Rival Queens*, the assault has physical consequences for the divas: "*The Queen loses her Head of Hair, and the Princess her Nose in the Skirmish*" (381). Finally, in a deus ex machina, the Goddess of Discord intervenes to encourage Queen Cuzzoni to fly away with Princess Faustina. Sensino concludes with a moralizing simile: the women are simply bulldogs fighting over a bone, and their ability to rule territory is completely forgotten. The quarrel was fought over a mere "Puff of Air"—in short, the ephemeral nature of celebrity—rather than something substantial.

Though the vehicle of *Contre Temps* is slight, the stakes were high in attempting to increase the receipts for the house, and the publicity emanating from the women's staged battle enhanced the already lucrative careers of the opera divas. Feminine ambition is made comic and visceral, and it is mocked as failed heroism. The audience, transformed into a participatory jury engrossed in the antique quarrel revisited for another round, shares fully in the public sphere of private aspiration. Alexander's winning the queens mimics his colonizing territory; each woman governs an empire of fame that he attempts to usurp, and reduces that desire to female lust. Like other actresses who played rival queens, the divas represent the imperial domain shrunk to the size of the stage, diminished by venereal analogies, and allegorized as female body parts, thus delegitimating women's aspirations for sovereignty, whether they fastened on the empire of romance, the theater, or actual territory and their corporeal selves. In short, they appropriate an embodied form of memory to reanimate the past and transform it into a vehicle for a new form of empire. The dramatic representation of an empire of weak masculinity and violent femininity appears to be parodied in ways that undercut the political reality of empire, but it may instead provide the impetus to bolster its force.

One more twist to the Alexander plot augments the original play's imperialist dimensions in George Alexander Stevens's light-opera farce, *The Court of*

Alexander.⁶³ This burlesque opera lends itself to a kind of liminality in which the women's rivalry is based on complexion color rather than the prior claim of the beloved. It demonstrates that the fable of Alexander the Great may absorb not only shifts in sexuality and genre, but that the original tragedy can absorb racial hybridity as well. The two-act opera in rhymed couplet opens as the conquering Alexander in search of India's wealth makes King Porus his captive. Little of the original plot remains: Alexander celebrates his victory with a drinking match, his procession involves drinking rather than war trophies. The rival queens Roxana (Mrs. Thompson) and the courtesan Thais (Mrs. Pinto) become secondary to the original subplot.⁶⁴ The Indian Porus, sometimes called Macedonian and caricatured as black, is transformed into Lysimachus's rival for the affections of the Persian princess Parisatis (Statira's sister played by Mrs. Mattocks). The argument to the opera notes, "As to the Complexion of Porus, Historians are divided: Some supposing him White, like the *Chinese*; others Copper-colour'd, like *Mangolans*: Some declare him to have been only Tawny, like the *Malays*. But we have followed the authenticated Commentaries of [Alexander's generals] Meleager and Gorgias . . . and they declare Porus to have been a Black" (vi). The role of Porus (played by Mr. Barnshaw) would almost certainly have been sung in blackface, thus complicating his courtship of Parisatis and figuring their potential union as miscegenation. There are further references to "India's sun-burn'd Sultan" (13), his "Mahogony"] color (28), his "Ink-Face" (36), and his "*Indian* Way of Wooing" (28). Lysimachus insults him as he threatens him: "I'll coit [throw] to Earth your Charcoal Carcase" (28). Porus's burlesqued blackness figures as a comic justification for defeating him. This combination of racial mockery with singing is an unexpected early example of blackface minstrelsy that first became popular in the character of the singing black servant Mungo in Isaac Bickerstaff's *The Padlock* (1768).⁶⁵ The men's rivalry, to be resolved through a backgammon game, remains undecided in the end, though Parasitis clearly favors the "sallow" Lysimachus over the dark Indian king, and the balance is given over to the lighter-colored man.

Regretting his impulsive act in stabbing Clytus, Alexander is borne off on his horse Bucephalus singing a mad song, a genre more frequently assigned to star tragic actresses. Mercury and Jupiter miraculously appear to resurrect Clytus and thus restore classical values. Nathaniel Lee's original criticisms of the French and Macedonian leanings of the court, thus seeking to cleanse the national identity of Oriental influences, are appropriated for more specifically racist ends; and the rival queens, rather than representing the seductive nature of the East, collude in this attitude. The play is, then, adapted to reinforce racial thinking as it emerges in embodied memory.

Conclusion

What then are the implications for "real, beautiful actresses" regarding the popularity of *The Rival Queens*, its sequels, and its parodies throughout the eighteenth century? Drawing analogies between the theatrical and the political, the strong female heroines act as ever-evolving proxies for the competition between nations and over the power to sway the sovereign ruler. When Colley Cibber spoke of "real, beautiful Women" attracting "new Admirers to the Theatre," he yoked their entrance to the stage to their influence on the court: "more than one of them [the actresses newly playing on the stage] had Charms sufficient at their leisure Hours, to calm and mollify the Cares of Empire" (*Apology* 1: 90). He was alluding, of course, to Restoration queans like Nell Gwyn who soothed the cares of Charles II. But his casual joke set up an opposition that, as we have seen in *The Rival Queens* and its revivals, persisted throughout the eighteenth century in attempting to confine a residue of raw reality to the erotic at the expense of women's political authority. Through anecdote, burlesque, and parody, the play insistently substituted sexual magnetism for the material labor and the economic power of actresses that, ultimately, contributed very substantially to the success of Drury Lane and Covent Garden.

In short, as highly visible signs of economic, cultural, and political change, eighteenth-century actresses were more central to the eighteenth-century stage in the age of Cibber and Garrick than has been previously recognized. We might then rewrite conventional wisdom to suggest that these real, beautiful women were leading contenders in representing modernity and the modern individual, as they turned these plays into commercial vehicles for producing an interiority effect as a viable commodity. In vying with the domesticated fictional woman for modern personhood, presenting models of female freedom jointly with decorous femininity, the exotic actresses who performed classical tragic roles traversed the temporal distance from past to present. As embodied forms of reiterated memory, animating past performances in new dress, they jolted history, seemingly stalled in heroic tragedy, into a reengagement with topical issues to skirt the agonizing implications of tragedy and testify to future possibilities. In their interactive relationship with the audience, not just as pitied objects or prostitutes but as persons, these women presented new models of subjectivity, alive with potential while fraught with danger, in alluring proximity. Roxana, who combines passionate spirit with imminent if illegitimate maternity, triumphs over the more domestically inclined Statira; and though Alexander conquered Persia, it is not clear that he conquers Roxana. At play's end Roxana is exiled but remains pregnant with the child who has a claim to become Alexander's successor.

The Rival Queens in all its versions places the actress front and center, redrawing the boundaries between tragic play and comic epilogue, between past and present, and between virtual reality and life. Rival queens, actresses all, ultimately provided a human, feminine face to the fluctuating market's competing values of reassuring stasis and dangerously seductive instability, to give them prominence in the theater. They resisted merely inhabiting the outdated ideologies of heroic tragedy. Played out across the century, the quarreling women revealed its tensions within their real and simulated subjectivities, and they challenged audiences, including the men who were seduced by them and the women who secretly sought to emulate them, to discriminate between the opposing values they represented. In fulfilling the audience's abstract desires, the paired actresses furthered their careers and promoted their self-commodification into the cult of celebrated individuality as they repeated their battles afresh.

CHAPTER 3

Actresses' Memoirs: Exceptional Virtue

> Even her indiscretions have, in some instance arisen from the best motives, the most warm and active benevolence.
> —*Critical Review*, April 1785

> Virtue has an existence, though like the phoenix, its appearance is very rare.
> —George Anne Bellamy, *Apology* (1786)

IN SAMUEL RICHARDSON's *Pamela* (1740), the Cinderella story of a servant girl's stubborn resistance and eventual marriage to her seductive master, the heroine's *virtue* is largely synonymous with her *chastity*. In the novel Pamela protests that she would willingly embrace "Rags and Poverty" rather than forfeit her virginity.[1] When Mr B ultimately succumbs to her irresistible charms and accepts her terms, her wedding gift to him is "an experience'd Truth, a well-try'd Virtue, and . . . [an unequaled natural] Meekness of a Temper, and Sweetness of Disposition" (337) which, the reader is encouraged to agree, serves as a legitimate exchange for his riches. Pamela is a chaste woman who manages to keep her distance from the commercial transaction in which she is engaged, in contrast to professional actresses who struggled to reconcile virtue with the commerce that they, of necessity, embraced.

Richardson's novel, as Jocelyn Harris has astutely noted, transformed contemporary erotica into more palatable moral fare with a persistent undertone of sexual sizzle.² But the anti-Pamelist readers who found Pamela's demurral unconvincing fastened onto this potential double meaning of the novel in order to mock it. They regarded the heroine of Richardson's novel, not as an innocent maiden defending her chastity, but as a skilled actress who cunningly enticed Mr. B into an improbable marriage. In Henry Fielding's parody of *Pamela* she was transformed into the loose-living Shamela who mockingly flaunted her "vartue," a cant word that implied self-interested manipulation of her lover's expectation of chastity rather than virtue itself. The attempt to define female virtue as something other than strictly interpreted chastity was consistently and fervently explored in the decades leading to Richardson's novel and beyond.

The early decades of the eighteenth century, witnessing the rise of fiction that frequently took women's defense of chastity as its subject, debated what it meant to be a woman whose sexuality was publicly displayed and evaluated in text and in life. The standard that regulated the behavior of men, especially aristocratic men, who participated in civic life in which their private life was nobody's business, did not pertain in the same way to public women who, by their gender and very nature were operating in a sphere that was not their own.³ Richardson's epistolary novel *Pamela* has in common with the biographies of actresses the morally inspired voyeurism, the urge to rectify behavior through interested surveillance characteristic of an age in which self-fashioning invited intrusion into private space. This invasion of interiority through print culture gave special impetus to pouncing on an unconventional woman's reputation.⁴

Actresses were, as we have seen, the near-constant subject of sexual gossip, while male actors were instead mocked for their lower-class origins, for self-love, for behaving like fools, or for lacking sufficient acting skills. The first biographies of women players on the Restoration and eighteenth-century stage were, perhaps surprisingly, not simply moral warnings that chastised actresses for loose behavior, but also entertaining accounts of female adventurers who managed to exhibit some semblance of "virtue" in spite of transgressive sexual mores and humble family origins. These theatrical memoirs ponder the extent to which virtue—a kind of deliberative prudence—involved possessing purity of heart as distinguished from having an untarnished history. This attitude involved a more expansive notion of virtue, closer to masculine *virtù*, marked by natural judgment, by the ability to deliberately carve out an autonomous identity, and to make appropriate ethical decisions based upon personal convictions.⁵ Such a view of virtue, emphasizing independence of mind and spirit, previously assumed to be confined to those of high blood, evaded the necessarily commercial nature of actresses' endeavors and highlighted instead the effects of an interiority governed by a special kind of integrity. The biographers of actresses in the several decades just preceding *Pamela,* instead of merely cautioning young ladies about the dangers of emulating the notorious promiscuity of women players, curiously attempted to explain and even justify their unseemly behavior in these terms. In this chapter I focus first on the lives of three celebrated actresses, Nell Gwyn (1642?–87), Lavinia Fenton (1708–60), and Anne Oldfield (1683–1730), in order to examine the way in which a generation of English actresses was memorialized, and how their virtue—or lack of it—was treated. I turn then to consider Charlotte Charke (1713–60), George Anne Bellamy (c.1731–88), and finally Sarah Siddons (1775–1831) to argue that the biographical and autobiographical descriptions of these actresses in the public eye implied—and not always with a touch of irony—that a woman's "virtue," broadly interpreted, could be kept distinct from her sexual history. As I have been suggesting throughout, this argument resists the conventional wisdom that Restoration and eighteenth-century actresses were consistently regarded as whores, and rather than equating virtue with an intact hymen, it redefines it to incorporate benevolence. Unlike the fictional Pamela, the real women of theatrical memoirs sought to improve their social class and economic situation through hard work, sociability, and often without benefit of marriage. Oldfield, Fenton, Bellamy, and others elevated their social position through cultivating wealthy and well-placed friends.

The biographical publications written about actresses, and the memoirs they themselves compose for the first time, allowed readers and audiences to peep behind the curtain. The memoirs take as their subjects Lavinia Fenton (1728), Anne Oldfield (1730, 1731, 1741), Eleanor Gwynn (1752), Charlotte Charke (1755), Margaret Woffington (1760), George Anne Bellamy (1785), and Sarah Siddons (1831). Often exploitative and notoriously unreliable, the memoirs explore the ways women players' lives contradicted or merged with their dramatic roles to offer scripts for private life as well as public performance. Actresses' memoirs written by others (during the eighteenth century almost always penned by men) attempt to suture together the ruptures between their public and private lives into a coherent whole, while autobiographical narratives tend to be more provisional and expose unstable aspects of their identity. As we have seen, the rise of a credit economy based on speculation and paper credit contributed to the sense of women players' fluctuating selves both on and off stage.[6] Actresses' memoirs, in helping to produce a consistent and recognizable public personality, closely linked women with their stage characters, publicized personal scandals, intensified competitive quarrels between players, and ultimately stimulated patronage of an increasingly commercial theater.

The Lives of Nell Gwyn and Lavinia Fenton

Though the actual life of Restoration actress Nell Gwyn, Charles II's mistress, occurs before the period being considered here, the first full-length memoir about her was not published until the mid-eighteenth century when the political consequences of her relationship with the king had significantly diminished. Broadsides, satires, and ballads on Gwyn abound and, as for most actresses of the period, factual information is often difficult to extricate from the many apocryphal tales. *Memoirs of the Life of Eleanor Gwinn, A Celebrated Courtezan, in the Reign of King Charles II. and Mistress to that Monarch* (London, 1752) by John Seymour, comedian, offered the first full-length life story of the actress at more than a half-century's distance from her death (Figure 7). The memoir predictably followed the pattern of popular whore and rogue biographies that greatly influenced the nascent novel during the early eighteenth century. Illustrated by a revealing frontispiece of a bare-breasted Gwyn, it traced her ascent from her beginnings as the daughter of a tradesman "in mean Circumstances" (1) to becoming the king's most celebrated courtesan. According to this version of her life, Gwyn turned to acting as the last refuge of a poverty-stricken girl struggling to find her way in London, a path that seemed natural for a strikingly beautiful woman with limited skills: "At least, if she could not wear the Buskin with Success, she could see no Objection to her appearing as a Lady in waiting, or one of the Maids of the Bedchamber to the Queens of the Stage" (7). Her preference, however, according to the anonymous memoirist, was to *become* royalty rather than merely impersonating it, "if not a Queen, a[t] least the Mistress of a Monarch" (7). The biography, in other words, described Gwyn as steadily improving her status in a calculated way by advancing from being the mistress of Thomas Betterton to the lover of a player named Deviel, moving on to Lord Rupert, the Earl of Meredith, Lord Wilmot, and finally the king, though in fact her actual catalog of lovers was even more extensive. The narrative portrays her as a conniving opportunist who managed her meteoric rise because of a dazzling talent for quick, sprightly

Figure 7. Possibly Nell Gwyn. Studio of Peter Lely (c. 1675), oil on canvas. © National Portrait Gallery, London.

conversation delivered with polite candor: "She inherited a great deal of Wit and good Sense; and had great Promptitude at Repartees" (21). She is praised, too, for having displayed the great good sense to realize that she could not aspire to be the wife of the nation's king, but only his influential mistress.

The memoir, then, is not so much the biography of an actress as a whore's progress toward her eventually impersonating a lady of quality. Though the narrative warmly praises her beauty, it faults her as a player on stage regarding elocution, dignity, understanding, and grace. In her brief acting career, Gwyn was best known for her ingénue roles in plays written by John Dryden, Robert Howard, and Charles Sedley. Seymour remarks that as an actress her greatest power lay at stage's edge when she was "speaking an Epilogue . . . with a striking Air of Coquetishness and Levity" (19), as if to emphasize the linkages between her role in the play and her life on the theater's periphery. Gwyn engaged the audience in character and in her own person when, for example, she played the tragic heroine who seemed to rise from the dead to speak a comic epilogue at the end of *Tyrannick Love* (1669) as Nell Gwyn, still wearing her costume as the character Valeria: "Here Nelly lies, who, though she liv'd a Slater'n, / Yet dy'd a Princess acting in S. Cathar'n."[7] The epilogue required a particular kind of skill, sufficiently removed from the tragedy itself, acting but not acting, to create a public persona that allowed an audience simultaneously to assess her as actress and person, as a real individual even while still in character.

In fact, of course, Gwyn's public identity as the king's whore and mother of his bastard children was common knowledge, and King Charles II underscored this identity by treating her as a mistress rather than as a respected professional. Though Gwyn was lacking in *chastity* according to these *Memoirs*, her virtue was several times bolstered with reference to her *charity*. She was credited with displaying her good nature through acts of generosity and philanthropy that would have been regarded as properly characteristic of a gentlewoman. In particular, her kindness to English Civil War veterans in providing care to the wounded was explained in some detail: "Another Act of Generosity, which raised the Character above any Courtezan in those or any other Times, was her Solicitude to effect the Institution of the *Chelsea* Hospital" (46). In sum, "she was a Lady of distinguished Talents: she united Wit, Beauty and Benevolence, and if she deserves Blame for want of Chastity, there are few who challenge such lavish Encomiums for other moral Qualities" (60). Chastity strictly interpreted, though perhaps the dominant measure of a woman's morality, was not the only gauge of a woman's virtue. The centrality of Gwyn's sexual life relegated her acting to something merely incidental in defining her more lasting identity, but the memoirist's attention to her benevolence made her "vartue" seem worthy of a prince.

In contrast, the anonymous *Life of Lavinia Beswick, alias Fenton, alias Polly*

Peachum (1728) maintained from the outset that acting was most important in Fenton's life. Among the first women celebrities, Fenton's singing and acting as the heroine in John Gay's *Beggar's Opera* (1728) skyrocketed her to fame. A raunchy broadsheet, *The Whole Life of Polly Peachum; Containing an Account of her Birth, Parentage and Education*, written just after the play opened, recounts how "Polly Peachum . . . jumpt from an Orange Girl to an Actress on the Stage, and from that to be a Lady of Fortune." As in the Nell Gwyn memoir, sexuality is again a dominant theme. During Fenton's young life, described with distant, amused irony, she early became "a Sacrifice to *Priapus*" (14). Comparing her to Daniel Defoe's fictional adventurers Robinson Crusoe and Moll Flanders, the memoirist notes with sympathy that she was a fatherless love child until her mother, a barmaid and an occasional frequenter of Old Bailey, married her stepfather Fenton. Having much in common with the popular amatory fictions written by Aphra Behn, Delarivier Manley, and Eliza Haywood during the same period, the memoir emphasizes Fenton's seductive charms and the sparks who pursued her, though the thread of her enduring love for a feckless Portuguese nobleman is interwoven throughout. Appearing to sympathize with her unfortunate plight, the biographer offers samples of the numerous missives from admirers that Fenton, like other prominent actresses, found herself having to scrutinize and fend off or acknowledge. In the memoirist's eyes, Fenton's real dramatic talents made her worthy of a stage career but also aligned her with prostitution: "Polly becoming now the most celebrated Toast in the Town, she gain'd new Admirers every Time she appear'd on the Stage, and Persons of the highest Rank and Quality made Love to her; insomuch, that by the Presents she has received, she lives in Ease and Plenty, keeps her Servants, and appears abroad in as much Magnificence as a Lady" (33). In other words, her achievement as an actress, her accumulation of wealth, and her sometimes passing for a woman of rank transpired because of her magnetic sexual attractiveness more than her talent. Her willingness to accept gratuities such as "a Diamond Ring, a green Purse, a Watch, . . . Snuff-Box or some valuable Trincklet" (34) from admirers is sneeringly noted. Her success is attributed to male patrons and mentors, as it is in other popular pamphlets or broadsides that condemn the high fees she allegedly charged, not for acting, but for prostitution: "*A hundred Guineas for a Nights Debauch*" (34). The question raised about Fenton, as for other actresses in their biographical accounts, concerns the legitimacy of the means by which they acquired wealth and whether their talent as players justified their apparent class mobility; but the possibility that Fenton possessed a certain kind of virtue in spite of her sexual behavior, and that she is absolved from being merely a common whore, is nevertheless forwarded as a plausible interpretation.

Fenton's memoir liberally criticizes her conduct, but the moral censure gives way near the conclusion to muted admiration for the high quality of her performance as Cherry in Farquhar's *The Beaux Stratagem*, for which she merited an increase in pay from a paltry initial salary of thirty shillings per week. Such a wage would indeed have been quite modest, but it would have been greater than a common laborer's pay, not counting the gifts patrons gave her or the benefit receipts she earned.[8] The memoir thus becomes less a story of poverty than one of a clever actress's ability to earn and accumulate funds sufficient to grant charity to neighbors, bail out her Portuguese nobleman lover from debtor's prison, and offer "*Humanity* to the *Distressed*," as the title page advertises. In fact, one could certainly argue that a significant theme weaving through the biography is polite admiration for Fenton's remarkable ease in seeming to be a lady of quality in spite of her modest beginnings and her marginal status as a working woman: "I think she may pass for an accomplish'd worthy Lady, *if the Publick will allow an Actress the Title*" (47). This ambiguous phrase—"if the Publick will allow an Actress the Title"—is no small caveat, but the gist of the biography is to assert that Fenton, though contaminated by the company she kept, through grit and ingenuity, earned the right to be remembered as a woman who improved her status through her own inherent merit. She thus is proclaimed to possess an exceptional virtue, a kind that no less a heroine than Richardson's moral exemplar Clarissa was to embody—though in Fenton's case, and the case of the other subjects of memoirs discussed here, without preferring death to marriage with a libertine in order to prove she possessed it.

Several of Lavinia Fenton's accomplishments are mentioned with some cynicism as expressed in a poem in which she defends her freedom to remain a mistress rather than become wife to a fop. But running counter to the sardonic tone of the narrator is substantial praise for Fenton whose name became permanently identified with her explosively popular role as Polly Peachum. The memoirist expresses considerable admiration—if tongue-in-cheek— not only for her stage career, but also her knack for attracting admirers.[9] Significantly, after promising to provide "Proofs of her *Ingenuity, Wit*, and *Smart Repartees*," he praises her politeness and genius as she witnesses to it in social situations. Here, as in later memoirs of Fenton and of other actresses, the biographer assigns considerable weight to the high caliber of her genial conversation. The memoir was somewhat prophetic, for Fenton left the stage shortly after its publication to become mistress to the Duke of Bolton whom she finally married after the death of his wife several decades later.

In sum, Fenton's memoir explained her being welcomed into the best circles of women of rank in spite of her sexual profligacy because of her discriminating taste, conversational skills, and considerable dramatic talent. Her sexual behavior was made to seem an inevitable consequence of her profession rather than a matter of perverse desire, and Fenton's memoir implies that a celebrated actress's worth might be evaluated separately from her passions. An actress's personal matters could under certain circumstances be assumed to remain appropriately private and exempt from public scrutiny. Curll similarly skirted the embarrassment of Jane Rogers's passionate relationship with Robert Wilks, for example, by declaring coyly that "in the *polite World, the Fair Sex has always been privileged from Scandal* for which Reason I shall here *let fall the Curtain.*"[10] Her questionable sexual life remained off-limits in order to preserve the fiction of purity of heart.

At some level, celebrity actresses understood that their lives were not reduced to sexual biography, and that given their talents and stature, and because of their ability to project the effect of a convincing interiority characterized by an essential generosity, other standards might be applied. Anne Oldfield, like other subjects of memoirs, is conveyed as possessing a virtuous essence as part of her appeal, taking pleasure in work and philanthropy rather than profit for its own sake; her value is assessed through her intrinsic quality. Other biographical memoirs similarly strain toward producing cohesive narratives that explain away misdeeds, while actresses' *auto*biographical writings, such as Charlotte Charke's *Narrative*, expose the contradictions of an unorthodox life, often justified by the unequal expectations of the sexes.

The Memoirs of Anne Oldfield

The recurring theme in the memoirs of Gwyn and Fenton of valuing these public women as virtuous in spite of their imprudent sexual behavior is also apparent in the several memoirs of Anne Oldfield. A star actress such as Oldfield claimed virtue of a special kind, or biographers claimed it for her; and that special exemption from proper femininity, along with the economic independence that came with celebrity, became a viable substitute for decorous behavior.[11] The various biographical tracts written about Oldfield justified her being treated as a woman worthy of mixing with the highest echelons in spite of her failure to satisfy conventional norms.

Oldfield was the subject of two biographies published shortly after her death, neither of which is reliable: *Authentick Memoirs of the Life of that celebrated Actress Mrs. Ann Oldfield* (1730) that ran to six editions in the first year;[12] and William Egerton [Edmund Curll], *Faithful Memoirs of the Life, Amours and Performances of That Justly Celebrated, and most Eminent Actress of her Time, Mrs. Anne Oldfield* (1731) (Figure 8). A later version of the "Egerton" memoir was abridged and added to Thomas Betterton's *History of the English Stage, from the Restauration to the Present Time* (1741). The later memoir had been announced at the time of publication of the first biography, and it attracted advance accusations of "pack[ing] together a gross Collection of Absurdities" (12). Curll's biography of Robert Wilks (1733) and Benjamin Victor's of Barton Booth (1733) were also written about the same time as these memoirs, and Colley Cibber complains in his *Apology* about the fashionable tendency to follow with unbecoming haste an actor's death with a published life story.[13]

Recognizing the commercial appeal of women writers in the 1720s and 1730s, Edmund Curll maintained a special interest in publishing the plays and fictions of early women writers including Jane Barker and Susanna Centlivre, as well as the poet Elizabeth Thomas. He especially encouraged printing texts that included biographical exposés or secret histories.[14] Small wonder then that he found writing the memoirs of actress Anne Oldfield appealing as a highly marketable commodity. In the various biographical accounts of Oldfield, an apparently irreconcilable division develops between the spirited private woman who was "worthy" of being a mistress to controversial political figures Maynwaring and Churchill, and the brilliant actress without equal, "The Brightest Actress *Britain* e'er did yield" (Curll, 77). But actresses such as Oldfield are somehow forgiven, excused at some level for their sexual freedom, as if to acknowledge that it is an inescapable demand of the trade, and that the truly remarkable feat was for someone like Anne Bracegirdle to manage to avoid it.

Oldfield's memoirs are especially remarkable because they are the first full-length biographies to describe an actress as a credible professional, and they testify that her talent and steady industry served to some extent as penance for her less than reputable activities. A critical part of the task for Oldfield's biographers was to extricate her person from the sexual sins, real and imagined, of her predecessors. *Authentick Memoirs* (1730), the first of Oldfield's memoirs

Figure 8. "Mrs. Oldfield the celebrated Comedian." Edward Fisher, mezzotint published by John Spilsbury, after Jonathan Richardson (c. 1760–85). © National Portrait Gallery, London.

to appear, was an encomium that took pains to rank her in both comedy and tragedy as the equal to Wilks, who frequently played opposite her. The popular and talented pair starred together as Plume and Silvia in Farquhar's *Recruiting Officer*; as Archer and Mrs. Sullen in Farquhar's *Beaux Stratagem*; as Valentine and Angelica in Congreve's *Love for Love*, and as Careless and Lady Dainty in Cibber's *The Double Gallant; or, The Sick Lady's Cure*. The sole exception to the memoirist's praise for Oldfield is the accusation that she engaged in one "ungenerous action" in having stolen a "Mr F--e" from his wife and children, but she later appropriately persuaded him to return to his family as she sincerely repented of her "misspent Life" (6th ed. 1730, 41). As in the case of Fenton, the memoirist explains her misstep as a professional hazard that ought to be excused by recognizing that she was surrounded by seductive flatterers. This is swiftly followed by proof of her excellence in having earned £150 each year, rising to as much as £500, plus substantial profits from benefit nights. Oldfield's worth as a woman was thus complicated and enhanced by her star power and her ability to earn an independent living. If her life story did not provide a model of sterling behavior for young girls, it did offer an enticing fantasy of independence and an escape from class restrictions.

Even more than is the case for Fenton's life story, the 1730 memoir emphasizes Oldfield's deserving to be the universal delight of the "beau monde" in spite of her extraordinary personal adventures. Inclined to the theater from an early age, Oldfield's ascent to the stage is ascribed to the special aura emanating from her acting abilities. Exhibiting an appeal across class divisions, Oldfield's acting charmed the boxes and delighted the pit, including "Ev'n the Pert Templer, and the City Prig, / Who come to Plays to show their Wit—or Wig" (44). The gentlemen and ladies in the audience, seeming to meld together with the theatrical properties and to share the stage with the players, were metonymically portrayed as wigs or costume accessories, when Oldfield (purportedly engaged in an acting contest with Elizabeth Barry) caused "Effusion among the *Toupees*, and fluttering of *Fans* among the *Ladies*" (20). Leveling out the distance between gentlemanly playgoers and the lowly female player, the narrative assumes that the reader shares the attitude of a captivated male spectator, enchanted by Oldfield's performance, who found himself longing to play opposite the convincing actress on the stage: "Who that has seen her *Angelica* in *Love for Love*, but would, like *Valentine*, have made away with all to have obtained her! . . . so irresistable was she in every Character she personated" (23). The reader, like the spectator, is encouraged to be swept up in the performance and to become assimilated to it in order to possess her.

The first of these several memoirs concerning Anne Oldfield also countered her eccentric if excusable sexual behavior with high praise for her discerning taste, including her superior standards in judging painting, poetry, and drama: "She is such a Judge of Painting, that the greatest of our Modern Artists in their Profession are glad to have her Opinion of a Piece before it is shewn to the World, knowing, that if it escapes her Censure, it will gain the Approbation of the whole Town; for she is so Nice in the Discovery of an Error, that it's as impossible to deceive her, as it is to express her Strength of Fancy" (6th ed. 1730, 43). Such natural ability to distinguish between art and artifice, and to develop aesthetic taste, helps explain her social class mobility. Similarly, her clever repartee meant that her wit could be construed as exceeding even her considerable beauty. Yet there is a double edge to the conclusion of the biography, "*A Poem to the Memory of Mrs. Oldfield*," in its assertion that Oldfield compelled the spectator or reader to ignore her untoward behavior because of the stunning quality of her thespian achievement: "She spoilt, against her will, the Poet's Aim; / Making those Follies which we should despise, / When seen in her, seem Virtues in our Eyes" (1st ed. 44). Irregular sexual conduct was transformed in Oldfield's performance into something ultimately exceptionally virtuous in her actual person through the theatrical magic of her dramatic characterizations.

The second narrative of Oldfield's life, *The Faithful Memoirs* (1731), consists of a miscellany of documents rather than a linear narrative. It includes highlights of her life, the principal parts she performed, and a defense of the English stage that hints at the beginnings of a dramatic criticism and counters antitheatrical sentiments. *Faithful Memoirs* defines Oldfield in terms of friendships, affairs, and politics as well as her parts and her epilogues. Sections on actress Mary Anne Campion, the Duke of Devonshire, and William Wycherley's marriage fill out the narrative with bits that were only tangentially related to Oldfield's life, but *Memoirs* returns to its subject to discuss her last original role as the eponymous Dido-like Sophonisba in Thomson's tragedy, as well as her illness, death, funeral oration, will, and effects. It includes her poems, some of which were commemorative, while others bore only the vaguest relationship to the theater.

In *Faithful Memoirs* the narrative switches course to suggest that Oldfield did *not* embody exemplary virtue because she lacked sufficient self-reflection about her behavior. At the outset the title page offers an apparent criticism of Oldfield's behavior, citing Rochefoucault: "The great Pains, which the Ladies of this Age take to commend Virtue, is sometimes a shrewd Sign that they take but very little to practice it. And, the greatest Part of those complaints against their Neighbours, are owing to the Want of Reflection upon Themselves." If the stage was supposed to inculcate morals, Oldfield was judged as personally derelict, at least with reference to this quotation. But at the same time the memoir suggests that she instructed the audience by moving their emotions and arousing their sensibilities through her many and varied parts, as was signaled with admiration in her funeral oration, also included: "What harden'd Heart wept not with *Andromache*? What Mother did she not instruct in Maternal Love when *Astynax*'s Danger wrings her Soul?". In fact, in mourning Maynwaring and becoming solely responsible for raising their son, Oldfield was described as having embodied her role as Andromache: "The *Distress'd Mother* seemed now to be the case of Mrs. Oldfield, both on and off the Stage" (1731, 153).

The didactic nature of her onstage roles helped to balance her personal inadequacies. Oldfield's principal parts served as sentimental examples of penitence and reformation flowing from a stage that aimed to inculcate virtue and punish vice. Just as the 1731 memoir argues that spectators benefited from watching Oldfield's instructive tragic roles as Andromache and Astynax, her comic roles allegedly challenged the receptive spectators to behave more honorably: "What Woman so lost in a Crowd of Cards, and good Company which the Repentance of my Lady *Townley* could not teach to reform? What Coquet so abandoned to her Folly whom the ridiculous Behaviour of Lady *Betty Modish* could not make detest her Vanity? What Character did she appear in private or publick Life which she could not make Amiable? On the Stage so easy did the Poets Language flow from her, it might well be taken for her own Sentiments; and in private all she spoke, all she did, carry'd that agreeable Air, that every thing sat upon her with the same genteel Neglect, her Cloaths did; unaffected gay, but politley Neat" (1731, 153). Because the sentiments of the dramatic character seemed to the audience to reflect Oldfield's personal indictment of Lady Betty's coquettish folly as she melded her acting skill together with her identity, she could be forgiven her affairs with Maynwaring and Churchill. In fact, as "A Poem to the Memory of Mrs. Oldfield" had ingeniously claimed, she set a decorous standard for actual gentlewomen rather than the reverse: "Such finish'd Breeding, so polite a Taste, / Her Fancy always for the Fashion past" (1730, 42).

By ending with "A Funeral Oration for Mrs. Oldfield," the 1731 biography finally seemed to claim that Oldfield was the exception to the ladies of the age, for "she taught Virtue in such persuasive Accents, that the Hearers have been with Immitation fired, and wished they so could Act that so they may Instruct, and so instructing be adored like her" (1731, 152). The memoir concluded with a panegyric in which she, like Fenwick, is judged to exceed the expectations of "woman"; she is instead, in a trope common to satires on women, compared to a phoenix, "for as far as Nature exceeds Art, so far did she excell all the Women of her Time" (1731, 153–54). In sum, her public fame ultimately took precedence over any quibbles about her private life.

Much more than the biographies of Gwyn or Fenton, Oldfield's memoirs depict her superior acting as central to her identity. The approach makes these biographies unique in the history of the early actresses' life stories. The final life story, *Memoirs of Mrs. Anne Oldfield* (1741), was published as a separate addendum to *The History of the English Stage, from the Restauration to the Present Time*, attributed to Thomas Betterton but compiled by William Oldys and Edmund Curll from his papers. This abridgement of the 1731 memoirs reiterated the principal narration of the earlier version but omitted the summation of her life; it included four poems on her death, the list of plays and epilogues in which she appeared, and the inventory of her estate and her effects. Both versions—full-length and abridged—emphasized Oldfield's epilogues, those occasions at the play's conclusion when the actress appeared to be most in synchrony with the times, and most herself, as she migrated toward the edge of the stage to establish greater rapport with the audience. As much a history of other actresses contemporary to Oldfield as her own exclusively individual biography, the memoir demonstrated the actress's courage in blazing the trail for other women in, for example, her epilogue on the parliament of women, her rant against vile husbands, and her argument for a woman's right to divorce and remarry when faced with an unfaithful husband. As the epilogue's speaker who resembled both the actress and the character, she acted as an intermediary to the audience but one who was not solely herself or her part.[15]

In particular, the comic epilogue to Ambrose Philips's tragedy *The Distrest Mother*, spoken by Oldfield as the widowed Andromache, became an opportunity to appear to defend her lover Maynwaring and their relationship after his death. The 1741 memoir includes this ribald epilogue, the gossipy afterpiece to which Richardson's Pamela famously took exception. The memoir terms the epilogue, in which Oldfield mocks her character's scrupulously moral decisions, to be "very humourous," an opinion quite different from Pamela's reaction to the "lewd, and even senseless *Double-entendre*." The shocked Pamela complained to Mr. B's sister, Lady Davers, "I was extremely mortify'd to see my favourite (and the only perfect) Character, debas'd and despoil'd, and the Widow of *Hector*, Prince of *Troy*, talking Nastiness to an Audience, and setting it out with all the wicked Graces of Action, and affected Archness of Looks, Attitude, and Emphasis."[16] Pamela of course does not comprehend Oldfield's ironic and even playful stance toward her character. Ignoring spectators like the fictional Pamela who might have been offended, the memoir glosses over potential moral harm that might result to the audience from the very popular epilogue.[17]

Similarly, Oldfield's reciting the comic epilogue to *Phaedra and Hippolitus* bridged the gap between classical history and contemporary eighteenth-century events to turn it into a witty injunction to modern women, whom she cajoled to remain chaste in contrast to the unfaithful Phaedra. Oldfield is depicted as attempting to elevate the flagging morality of the theater for people of quality, "especially the Ladies" (1731, 1741, 10), an idea that, even if ironic, runs counter to the assumption that her performances pleased primarily male spectators. These epilogues made the plays seem startlingly personal and current: they helped to bridge the temporal gap between an older play and its current moment of performance, as well as between the classical characters and the modern women who embodied them.

Oldfield justly earned a reputation as a consummate actress, and her modern sexual attitudes paradoxically became a sign of her brilliant natural talent, as if she had not labored for many years to learn a demanding craft or to pursue the mundane task of earning a living. In the first memoir, the reader is encouraged to generously grant her the "Grains of Allowance to those whose excentric Genius move about their Orb, that is to say, to those whose petty Failings have superiour Excellencies to all such Cavillers" (1730, 26). The memoir also relates the unconventional love story of Oldfield and Maynwaring (and later Charles Churchill) in a manner designed to rationalize a nation's star-struck idolizing of the star actress. Maynwaring, though rendered blameless because of his nobility, is acknowledged to be an alcoholic spendthrift, and much of the memoir rather peculiarly turns out to be a defense of him, in part as a reformed Jacobite, rather than of her. The two actors' fates and public reputations were, of course, closely intertwined, to such an extent that his death was attested to have resulted not from venereal disease in order "to clear up the unjust Aspersion cast on Mrs. *Oldfield*" (1731, 40; 1741, 29), and perhaps to dissociate her from any resemblance to Nell Gwyn whose death was similarly suspect. Neither is Oldfield's having given birth to illegitimate progeny, one son each with Maynwaring and Churchill, condemned. Portrayed as both a legitimate object of desire and a moral teacher, the actress is represented as an ideal mother whose generosity prompted deep affection from the men of means who fathered her children. For example, her willingness to bequeath money to her children, including sufficient funds for one son to purchase a coveted place in the horseguards, is transformed into a sign that her character was worthy of Maynwaring who was "a Gentleman of one of the best Families in *Great-Britain,* as well as a Man of the most exquisite and refin'd Taste, and most unquestion'd Judgment" (1730, 24). In that way the memoirs are testaments to Oldfield's maternal generosity, and to her ability to amass a fortune including the rich tapestries, fine jewels, and Dutch paintings among her possessions, equal to twice the estate that Maynwaring left.

Oldfield's affinity for her dramatic parts, whether seduced maiden or aristocratic lady, allowed her to manipulate the tensions between stage and life for maximum benefit to her career. Like other star actresses she was credited with making social comedies and she-tragedies seem to parallel actual people's lives and thus cause theatrical illusion to disappear. When Oldfield acted as Calista in Rowe's *Fair Pentitent* (1725), "she appear'd with such a noble Grandeur in her Person, that it were to be wish'd some of our modern Ladies of Quality could learn in their Turn to personate Mrs. *Oldfield*; So infinitely did the Copy transcend the Original, and so much more amiable did they appear when represented by Mrs. *Oldfield,* when at home with their Lords" (6th ed. 1730, 38). Her sympathetic portrayal of the seduced maiden of she-tragedy speaks to her ability to reflect the complexity of combining virtue with lost chastity when she finally succumbs to the cunning Lothario rather than accepting her betrothed Altamont. William Chetwood wrote of Oldfield's Calista, "Her excellent clear Voice of Passion, her piercing flaming Eye, with Manner and Action suiting, us'd to make me shrink with Awe . . . and though Mr. *Booth* play'd *Lothario,* I could hardly lug him up to the Importance of triumphing over such a finish'd Piece of Perfection, that seemed to be too much dignified to lose her Virtue."[18] Calista afforded a splendid role for Oldfield that enticed audiences to assume her interiority imitated the she-tragedy heroine, and she played the part at least twice a year until she wisely chose it for her benefit night in 1730, her last year of performing. In yet another dramatic part that mourns the loss of the heroine's virginity, Oldfield was credited with actually *becoming* Jane Shore, at once a queen and a woman who sought vindication, as the epilogue to the play makes clear: "Then judge the *fair Offender* with good Nature, / And let your Fellow-feeling curb your Satire. / What if our Neighbours have some little Failing / Must we needs fall to damning and to railing; / For her Excuse too, be it understood, / That if the Woman was not quite so good, / Her Lover was a King, she Flesh and Blood" (1731, 75). In pitying Oldfield who made the plea in character as Jane Shore, a prototype of the actress, the audience was coaxed into forgiving her own moral lapses.

But perhaps the most noteworthy and memorable character that Oldfield played was that of the charmingly duplicitous Lady Betty Modish in Colley Cibber's sentimental comedy, *The Careless Husband*, produced for the first time at Drury Lane, 7 December 1704. On that occasion she shared billing with her frequent costar Robert Wilks as Sir Charles Easy, the careless husband of the title. In writing the play Cibber almost certainly modeled the role after Oldfield, who owned the part during her lifetime; and the play, like *Fair Penitent* and *Jane Shore*, teases the audience with its close blending of life and legend. The *Faithful Memoirs* includes verbatim an entire scene between Lady Easy and Lady Betty Modish (2: 1); and though the 1741 version omits the scene, it dates Oldfield's birth as an actress from her performance of this part. The memoirs imagine that her "*real Character*" is revealed through the "*imaginary one* of Lady *Betty Modish*" in regard to her dress, charm, "Wit, Raillery, and Conversation" (1731, 11). The part splendidly illustrates the potentially comic effect when Oldfield straddled her public and private identities. Though Cibber created the part with her in mind, Thomas Davies admiringly remarked in his *Dramatic Miscellanies* that Oldfield seemed to have invented her character's words as if she had spoken them in her own life: "By being a welcome and constant visitor to families of distinction, Mrs. Oldfield acquired an elegant and graceful deportment in representing women of high rank. She expressed the sentiments of Lady Betty Modish and Lady Townly in a manner so easy, natural, and flowing, and so like to her common conversation, that they appeared to be her own genuine conception."[19] *The Careless Husband* also animates the ongoing debate over an actress's virtue versus her chastity, seeming to allow the character Lady Modish's rank to compensate for Oldfield's unconventional sexual behavior.

Demonstrating that Oldfield's natural character made her equal to the peer's daughter she played, Cibber set the play's scenes of vigorous exchange in Windsor Castle where he imagined that the actress had actually engaged in similar conversations with ladies of quality. Lady Modish relishes the power of her beauty to torment Lord Morelove, whose solid morality contrasts with Sir Charles Easy's libertine tendencies and at the same time with the studied extravagance of Lord Foppington (played by Cibber in full-bottomed periwig), with whom she shares delight in employing her à la mode status as a means of accruing power. Because Lady Modish's authority resides in her stylish dress, she boldly asserts that "A new fashion upon a fine woman is often a greater proof of her value than you are aware of" (2: 1). Pragmatically manipulating this power, in a feminine counterpoint to Sir Charles Easy's casual infidelity, she displays apparent indifference to the adoring Morelove for the bulk of the play. Though Lady Modish publicly expresses contempt for reputation, the play reins her in to exemplify virtue at its end. If the play draws upon racy Restoration themes in a toned-down eighteenth-century context that requires a reformation scene, then Lady Modish stands between Restoration heroines such as Congreve's Millamant and eighteenth-century comic sentimental heroines in what is arguably the first sentimental comedy.[20]

Lady Modish's power emanates in considerable part from her studied attention to high fashion, a trait for which Oldfield herself was also famous. In the *Memoir* Oldfield's well-known attention to elegant clothing is imagined to be the outward reflection of inner stability: "however she was apparell'd, her self was the same. For there is so immediate a Relation between our Thoughts and Gesture, that a *Woman* must *think* well to *look* well" (1741, 45). Wearing beautiful clothing brought feminine sway, while public reputation—for which Lady Modish claimed to care not a fig—resembled exotic deformity: "One shall not see an homely creature in town but wears it in her mouth as monstrously as the Indians do bobs at their lips, and it really becomes 'em just alike" (2: 1). The plot relies for resolution on a costume stage property, the famous steinkirk scarf that Lady Easy dangled from her philandering husband's neck as material proof of his adultery. The lady's scarf—rather than the fop's periwig, cravat, or hat—unfolds the moral of the drama. Yet the play's other fashion plate, Lord Foppington, comes to possess a masculine piece of stage property that threatens Modish's relationship with Morelove, and she demands its return. The snuff box Morelove gave Lady Modish as a talisman of his love is transformed into "a lady's utensil" (3: 1). In short, even traditionally male properties could become female possessions in the theater. The male characters challenge Lady Modish's reckless courage, and the women are jealous of it, making her character a double for the actress who plays her.

When it becomes clear that no amount of new-fashioning of the scarf will change the circumstances of Sir Charles's exposure, the women show themselves to be reformers of the men, though not before the chastened Sir Charles Easy lectures Lady Betty Modish in a speech that points directly at Oldfield herself: "But the noble conquest you have gained at last, over defeated sense of reputation, too, has made your fame immortal. Ay, madam, your reputation.... I say, your reputation; 't has been your life's whole pride of late to be the common toast of every public table, vain even in the infamous addresses of a married man, my Lord Foppington; let that be reconciled with reputation" (5: 7). Particularly regretting the *public* nature of the slights she had shown Morelove, Lady Betty wins her lover and regains her reputation.

Empowered by her quick tongue and sheer attractiveness, the illustrious Oldfield embodied the contradictions of an actress who exploited her personal character and competed with it. Her memoirs drew the parallel even more tightly in Cibber's words when he gloated "that almost every Sentence, in the Part, may with Justice be said to have been heard from her own Mouth before she pronounced it on the Stage. In short, it was not the Part of Lady *Betty Modish*, represented by Mrs. *Oldfield*; but it was the real Mrs. *Oldfield* who appeared in the Character of Lady *Betty Modish*" (1731, 3). In other words, as the subject of early theater biography, Oldfield was credited with a nearly seamless assumption of a role *and* a social class that was attested to be essential to her character even while her less-than-perfect sexual reputation was acknowledged.[21] According to Charles Macklin, she possessed the authority of class without the gravitas, energizing any given role stage with "the *rage* of fashion and vivacity," speaking "with a rapidity and *gaieté de Coeur*, that electrified the whole house," and revealing "*high-bred manners*" in which she was unequaled, even among women born into privilege.[22] Cibber adds in the preface to his version of Vanbrugh's *The Provok'd Husband* (1728) that "her natural good sense and lively turn of conversation made her way so easy to ladies of the highest rank, that it is a less wonder if on the stage she sometimes *was*, what might have become the finest woman in real life to have supported."[23] In Oldfield's 1730 memoirs, "modern Ladies of Quality" were enjoined to impersonate *her*, "so infinitely did the Copy transcend the Original, and so much more amiable did they appear when represented by Mrs. *Oldfield*, than when at home with their Lords."[24] Her impersonations of them in performance were alleged to be superior to the elegant manners of the authentic elite.

Even in death Oldfield was dressed as a fashionable gentlewoman: in her coffin she wore "a very fine *Brussels* Lace Head; a Holland shift with a Tucker, and double Ruffles of the same Lace; a Pair of New Kid-Gloves, and her Body wrapped up in a Winding Sheet" (20). Though Elizabeth Barry and Anne Bracegirdle were her rivals, Oldfield remained "*sole Empress of the Stage*" (74). She was "the *Greatest Lady* in *England*" (1731, 38) and "the Brightest Actress *Britain* e'er did yield" (1731, 146). Spurred by the xenophobic preference for English theater over Italian and other foreign influence, the theater was "aptly calculated for the forming a free-born People," according to *The History of the English Stage* (124), and Oldfield became its national treasure. Oldfield was consistently put forward as a woman, worthy of symbolizing the English nation, who richly deserved the honor of burial in the national monument, Westminster Abbey.

In sum, the taint of the whore followed Nell Gwyn, Lavinia Fenton, and Anne Oldfield into their social mingling with persons of high rank, and it would be too simple to say that the memoirs absolved them of their sins simply because they traveled in circles of quality. The memoirs—and some of the plays in which they acted and the epilogues they recited—offered exoneration for the actresses' lapses rather than condemnation; they suggest, in a not entirely uncomplimentary fashion, that actresses aspired to a category not contained by "woman." As Fenton's biographer put it, "*For sure she was more than Woman.*"[25] This sentiment is both derisive and admiring, indicating that all of these actresses were moving in previously untrod territory. But identifying these women primarily by their affairs or lack of them—as prostitutes, mistresses, or even as chaste women—is, if we attend carefully to the subtleties of their biographies, a skewed and inadequate view of how they were perceived. Oldfield's 1730 memoirist argues this most forcefully: the celebrated actress "endeavour'd by a sincere Repentance to make all the Atonement that lay in her Power for a misspent Life; and indeed how could it be expected otherwise, from a Person who had been from her Youth immersed in Vanity, surrounded with Flattery, and inur'd to a profuse Way of living? most Women, I believe, in her condition would have done as much, few would have done better, and many would have done much worse" (6th ed. 1730, 41). Though sexually renegade in private life, each of these actresses was purported to be charitable and generous; and in the cases of Fenwick and Oldfield, they were believed to possess an immense natural talent that somehow allowed them to display social ease and to merit social mobility. In addition to providing fashionable models for ladies of quality, as public women they were also surrogates for a growing bourgeoisie aspiring to assume a kind of celebrated, impersonated nobility that could be achieved rather than inherited, that took its impetus in wage labor and attached an actress's personal worth to its exchange value in the marketplace. No wonder then that the theater audience, hungry for juicy tidbits and private information about these strong-minded women, interpreted their roles as well as their spoken prologues and epilogues as affording authentic glimpses into actresses' private lives even as they redefined virtue. Exceptional virtue helped mold a new kind of double standard for a commercial age in which the extraordinary talent of star actresses opportunely substituted for respectability.

Later Lives

The memoirs of Anne Oldfield offered the first substantial accounts of an actress's life, but the first extended autobiographical narrative in which an actress tells her own story did not appear until *A Narrative of the Life of Mrs. Charlotte Charke, Written by Herself* in 1755. Until that time, the narratives that most resemble autobiographical histories were Jane Rogers's short memorial (1712) and Kitty Clive's protests concerning her professional mistreatment (1744), mere fragments of self-representation but courageous defenses of their rights as working women.[26] The burgeoning interest in autobiography in the eighteenth century, "a quintessential form for demonstrating . . . the art of self-dramatization," as Thomas Postlewait has aptly termed it,[27] developed as a genre justifying the growing fascination with players' lives as avenues into their unplumbed interiorities and to make them cohere with performances.

It is significant that the publication of actresses' lives anticipated the more general popular demand for biographies of political, historical, and literary figures. The market was tested with Samuel Johnson's *Life of Savage* (1744) and the early lives of Alexander Pope, which were soon followed by the formal biographies of public women distinguished in the republic of letters that came to fruition in George Ballard's *Memoirs of Several Ladies of Great Britain* (1752).[28] Ballard's biographical accounts most resemble the conduct books that provided the cultural context for Richardson's mid-century novels; but Ballard's collection did not rival the popularity of the many editions of Oldfield's memoirs until it became more popular much later in the century. Unlike *Pamela*, Ballard's biographies do not intermix exemplary models with titillating boudoir scenes, but his lives of eminent women paved the way for similar compilations such as Thomas Amory's *Memoirs of Several Ladies of Great Britain* (1755) and *Biographium Faemineum: The Female Worthies* (1766), among many others. These publications featured characterizations of learned ladies who were illustrious in a markedly different way from actresses who were, however, like them, anomalous.

The proliferation of new media as gossip outlets and the increasing numbers of women entering the public sphere aroused a greater appetite for insider information. Charlotte Charke surely sensed the confluence of these conditions in the marketplace when publishing her *Narrative*, the first of its kind written by an actress. While Charke recognized that women's secrets were most often assumed to be sexual, she cannily traded on creating a sense of public mystery crucial to attracting attention and improving her status. Charke's autobiography delights in tantalizing the reader with unanswered questions as she mimics in life her onstage roles and seeks through memoir the publicity that might alleviate her poverty and win her acting roles again. Yet the appeal of the *Narrative* lay elsewhere. Charke essentially makes feminine virtue irrelevant to her narrative of indeterminate gendering: in fact, the word "virtue" does not appear in the *Narrative* with reference to any aspect of character. The originality of the autobiographical account rests in large part on her refusal to define herself as a traditional female whose public identity depended upon chastity or modesty. From early childhood she contests a determining difference between the sexes as she teases the reader regarding the hidden reason for her masquerading in breeches as Mr. Brown and taking a "wife": "I rather chuse to undergo the worst Imputation that can be laid on me on that Account, than unravel the Secret, which is an Appendix to one I am bound, as I before hinted, by all the Vows of Truth and Honour everlastingly to conceal."[29] She insists that the real-life roles for women extended far beyond those of the chambermaids, penitent prostitutes, distressed mothers, and tragic queens dominating the stage at mid-century, and she imitated in life her travesty roles as Lord Foppington, Captain Macheath, Lord Townly, Sir John, and Lothario. Rather than claiming virtue in any of its forms, Charke parodied the reader's expectation of the biographical memoirs that preceded her autobiographical writing, just as she had parodied her father and brother on stage, to flaunt her violation of the typical biography and its assertion of exceptional virtue. Her eccentricity allowed her to avoid the usual protestations regarding proper female conduct, and she sought only to justify the public disrespect she dared to direct at the disapproving Colley Cibber.

As we have seen in Oldfield's memoirs, the heroine of Nicholas Rowe's *The Fair Penitent*, Calista, became a kind of prototype of the celebrated actress who had strayed from traditional moral paths. For Calista as well as for the actresses who played her, "pride and shame were struggling for superiority." This struggle appears in somewhat altered form in the ghostwritten *Apology for the Life of George Anne Bellamy*, a multi-volumed defense of the actress, letters ostensibly written to the Honorable Miss ---, that parallel the emerging novel in its epistolary form.[30] Bellamy, the lovechild of Lord Tyrawley, was made legitimate when her mother married Captain Bellamy. She was herself twice married and bigamous. In a largely sympathetic discussion of the memoirs, Kristina Straub emphasizes Bellamy's self-proclaimed victimization and finds that the actress impersonates a sentimental heroine of a passionate romance fiction that "render[s] her vulnerable to the predations of an unfeeling world and the ill effects of her own 'innocent' mistakes" (113) in her affairs with George Metham, Thomas Calcraft, and West Digges.[31] Through her ghostwriter, probably Alexander Bicknell, Bellamy pits being an object of desire against inhabiting a more conventional societal role as a passive but sympathetic victim. In Bellamy's impassioned biographical tale the narrator is torn between presenting herself as a beleaguered heroine in distress, and describing a more active agent in charge of her own self-commodification. Straub puts it this way: "By making a spectacle of herself, Bellamy compromises the very credentials as sentimental heroine that she seeks to establish" (122). She interprets Bellamy's violation of the rules of femininity and her wish to control her public persona as indicative of an ambivalent identification with both masculine and feminine roles. In spite of the many strengths of this interpretation, Straub underestimates, in my view, the potential agency available to actresses even when they are "raped" onstage and off in both the ocular and literal senses, and the way they manipulated "masculinity" as critical to their success.

Pushing at the limits of available narratives of femininity, Bellamy actually assumes substantial responsibility for the imprudent choices that contributed to the unfortunate progress of her life, and she regularly resists adopting the victimized position. Because Bellamy is writing autobiographically, even if pseudonymously, she affects to reveal her authentic personal feelings and uses the occasion to correct popular misapprehensions about her, unlike the biographical narrators in earlier memoirs. The lengthy *Apology* affects an intimacy with Bellamy's reputed female correspondent, as well as her larger audience of readers, that parallels and reinforces the actress's stage performance of easy familiarity. Though the line is narrowly drawn between sentimental appeal ("May Sterne's recording Angel drop the tear of pity and obliterate my faults!" 5: 149) and confession, Bellamy attributes most of her misfortunes to "a train of untoward events" because "my misconduct has been more the result of thoughtlessness and imprudence than of a depraved disposition" (5: 148). Women fall, she argues, because they unwisely trust unreliable men. Although she asks for sympathy for being unfairly maligned in popular opinion, she publicly defends herself as when, for example, a "gentleman," Mr. Medlicote, "vilely traduced" her character in pressing himself upon her (1: 151). Bellamy does not exonerate herself by suggesting that she is the unwilling prey of lecherous men but instead transforms the concept of virtue into one sufficiently elastic to fit her own experiences. Bellamy consistently attempts to wriggle out of the restricting mold of decorous femininity to insert herself within a more manly form of virtue—one based upon an ethics that derives from a highminded, if unorthodox, rationale—even while she readily acknowledges more conventional definitions as they are applied to most actresses: "There were many, I was persuaded, who trod the stage, and were truly virtuous. I brought as examples a [Hannah] *Pritchard* and a [Kitty] *Clive*" (1: 162). Women players seeking a livelihood endure special testing, she animatedly asserts: "I thought a woman who preserved an unblemished reputation on the stage, to be infinitely more praiseworthy, than those who retained a good name, merely because they were secured by rank or fortune from the temptations actresses are exposed to" (1: 163). But, though she claims to value chastity highly and regrets her own "loss of innocence," she separates that physical loss from her virtuous *essence*: "my mind still retaining its native purity" (1: 164). In addition, reviewers of the *Apology* concentrated on the romantic and yet instructive nature of Bellamy's memoirs ,which included "many an useful lesson of virtue." It is not Bellamy's victimization that made the book a runaway best seller, but her ready acknowledgment of her imprudence—the "vanity, pride, self-consequence, and extravagance" that dominated her life—and her demand to be judged by an alternative measure that sidestepped proper femininity.[32]

Echoing the sentiments of the earlier memoirs of Oldfield and Gwyn, William Chetwood's *History of the Stage* twice commends Bellamy's compassionate spirit for the distressed and her generosity as indicative that she is possessed "with every moral Virtue" (113). As an actress soaring beyond "*slavish Rules, mechanic Forms,*" he praises her for exhibiting on stage a grace beyond the reach of art that recalls Milton's Eve. Chetwood also cites approvingly some lines from a panegyric that drew parallels to an earlier virtuous exemplar, though one with a similarly uneven character: "*Each magic Charm, lamented* Oldfield *knew, / Inchanting* Bellamy! *revives in you*" (113). In both cases the actress's capacity to ease the miseries of others restores her virtue in spite of her unseemly reputation. Bellamy's virtuous core, then, might be regarded as an extension of her claim to an interiority effect, one which she contrives onstage to enhance her marketability. As in the earlier biographies of actresses, in her self-vindicating account Bellamy opts for an alternative definition, an exceptional virtue, that corresponds more closely to a masculine *virtù* rather than to one resembling private forms of proper femininity. Her exceptional virtue contrasts not only to domestic heroines of the mid-century realist novel, but also to the classical public virtue most exemplified in women of letters such as Bluestockings Catherine Macaulay, Hannah More, or Elizabeth Montagu.

Unlike those learned ladies or Richardson's fictional exemplars, Bellamy cordons off her sexual affairs, illegitimate children, and financial troubles into a category distinct from her bedrock character to demonstrate that she is superior to the men with whom she traffics. Unwilling to relinquish her claim to public virtue, Bellamy redefines and rationalizes it to incorporate her freewheeling behavior.

In this way, though the early biographies of actresses attempted to recuperate actresses into femininity, those in which the actresses shape their own images are less cohesive. Bellamy's narrative, as I have been demonstrating, is unevenly split: there is the cultural authority she derives from acting versus her inability to control her debt and her lovers. The tension between public and private life remains unresolved, for Bellamy attempted to conflate her personal adventures with the sufferings of the tragic heroines she played; but she prided herself on the indomitable resilience with which she faced regular challenges that allowed her narrative, and her life, to avoid becoming a tragedy. For example, she reports that she formed a little party of men and women of learning, called the Nonsense Club, that met weekly at her home for the exchange of "mirth, wit, and good humour" (4: 80). At first refusing to participate in political activities usually unavailable to women, Bellamy eventually changed her mind to become the only woman in attendance at Charles James Fox's political junto "where the national concerns were talked over" (3: 119). Regularly attending the House of Commons where she employed her prodigious memory honed through acting, "my retentive faculties being almost as extraordinary as his own" (3: 136), she made herself indispensable to Fox as amanuensis and trusted confidante. Developing a political consciousness, she soon "studiously sought to acquire a knowledge of the laws of nations" as a result of meeting Lady Rochford at Holland-house (3: 136).

Bellamy by her own report (or the report of her pseudonymous interpreter) finally worried much less about losing her virtue than losing her theatrical patronage. Like all of the memoirs discussed here, Bellamy's *Apology* is a commercial venture, and the author does not attempt to hide her economic motive for publication as an appeal for ancillary support. The final volume of the 1785 edition includes favorable reviews that tout the biography's success: "The five preceding Volumes of this Work, have met with the most favourable reception from the Public, and experienced a rapidity of sale scarcely ever equaled" (1785, 6: 171). Relinquishing the claim of exceptional virtue would have brought potentially disastrous commercial consequences. Ladies of quality attended plays starring profligate actresses without hesitation, but they sometimes threatened to put restrictions on other more lucrative forms of patronage if the actress's reputation became questionable. For much of her career Bellamy was surrounded with adoring female benefactors, and she cites these friendships as evidence of their tacit agreement as to her social acceptability. For example, she openly delighted in being given a valued token of esteem by the Countess of Kildare, later Duchess of Leinster (4: 124), a much-prized gold enameled snuff box. Bellamy similarly boasts of her friendship with patron Mrs. Butler in Dublin, and with the Duchess of Montague and the Duchess of Queensberry in London. According to the memoir, her acquaintances included Viscountess Townshend, the Duchess of Douglas, Lady Tyrawley, and Mrs. Cracroft. She especially cherished the Misses Meredith, St. Leer, and Conway as models of female friendship; they did not shy away from Bellamy's company and returned her visits. If the narrator is to be believed, in Scotland she was "caressed by ladies of the most exemplary character, as well as of exalted rank" (4: 81) who did not worry about being "contaminated by an intimacy with a much-injured woman, that [they] knew had been grossly imposed upon, and most wickedly traduced" (4: 126–27).

Chastity then, Bellamy argues, is not the sole measure of virtue, and it ought not to be the determining factor in judging a woman's worth: "I have always observed that the *really* virtuous of our sex, ever view with compassion the errors of those, who have been seduced by the artifices of designing men; and, though totally unacquainted themselves with the frailties of human nature, in this point, can bestow a tear of pity on the martyr of an unguarded moment.—Chastity is undoubtedly the brightest ornament that adorns the female mind . . . But I can by no means allow, as the censorious part of the sex seem to consider it, that this virtue is the *only* needful one; and when a person has been unhappily deprived of it, though by the most seductive arts, every other good qualification takes its flight with it" (4: 127). Bellamy exposed feminine virtue as a slippery cultural construct that she reconfigured in life and in text to claim its extraordinary possession as integral to comprehending her interiority.

The fact that novelist Elizabeth Griffith's heroine in *The Delicate Distress* (1769) engaged in similar special pleading regarding exceptional virtue suggests that such reasoning among thinking women throughout the period was not uncommon. A breach in chastity is "the most unpardonable folly," but the essential virtue of a woman is not irremediably contaminated by a sexual slip. Griffith, herself an actress and a playwright, wrote, "I believe there are many women, who have erred, in that point, who may have more real virtue, aye, and delicacy too, than half the sainted dames, who value themselves on the preservation of chastity; which in all probability, has never been assailed. She alone, who has withstood the solicitations of a man she fondly loves, may boast her virtue; and I will venture to say, that such an heroine will be more inclined to pity, than to despise, the unhappy victims of their own weakness." One hears again in Griffith's entreaty an appeal for compassion for those who have been severely tested and tempted: "There is no character I so heartily abominate as that of the '*outrageously virtuous*' who malevolently repeat such stories."[33]

The various biographical and autobiographical memoirs I have considered here attest to the ways in which the character of these actresses, aligned with a simulated interiority, was legible through their dramatic roles and other public appearances. In the early nineteenth century James Boaden resolved the separation between public and private virtue differently in his memoir of Sarah Siddons by restricting his discussion almost exclusively to her public life. He insisted that, at least in the case of someone of Siddons's stature, stricter codes of separation between the public and private lives of actresses pertained, for private life should be kept separate from celebrity. "Her PRIVATE life!" he exclaims, "What is there, then, in the private life of the *most* excellent wife, mother, sister, friend, the *detail* of which could be interesting to the public? The duties of such a character are unobtrusive, unostentatious, and avoid the pen of history. They confer the BEST OF BLESSINGS; but they shun all record and reward, save the internal consciousness, which renders every other, in this life, of little moment."[34] At the same time, Boaden boasts that Siddons's intrinsic character rather than her personal idiosyncrasies permeated her performances and revealed "the actual possession of such qualities in the WOMAN." He continued, "Her spectators *here* inferred, at least, that ALL was *not seeming*; and that in any signal crisis of her own life, she would be found indeed the noble creature she appeared to be upon the stage" (1: 315). For Siddons, then, he believed her performative interiority was authentic rather than an affectation.

An incident in which Siddons was publicly insulted and embarrassed by Thomas King elucidates the complications involved in drawing these elusive boundaries as the demands of celebrity intensified. After agreeing to act at Mr. Brereton's benefit for a lesser sum than she usually commanded, Siddons had to forgo the performance when she was suddenly taken ill. When rumors circulated about her alleged greed and arrogance in disappointing Brereton and her fans, her husband, a spokesperson "under whose directions she might fairly be presumed to act, as every theatrical engagement could only be made by him or by his power," placed an article in the newspaper to defend her "private character" against scandalous assertions (2: 106). Mr. Siddons rigidly distinguished between the theatrical domain of her paid labor and the domestic sphere he wished to protect, insisting that only her acting was a legitimate basis for public criticism. In this way he claimed for her a masculine privilege and denied access to a public intimacy. Siddons's memoirist Boaden, however, counters that her husband ludicrously misconstrued the situation in defending her character (2: 108). Sarah Siddons's response, in spite of her husband's assertion that private and public were totally distinct, involved an insistence upon openly defending herself from the stage. She testily delivered onstage a nervy self-vindication in propria persona, labeling as "calumnies" the stories circulated about her, leading Boaden to praise her courage as a brave and manly action: "It was not very usual to hear a *lady* on such occasions; the delicacy of the sex, while it becomes accustomed to repeat the sentiments of others, shrinks from the seeming boldness of publicly uttering their own. But there was a male dignity in the understanding of Mrs. Siddons that raised her above the helpless timidity of other women" (2: 116). Siddons's defense in addressing the audience reflects her apparent belief that a rumored unwillingness to perform as scheduled reflected a personal flaw, but her public assertion of innocence also slyly contradicted her husband's zealous assertion that the spheres were always completely distinct, and it testifies to the equivocally gendered space that Siddons commanded.

Siddons was invincibly chaste, and she cultivated a public persona of wifely and maternal devotion. In contrast to Colley Cibber's admiration of the way Anne Oldfield impersonated Lady Modish onstage and off, thus uniting private and public character into one person, Boaden asserted that Siddons possessed no private life outside of the theater that was relevant to her public identity. As evidence that she too exhibited a singular brand of virtue, he wished to erase completely her domestic circumstances: "But on the stage, I never felt the least indication that she had a private existence, or could be any thing but the assumed character" (1: 159). Boaden unsurprisingly aligned the exceptional virtue granted to an actress with her role as Calista; the tragic heroine familiar from earlier biographies who again exemplified the struggles characteristic of actresses' lives. As Rowe's fair penitent, Siddons possessed "a haughty affectation of being above control, which a deviation from virtue ever produces in a great but proud woman; the conscience is stilled by an assumption of superiority—she does not deny the RULE, but conceives herself an allowed exception" (1: 338).

As any number of critics over the past decades have demonstrated, eighteenth-century women bore the cultural weight of alternately personifying and protecting virtue, and serving as an index to civilization's progress; but the definition of virtue was anxiously molded and reconfigured in the hands of actresses to take on a more manly, or at least a more ambiguously gendered, cast. The biographies of these players negotiate the split between the scandalous fallen woman and the respectable public icon to define their possession of an uncommon quality that refined civil society in unexpected ways. The actress's body on stage, a vital instrument that combined the labor of acting with sex work, bonded exceptional virtue together with public display in unstable proportion. These actresses' memoirs convey contradictory impulses to explain and to forgive, to condemn and yet to entertain the possibility that celebrated women of the theater could prosper while living their ostensibly "private" lives according to an inconsistent moral standard that reigning definitions of "woman" could not contain. The biographers attempt to make the actresses appear to be consistent personalities with accessible interiorities reflected in their stage performances; they seek to make their unconventional lives more nearly resemble realist fiction, thus producing the kind of interiority, more easily condensed and molded into coherence, that we have come to expect from eighteenth-century novels. But the kind of virtue the subjects of these lives represent is virtue shaped by their own efforts and rewarded in the theater rather than in the marriage market.

When Bellamy remarks in her *Apology* that "These Memoirs, however, are *uncommonly instructive*," perhaps the nature of that peculiar sort of instruction is more nuanced than we might have imagined. Actresses' exceptional virtue resembled masculine virtue in that it was limited to a small elite; but rather than constituting a group deriving entitlement principally from land or rank, these few star actresses, with influence far in excess of their numbers, found that commercial success distracted from their sexual transgressions and afforded them a special category of virtuous commerce that gained them entrance to the world of polite refinement. In short, the biographical histories of the generation of celebrity actresses who first opened their lives to public scrutiny reveal that their talents meant that public fascination afforded them a special category: "vartue" was transmogrified into virtue and even, on occasion, into *virtù*.

CHAPTER 4

Actresses and Patrons:
The Theatrical Contract

> As the Stage is a Representation of the World, so is the World but a more extended Stage: And every Body, who knows that World, is sensible there are very many more personated than real Characters in it.
> —Sir Richard Steele, *The Theatre*, no. 2, 5 January 1720

IN SIR RICHARD Steele's short-lived periodical *The Theatre*, his depiction of a broad-based audience engaged in the critical assessment of drama adds new dimension to our understanding of audience-actor relations. In the first issue, Sophronia, a sophisticated lady of high quality, attends the theater with a *belle assemblée* of three female friends who share her passion for drama.[1] In a subsequent issue, Steele's exalted persona, Sir John Edgar, proposes that a small number of theatergoers like Sophronia and her companions should be elected "*Auditors of the* Drama" in order to characterize public taste to the management and to speak as the "real Representatives of a *British* Audience" (no. 3, Saturday 9 January 1720, 10). Though Steele's proposal is a lightly satirical attempt to fend off more draconian censorship and to protect actors' autonomy, it attests to the importance of women in the audience, to the emergent nationalism in the theatre, and to the multifarious attitudes represented by the full spectrum of social classes seated in pit, gallery, and boxes. "The Players," he writes, "shall chuse two of their own Society, *viz.* one Male, and one Female, to take care of their Interest, and for the better information of these *Auditors*, in Matters immediately relating to their Customs and private Oeconomy" (10). According to this scheme, women representatives would have outnumbered the men seated in the boxes, affirming the vital interest of ladies in the theater: "Three of the Fair Sex shall represent the Front-boxes," while "Two Gentlemen of Wit and Pleasure" (10) will occupy the side-boxes. The pit would elect three citizens, the first gallery would choose a lawyer's clerk and a *valet de chambre*, and the upper gallery would select a journeyman baker along with a literate footman messenger. The motley group thus constituted as critics and censors would exercise "full power, in the Right of the Audiences of *Great Britain*, to approve, condemn, or rectify, whatever shall be exhibited on the *English* Theatre" (10). The whole evening's entertainment—including prologues, epilogues, interludes, and afterpieces, as well as music and dance—has come into prominence in recent reassessments of the eighteenth-century theater. In addition to envisioning the night's activities as encompassing a full range of performances, we might also consider the stage and audience in tandem as the "full assembly," a term that the character Jupiter in John Crowne's popular masque *Calisto* (1675) early applied in a slightly different context.[2] Such a perspective enlarges the space of the theater to include all of the playhouse participants—audience and actors, stage and backstage, bound together in spite of the distinct cultures of taste emerging.

Players and spectators thoroughly intermingle in Steele's account as the narrator considers which candidates might deserve to become auditors. Taking the occasion to slyly introduce several characters he would invent for his popular sentimental comedy, *The Conscious Lovers* (1722), and to puff the play, Steele imagines seating Mr. Sealand and Lucinda as prominent members of the audience. Sealand, a quintessential Whig, East-India sea merchant, and "a kind of third Gentry," would stand for election from the pit, while his daughter Lucinda would represent the boxes. Magnificently conspicuous in her white suit trimmed in cherry-colored silk, Lucinda turns her sartorial splendor into a political stance to insist that costumes should be made only from homegrown goods and manufacture. In spite of her privileged standing, she serves as a democratizing, patriotic force that makes the theater "serviceable to all Parts of Life, and all Trades and Professions" (11). The essay's narrator testifies to the quality of upwardly mobile merchants and traders who, like Lucinda, are "so far from being below the Gentry, that many . . . deserve the Imitation of the modern Nobility" (12)—a description that could easily describe both her upstart character and the actress who plays her.

The close proximity of the actors to the spectators, at times indistinguishable from the characters on stage, underscores their mutual interdependence in the eighteenth-century theater. Steele, for example, notes that players found themselves compelled to respond to the noisemaking rabble that pressured them to drop out of character. The rabble attempted "to disconcert and push [an actor] out of a personated Character of Liveliness and Mirth, into his private one of Grief and Dejection" (6). Jeremy Collier in *A Short View of the Immorality and Profaneness of the English Stage* (1698) had earlier cautioned that this kind of engagement with the actors threatened the moral standards of the most vulnerable audience members. Collier, ever quick to legislate the theater's moral tenor, had charged that loose dealings at stage's edge were particularly likely to arouse female playgoers' worst impulses: "Now here properly speaking, the *Actors* quit the *Stage*, and remove from Fiction into Life. Here they converse with the *Boxes*, and *Pit*, and address directly to the Audience. . . .But here we have Lewdness without Shame or Example. . . . And to make it the more agreeable, Women are commonly pick'd out for this Service."[3] While he determined that it could be dangerous for actresses to initiate close attachments with lady spectators, the continual renegotiation of those kinds of relationships indicates that a strong, interactive connection pervaded much of the century. As is well known, the audience, including the ladies, sometimes conversed loudly even during the actual performance. The prologue to Nathaniel Lee's *The Rival Queens*, like many others of its kind, addressed the audience's disorderly self-absorption and attempted to silence the fashionable sparks who gossiped audibly about their conquests: "Hither come each day / To act your own and not to mind our play, / Rehearse your usual follies to the pit, / And with loud nonsense drown the stage's wit."[4] Similarly, the *Gray's Inn Journal* chastises Lady Tittletattle, who situated herself in a sidebox near the stage and "talked louder than the Actors."[5] This unruliness in the eighteenth-century playhouse sometimes occasioned a near-exchange of roles between audience and actors, having the effect of redistributing and expanding cultural authority to all parts of the theater.[6]

The women in the full assembly who competed with actresses for celebrity's mystique included not only the ladies of quality, and the milliner apprentices discussed in an earlier chapter, but also the middling ranks. The *Grub-Street Journal*, no. 359 (Thursday, 11 November 1736) tells of Mrs. Mapp, a renowned bone-setter, who attended Lincoln's Inn Fields to see *The Husband's Relief*, a play that mocked a woman of her unusual trade. Her mere presence at the theater "occasion'd a full House."[7] Known as "Crazy Sally," Mrs. Mapp, née Sarah

Willon, was married to a mercer's footman, but she affected the trappings of higher quality. A celebrity in her own right, Mrs. Mapp had performed such miraculous cures that the town of Epsom awarded her an annual stipend of one hundred guineas to entice her into becoming a permanent resident. Mrs. Mapp performed "surprising Cures . . . before Sir Hans Sloane at the Grecian Coffee-house (where she comes once a Week from Epsom in her Chariot with four Horses)" to heal a man's broken back and another's lameness.[8] At the play, she and her oculist companion competed with the actors as spectacular objects of the audience's attention, and the *Grub-Street Journal* implies that she took the staged satirical barbs referring to her alleged quackery with good humor. In reporting her presence at the play, the account puts her on the same plane as the theater's more noble patronesses, but slyly questions whether Mrs. Mapp's skills at bone-setting also qualified her to become, like them, a connoisseur of drama. The correspondent A.B. asks how bone setting might resemble acting, and the journalist responds, "Tho' the displayer of my Candour as well as Wit, owns, that he does not understand the distinction, (what distinction I know not, unless it be between Mrs. Mapp and persons of Quality) yet I must continue to think, that as it is the highest compliment the managers of a Theatre can pay to persons of Quality and Judgment, to act a Play at their request, therefore it is an affront to, and sneer upon them, to pay equal respect to Mrs Mapp, who has no claim either to Quality or Judgment in dramatick writing" (11 November 1736). Her near-miraculous power of healing attracted gossipy anecdotes to the eccentric woman to trouble the relationship between fame and infamy, between critical acumen and patronage, issues that became ever more acute in shaping the theatrical taste of the town.

There are further hints in anecdotal reports regarding just what the bone-setting trade might have had in common with dramatic performance and its critical evaluation. Not only had Mrs. Mapp's character been represented on stage and woven into a ballad, but in real life she had frequently been mistaken for a woman of quality: "A Lady passing Kent-street in her Chariot towards the Borough, dressed in a Robe de Chambre, the People gave out she was a certain Woman of Quality from an Electorate in Germany, whereupon a great Mob followed, and bestowed on her many bitter Reproaches, till Madam perceiving some Mistake, look'd out and accosted them in this familiar Manner, *D--n your Bloods, don't you know me! I am Mrs. Mapp the Bone-setter*. Upon which they sudden chang'd their Rivilings into Loud Huzzas."[9] Her simulation of the celebrity of actresses, combined with appearing to possess elevated standing, within and without the playhouse, meant that theatricalized notoriety had seeped into the middling ranks and settled upon an ordinary woman.

These passages from Steele's *The Theatre* and the *Grub-Street Journal* are instructive in several ways regarding the public behavior of women of various social classes in the theater audience. Managers, the *Grub-Street* notice confirms, warmly responded to persons of quality who supported favorite plays, and it attests to their discriminating judgment. The notice in the *Journal* divides women spectators from each other according to social rank as a means of disciplining Mrs. Mapp and charlatans of her sort while reserving legitimate influence for women of quality, and it disparagingly concludes that Mrs. Mapp and the people of quality shared at least one undesirable characteristic—a déclassé wish to be ogled in public: "It seems the facetious Considerer is of opinion, that they are advertised to be seen in the boxes, to the same end with Mrs. Mapp the famous Bone-setter, that is, only to draw people together to stare at them, which certainly is a very great and real compliment to all high personages." If the middling classes in the theater imitated the social graces revealed in the simulacrum of aristocratic manners on stage, it seems entirely plausible that the ladies of quality also learned something about being modern women from the actresses who boldly contested the bounds of gender and shared their capacity to cultivate connoisseurship and philanthropy.

In this chapter I continue to assess the relationship between actresses and women patrons of the drama, both in and out of the theater, to reveal that their associations—indicative of the evolving sociability between ranks—were ongoing, reciprocal, and mutually beneficial. Like the actresses they championed, female patrons shaped the economies and repertoires of the playhouses as well as the theatrical event itself. Prominent among those patrons, the ladies of quality, women of means and privilege, were not merely passive observers and moral arbiters: they were active participants in creating eighteenth-century theater culture.

As older forms of social interaction continued to coexist along with increasing commercialization, both actresses and ladies of quality created their own dramatic moments by curtseying to friends and patrons, and engaging in cross-talk or verbal outbursts that competed with the play and could even bring it to a halt. For example, Susannah Cibber as Ophelia in *Hamlet* reportedly "rose up three several times and made as many courtesies, and those very low ones, to some ladies in the boxes," according to the *Volunteer Manager* (24 April 1763), and a reviewer mocked Mrs. Cibber for stepping out of character: "Pray, good Sir, ask her in what part of the Play it is Said, that the

Danish Ophelia . . . is acquainted with so many British ladies?"[10] In addition to addressing audience members, the actors onstage also engaged in chatting amongst themselves: "Not only the Supernumeraries . . . or Attendants, mind nothing of the great Concern of the Scene, but even the Actors themselves, who are on the Stage, and not in the very principal Parts, shall be whispering to one another, or bowing to their Friends in the Pit, or gazing about."[11] Actors or former actors in the patent theaters sometimes attended performances as members of the audience and often in disguise. David Garrick reports that "Mr Barry & Mrs Cibber came incog[nito] to see Us," after having played the lead parts in *Romeo and Juliet* themselves.[12] Furthermore, the comments of audiences attending a premier performance could actually spark revisions to the script for subsequent productions. In rehearsal but also in performance, actors "responded to the audience on their level, answering the regular (and expected) heckling, but also making points in propria persona about the nature of the performance itself. . . . Audiences were actively involved not simply in approving or condemning a play, but in revising it."[13] As we have seen, epilogues offered special opportunities for actresses to spar with the audience and sometimes to suspend theatrical illusion by breaking character or interjecting improvisational comments. Their comic speeches—addressing coquettes or fine ladies or calling out to pit, gallery, and boxes—could specifically implore the ladies in the audience to approve the play, or, on occasion, could cause the audience to respond with disruptive retorts.[14] At many levels, then, the full assembly participated in determining the nature of the performance onstage and off.

In another example of lively theatrical interactions, when Colley Cibber's enemies booed the 1727 adaptation of Vanbrugh's *The Provok'd Husband*, legend has it that actress Anne Oldfield was forced to contend with the rude hissing of a disorderly playgoer as she delivered the prologue: "She fixed her eye upon him immediately, made a very short pause, and spoke the words *poor creature!* loud enough to be heard by the audience, with such a look of mingled scorn, pity and contempt, that the most uncommon applause justified her conduct in this particular, and the poor reptile sunk down with fear and trembling."[15] The *London Daily Post* reported an even more spectacular disruption of Mr. Pritchard's *The Fall of Phaeton* (1736) when actress Kitty Clive broke off her singing to rescue a lady in the pit who had fainted: "In great Concern [Clive] ran off the stage for a Glass of Water and procured it to be delivered to the poor Lady who, by this means, recovered. I could not but be delighted to see Her (who enters so thoroughly into all her Part and is really the very Character she assumes) the first to take notice of an accident of this kind: nor could I help feeling better pleased when the Audience applauded her Action."[16] On another occasion in a spirited address directed to ladies of quality seated not onstage but in the theater boxes, Clive recited "The Author Written by a Lady," later reprinted in *The Theatrical Bouquet* (1778), a collection of the most popular prologues and epilogues from plays produced earlier in the century. Having thrown off the mask of her dramatic character, speaking the epilogue in her own person, Clive commends the ladies' aesthetic taste; she welcomes their temporarily putting aside their refined sensibilities to revel in the play's satire, and she testifies that their theatrical gossip enlivens the mutual give-and-take of the performance:

> Cou'd we suppose this circle so refin'd,
> Who seek those pleasures that improve the mind,
> Cou'd from such vulgarism feel delight,
> Or laugh at characters so unpolite?
> Who come to plays, to see, and to be seen;
> Not to hear things that shock, or give the spleen;
> . . . .
> Thus ridicule is bounded like a ball,
> Struck by the great, then answer'd by the small;
> While we at times, return it to you all.
> A skilful hand will ne'er your rage provoke;
> For though it hits you, you'll applaud the stroke;
> Let it but only glance, you'll never frown;
> Nay you'll forgive, tho't knocks your neighbour down.[17]

It is commonplace to argue that Restoration and eighteenth-century audiences attended plays "to see, and to be seen," as Clive's epilogue put it. Clearly verbal banter ricocheted from stage's edge to the audience and back, and the actress's words reflect a shared immersion in the theatricality of the event.

Though women of the middling and upper classes ordinarily occupied the boxes and the middle gallery, both sexes sometimes sat on the eighteenth-century stage itself, especially during benefit performances, to constitute a second audience visible to the pit, gallery, and boxes. Female servants were among those who occupied the upper gallery. The spectacular presence of ladies from the court in attendance purportedly testified to the nation's claim to superior women: "the Whole is illuminated to the greatest Advantage," unlike the theaters abroad where only the stage was lit, "and indeed the *English* have reason in this, for no Nation in the World can shew such an Assembly of shining Beauties as here."[18] This nationalist fervor would have resonated differently in Ireland: at a Dublin charity benefit of Rowe's *The Fair Penitent* in January 1746, "a hundred ladies of the first distinction, dressed in all the elegance of fashion, who, unable to obtain places in the pit and boxes, had, in order to assist and support the manager, accepted of accommodations on the stage, the clamour was so great that Mr. Sheridan was obliged to withdraw without speaking."[19] Even after the audience was banished from the stage, the brilliantly lit house of the Dublin theater, shaped in a semicircle, put the ladies and gentlemen of quality on display in the same manner as the actors.[20] Like the fictional Sophronia introduced in Steele's *Theatre*, sometimes the "fine ladies" attended together in a theater party conspicuously seated in the side boxes, though women of elevated social standing often appeared in vizard disguise until audience members wearing masks were banned in the early eighteenth century.[21] The public liaisons reputed to occur in pit and gallery may have led theatergoing women to avoid those seating areas because of the potential sexual danger. Susan Cannon Harris imaginatively characterizes the political and social stakes for women in the mid-century Dublin theater as potentially subversive when the women spectators sat onstage as the fair penitent actress-heroine performed Rowe's play. Female spectators and actresses in close proximity were, she argues, united in recognizing their vulnerability to sexual coercion and violence in spite of their social differences, to "carve out a cause, and a subjectivity, of their own."[22] That kind of consolidation of women's interests in the public sphere, Harris contends, threatened to supersede other national, regional, or class loyalties. This close identification between the ladies and the actresses and their formation of a shared subjectivity, I suggest, was not limited to the Irish theaters at mid-century but was ongoing even from women's first appearance on stage.

At other times as well, the *Dublin Gazette* (January 1743) complains, actors and audience could scarcely be distinguished from one another. The jumble of people present on stage was particularly bewildering to a novice actor because, as the paper reports, "the Confusion which a Person must necessarily be under on his first Appearance, will be greatly heighten'd by having a Number of People about him, and his Perplexity on his Exits and Entrances . . . must be greatly encreas'd by having a Crowd to bustle thro'."[23] Such seating resulted in bizarre effects such as when, according to Tate Wilkinson, the funeral scene in *Romeo and Juliet* was sandwiched between onstage and offstage audiences:

"Romeo was breaking open the supposed tomb, which was no more than a screen on those nights set up, and Mrs. Cibber prostrating herself on an old couch, covered with black cloth, as the tomb of the Capulets, with at least (on a great benefit night) two hundred persons behind her, which formed the back ground, as an unfrequented hallowed place of *chapless* skulls, which was to convey the idea of where the heads of all her buried ancestors were packed."[24] The dark tomb surrounded by fleshless skulls contrasted in a macabre fashion to the two hundred playgoers, very much alive, who shared the stage and seemed to be performers themselves. The problem was especially vexing during benefit performance when, for example, Lavinia Fenton, acting as Cherry in *The Beaux Stratagem* for her benefit (29 April 1726), reported that she "offended the best Part of her Friends, by laying Pit and Boxes together" to increase the number of seats available and thus the evening's receipts. The offense was sufficiently heinous that many tickets for the performance had to be refunded.[25]

The memoirs of actors, theater managers, and theater historians abound with similar anecdotes describing startling interruptions and boisterous exchanges among authors, managers, actors, prompters, and spectators that gave texture to the eighteenth-century theatrical arena. The vocal, often rowdy, audience who participated jointly with the players in an evening's entertainment in Covent Garden or Drury Lane is, then, more typical of the period than the image of a theater filled with bemused spectators regarding a proscenium stage would suggest, and women on both sides of the stage engaged with the actors in multiple ways. Because of the full assembly's participation in theatrical repartee, the confusion of the stage's boundary, and the bonds of patronage between actor and audience, it is misleading to regard the eighteenth-century theater primarily as a picture stage upon which a distant audience gazed with relative detachment, especially with regard to women actors and spectators.

The Theatrical Event

Among the most influential of those who have described the stage as spectacle and emphasized the visual nature of the theatrical relationship is Kristina Straub in *Sexual Suspects: Eighteenth-Century Players and Sexual Ideology*. Identifying the ocular as the dominant metaphor ("the economy of the gaze"), Straub's seminal interpretation draws on Michel Foucault's theories to stress the victimization of players by audience members who subjected the actors to a policing gaze and brought them into line with regimes of taste, including the performance of a modern (hetero)sexual difference.[26] The theater of Cibber, Garrick, and Sheridan served, according to her persuasive description, as a cultural location where male actors in particular sought to circumvent the degradation inherent in a profession that objectified and sometimes mocked them. Straub's rendering seems to assume, perhaps unwittingly, that the audience included principally male spectators who witnessed a feminine or feminized onstage spectacle and exercised a controlling masculine gaze. Straub contends that both actors and actresses were forced to submit to the spectator's judgment, bowing and scraping in apology when they displeased the playgoers, and even on occasion having to bare their buttocks to the audience for a literal thrashing; she stresses the way the pain of the player, subjected to the spectator's gaze, tends to curtail the possibility of the actor's agency.[27]

Here I would like to emphasize instead a broader-ranging theatrical contract—visual, auditory, and economic—that emerged from the active negotiations between stage and audience. P. David Marshall, though he was not speaking specifically about the eighteenth century, helpfully employed the term "audience subjectivities" to describe the shared exchange that transpires between audience and actors in the theater, and that collectively attaches itself to celebrity to promote its survival.[28] Similarly, Robert Weimann was among the first scholars to discuss theatrical interaction as generating a situation in which "the spectator remains a potential actor and the actor a potential spectator";[29] and Willmar Sauter has defined theatricality as descriptive of the nuanced relations between performers and spectators in the making of "the theatrical event," which includes all the actions that are exhibited, encoded, and embodied throughout the dramatic space.[30] It is worthwhile, then, to apply the concepts of a theatrical contract and a collaborative assembly to the eighteenth-century theater, augmenting them with performance theory, and revising them to include the special relationships of actresses to their patrons and audiences, especially in relation to women's subjectivity.[31] This approach emphasizes the expansive sociable and fluid elements of the whole theatrical event.

The ill-mannered behavior of spectators assembled in the eighteenth-century theaters was often justified, like the splendid display of ladies of quality onstage, as an embodiment of the nation's diversity in all its volubility. In fact, the right to exercise freedom of speech and action in the Drury Lane or Covent Garden Theatres, even in their most disruptive forms, was touted as a public display of Britain's status as a free country versus its more repressive neighbor, France. For example, Theophilus Cibber in an open letter to David Garrick found the amorphous "Town" to be widely representative of the nation: "I think, the Town may be supposed to include all Degrees of Persons, from the highest Nobleman, to the lowly Artisan, &c. who, in their different Stations, are Encouragers of Dramatic Performances:—Thus all Persons, who pay for their Places, whether Noble, Gentle, or Simple, who fill the *Boxes*, *Pit*, and *Galleries*, in a Theatrical Sense, form the *Town*; as K--g, L--rds and Commons, in a Constitutional one, make that Great Body, the Nation."[32]

While distinctions of rank were not of course actually suspended during the course of a performance, the theater could produce a democratizing effect: lowly footmen sometimes voiced approval or disapproval, and apprentices or middling citizens could weigh in concerning the merit of particular actors or performances and even publish their opinions. Like Theophilus Cibber, Sir Richard Steele labeled this kind of disturbance among the assembled audience characteristically English and boasted of its contrast to French despotism, "we being more at the Mercy, even of the lowest People, than any other of his Majesty's Subjects" (*The Theatre*, no. 2, Tuesday, 5 January 1720, 6). Steele lamented that the theater's toppling of the social hierarchy meant that "our Audiences are often disturb'd by the Caprice of two or three unruly People," who could quickly transform the theatrical space into a carnivalesque upside-down world: "Nay, here the very Footmen give Laws to their Masters, and will not suffer any one but themselves to be heard, till they are easy in their Places, tho' they never pay for them."[33] Colley Cibber also shared the conviction that audience disruptions were an annoying but necessary component of English liberty. The price of freedom, he forcefully declared, was that actors and audience alike had to tolerate catcalls, booing, and clapping emanating especially from the upper gallery. In his *Apology* he sardonically acknowledged the pleasure of a hushed theater while defending as characteristically British the leveling effect of collaborative participation: "Now, though I grant, that Liberty is so precious a Jewel, that we ought not to suffer the least Ray of its Lustre, to be diminish'd, yet methinks the Liberty of seeing a Play in quiet has as laudable a Claim to Protection as the Privilege of not suffering you to do it, has to Impunity. But since we are so happy as not to have a certain Power among us, which in another Country is call'd the *Police*, let us rather hear this Insult than buy its Remedy at too dear a Rate. . . . In a Word, when Liberty boils over, such is the Scum of it."[34] In short, in spite of the distraction and inconvenience, allowing the full assembly its all-embracing freedom of expression was often construed as an unassailable right that signified British liberty, bolstered national pride, and was a palpable measure of the nation's health. Such displays of freedom also prepared the way for actresses and female spectators to achieve liberties seldom experienced elsewhere.

Throughout the century there continued to be heard claques who shouted or booed, as well as spectators who issued catcalls, threw orange peels, potatoes, oystershells, pippins, and glass bottles, and sometimes occasioned riots. The process of ridding the stage of rowdy spectators was more gradual than we might suspect. Despite the 1704 regulation that no ladies or gentlemen of quality were allowed to step onto the stage or go behind the scenes, James Ralph notes in an essay on audiences decades later that "Hermaphrodites of the Theatre, being neither Auditors nor Actors perfectly and imperfectly both," continued to defy the ruling that forbade them the stage. He continued, "I mean those Gentlemen who pass their Evenings behind the Scenes, and who are so busy in neglecting the *Entertainment*, that they obstruct the View of the Audience in the just discernment of the Representation."[35]

Theater manager John Rich's decision to foreshorten the stage and to move productions behind the proscenium arch at the Theatre Royal, Drury Lane, was designed to increase seating space for commercial ends. By the mid-eighteenth century, architectural innovations for the first time prevented easy access to the greenroom and to actresses' dressing rooms, and there was a more consistent effort to avoid seating spectators on the stage. In Dublin after the Kelly Riots of 1747, Sheridan secured the stage from gentlemen playgoers' intrusion and established an invisible curtain, a "fourth wall," between actors and spectators that also, incidentally, encouraged actors to address the audience as constituting one indivisible unit. By restricting spectators from the stage, especially aggressive suitors in pursuit of actresses, Garrick continued to try to prevent would-be beaux from wandering behind the scenes, but not until 1762 did he forbid the sale of tickets for seats onstage. Actors consequently had to forfeit the gratuities that had resulted from closer proximity to the audience, "being willing to forego that Advantage for the sake of rendering the Representation more agreeable to the Publick."[36]

But even though Garrick refused to allot onstage audience space during benefit performances, and actors complained of frequent interruption when playgoers were seated on the stage, as late as 1768 Hannah Pritchard's benefit sold such seating for "the first People of Distinction at *advanced* Prices." The barriers to the later eighteenth-century stage remained porous in spite of theater managers' best efforts: in 1774 Charles Macklin sought to bring legal charges against members of the audience who formed hissing claques or edged forward to threaten the actors so "that any Person who forced his Way behind the Scenes . . . if that Person was apprehended, and brought into that Court, and the Fact proved there, he should feel the utmost Severity of the Law."[37] And in 1789 a well-known German commentator on London, William Archenholz, remarked on a scene of ensuing confusion with amazement: "The common people in the galleries, where the din is greatest, are simply bent on making a noise to pass the time, and since several hundred people are crowded together who have no conception of decorum, but so much the more of personal liberty, the disorder is only natural."[38] He tells of their pocketing oranges to throw at the pit and the actors.[39] Even as late as 1809, according to a witness reflecting on the free-for-all atmosphere of the eighteenth-century theater, "Pits, boxes, and galleries became stages themselves, with perorations, dances, mock battles, and demonstrations."[40]

For most of the eighteenth century, then, the stage—and especially the actors—were not actually walled off from the audience, nor the principal target of the spectator's gaze, but were involved in a kind of raucous sociability, a reciprocal give-and-take, in determining the nature of the evening's entertainment and the choice of plays, and in satisfying the taste of the Town. In short, from the beginning of the century until at least the 1770s, the social and spatial relationships between actresses and their audiences remained unsettled as both forces shaped the whole theatrical event. This mutual exchange, between an engaged if noisy audience and a company of actors necessarily attentive to its demands, became a significant component of a successful commercial theater that persisted well into the later decades of the eighteenth century. These improvised social relations of cultural exchange did indeed constitute "a new social contract between itself [the emergent market culture] and its audience," as Jean-Christophe Agnew has argued;[41] but in establishing what we might call "the theatrical contract," the commercial theater also harkened back to the increasingly antiquated support system of patronage. We will now turn to concentrate more specifically on the entangled relationships that pertained among actresses and patrons, especially women theatergoers.

The Jury of Women

If England lagged behind other European countries in welcoming women's bodies onto the stage, its star actresses as we have seen soon wielded unprecedented influence over spectators of both sexes. Women in the audience, able to see public models of their own sex acting in a variety of characters, actively participated in ongoing validation and critique. Even as early as the Interregnum, ladies of quality actively anticipated actresses' inaugural appearance in the legitimate Restoration theaters. The interactions between aristocratic and courtly women, including the Stuart and Caroline queens, took root in the amateur and private theatricals that enabled women to participate in their self-representation. Between Elizabeth I's reign and the Restoration period, the court and the stage were linked in previously unacknowledged ways. "In the Caroline period," Sophie Tomlinson convincingly maintains, "the concept of the woman actor, in the senses both of a female player on the stage and an active woman, gained a partial acceptance in drama and elite society, albeit with a concomitant tendency to be mocked and satirized."[42]

Female spectators, with a few notable exceptions, have been thought to have adopted a uniformly judgmental attitude toward actresses and the bawdy Restoration comedies in which they played, and to have instigated the turn to moral reform in the early eighteenth-century theater. J. H. Smith has argued that after William and Mary's ascension to the throne, a specific group of powerful women played a critical role in turning vulgar plays toward sentimentality, though other scholars have been more skeptical of their degree of influence.[43] The Jeremy Collier controversy resulted in less offensive comedy productions that enabled women to justify attending the theater in more substantial numbers, and a certain way to kill a Restoration play was to label it as unfit for the ladies who served as the index to social mores. That women in the Restoration audience took offense at vulgarity was often mentioned in the plays and epilogues: women spectators enjoyed the double entendres on stage but employed canny ways to escape being blamed for taking pleasure in them.[44] The ladies were damned if they caught the risqué jokes, and assumed to be feigning ignorance if they did not. But the considerable influence female spectators exercised in shaping the eighteenth-century dramatic repertory extended well beyond demanding decency and propriety.

Many models of theatricality begin, as Tracy Davis and Thomas Postlewait have pointed out, with an assumption that although plays and other performances generate thousands of potential meaning, they "are often described as if there were one idle spectator who would (or should) see and read all of the signs"; but once we recognize "that each spectator perceives a performance in an idiosyncratic manner" any "grand semiotic project of total description" has to be abandoned (*Theatricality*, 25). Assumed to be morally lax because of their inherently corrupt nature but paradoxically positioned as moral censors of the drama, even women spectators of a certain rank cannot be assumed to have always responded in a predictable or consistent fashion. Ladies in the audience were, like actresses, carefully monitored for their reactions, which also constituted a kind of performance. Although a group of women of high rank had formed a cabal to protest the immorality of Wycherley's *The Country Wife* (Roberts, 36), when playwright Aphra Behn previewed her bawdy play, *The Luckey Chance* (1686), before several ladies of quality, they did not find it indecent. According to biographer Janet Todd, there was no objection when Behn asked "some noble ladies to read [the play] before she put it on, and neither they nor Sir Roger L'Estrange, who licensed it, nor Killigrew's son Charles, now Master of the Revels, had found it indecent."[45] This telling anecdote points to another often neglected aspect of female theatergoers' responses—that ladies of quality rapidly developed into nascent drama critics with a budding critical sense.

Rather than defining elite women solely as measures of virtue, popular plays as well as prologues and epilogues addressed female spectators as the intelligent and discerning judges that they were becoming. While the Collier controversy had questioned whether women playgoers tolerated earthy allusions,[46] the speaker of the prologue to Farquhar's *The Constant Couple; or a Trip to the Jubilee* (1699) seems to mock this possibility when he declares that ladies "leave all the regards to Decency and Conscience behind them when they come to the Play-house." The prologue reassures the ladies of quality that they nevertheless need anticipate no naughty jokes in the play: "The Ladies safe may smile: for here's no Slander, / No Smut, no lewd-tongu'd Beau, no double Entendre." Directly addressing women as a group, the prologue bundles the women in the audience together to assume that they possess a uniform attitude: their principal function was either to censor the play's ribaldry or to sanction its decency. The prologue specifically mentions that women in the audience will be important judges of the play's success: "Poets will think nothing so checks their Fury, / As Wits, Cits, Beaux, and Women for their Jury."[47] The interaction between the "jury of women" in the audience and the women on stage, particularly in the early eighteenth-century theater, might be regarded then as a joint endeavor in which cultural meanings circulating within the theatrical arena took new shapes.

Significantly, noblewomen, including Henrietta Maria and the Cavendish sisters (Lady Jane Cavendish, Lady Elizabeth Brackley, and Margaret Cavendish) closely collaborated in the theatrical culture of the early Stuart court and formed small coteries of literary and dramatic patronage. Other women of rank who offered support and exerted influence after the Interregnum included Sarah Jennings (later duchess of Marlborough), poet Anne Killigrew, Carey Fraizer, Elizabeth Godolphin, Dorothy Howard, Anne Howard, Henrietta Price, Frances Sheldon, Phillipa Temple, and Ann Walker (Roberts, 108). The fact that Elizabeth Pepys, long-suffering wife of the famous diarist, attended the theater more frequently toward the end of the seventeenth century may indicate that dramatic performances became increasingly oriented toward encouraging women's presence. Fourteen women patrons held sufficient sway to be specifically named as the objects of dedication in plays written between 1660 and 1700, including the princesses Mary and Anne and the duchesses of Newcastle, Ormond, and Richmond (Roberts, 98), but when David Roberts notes that no more than eighty of the four hundred or so patrons of the Restoration theaters were women, "in a city which contained thirteen women for every ten men" (65), he may well be significantly underestimating their cultural authority. Taking into consideration the economic and social strictures on women, an audience that included at least 20 percent women, many of whom occupied exalted rank, would have been a significant number. Though the full range of theatrical patronage that women of rank exercised at the turn into the eighteenth century may never be fully known, the itinerant observer John Macky mentions specifically Lady Fretcheville, the duchesses of Somerset, Ormond, and Devonshire, and the countesses of Burlington, Rochester, Scarborough, Abingdon, and Cardigan as accompanying the queen in public spaces.[48] In the early decades of the eighteenth century, women supported theatrical production in print as well as performance: to take just one example, eighteen women were numbered among the subscribers to the Dublin edition of *The Dramatic Works of Thomas Shadwell* (1720).[49]

Women spectators outside of court circles or the elevated ranks would not have significantly influenced the stage repertoire in the Restoration period, nor would they have voiced their views publicly. From 1660 to 1700, the requests for special performances of plays from ladies of quality, or any other theatergoers, are not specifically recorded, largely because the Restoration theater was a court theater supported by Charles II who acted as its protector and patron, but such requests—often publicly advertised—from gentlemen of quality, ladies of quality, and gentlemen and ladies of quality abound in the eighteenth century.[50] Under James II's reign, drama began to lose its status as the preferred form of entertainment for the nobility and gentry. The audiences attending the royal theaters after 1688 became "patently more bourgeois and Whiggish" as they increasingly turned for support toward the marketplace economy, and dramatists, previously dependent upon the court, found themselves disoriented in their attempts to secure sufficient patronage to be successful.[51]

In addition to women's growing interest in attaining legal and political rights in the 1680s and 1690s, shifts in comic taste reflected economic fluctuations. Focusing on popular plays like Southerne's *The Wives Excuse* (1691), Cibber's *Love's Last Shift* (1696), and Farquhar's *Constant Couple* (1699) as examples of comedies that specifically address women's compromised situation because of their sex, David Roberts determined that these comedies were designed "to enlighten and equip" the audience to cope with evolving sex roles in a new modern age (*The Ladies*, 156). Armed with convincing evidence, he attributed the dramatic change, not to the effect of one identifiable female faction, but to a broader social evolution across the population at the turn into the eighteenth century, and he aptly questioned whether all female theatergoers—young maidens, city wives, whores, ladies of quality, or other kinds of women—would have uniformly shared this transformation in taste. Women playgoers ranged from orange girls to ticket-takers, from apprentices and tradeswomen to city wives, whores, and courtesans. The Restoration audience, he reminds us, encompassed "duchesses, royal mistresses, the wives of the aristocracy, and members of their households; the wives, daughters, sisters, and nieces of Members of Parliament, playwrights, professional men, craftsmen, merchants, and shopkeepers; [and] a large contingent of lady's companions and maidservants" (94). Women would have certainly been numbered among the milliners, seamstresses, mantuamakers, shoemakers, and staymakers necessary to keep a theater in business, and they would undoubtedly have been a visible presence. Women attending the Restoration and eighteenth-century theater included, then, not only ladies of distinction, but also city wives and younger women from more lowly social origins who may not have shared a homogeneous taste and who formed multiple factions, as numerous as the mountings of fresh productions.[52]

Ladies of distinction, then, preferring certain plays and regularly requesting them, comprised a diverse group who were not solely or perhaps even primarily, interested in bringing a halt to theatrical indecency. The most successful plays, staged to respond to the requests of playgoers at large rather than to a particular female faction, were those that offered tantalizing seduction plots while avoiding explicit sexual references, thus allowing the audience to have it both ways. While Roberts concludes that "the court, for all the benefits of company and education it conferred on its ladies, provided them with no immediate tradition of sustained or organized influence over the stage" (126),

I suggest that after the Restoration and throughout the eighteenth century, ladies of quality especially, but also women of other social classes, developed special relationships with the theater and with the actresses whom they patronized and whose social cachet they wished to possess. Women of varied social standing, onstage and off, recognized in each other an expanded range of imagined subjectivities witnessed in a public space.

Any number of stereotypes regarding women's reactions circulated as commonplace assumptions. In an oft-cited passage in his *Original Letters, Familiar, Moral and Critical* (1721), John Dennis cynically alleges women's insincerity and moral duplicity in their reactions to she-tragedies:

> I would fain know from you . . . for what Reason the Women, who will sit as quietly and passively at the Relation of a Rape in a Tragedy, as if they thought that Ravishing gave them a Pleasure, for which they have a just Apology, will start and flinch like unback'd Fillies, at the last Approach of *Rem* to *Re* in Comedy. . . . I have been sometimes apt to entertain a Suspicion, that 'tis not the luscious Matter which disturbs them in Comedy, but the secret implicite Satire upon the Sex. . . . For a Woman in comedy never grants the last Favour to one to whom she is not marry'd, but it proclaims the Man's Triumph and her Shame. It always shews her Weakness and often her Inconstancy, and sometimes her Fraud and Perfidiousness. But a Rape in Tragedy is a Panegyrick upon the Sex: For there the Woman has all the Advantage of the Man. For she is suppos'd to remain innocent, and to be pleas'd without her Consent; while the Man, who is accounted a damn'd Villain, proclaims the Power of Female Charms, which have the Force to drive him to so horrid a Violence."[53]

Dennis assumes that women, reacting with one voice, took surreptitious pleasure in innocently observing the spectacle of a rape, and that they delighted in witnessing libertine desire while denying their own passions. Jonathan Swift appears to parrot Dennis's view when he avows that women spectators preferred tragedy where they were "deified and adored, [while] in comedy [their sex is] exposed and ridiculed."[54] But these harsh assessments also signal that female playgoers' reactions to tragedy and comedy were closely scrutinized. They follow the well-rehearsed arguments we have outlined here: that women spectators reacted uniformly in a predictable manner, that they privately harbored secret desires while pretending to be moral arbiters, and that their preference for tragedy over comedy was an affectation rather than an aesthetic judgment. Instead, I suggest, many eighteenth-century women theatergoers were willing patrons and perceptive critics of the drama in ways that extended far beyond the simplistic responses Swift, Dennis, and others ascribed to them. Their expressed preferences in the London theaters ranged over a large repertoire of plays that proved to be among the best written and most beloved over decades of performances.

The Full Assembly

The power of the ladies of quality—women of the court, noblewomen, and women of the upper gentry—was most fully realized during and after Queen Anne's reign when the theater became a commercial venture. By the early years of the eighteenth century, command performances could be requested or the rehearsal of a new play could be authorized by persons of distinction. The evidence regarding women in performance and in the audience is much richer for the eighteenth century than for the earlier period. Returning to Steele's commentator, Sir John Edgar, in *The Theatre*, no. 3 (9 January 1720), we find that he clearly links the "quality" with aesthetic taste: the actors took pains "to know who were properly the Town, and who not; they having been often under the nicest Perplexities, form the very different Opinions of People of Quality and Condition" (9). Ladies and gentlemen of distinction did indeed endorse particular plays, sometimes at the request of the performers themselves; they sponsored actors' benefits not only with their financial resources, but also their presence and their social influence in filling the seats with friends. These improvised relationships were part of both tacit and explicit agreements that constituted an evolving form of theatrical patronage, largely among the privileged ranks, that has not received as much attention as literary and artistic patronage. From the beginning of the eighteenth century until the later decades, I am arguing, the commercial marketplace operated concurrently with a still vital, if waning, patronage system that included the support of high-placed women.

As court patronage for the theater decreased during the reign of Queen Anne, women of quality began to request—that is, to "desire"—certain performances each season. The practice of aristocratic men and women requesting a particular play, often as a charity benefit, extended to Dublin; there were almost 180 such requests between 1720 and 1745, along with eighty charity benefits.[55] Filling the boxes mattered greatly to insure the success of an evening's entertainments and to salvage the reputation of the patron who had sponsored a benefit. One way to determine the total receipts on a given night might be to calculate the total number of boxes, each of which ordinarily seated about twenty people, but actual attendance does not reveal the whole story.[56] Patrons bought up seats even if they were unable to occupy them, in order to support a particular actor or play, and tickets were sometimes refunded. Hannah Pritchard, for example, directed patrons displeased by her benefit performance as Lady Macbeth to her residence to have their money returned: "those Ladies and Gentlemen who have taken places and paid for their Tickets will have the difference return'd if they will please to send for it at her House in Great Queen Street Lincoln Inn Fields."[57]

Producing a favorite play in response to a particular request sometimes involved the corrupt and often covert practice, according to the *Grub-Street Journal* (Thursday, 28 October 1736), of encouraging the Town to emulate their superiors in frequenting a particular play: "If the word, Desire, were only used by People of Quality, as the word, We, from the Crown, then indeed it might be well construed an Affront; but when we have seen it particularly and often given to people of a lower Class, it cannot bear the least colour of resentment." According to the *Journal*'s notice, the "desire" for a particular play could on occasion be planted by the performers or the theater managers, thus suggesting the commercial viability of seeming to effect a collaboration between the town and the theater regarding the choice of repertoire: "Besides it is notorious, that Managers of Theatres have prefixed Desires of Persons of Quality, Ladies of Quality & c. when no such Desire has been made; which I take to be a Greater Affront to all Persons of Quality, than can possibly be made from the Desire of a Person eminent in her Way . . . and are not most Desires acquired by soliciting for them?" If this account is to be trusted, we cannot firmly rely upon playbill notices announcing that ladies of quality requested a specific play. Advertising "desire" thus became a means of attributing pleasure and patronage in a convenient though not always authentic way. Still, the likelihood of their consistent interest in a given play is surely indicated by a manager's assumption that their endorsement would seem credible.

The practice of addressing female patrons of the drama before or after the mainpiece, whether complimentary or satiric, also points to the continuing importance of building patronage among the women of quality. In the prologue to Susanna Centlivre's *The Wonder: A Woman Keeps a Secret*, the actress-speaker, believing that the pit or stalls are prejudiced against her, appeals to female solidarity and speaks directly to the ladies. She turns to "the bright Circle of the

Fair," the women of quality seated in the boxes, to whom she "Commits her Cause, with Anxious Doubts perplext. / Where can she with such hopes of Favour kneel, / As to those Judges, who her Frailties feel? / A few Mistakes, her Sex may well excuse, / And such a Plea, No Woman shou'd refuse: / If she succeeds, a Woman gains Applause, / What Female but must favour such a Cause."[58] This kind of bonding among actress, female playwright, and patroness through text and speech was a common theme throughout the century.

Some ladies of quality in both London and Dublin regarded providing financial assistance as their civic duty and also expressed aesthetic opinions through endorsements of particular plays. In the process they contributed to professional advancement for the most celebrated actresses. Though we cannot fully trust existing statistics for the reasons I have outlined, and the *London Stage* records are currently being revised, a rough tally of the known requests by "ladies of quality" for specific plays between 1700 and 1770 reveals that women of high standing were active participants in determining the repertoire. Their favorite choices included the extremely popular *Careless Husband* (28 requests), *The Constant Couple* (27 requests nearly every season, including 3 by both "Gentlemen and Ladies"), and *The Orphan* (25). Their requests ranged from the popular tragedies *Venice Preserved* and *Distress'd Mother* (19 each), *Jane Shore* (16), and *The Mourning Bride* (12), to comedies such as *The Beaux Stratagem* (20 times), *The Man of Mode* (18), *The Tender Husband* (18), *Rule a Wife and Have a Wife* (13), *The Devil to Pay* and *The Busy Body* (12 each). Other favorites of the ladies of quality, occasionally requested along with gentlemen of quality, were *The Relapse* (13 requests), *The Fair Penitent* (13), *Love for Love* (11), *The Indian Emperor* (11), and *The Provok'd Husband* (11). *Mithradates*, *The Scornful Lady*, *The Provok'd Wife*, *The Way of the World*, *Conscious Lovers*, *The Beggar's Opera*, and *The Fatal Marriage* merited 9 requests each. These choices reflect an increasingly acute critical sense among women who possessed sufficient means to underwrite productions they "desired," as well as their avid interest in seeing dramatic models of femininity. Other examples of the ladies' support are perhaps more surprising: John Gay's 1715 farce *The What D'ye Call It* (14), as well as *The Spanish Fryar* (13), *The Stage Coach* (13), *The Committee* (12), *The Hob; or The Country Wake* (11), *The Funeral* and *Wit Without Money* (10 requests each), *Tamerlane* (9), and *The Royal Merchant* (8).

The ladies' preferences for Shakespearean plays included *Hamlet* (ranking at the top with 23 requests, a preference that the men shared) along with *Macbeth* and *Othello* (13 requests each), *King Lear* (12), *Julius Caesar* (11), and *The Merry Wives of Windsor* (8).[59] The Shakespeare Ladies Club, flourishing around the time of the 1737 Licensing Act, may have supported many of these revivals as alternatives to new plays that would have been subject to censorship.[60] The Club included among its members Susannah Ashley Cooper, Countess of Shaftesbury; Lady Mary Churchill, Duchess of Montagu; and Mary Cowper, also a poet and cousin to William Cowper.[61] A poem addressed to the Club applauds the ladies for demonstrating sound British sense in studying the bard in contrast to the Frenchified effeminate men who fritter away their time on fashion: "Coxcombs shall listen to the Stage, / By you instructed, Wits commence, / Ev'n *Beaux* your *Beauty* shall engage, / To join the Banner of *Good Sense*."[62] Expressing patriotism through bardolatry, these female devotees made it a *"Fashion to be Wise"* (179). Similarly, "An Ode to her Grace the Dutchess of Montague, and the Rest of the Illustrious Ladies of Shakespear's Club" praises the noblewoman as preeminent among the "Heroines gloriously ally'd [in the Club] / To raise our Taste, improve our Sense, *Great-Britain's* Pleasure, and its Pride!"[63] Even more significantly, the ode asserts, she sponsored the formation of new genius through her efforts: "Beneath your Nurture comes the Hour, / New *Bens* [Behns] and *Shakespeares* shall arise" (112). The ladies' predilection for Shakespeare has the effect of extending Britain's influence beyond its shores and throughout its imperial domains by virtue of its maritime strength: "Our Sails, throughout the distant Main, / Shall spread the Virtue of your Charms, / And tell them how supreme we reign / In Wit, as heretofore in Arms" (113). While the emphasis in previous discussions of the Club has been on their attempt to restore virtue to the stage through reviving Shakespeare's plays, such women were unquestionably powerbrokers in the theatrical world, becoming increasingly discriminating supporters who nurtured dramatic talent and who, in encouraging performances of Shakespeare's comedies and tragedies, and gracing the theater with their attendance, supported vital roles for star actresses such as Clive, Cibber, Pritchard, and Woffington.

On the Dublin stage as well, the plays specifically requested in 1720–45 by "several Ladies of Quality" featured similar preferences for Shakespearean productions (*Twelfth Night, Merchant of Venice, Julius Caesar, Hamlet, Macbeth, Henry IV* with *The Humours of Falstaff, Henry V*), but also a substantial number of requests for new and restaged plays with major roles for women, including *The Recruiting Officer, The Constant Couple, The Conscious Lovers, Love for Love, Jane Shore, Pasquin, The Distress'd Mother, The Relapse, The Provoked Wife, The Careless Husband, The Double Dealer, The Scornful Lady,* and *A Bold Stroke for a Wife*.[64] Subscribers to the Dublin theaters acting as patrons for benefit productions could, even as late as 1758, vote on the plays that were chosen for presentation, and women participated in the process by proxy.⁶⁵ The list of plays requested in London and Dublin demonstrates the ladies of quality's support for a wide range of productions that reflect a larger cultural uneasiness—but also fascination with—the changing status of women. In short, though the theater during the early eighteenth century was much criticized for its degenerating taste and the popularity of low entertainments such as farce and pantomime, it also afforded a public space where women's aesthetic judgments could be molded and sharpened. The ladies of quality were, then, not merely passive spectators: in groups of women and sometimes with gentlemen of their acquaintance, they became public benefactors who attempted to fill the theater and guarantee a full house, even on occasion buying up unsold tickets or overpaying to keep an actress solvent: at one of Sophia Baddeley's benefits in the late 1760s, "so many people of rank and distinction patronizing her, all the boxes were engaged, and many of them at a price, which seemed more like a magnificent present than a consideration for the seats."⁶⁶

Women patrons also sponsored privately staged plays as diversions intermixed with their social gatherings, meeting to converse while informally rehearsing and performing plays. To take only one example, Elizabeth Carter recounts a relatively intimate occasion on which she and her female friends acted *The Royal Convert* and *The Distress'd Mother* in Canterbury, on 1 April 1742 "before an Audience of about 20 Ladys" when it "came off with flying Colors." She animatedly describes her successful performance in the amateur theatrical: "Miss [Molly] Lynch played the Fury a merveille, & Seofrid had such a well acted expression of Concern on her face at seeing me bleed that it actually struck me & I fancied my self dying in good Earnest. Do not you think we shall be *lampooned*?"⁶⁷

The testimony of actresses, and those who supported them, indicates that aristocratic patronage for the theater persisted throughout the period in question. The *Morning Chronicle and London Advertiser* (March 1788) testifies to the considerable cultural authority that continued to be exercised by fashionable women of means, in this case a female playwright, late in the century: "When a lady of fashion, supported and encouraged by a large train of persons of the first rank in life, brings a piece to the manager, his door must be opened to her; and unless her production should appear prima facie, to be altogether destitute of claims to commendation, and such as would equally disgrace her and discredit the theater, her piece ought to be prepared for representation; at least every prudent manager would produce it and suffer the author to have a fair trial." Near the end of the century George Anne Bellamy testifies to her dependence upon the ladies of quality and their power to affect an actress's fate and her choice of plays: "My theatrical expectations, this season, were far from pleasing. Most of those ladies who had usually honoured me with their encouragement at the Theatre, being either indisposed, gone abroad, or dead, it made a material difference in my situation, and foreboded but an indifferent season."[68] The moral objection of a lady of quality apparently caused Lady Wallace's first play *The Ton* to fail in the late 1780s.[69] Similarly, in her novel *Walsingham* (1797), Robinson attests to fashionable women's power to scuttle certain plays, almost certainly because of her experiences with her own play, *The Nobody*, which was withdrawn in the 1790s because of their interference.[70] This kind of ongoing reassessment of older aristocratic values that had been characteristic of the earlier court theater vis-à-vis newer commercial practices occurs regularly throughout the century among playgoing women, as well as among those who financially support it, write for it, and act in it. Even Sarah Siddons was prominent among those who were beneficiaries of this kind of patronage system, which relied upon the ladies' hope of contracting an infectious, transmittable celebrity.

Female Patronage

The extent to which *literary* patronage became an outmoded system during the eighteenth century has been a matter of considerable scholarly debate. As I have been arguing, the shift from aristocratic support of the arts toward a more dynamic marketplace, in the dramatic as well as literary spheres, was less sudden than we might expect, in part because the patronage arrangement was beneficial to all parties and was practiced concurrently with the development of a commercial theater. Margaret Ezell has helpfully recovered the networks of informal friendship and manuscript circulation at work in perpetuating the patronage system in relation to literary texts, and it seems likely that similar networks existed for dramatic texts and productions.[71] And although Dustin Griffin excludes the drama from his analysis of literary patronage because he believes it operates under a different economy (largely because he considers the patronage of playwriting but not dramatic performance), the definition he provides of patronage as "a personal relationship between two parties unequal in status and resources, designed for mutual benefit of the two parties, and ultimately as a means of socio-political organization," seems accurately to describe the close association between patrons and celebrated actresses as they gathered symbolic capital through such relationships.[72] In short, the eighteenth-century theater, especially in relation to actresses, presented a complicated confluence of patronage and commerce of social networks alongside commercial pressures. For actresses, the continuing power of patronage, even as the democratization of the theater took hold, is a significant aspect of the theatrical contract.

Patronage, of course, relies on the hierarchical social order that it preserves, but it may also paradoxically have contributed to a kind of leveling in certain situations. Griffin argues that literary patronage operated as a conservative force, but it is not clear whether it consistently had this effect in the theatrical realm. Given the many actresses who were supported by patronesses in spite of their unconventional conduct, this seems an unlikely conclusion when consideration is brought to bear on star actresses who frequently challenged social mores. Clearly actresses and women playwrights attempted to please patrons and subscribers to keep themselves and their companies afloat. Imparting their special mystique to those aristocrats who began to fade from influence and public favor, and rising in influence in their stead, celebrity actresses threatened to usurp the place of noblewomen and gentry in the cultural order, while at the same time providing less rigid models of social behavior. In spite of the commodification of these relations there emerged, on occasion, a kind of magical equalization, a temporary suspension of ordinary hierarchies. Within that splendid congress of the social classes in the theatrical forum, a realm of "pure possibility" could arise and evoke "novel configurations of ideas and relations," as Victor Turner more generally characterized the liminal threshold between the real and the imagined.[73] Celebrity took hold in this kind of interaction, in which the fantasies conveyed between the charismatic actor and the enthralled spectator extended to a romanticized exchange of places and an extraordinary relationship of mutual, if sometimes asymmetrical, regard. This double identity, according to Josette Féral, "attends theatricality, not only in the paradox of the actor—the profound duality of the body in performance—but also in the 'play of ambivalence' that relates performance to perceiver."[74]

In short, the antiquated patronage system persisted through mid-century in sometimes startling contrast to the modern commercialism typical of the actress's profession. Becoming a celebrated actress depended, then, not solely on talent but also on developing an acute political sense in relation to benefactors. Although male actors also solicited patronage for their benefits, the sexual and social dynamics were inevitably more highly charged for actresses whose reputations were at stake. Actresses' memoirs indicate that they personally visited their patrons' homes in pursuit of benefactors. Ladies of quality hospitably entertained playgoers at the theater itself on benefit performance evenings, as if they imagined the sociable occasion to be the equivalent of maintaining a salon. In Dublin, for example, "leading actors attached themselves to some lady of quality, who took on herself the management of his 'night,' canvassed her acquaintances, disposed of tickets, and received the fashionable part of the audience in the box-room, as though she were the hostess."[75] The Aungier Street Theatre in Dublin offered a space suitable for conducting a salon, a "commodious *Box-Room* . . . finely ornamented and large enough to hold all the company that can sit in the Boxes; from whence they all immediately retired at the end of the Play, as to a Drawing-Room where they conversed with each other till they are called to their Carriages."[76] Adding to the patroness's proprietary sense over the night's event, such occasions were called "not the actor's but 'Lady--'s night'," and a kind of competitive edge was maintained in order to make one lady of quality's night more successful than that of others in her circle (Raymond, 167). This sociable space would have encouraged private conversations among the elite theatergoers, especially the ladies of elevated standing whose status was further enhanced by sustaining relationships with celebrity actresses.

Influential patronage was often exchanged for glamorous clothing and fashion expertise in a mutually beneficial arrangement. Elizabeth Barry's performance as Queen Elizabeth was said to have flattered her patron, the Duchess of York, by impersonating the spectator monarch. Delighted by Barry's acting and manner of speaking, the duchess consequently "learned to improve in the *English* Language" and "made her a Present of her Wedding-Suit, and favoured her in so particular a Manner, not only whilst Dutchess, but when Queen, it is said, she gave Her Coronation Robes to act Queen *Elizabeth*, in the Earl of *Essex*."[77] Susannah Cibber's biographer, Mary Nash, maintains that the tragic actress was unusual in insinuating herself with ladies of quality, but as I have been demonstrating, these affiliations suggest that Cibber's close interaction with audience members, and especially women, would have been typical behavior for celebrated women players. Publicly humiliated by her husband who brought criminal conversation charges against her, Mrs. Cibber was "prevented paying her Duty to the Ladies of Quality, etc., in Person, as She intended, [and] she relie[d] entirely on their Candor and Good Nature" for support of her benefit performance. When Theophilus Cibber's commercial greed at Drury Lane won out over his animosity to his wife, he alluded to Susannah's loyal following of ladies whose help he wished to continue to cultivate: "I should . . . decline giving her any Disturbance, were it from no other Motive than my complaisance to those Ladies who are desirous to see her act."[78]

Ladies of quality who granted patronage to star actresses could also turn that connection into a vindictive assertion of their superior taste. Lady Coventry (who was actress Maria Gunning before her marriage) interrupted George Anne Bellamy's performance of *Romeo and Juliet* with loud laughter (*Apology*, 3: 98). The rude intrusion, causing the actress to be flustered enough to flee the stage temporarily, erupted at the moment when Bellamy as Juliet was about to poison herself. In addition to causing public embarrassment, these kinds of encounters also aimed to settle long-standing grievances between women in the public space of the theater. When Bellamy retaliated against Lady Coventry by calling in a debt, the noblewoman threatened that she would form a claque to hiss Bellamy off the stage for her impertinence if she persisted in her demands for repayment (3.100). Other forms of manipulation included battles between rival camps of ladies of quality who supported the two competing Dublin theaters, Smock Alley and Crow Street, forcing tradesmen into patronizing one theater over the other if they wished to maintain their business with the ladies (Stockwell, 187).

Patronesses could also collude with actresses to interfere with a rival actress's wish to play a particular role. One of the relationships about which we have the fullest information is that between Bellamy and the Duchess of Queensberry, friend and patron of John Gay, who pointedly reminded the actress that she was heavily obligated to her for launching her career. The duchess chided Bellamy, "I suppose you recollect I was one of the first that noticed you?" (*Apology*, 4: 182). When the patroness and the actress amicably discussed the selection of possible plays for Bellamy's benefit performance, several parts were rejected as too demanding in light of the actress's rather frail health. They eliminated from consideration the part of Andromache in *The Distress'd Mother* as inciting jealousy in Mrs. Yates who, feeling she owned the part, had registered her chagrin in the newspapers. The Duchess along with her friends dryly reviewed the other options in Bellamy's repertoire: "'Your Queen of Troy is left alone; for the Grecian Princess has declared that she shall meet her Hector on the other side of the Stygian Lake, before she will assist her.' The universal laugh which this droll speech excited, was greatly increased by the inflexibility of the lady's countenance. As soon as the laughter was subsided, her Grace remarked, that notwithstanding the pleasantry which had just passed, the determination was of as much importance to *me*, as that of the great Douglas cause was to them, as I played under a letter of licence, and had nothing to support me but the produce of my benefit" (4: 184). Queensberry and the two Duchesses of Douglas (of the famed Douglas legal cause) avowed that Bellamy's choosing a play for her Covent Garden benefit was as momentous a decision as the case of inheritance being adjudicated in the House of Lords. The analogy between affairs of state and the stage continued: "At last her Grace concluded, assuming at the same time an air of as much importance, as if she had found a method to pay off the national debt, that it must be the 'Albion Queens'" because "I was like Mary, Queen of Scots" (4: 184). Bellamy, flattered by the comparison even to so tragic a queen, protested. In spite of the duchess's mixed feelings toward Bellamy, she rewarded her with "pecuniary advantages" that exceeded the actress's expectations. The dialogue between them suggests that the duchess had followed Bellamy's career closely and also exerted considerable and even decisive sway regarding her professional choices. The patroness role for women like the Duchess of Queensberry had little to do with being a moral arbiter: her decisions were based instead based on her well-considered aesthetic preferences, on personal friendship, on her ability to influence the repertoire, on her intimate knowledge of Bellamy's acting skills, and on a finely honed understanding of theatrical politics.

Patronesses Queensberry and Douglas were clearly not entirely benevolent in their intentions. Mortifying Bellamy with their outbursts at her benefit performance and making it difficult for her to avoid breaking character, Queensberry loudly ordered Bellamy's onstage character to be seated instead of curtseying: "Her Grace [the Duchess of Douglas] being in high good-humour, she kept calling out, occasionally, loud enough for me to hear, 'Well said, Mary [Queen of Scots]!' 'Bravo, Mary!' which, united with the former, was very near turning the said story we were enacting, into a Tragi-Comedy; for it was with the greatest difficulty I could keep my risible faculties in any decorum" (4: 186). The unseemly interjections were blatant public declarations designed for public consumption of the special bond that obtained between the eccentric duchess and the savvy actress who depended upon her.

Patronesses declared themselves to be devotees of a particular actress, but their support remained contingent upon their continuing to have cordial relations. When Bellamy acted on the Irish stage in Dublin, she was introduced to a small circle of quality, including most prominently Mrs. Butler, an elegant woman of means who "avowed herself my patroness" (2: 105). She writes, "As I was now in a circle with some of the first people of distinction, besides those who had hitherto been my patronesses, I was honoured with the patronage of the *Essex* family; the Lady Capels were as partial to me as the Lady Keppels;

particularly Lady Mary" (2: 134). Delighted with the lucrative returns from her benefit, Bellamy ascribed its success directly to her female fans who felt they were purchasing shared celebrity and demanded a proper return on their investment. She writes, "I had for some time been allowed to be sole dictatress among the polite ranks in the article of dress. My judgement in this point was held in so much estimation, that the ladies would have been wretched who did not consult me relative to their birth day or fancy cloaths" (3: 1). She complains that crowds of ladies, including Lady Kildare and Lady Granby, had applied to borrow masquerade dresses from those she had worn onstage, and she found it was difficult to favor each with a distinctive dress. Bellamy knowingly bartered for support in the exchange, as "each of them made a point to employ all their interest to increase the emoluments" of her benefit night (3: 2). The ladies of quality attained newfound visibility in a theater that advertised their social importance and substituted for their waning aristocratic authority.

All female theatergoers, but especially ladies of quality, played a critical role in fashioning critical dramatic taste: playwrights, managers, and actors solicited their influence and cultivated their economic support. The competing paradigms of the eighteenth-century theater—patronage and profit, formal spectacle and informal exchange—were reconciled in an uneasily collaborative theater that dominated the first half of the century and extended well into the later decades. In short, the interactions between actresses and their female audience were central to the eighteenth-century theater as women clustered in networks of patronage to provide clothing, endorsements, substantial remuneration, and a developing critical appraisal of the drama. Their relationships, founded on mutual flattery, affection, and need, provided the social glue that eased the transition to a commercial theater which, given new life in the bonding between actresses and female fans, coexisted with the patronage system for many decades before eventually supplanting it. Fostering an animated exchange and a new sociability within the theater and outside its walls, ladies of quality—as well as their impersonators—middling women, female apprentices, and even actresses themselves engaged with each other in sufficient numbers to reconfigure theatrical relations. The patronage system, fading and evolving but still very much in evidence among actresses and their female spectators, violated any rigid separation between stage and audience, or between private and public spheres. The eighteenth-century commercial theater involved, then, into a full assembly in which women onstage and off actively engaged in negotiating a theatrical contract regarding the public representation of modern female subjectivity.

CHAPTER 5

The Actress and Performative Property: Catherine Clive

> I shall as soon expect to see another Butler, Rabelais, or Swift, as a Clive.
> —Thomas Davies, *Dramatic Miscellanies* (1783–84)

> I curse all Squibs, Crackers, Rockets, Air-Balloons, Mines, serpents & Catherine Wheels, & can think of nothing & Wish for nothing, but laugh, Jig, humour, fun, pun, conundrum carriwitchet & Catherine Clive!
> —Letter from David Garrick to Clive [26 August 1774]

> Clive, sir, is a good thing to sit by; she always understands what you say. In the sprightliness of humour, I have never seen her equaled.
> —Samuel Johnson in Boswell's *Life of Johnson* (1791)

As NEW FORMS of patronage developed alongside the increasingly commercial theater in the eighteenth century, the spirited Catherine Raftor Clive (1711–85) took full advantage of the situation to rival her manager as well as other actors and playwrights, and she deserves to be treated as their talented equal. Born to an Irish father and an English mother in 1711, Clive debuted on the stage a scant two years before Anne Oldfield died, thus inaugurating a second generation of actresses who followed upon Elizabeth Barry and Anne Bracegirdle;

she was the heir apparent to these extraordinarily gifted performers, many of whom were employed by David Garrick. This chapter focuses on Clive's expert management of her acting and singing career and her remarkable accumulation of theatrical property. Attempting to avoid being construed as the possession of her employers or her devoted audiences, Clive served as her own agent, propelled by confidence in her prerogative to appropriate her own labor and to possess her own self. Clive constructed a consistent simulated personality that defined her character on stage, and that allowed audiences to believe they might claim access to her subjectivity. Clive created an illusion of coherent identity or an "interiority effect" that referred, not to a preexisting "real" person or to a fixed and knowable identity, but to a fabrication of self. Her person, social standing, costuming, and national affiliations worked together to shape this virtual intimacy into a cohesive, recognizable, and yet supple theatrical personality.

Clive's promoting an "interiority effect"—granting audiences the sense that they might indulge in the privilege of fathoming her multifaceted "self" was a response to the commercial theater's demands to innovatively advance her career. For Clive as for other celebrity actresses, I am arguing, private identity exposed in public had the potential to metamorphose into a marketable personhood that became a new sort of commercial property worthy of the high wages she commanded and that could be transformed into hard currency. Clive sought to develop an alternative notion of value—one based not on sexual exchange, land, or inherited property, but rather founded on work, her labor—as a singer, playwright, and actress—combined with unprecedented social leverage. In the theater Clive converted what might be called *performative* property into a kind of specie that we might locate somewhere between "real" property and paper credit. This action extended to her proprietary right to "own" certain roles, to invent idiosyncratic actor-character parts for herself in her own compositions, and to promote herself as a transnational Anglo-Irish character. Seeking ownership of her creative activities, Clive's astute recognition of the shifting forms of mobile property—a shift which paralleled the historical development of authorial copyright law beginning with the 1710 Statute of Anne, enabling legal ownership over one's published work for a limited term—allowed her to keep pace with changing times in the emergent market economy.[1] This strategy enabled the celebrated actress to sustain her career over four decades and to transform potential liabilities—including her Irish heritage, coarse humor, fiery temper, faulty education, fading beauty, and diminishing powers—into strengths that contributed to an ever-maturing formulation of a recognizable yet protean identity.

It is especially noteworthy that Clive largely managed to escape unflattering innuendoes about her personal life. The difficulty, of course, was for an actress to appear sufficiently distant from commercial transactions to develop a reputation for uncommon virtue. Clive heightened her marketability by aligning decorous womanhood with theatrical femininity at the very time when the larger culture was struggling with the incongruous linkage of these terms.[2] Clive separated in 1732 or 1733 from barrister George Clive of Hereford (second cousin to Robert, Lord Clive), shortly after their marriage; and though they maintained amicable relations, she was never to live with her husband again. If *The Life of Mr. James Quin, Comedian* is to be believed, Clive endured indecent advances from male admirers, but the anonymous memoirist makes even a fellow actor's "taking some liberties with her in the dressing room" an occasion to buttress Clive's reputation for virtue.[3] Bolstered by her economic independence, she frequently gave voice to her strength of mind, brushing off the fact that an expected annuity did not materialize upon her husband's death. In her letters she casually excuses the slight and asserts her self-reliance: "I am quite happy and contented, and don't feel the least malice to his memory. I have fortune enough to purchas every thing I *cannot* do without."[4] Virtue and commerce, in spite of the corrupt reputation surrounding her profession, were together embodied in Clive who managed to remain largely untainted by commercial transactions even as she founded her livelihood upon them.

Clive's ability to manage her public reputation and to project it to theater audiences brought her extraordinary longevity on stage from 1728 to 1769 (twenty-two years of which David Garrick served as her manager). According to actor-manager Tate Wilkinson, "Mrs. Clive was a mixture of combustibles—she was passionate, cross, vulgar, yet sensible, and a very generous woman, and as a comic actress, of genuine worth—*indeed, indeed*, she was a diamond of the first water . . . . The valiant Boadicea never hurled her spear with more furor than Clive, that Amazonian Thalestris of Drury-Lane theater, [who] pursued that great general, Garrick, whenever he offended her; indeed the whole green-room dreaded her frowns."[5] Her quick temper may have been not just a personality quirk or an Irish stereotype but an indication of her understanding that women needed toughness to manipulate the convoluted power relations in the eighteenth-century theater. Known as "the Clive," having been awarded the honorific article applied originally to opera divas, she acted and sang on the stage for forty-one of her seventy-four years, retiring to Cliveden cottage (the name wittily parodying the court seat at Clivedon) at Strawberry Hill purchased by her enthusiastic but platonic admirer, Horace Walpole (Figure 9). After moving to London and joining Cibber's troupe at Drury Lane, the young actress debuted in drag as the page Ismenes in Nathaniel Lee's *Mithrades, King of Pontus*, in 1728. In her first season alone she acted multiple roles as Bianca in *Othello*, Minerva in *Perseus and Andromeda*, Honoraria in *Love Makes a Man*, Valeria in *Whig and Tory*, and the heroine of Beaumont and Fletcher's tragedy *Bonduca*. Beginning at a mere 20s. per week, Clive quickly gained a substantial salary and reputation through hard work.

As a consummate actress, accomplished singer, and innovative playwright, Clive posed a triple threat to her manager and to fellow actors of both sexes. By her own account, Clive was stagestruck from an early age, tagging after Robert Wilks and gaping "at him as a Wonder."[6] One unlikely and much repeated version of Clive's discovery as an actor recounts that she was a lodger with Miss Eleanor Knowles, happily scrubbing the porch steps, when her lovely singing enchanted theater patrons in the Beef Steak Club that met opposite in

Figure 9. "Residence of the late Mrs. Clive at Twickenham (Cliveden)." Harvard Theatre Collection, Houghton Library.

Figure 10. "Mrs. Clive from the Picture at Strawberry Hill." Alexander Van Haecken, engraving after Joseph Van Haecken. Harvard Theatre Collection, Houghton Library.

the Bell Tavern. This anecdote reinforces Clive's popularity as a singing chambermaid on stage (until 1747–48) and testifies to the extraordinary sweetness of her voice. She was the best-loved female comic singer of her time, making entr'acte songs her special property (Figure 10). As the hero of *The Comedian* (1732) remarked admiringly, only Italian opera singers could rival her: "Miss Raftor is without a *Superiority*, if we except the foremost Voices in the Italian Operas."[7] Clive early sang Handel's oratorios, including *Deborah*, and helped to popularize his music with admiring English audiences.[8] Clive's most frequently performed roles included Phillis in *The Conscious Lovers* (36 seasons); Lappet in *The Miser* (29 seasons); Edging in *The Careless Husband* (30 seasons), Miranda in *The Busy Body* (19 seasons); the singing servant Lettice in Fielding's comedy, *The Intriguing Chambermaid* (28 seasons); the high-bred Lady Fanciful in *The Provoked Wife* (27 seasons), and Lucy in *The Beggar's Opera* (18 seasons). She successfully played the singing shepherdess Phillida in Cibber's *Love in a Riddle* (1729), but her greatest triumph came as the cobbler's wife Nell rising to the lady of the manor in Charles Coffey's *The Devil to Pay, or the Wives Metamorphosed*, a character she debuted in 1730 that established her reputation, doubled her salary, and guaranteed that the farce would become a fixture of the repertoire for the rest of her career (35 seasons).[9]

Part of what may have driven Clive's ambition and sometime snobbery was a sense of entitlement because of her father's obligatory forfeiture of an estate to which he had been heir.[10] She was the daughter of William Raftor, an Irish lawyer from Kilkenny who, according to William Chetwood, was forced to surrender his land after fighting on the losing side with James II at the Battle of the Boyne (1690), though he was later pardoned by Queen Anne. This personal history may well have influenced Kitty's political views; in the 1740s especially, her stage persona included Patriot opposition to Robert Walpole.[11]

Clive's onstage performance of social class was remarkably labile. Frequently recruited from the lower classes, actresses sometimes slipped into acting from allied trades such as millinery. As a comic actress Clive was able to impersonate servants, women of quality, and characters in between, offering a consistent thread that simultaneously enlivened her characters from knowing chambermaids to fine ladies, and connecting them to her offstage self (Figure 11). Best known in her early career for chambermaid roles, Clive often mimicked the airs of her onstage mistress while outwitting her. In her parts as would-be fine ladies her characters imitated—but could not fully inhabit—the genteel manners and latest fashions that signaled their characters. Clive played on this doubleness by alternating between chambermaid and fine lady,

Figure 11. "Mrs. Clive as the Fine Lady of *Lethe*." Harvard Theatre Collection, Houghton Library.

their intermixture appearing to occupy the same woman's body in subsequent iterations. The social rank coding for Clive, as for many actresses, signaled in part by her conspicuous display of accoutrements such as carriages, clothing, and jewels, was remarkably elastic; her theatrical movement up and down the social scale appealed to a diverse audience. Cosmopolitan, thoroughly outré, and ultimately a wealthy woman, Clive was among the few women to achieve real social mobility by dint of their talent and labor. Clive's professional innovations as a consummate professional deserve fuller attention before we consider specific roles that demonstrate her ability to integrate individual parts into her consciously molded star personality.

Common Law and Performative Property: *The Case of Mrs. Clive*

Kitty Clive achieved unparalleled status as the finest comedienne on the eighteenth-century stage: her comic abilities, including her improvisational skills, according to Thomas Davies, "have not been excelled, or indeed scarce equalled, by any performer, male or female, these fifty years."[12] Enormously successful in comic roles accompanied with ballads and airs, she joined Garrick's company in 1747–48 at Drury Lane after having worked briefly for manager Fleetwood. When Samuel Johnson famously compared the ambitious and talented Clive to Garrick, he backhandedly acknowledged that actor and actress could compete in the same league: "What Clive did best, she did better than Garrick; but could not do half so many things well; she was a better romp than any I ever saw in nature."[13] Oliver Goldsmith, on the other hand, found her comic acting was without parallel: "Without the least exaggeration, she has more true humour than any actor or actress on the English or any other stage I have seen."[14] The debate over thespian superiority continued to rattle Garrick throughout his career, and his professional jealousy was legendary. It is not surprising, then, that Clive would have aggressively sought to protect herself from unfair practices in Garrick's theater and throughout her career. Yet on at least one occasion Clive recognized that in spite of Garrick's competitive streak, he held a grudging affection for her ("a sort of sneaking kindness for your Pivy") expressed in what she termed a "love letter" (27 November 1768). She wrote, "I suppose I shall have you tapping me on the shoulder, (as you do to Violante,) when I bid you farewell, and desiring one tender look before we part, though perhaps you may recollect and toss the pancake into the cinders."[15]

The identity of a star actress, we have seen, was both public property and her own private possession, though it was vulnerable to being purloined by actors of both sexes. Theater managers frequently acted as if they owned the services of actresses, and faced with gentlemen admirers who enticed them away from their profession, managers "considered female perfections as almost a property, and . . . ventured upon even rude expostulation with the intended monopoliser of their charmers."[16] Arguing that talent requires "the frequent attestation to its preeminence to secure self-esteem," James Boaden vouched for the public's powerful claim on an actress as more legitimate than a suitor's. Women who left the stage for marriage regretted returning to domestic life, he wrote, for "the independent has become dependant" (1: 191). His remarks pinpoint the dilemma star actresses faced when they sought to claim their own personhood from the public on which they relied.

Newfound celebrity unsettled established hierarchies because it came to define star power as intangible but negotiable property. In his classic formulation of eighteenth-century economic change, J. G. A. Pocock linked identity to property, arguing that "property was both an extension and a prerequisite of personality"; property afforded a citizen the autonomy "necessary for him [sic] to develop virtue or goodness as an actor within the political, social and natural realm or order."[17] "Actor" used in this way describes an agent of action rather than a dramatic player, but the theater was central in grappling with these cultural issues. Women were classified as unable to possess property themselves, as Blackstone's *Commentaries on the Laws of England* (1765–69) made clear, and they were legally required to subsume themselves and their right to property upon marriage within their husbands' identity. Thus actresses who through self-commodification legitimately possessed property in their own persons and talents functioned in largely uncharted territory. "Once property was seen to have a symbolic value, expressed in coin or in credit," Pocock contends, "the foundations of personality themselves appeared imaginary or at best consensual: the individual could exist . . . only at the fluctuating value imposed upon him by his fellows."[18] The public personhood that star players created was an enabling fiction, an effect of performance, but it also acquired economic reality as a tradable commodity in the marketplace.

As Carole Pateman argued definitively in *The Sexual Contract*, Locke implicitly limited the possession of one's self to the male sex. Locke wrote, "Every Man has a *Property* in his own *Person*," and a person can only claim an object as property insofar as he intermingles it with labor and thereby "fix[es] a *Property*" within it: such a self was determined not by its substance but by its identity with a consciousness that appropriates self to itself.[19] Analyzing the relationship between Locke's use of "self" and "own," Etienne Balibar conceptualizes the problem in this way: "the self is one and the same, 'the same to itself,' because it 'owns itself' or is its 'own self'."[20] Coming into possession of her commodified *self*, Clive, along with other celebrity actresses, adopted this definition of self-possession as her own. Throughout her career she regularly sought restitution of her rightful property and redress of her grievances, as an actress, playwright, singer, and Irishwoman, and her relationship to her own celebrity evolved as her performances gained in commercial value. Clive openly queried the relationship of self to person and property, jockeying what might be termed "the uneasy relationship of identity and difference," as Balibar recently described the philosophical dilemma (33). Clive created a persona with an identical name, performed by her self-same person; she jockeyed what she had named as herself (by appearing in her own person) and at the same time disowned it (by claiming not to be herself when in character).

When Clive referred to the "customs" of the theater with respect to property relations in *The Case of Mrs. Clive submitted to the Publick* (12 October 1744), a pamphlet to which we shall return, she drew on the longstanding English reliance on custom and common law.[21] As is well recognized, common law derived from precedent rather than statute, and it assumed a more permanent shape as local practices became more fully entrenched and accepted as authoritative. Common law rests on oral transmission, and as such, it is informal and arbitrary. Clive sought throughout her career to insist that the existing body of practices relating to acting should be fairly and consistently applied, and that establishing those practices was crucial to the wellbeing of women players, who were especially vulnerable to exploitation—a situation especially relevant to Clive's case because, in spite of having separated from her husband, her property could be subsumed into his.[22] Thomas Davies laments the ambiguous legal position of actors who "have,—till very lately, been as neglectful of themselves and their interest . . . *as the legislature itself.* They were governed by no particular rules and orders, which cement a society for its own advantage or preservation. No laws were thought of by them, to secure them from want, injustice, or oppression."[23] It is just this situation that Clive recognized in *The Case of Mrs. Clive* decades before Davies, who does not of course credit Clive's contribution to increasing public awareness about actors' predicaments.

Clive was not alone in staging disputes over theater practices. An anonymous pamphlet, *The Disputes Between the Director of D--y, and the Pit Potentates*

(1744), described the plight of actress Mrs. Roberts, who, in addition to enduring insults, was capriciously denied her benefit performance and discharged in spite of successfully acting the role of Andromache. Similarly, in the case of Mrs. Horton, it was "a shocking Affair, that a Woman who makes so Amiable a Figure, and understands her Business so well" is deprived of a living wage.[24] The pamphlet consequently issues a plea for women to be treated civilly and paid as respected professionals instead of being reduced to penury. Though respecting an actor's right to a role was the generally accepted practice, in fact celebrated infringements of this tradition suggest that actresses were more susceptible to its abuse than actors. The potential for difficulty seemed greatest when an actress returned to the stage after a leave of absence such as for pregnancy or illness, leading another actress in the company to assume her roles in the interim. As in marriage in which legal existence was suspended, or subordinated to that of the husband, women were unquestionably at a disadvantage for both wages and inheritance. Nor were women players consistently granted their spouse's pensions. According to historian Amy Erickson, "No amount of equal inheritance could counteract the law of coverture and its legal 'fiction' that a husband and wife were one person—the husband—and therefore their property was his."[25]

Clive fought throughout her career for her right to "own" parts, paratexts, and her celebrated identity. Fellow actress George Anne Bellamy shared Clive's views when she remarked, describing the situation at mid-century, that "the possession of parts at that time (except when permitted novices for a trial of their theatrical skill)" was "considered as much the *property* of performers, as their weekly salary."[26] Performative property, differing from real or mobile property, is embodied within one's person, and avoids the alienation intrinsic to contractual prostitution. Inherent within the actress's body and personhood was her right to act a given role in perpetuity (including performing the part at lucrative benefit performances), and it could not be transferred without permission. Performative property, then, was among the very first properties—both intellectual and embodied—that a woman could possess in her own name and that depended upon her personal identity rather than her husband or family. An upstart woman from the least privileged classes could thus rival the elevated standing that the aristocracy possessed because of its claim to land, and her economic and social mobility could even surpass that which accruing moveable property had made available to the trade and merchant classes. As a property abstracted from the real, its actuation was realized in a unique performance that could never be exactly replicated.

Clive countered the erosion of women's legal rights perhaps also as a response to women's economic decline, represented most notably in fictional heroines in eighteenth-century novels such as Richardson's Clarissa who, like the real women who found themselves dispossessed, were subject and witness to the "great disinheritance."[27] Tracing a trajectory of progress for eighteenth-century women followed by later retrenchment, Susan Staves describes women's legal status regarding property during the century as having first moved within the courts through a stage of experimentation. In a second later stage (1778–1800), "separate maintenance" developed as a viable alternative to marriage, and women sought to enter into contracts on their own.[28] During this revolution at the turn into the nineteenth century several celebrated actresses attempted to erode masculine privilege under married property and dared to contract independently as *femes sole,* as single women independently able to make contracts in their own name.[29] But Kitty Clive had earlier anticipated this shift in asserting her rights as a *feme sole* in *The Case of Mrs. Clive* where she had argued in the court of public opinion for all professional women regardless of their marital status.[30]

Attempting to codify common law in her treatise, Clive attacked the legitimacy of patriarchal power and its sovereign authority. Her cogent argument insisted upon the right to *own* her own labor outside the domestic sphere and, by virtue of that labor, to own her "self" as a subject with rights. Clive generated properties in her various impersonations on and off stage, inside and outside the theater, in Dublin and London. When, for example, the manager insisted that Susannah Cibber should replace Clive as Polly in *The Beggar's Opera* (1736), Clive at first averred that she preferred to keep such theatrical disputes behind the scenes.[31] Yet she publicly aired her grievance in the *London Daily Post* (19 November 1736), writing that she was unwilling to surrender her role as Polly, and voicing her suspicion of a conspiracy: "The true and only Reason is this: Not only the Part of Polly, but likewise other Parts (as could be made appear) have been demanded of me for Mrs. Cibber, which made me conclude (and I think with Reason) that there was a Design form'd against me, to deprive me by degrees of every Part in which I have had the Happiness to appear with any Reputation; and, at length, by this Method, to make me so little useful to the Stage, as not to deserve the Sallary I now have." In this public declaration she anticipated the principle she would assert several years hence: "*That no Actor or Actress shall be depriv'd of a Part in which they have been well receiv'd until they are render'd incapable of performing it either by Age or Sickness.*"[32] Theophilus Cibber's defense of his wife and the ensuing Polly war between the rival queens (Mrs. Squeak and Mrs. Squall) was parodied in Henry Woodward's farce, *The Beggar's Pantomime; or, the Contending Columbines* (7 December 1736), in which the manager granted Clive preference over the contesting diva: "Why, they are not angry with each other—'tis only to make themselves more considerable—all this Bustle is like that of two Prize-fighters, who, in order to draw the Curiosity of the Town, sit lovingly down in an Alehouse, to club the Penning of their challenges."[33] A paper war between the rival queens ensued as Kitty Clive boldly took her case to "The Town," a jury whom she sweet-talked into approving her, and she eventually became the sympathetic audience's favorite after a tearful appeal at stage's edge.[34]

From early in her career, Clive defended her rights as a celebrated actress. The precariousness of actors' remuneration was the subject of two disputes in which Clive was famously involved. In 1734 Theophilus Cibber spearheaded a revolt at Drury Lane, taking most of the troupe to the New Haymarket in a dispute over profit-sharing with the actors, and attacking Clive in the popular press. But Clive, along with Charles Macklin, refused to move because she believed that it was in the actors' best interests to remain at Drury Lane in order to avoid offending loyal audiences.[35] The dispute continued until the incompetent Charles Fleetwood finally succeeded manager John Highmore. Clive's loyalty to her audience in spite of Highmore's incompetence, and to fellow actresses Mrs. Wilks and Mrs. Booth, "would have given [her] the reputation of the greatest heroine of the age," Henry Fielding suggests, had she been a woman of privilege.[36]

A second dispute arose later when Clive, along with the leading actors of the Drury Lane Company, including Garrick, Macklin, Mills and his wife, and Hannah Pritchard, sought redress for their grievances against the manager Charles Fleetwood in late summer 1743.[37] The actors were subject to the monopolistic practices of Fleetwood and John Rich, managers of the two patent theaters, who secretly conspired to slash their salaries.[38] Prevented by the Licensing Act of 1737 from forming a competing troupe, they nevertheless attempted to establish a third company in the Haymarket.[39] Trapped between Rich and Fleetwood who conspired to mistreat her, Clive complained that her salary was in arrears, and she publicly embarrassed Fleetwood for cheating her of £160 12s. back pay. The Drury Lane actors rebelled against their managers because of the terms of employment, salary delays, and disputes about working conditions. An ensuing paper war of impassioned pamphlets debated actors' rights and claims against those of the management.[40]

In response the incensed Clive adamantly insisted in *The Case of Mrs. Clive* that an actor-manager relationship must not resemble a master-servant one as it had during the Restoration. Neither did she have had any patience with the 1728 law that had declared unlicensed actors to be "Rogues, Vagabonds and Surly-Beggars."[41] Rejecting the usual position of abject servitude enacted through apology, Clive categorically refused to be confused with goods that someone else could possess; she demanded the right to be regarded as a woman professional rather than a servant, a lackey, or a whore. Voicing a similar sentiment, an anonymous 1759 biographical memoir elaborated upon the view of actors that Clive rejected: it compared them to servants who were accountable not only in the theater "but in their private Behaviour when our Business has been transacted to the public who ostensibly paid them . . . Actors are Servants of the Public . . . and when they faithfully discharge the Duties of their Offices, we respect and reward them; if they neglect them, we punish and despise them." The anonymous author continued, "Good Servants of any Kind, whether Butlers, Stewards, or Footmen, House-maids, Chambermaids or Cooks, have no Right to withdraw themselves from their respective Masters, and act in an unbecoming Manner when their Masters Business is finished."[42] Calling on precedents that had redressed similar attitudes, Clive defended herself against charges of presumption and elevated her claim to the level of basic human rights: "Injustice and Oppression are by no means thought Matters of Indifference by any who have Humanity" (*Case of Mrs. Clive*, 6). In fact, in the years before abolitionist discourse, it was not uncommon to compare an actor to a slave. In one of the pamphlets inspired by the theatrical dispute, *An Impartial Examen of the Present Contests between the Town and the Manager*, "Mr. Neither-side" sympathized with a player's abjection that resulted from the Licensing Act's restrictions: "For the Actors are a People, from the highest to the lowest, the most to be pitied of any of his Majesty's Subjects; because the last Theatrical Act of Parliament has made them the only Slaves in the Nation."[43] Clive subtly distinguished between the theater audience—the jury she respected and whose verdict she would accept—and the theater manager or other sovereign authority to whom she refused to be enslaved.

Clive's pamphlet rails against the patent house managers' unfair treatment and working conditions. More than exposing Clive's individual plight, *The Case* is remarkable in insisting that acting involves real labor, the kind of demanding work that deserves a living wage. What other recourse, Clive asks, do players who have acted since infancy have with "no other Professions to live by, and very numerous Families to support?" (17):

It has always been a Custom in Theatres, that if ever any Actor or Actress was to be discharged, or their allowance lessen'd, they were acquainted with it at the End of the Season; the Reason of this will appear to be the giving them a proper Notice to provide for themselves: This the Manager of Covent-Garden did to all his Company whom he designed to discharge, or whose Allowance was to be lessen'd, except to me, which made me actually then conclude he determined I should continue with him, 'till I was undeceived by his Play-Bills with the Names of other Actresses in Parts I used to perform; so that he has not only broke thro' the Customs of the Theatre, but those in practice almost every where, in dismissing me, and has done me a real Injury in such an unprecedented Act of Injustice; for had I been informed of his Design at the End of the Season, I could have made Terms to have acted in *Ireland*, where I had met with most uncommon civilities, and received very great Advantages. (13–14)

In addition she protested that Fleetwood had overestimated her income from benefit nights, and underestimated actresses' outlay for costumes and other expenses. Grudgingly accepting a position at the Covent Garden price-fixed salary, she was denied the benefit free of house charges that had been granted over the preceding nine years. Again appealing to common law, Clive noted that an actor having to pay benefit charges broke a thirty-year tradition. She argued that actors' salaries were not really disproportionately large when prorated for the time that the theater remained dark, and when one allowed for out-of-pocket expenses. The large sums commanded by Garrick and Clive—whose salaries, "monstrous Sums," greatly exceeded those of the minor actors and dressers—began to tell on the company and the theater. Still, Clive's constant economic concerns highlighted her commercial value as one of the highest paid actors, and she needed the money, having no husband or patron to support her.

In short, theater "customs," as Clive fully understood, required regularizing because they were being violated and ignored. Not having been given proper notice that her contract would be terminated, Clive had been prevented from engaging herself to another theater for the following season. She was, in effect, a prisoner of her unjust contract, and she was being punished for others' jealousy of her celebrity. She and the other unemployed actors took up collections in order to keep from starving, to stave off debtor's prison, and to bury their own.[44] The actors also sought to extend benefits to include pensions for the widows of dead actors and the right of married actors to remain together in the same city, eventually commanding an actor's pension fund later in the century. Rich's action, as Clive brilliantly argued, extended the insult against one actor into an infraction against all actors, the craft of acting, and the longstanding agreements that had made the theater an attractive option. She fearlessly demanded fair labor conditions not only for herself but also for her guild, including timely payments, accurate playbills, and proper notice of dismissal.[45]

Clive's trust in the beneficence of the theater public—as opposed to the unjust dealings of the managers—was amply repaid when the "Ladies" (perhaps among them the women of rank whom she would accompany to George III's coronation), who had promised protection, convinced Rich to rehire her, and even within a month after the publication of her *Case*, "the Prince of Wales and his Princess sponsored at the Haymarket a concert for her benefit" (*Case of Mrs. Clive*, ix). In short, Clive's polemical pamphlet marked a historic moment when an actress first made an extended public plea to be treated as a respected professional, and to be granted appropriate commercial reward. Clive returned to Drury Lane in the upcoming 1744–45 season, where she acted for the next twenty years. Yet late in her career, she apparently had to fight the same battle again. Writing to Garrick on 14 October 1765, she entreated him to pay her what she was owed: "I beg you wou'd do me the favour to let me know if it was by your order that my Monney was stop'd last Saturday; . . . the publick are witness for me, wether I have ever neglected my buisinness, you may (if you please to recolect) remember I have never disapproved you four lines since you have been a manager . . . . I hope this stoping of Monney is not a french fassion; I belive you won't find any part of the English laws that will support, this sort of treatment of an actress, who has a right from her Character and Service: on the Stage to expect some kind of respect."[46] Once again her appeal rested on common law and civil rights. Clive may have been poorly educated, but she was no one's fool.

Fine Ladies and Chambermaids

Clive's insistence on getting her fair share from her manager is nowhere more in evidence than in an anecdote regarding Garrick's popular afterpiece *Lethe; or, Aesop in the Shades*, first produced on 15 April 1740 following Cibber's *The Careless Husband*. When Garrick highlighted his part and excluded her from the play-billing, Clive's alleged response, though usually attributed to hubris, is more properly interpreted as that of an astute businesswoman who fully understood the value of advertising: "Madame Clive at noon came to the theater and furiously rung the alarm bell: for her name being omitted was an offence she construed so heinous, that nothing but vengeance, and blood! blood! Iago was the word! And it was no more strange than true that Garrick ever feared to meet that female spirit" (Wilkinson, *Memoirs*, 3: 41–42).

Clive played various parts in *Lethe*: she mockingly acted the fine lady with operatic exaggeration nineteen times, and she delivered Garrick's epilogue as the sprightly maid Lucy. She first sang as Miss Lucy in 1745 (a character who had appeared in Fielding's *Virgin Unmask'd*) and later acted as Mrs. Riot (introduced in 1749), as Mrs. Tatoo (1749), and as the Fine Lady (introduced in 1757). Revised and revived in various versions from 1740 to 1777, *Lethe* was performed 263 times in twenty-six seasons.[47] Satirizing James Miller's *An Hospital for Fools* (15 November 1739) and borrowing from Vanbrugh's *Aesop* (1697), the farce features a hero who attempts to improve a whole stage full of fools (tradesman, tailor, Frenchman, drunkard) who represented London society. Only Lord Chalkstone, a late addition played by Garrick, resists their nonsense. At the conclusion, Mercury encourages them all to abandon their vices by drinking from Lethe, the river of forgetfulness.

In *Lethe* the references to Clive's private personality abound and the epilogue, like many paratexts written specifically for her, exploits her liminality between stage and life. Speaking and singing in the beloved role as a would-be fashionable lady who despises her boorish drunken husband, Clive was immortalized in a china figurine holding the fat pug dog mentioned in the farce. Anticipating Mrs. Malaprop in Sheridan's *The Rivals*, Clive as the Fine Lady misspeaks and misspells, reminding the audience of the actress's lack of formal education. Dr. Heartfree's characterization of Mrs. Riot's full-blown eccentricity in a puff for the afterpiece *Lethe Rehears'd* (1749) is typical of the stock character: "Mrs. *Riot* is come to Maturity in Madness . . . —a Woman of Fashion equally *distracted* in her Notions and corrupted in her *Manners*."[48]

In the epilogue to *Lethe*, Clive shifted roles to speak as the maid Lucy, and her real brother James Raftor joined her on stage in the character of Thomas, Lucy's ne'er-do-well footman husband. Though a social underling, Lucy dares even in her husband's presence to choose a lover from the audience. Clive herself did not, of course, marry a footman, but her actual husband was known (like her brother Thomas who exits, exasperated) to have early "retired" from her presence, and it is in her person as a "free" wife that she blatantly flirts with the audience. Turning the epilogue into a nationalist plea directed at the pit as well as the boxes, Clive as the coquettish chambermaid encourages the audience's interaction. As her eyes and voice penetrate the audience, the spectator role is not only reversed but thoroughly interrupted: in delivering the epilogue, she becomes hunter rather than prey. Any man in the theater could fantasize bedding or marrying her; any woman could playfully imagine retiring her own husband. Clive thus laid open her personality to seem emotionally and physically accessible to audience members of all ranks and both sexes, as the actress-character surveyed the audience in search of potential lovers, mischievously identifying real acquaintances to embarrass or charm:

> Besides, of all things, I abhor a beaux [sic];
> For, when tried, 'tis doubtful whether man or no.
> Next, let me view my last resort—the pit;
> Here's choice enough: the merchant, soldier, cit,
> The surly critic, and the thread-bare wit.[49]

Debating between merchant and soldier, Clive/Lucy opts for the patriotic choice by settling on *both* possibilities: "Applaud me, Britons, and approve my choice" (34). The actress's favored roles—including especially Mrs. Riot, Mrs. Heidelberg, and Lady Fuz, socially ambitious, modishly dressed ladies who strove to be accepted as authentically elite—similarly allowed Clive as the fine lady in various incarnations to enact and reenact the plight of celebrated eighteenth-century actresses.

According to actor-manager and dramatist Samuel Foote, however, Clive lacked the requisite delicacy and elegance necessary to portray a true gentlewoman. He complained that Clive "expressed herself behind the Scenes in too loud and forcible a Manner."[50] Though Foote assumed that ladies of quality avoided contact with actresses in private life, Clive's company was, according to Thomas Davies, "always courted by women of high rank and character, to whom she rendered herself very agreeable" (*Memoirs*, 2: 203). As a celebrated actress Kitty achieved enviable status, though she was believed by some observers to take unseemly pride in her high acquaintances: "Her brilliant face was seen for a whole day in Palace Yard, where she sat to see the coronation procession of George III, with her great friends around her,—Lady Hertford, Lady Anne Conway, Lady Hervey, Lady Townshend, Miss Hotham, Mr. Chute and also her brother . . . [as well as Garrick and other actors, with Governor Johnstone and his wife. Later they] met at Little Strawberry at dinner, and laughed over past perils."⁵¹ When the Earl of Radnor left her the small sum of £50 in 1757, she is reported to have been excessively pleased at the attention afforded by an aristocrat: "You never saw anything so droll as Mrs Clive's countenance, between the heat of summer, the pride in her legacy, and the efforts to appear unconcerned."⁵² Having played a significant number of ladies of quality manqué on stage, Clive developed a deep reservoir of patrician mannerisms from which to draw. In retirement at Cliveden, Clive produced in her letters a consciously developed persona, an affected demeanor rather than an authentic identity, of a country gentlewoman engaged in philanthropic activities, needlework, and gardening.⁵³ But limiting Clive to such an identity is too restrictive for such a strong-willed, buoyant spirit who understood the performative nature of social roles.

When Clive reached her fifties, she continued to perform boldly and sensually with an under-self that easily accommodated to parts as ladies or maids. In 1765 George Colman and Garrick together wrote the comedy, *The Clandestine Marriage*, a popular vehicle for the company of actors including Clive, Mrs. Palmer, Miss Rogers, Mr. King, and Mr. Ackman.⁵⁴ First produced on 20 February 1766, *The Clandestine Marriage* ran for thirteen performances and continued for eleven seasons, totaling a noteworthy eighty-seven performances at Drury Lane, and seven performances through six seasons at Covent Garden. Clive's much-admired role in the play was as Mrs. Heidelberg, the wealthy sister of Mr. Sterling, father of two marriageable daughters. Comically embodying women's desire for sway, Clive as character and actress is an independent, impudent woman with considerable funds at her disposal. The play blends the character Mrs. Heidelberg with the actress Clive, both of whom are strident and ill-educated but also wealthy and good-hearted, to make the audience believe that they "know" both. Testifying to the play's success, Clive later chose the piece to be acted at her benefit. The comedy focuses on the barbaric behavior of the money-grubbing family controlled by Mrs. Heidelberg, a pretentious, domineering Dutch merchant's widow who mocks "everything that does not relish of what she calls Quality," a word she persists in pronouncing "Qualaty" (1: 1). Reminiscent of Clive's other roles as a Fine Lady, the satire on manners arises principally from the would-be fine lady's mispronunciations, misusages, and haughty self-assertion.

In *Clandestine Marriage* Sterling's daughter Fanny is secretly married to Lovewell, a penniless clerk in Stockwell's counting house. The virtuous, sentimental, and "civilized" Fanny seeks to keep Mrs. Heidelberg's money within the Sterling family, whose crude mercenary attitude leads them to anticipate receiving "three or four very good mortgages, a great deal of money in the three per cents. And old South-Sea annuities, besides large concerns in the Dutch and French funds" (4: 2). Sterling, himself the object of satire, claims that his status as a *nouveau riche* merchant is characteristically English: "Money, money, that's the stuff that makes the great man in this country" (1: 1). The family fears that marrying either of their daughters to a nabob would contaminate them, and the play extends the xenophobic attitude to French, German, Dutch, Swiss, Turkish, and African stereotypes. When Sir John Melvil, a man of fashion, opportunistically transfers his affections from the elder daughter to the younger, Sterling angrily protests: "Do you think that I will suffer you, or any man in the world, to come into my house like the Grand Signior and throw the handkerchief first to one and then t'other, just as he pleases? Do you think I drive a kind of African slave-trade with them?" (3: 1). Central to the play—peppered with references to the Royal Exchange, stocks and bonds, shopping and fashion, and East India trade—is an exploration of the uneasy relationship of fashionable women to the commodity culture. Mrs. Heidelberg/Clive sublimates her sexual desire to consumption and, drawing a familiar linkage, her passion for goods spurs the nation's prosperity through global trade. She pompously asserts her superior class position: "I would not demean myself to be slobbered about by drunken shoemakers, beastly cheesemongers, and greasy butchers and tallow-chandlers" (3: 2).

But the family is also tainted because clandestine marriages lacking the sanction of the Anglican Church, such as Fanny's to Lovewell, were illegal. Though Mrs. Heidelberg/Clive is at first appalled to learn of the clandestine marriage, she ultimately exhibits the actress' celebrated generosity and forgives the young couple. Rather than offering an epilogue, several characters substitute a short afterpiece on cardplaying, one of Clive's favorite activities, to reiterate the association between women and the credit economy (4: 2). Clive's role as Mrs. Heidelberg in *The Clandestine Marriage* replaces the idea of the actress as whore with that of the actress as fine lady manqué, at home in a consumer economy.

Another of Clive's very popular fine lady roles was as Lady Fuz in Garrick's hit farce, *A Peep Behind the Curtain; or, The New Rehearsal* (1767), a rehearsal play in the tradition of the original *The Rehearsal* (1664, revised 1667) by George Villiers, Duke of Buckingham. Rehearsal plays underscored the collaborative aspect of readying a play for production, since by the 1730s actors were encouraged to combine their private preparation with rehearsing publicly in a group.[55] *A Peep Behind the Curtain*, in first production paired with George Lillo's bourgeois tragedy, *The London Merchant* (1731), was performed at least fifty-seven times. Garrick added a burletta, a burlesque comic opera, to the rehearsal farce in 1776–77. Combining singing and acting, the burletta—technically a rhymed musical drama in three acts including at least five songs—deals in a comical way with classical myth.[56]

Most significantly, *A Peep Behind the Curtain* resembles and even imitates Clive's *The Rehearsal: or, Bays in Petticoats* (1750) and her other dramatic writings, suggesting Clive's influence on Garrick rather than the reverse. Like the audacious Mrs. Riot and Mrs. Heidelberg of *Lethe*, Lady Fuz/Clive acts as an eccentric theater critic, a would-be fine lady, who watches the rehearsal of the burletta called *Orpheus*, along with her husband, daughter, and Sir Macaroni Virtu. Mr. Glib, the poet character, completed only one act of this burletta, and he is, as Phyllis T. Dircks has pointed out, "both the agent and object of the satire."[57] In the musical farce that the characters witness, Orpheus lulls his rejected harlot Rhodope to sleep with his magic lyre and seeks his wife Eurydice in hell. The play is interrupted with an absurd pastoral scene complete with cows, sheep, goats, and ballet-dancing shepherds.[58] In the second, unfinished, act, Mr. Glib suggests that Orpheus should exchange wives with Pluto in a hell that resembles the theater itself, peopled with "all degrees, and occupations—say, and of both sexes."

The farce splits actress and role briefly, only to reunite them with comical metatheatrical queries: "Is Clive there?" When told that she does not linger about the theater, Lady Fuz/Clive ironically responds: "Bless me! If I was an actress I should never be a moment out of the playhouse." She continues in a self-mocking vein, "I wish I could have seen Clive! I think her a droll creature. Nobody has half so good an opinion of her as I have" (1: 2). Known as an astute businesswoman, Clive as Lady Fuz asks the box manager to reserve her opening night place and coyly adds a self-promoting puff: "And don't forget Clive's benefit" (2: 1). When Lady Fuz is distracted by Mr. Glib's play, her daughter Miss Fuz takes the opportunity to act on her mother's repressed sexual desires and run away with her would-be actor. A hopeless romantic, Lady Fuz remains faithful to Sir Toby—a fat, faded libertine who amused pit and galleries by snoring loudly in his box seat—like Clive herself who had remained faithful to her husband even after their separation.

Because Lady Fuz's feelings are assigned an imagined home in Clive's actual body, the play's dialogue posits a plausible performative identity for the actress herself—one who delights in the feigned romance of the stage, freely expresses sexual desire, frankly acknowledges her husband's infidelity, openly seeks the audience's patronage, and knows her own value. Further, because certain recognizable personal traits such as her generosity and good-natured self-mockery travel from play to play, character to character, via Clive's knowing embodiment of them, they constitute a coherent identity made accessible to the audience. Acting the parts of fine ladies and chambermaids demonstrates how clearly Clive understood the significance of conveying a consistent theatricalized character, even though that character represented a social standing very much in flux.

In short, the most successful eighteenth-century actresses, their rank in the world mediated through struggles within and without the theater, publicly personified the contest for dominance and the ethical debates between commerce and property facing the ascendant middling class and the increasingly dissolute aristocracy. For male actors "the boundary between the nobility and gentleman had become blurred or even permeable," as Peter de Bolla accurately concludes;[59] and when Thomas Sheridan famously declared that he was "*as good a gentleman as any in the house*,"[60] he simultaneously claimed to be a gentleman and recognized that he would never be one. This "intense scrutiny of the category 'person' which occurred on the restoration stage" prefigured the modern divided subject which is self-evidently, in de Bolla's view, "most energized and exercised by [the] male person" (157, 165). Yet surely the nuanced meanings of personhood were most fully animated by *actresses* whose relationships to property and sexuality were, as we have seen, evolving in at least as complicated a way as those of male players.

Other Epilogues

Clive engaged in yet another form of hybridization: for example, the virtuoso comedienne yoked genres together within the same performance when she carried over the comic features of her chambermaid characterizations to the ordinarily serious role of Portia in *Merchant of Venice*. Though Shakespeare's play often teeters on the brink of tragedy, the full title is *The Comical History of the Merchant of Venice, or Otherwise Called the Jew of Venice*.[61] Still Clive/Portia, cross-dressed as the young lawyer Balthasar, was much criticized for her humorous rendering of "the quality of mercy is not strained speech" in the trial scene. Many judged her harshly for choosing to transform Portia's function into a comical one, yet she stubbornly insisted on repeating the unusual interpretation over seventeen seasons from 1739–40 to 1759–60, even opening one season with the play. According to *The Dramatic Censor*, she attracted applause even though she presented "a ludicrous burlesque on the character, [for] every feature and limb contrasted the idea Shakespeare gives us of Portia; in the spirited scene she was clumsy, and spoke them in the same strain of chambermaid delicacy she did Lappet or Flippanta; in the grave part—sure never was such a female put into breeches before!—she was aukwardly dissonant; and, as if conscious she could not get through without the aid of trick, flew to the pitiful resource of taking off the peculiarity of some judge, or noted lawyer; from which wise stroke, she created laughter in a scene where the deepest attention should be preserved, till Gratiano's retorts upon the Jew, work a contrary effect."[62] Just why Clive determined to portray Portia in a playful style while mimicking contemporary judges remains something of a mystery. Acting opposite the comic actor Charles Macklin as Shylock, she may have felt justified in lightening the role—though Macklin apparently interpreted his part with unrelieved seriousness.

Mimicry was Clive's forte, and she was among the most popular speakers of epilogues, most often high-spirited romps filled with topical references to current affairs and public personages. Innovatively (but perhaps ill-advisedly) inserting the tone of the comic epilogue into Portia's characterization in the fourth act trial scene, Clive may well have assumed that she could carry the power of her droll personality into the inner workings of Shakespeare's play as the transvestite character of Portia: breeches parts were, after all, usually comic ones. Flaunting her independent spirit, she acted freely and with originality in reconciling Jew to Christian, and comic to near-tragic, as the joking Portia assessed the contradictions in the scene before meting out mercy. In portraying a humorous rather than a solemn and judicious Portia, Clive challenged the confinement of cross-dressed characters to predictable generic expectations. The answer to this generic hodgepodge may lie in the fact that even the most deeply tragic plays staged in the Restoration and eighteenth century usually concluded with comic epilogues delivered by actresses.[63] For example, "A Prologue upon Epilogues, Spoken at a Private Benefit" remarks on the practice, especially associated with women, of ending a tragedy with a comic paratext:

> The epilogue, which always deck'd with smiles,
> In female accent, tragic care beguiles:
> That when exalted thoughts, the mind impress,
> A trivial jest must make the pleasure less.
> Ludicrous custom, which compels to show,

The cap of folly, in the rear of woe;
Portrays a smile, emerging from a sigh,
And pleasure starting from affliction's eye;
Makes joy's bright beam in sorrow's face appear,
And Quibble dry the sentimental tear.[64]

Clive, speaking as a "modern Sinner," questions the tradition of concluding tragic plays with naughty comic epilogues. After a performance of Cibber's *Papal Tyranny in the Reign of King John* (15 February 1745), she performed "With flirting Fan, and pointed Wit, so jolly, / Crack Jokes on Virtue, as an unbred Folly," leading vulgar rakes and witlings to laugh openly while the "boxes" blushed in response to the epilogue.[65]

Clive fought for her right to "own" epilogues as well as parts. Henry Fielding, David Garrick, Horace Walpole, and many others composed epilogues specifically for Clive, which allowed her to project a subjectivity united in the fine ladies and singing chambermaids that, as I have shown, drew attention to an actress's professional and personal quandaries. Clive, like other celebrity actresses, frequently "kept a distinguishing role in epilogues, creating a character quite as definite as those which she represented in the play itself, and authors wrote their epilogues to suit the speaker," as Mary Knapp has pointed out in her important study.[66] Clive was legitimately famous for the dozens of epilogues she skillfully performed, and was known to be "the most amusing as well as the most consistent of all speakers of such epilogues" (Knapp, 68).

By some accounts Garrick strictly regulated the acting methods of his players, yet speaking epilogues may have offered an opportunity for his most enterprising actors, especially women, to improvise. The epilogue speaker sometimes claims to share an intimate relationship with the playwright and to wield considerable influence over him. Clive's close ties to Fielding led him to design both the part of Chloe as "Maid, Wife, and Widow, all in one" and the epilogue to *The Lottery* (1 January 1732).[67] The actress-character, only mildly indecent, seems promiscuous and practical at once, seeking in the epilogue a new husband and an estate from the audience gallants. Similarly, after sexy double entendres regarding Turkish women and their guards, the epilogue to Aaron Hill's *Tragedy of Zara* (12 January 1736) enjoins gentlemen in the audience to woo an unfaithful wife with trust: "If you would FIX th' *inconstant Wife*—RESPECT her."[68] Clive also sang a comic chorus or interlude between the acts of *Zara* to prevent the boxes from dozing off, adding some "spirit" to the tragedy. Other epilogues allowed Clive to separate from her character in the play to expose her "self" as she transported the audience from the play's fiction to the actual moment of the epilogue's delivery. For example, in the epilogue to James Worsdale's afterpiece, *A Cure for a Scold* based on *The Taming of the Shrew*, Clive complains about her role as Kate: "It vexes me to th' Heart / To act unwomanly—so mean a Part / What . . . to submit, so tamely . . . so contented / Thank Heav'n I'm not the Thing I represented."[69] To be an obedient and submissive woman was seldom part of Clive's regular epilogue character.

Clive's epilogues energetically set out audacious comic or satiric commentary, both feminist and misogynist, regarding the status of women. Many of the epilogues allude to her writing talent and prod Clive toward producing her own original theater pieces. In the epilogue that followed Frances Sheridan's *The Dupe* (1763), speaking openly as herself, a "Sister Scribbler" ("Not Mrs. *Friendly* now, I'm Mrs. *Clive* / No Character from Fiction will I borrow"), she shares the female playwright's lament that she cannot convince a man to write the epilogue. Consequently Sheridan begs Clive as actress and playwright to produce one on the spot: "Can't *you* endeavour / To say some pretty thing?—I know you're clever."[70] Similarly Garrick's epilogue written for the 19 March 1751 (?) performance of Clive's two-act afterpiece, *The Rehearsal*, is a rowdy call to action on behalf of women writers:

> But pray, Sirs, why must we not write, nor think?
> Have we not Heads and hands, and Pen and Ink?
> Can you boast more, that are so wondrous wise?
> Have Women then no weapons but their Eyes?
> Were we, like you, to let our Genius loose
> We'd top your wit, and Match you for abuse.[71]

Speaking for modern women and addressing the epilogue to skeptical men, the speaker touts women's superior wit: "Name but your Arms, the time & place—we'll meet you, / Fight us but fair, & on my Life we'll beat you" (367). The richness of the epilogue in performance, spoken by Clive as Mrs. Hazard, would have arisen from its multiple layers of reference to actress, playwright, character, and private person, thus extending the joke of the play. Though the feminism of the epilogue is complicated by its misogynist assertion that frivolous women never tire of public pleasures, the force of Garrick's prologue is at least as much, I think, a grudging recognition that Clive's comic talent threatened to rival his; the delivery of the words reinforces the way her arguments for women's equality constitute part of her continuing epilogue persona.[72] Garrick's avoidance of a "struggle for victory" with Clive, according to Thomas Davies, could be "attributed to his dread of her getting the better of him" for "Mr. Garrick dreaded an altercation with her as much as a quarrel with an author whose play he had rejected" (*Memoirs*, 2: 200). Recognizing the feminine power lodged within the tradition, Clive allegedly stormed the greenroom to demand that she, rather than the nun character, should be allowed to speak the epilogue to Fielding's *Covent Garden Tragedy* (1732) that Walpole had written expressly for her: "I storm'd—for, when my honour is at stake, / I make the pillars of the green-room shake."[73] In fighting for her entitlement to speak epilogues, many of which asserted women's authority and underscored their ability to cultivate critical and aesthetic opinions, her performances hinted that women might assume intellectual property rights over their own judgments.

In James Miller's *The Universal Passion* (28 February 1737), Clive claims to have teased the playwright into writing the epilogue. She turns to advantage the misogynist assertion that women, speaking the epilogues, always have the last word. The epilogue to Miller's unsuccessful *Art and Nature* (16 February 1738) proclaims that two different epilogues have been written, one damning the play, the other saving it; but Mrs. Clive speaking as the chambermaid Violetta insists that she memorized only the pejorative one. Her speech promises not to embarrass the ladies who, she claims, hold the power to keep the play on the boards.

> Ladies, our Bard, with humbler Rev'rence, says
> Chiefly for you he has written all his Plays;
> Cautious that no loose Scenes should e'er appear,
> Or Line be spoke which you might blush to hear. (Danchin, pt. 3, 5: 29–30)

Speaking directly to the women, she chides them to extend the play's run: "Gad! we'll defy the World to keep away the Men; / So Ladies, if you smile, To-morrow will be acted This again" (30). The epilogue characteristically calls attention to the tedious work of rehearsing "Thro' Cold and Wet for Forty Morns together" (29). In a similar epilogue to *The Intriguing Chambermaid*, Clive as the eponymous character argues for the "occasional" features of the epilogue form but also affects to condemn its catering to crass tastes in contrast to the theater's former "ancient hospitable seat."

In short, the epilogue form enabled Clive to appear to be a drama critic. Acting the part of her namesake Miss Kitty in Robert Dodsley's *Sir John Cockle at Court* (23 February 1738), a comic afterpiece to the tragic *Venice Preserved*, Clive plagues the author to compose the very epilogue she speaks. When he refuses, the speaker / Clive determines to create it herself (pt. 3, 5: 32). The epilogues after Fielding's *The Author's Farce* (15 January 1734) and William Paterson's *Arminius* (4 January 1740) good-humoredly suggest that after every play an actor should be given a choice of two epilogues, depending upon the play's success or failure: "To each new Play a double Epilogue." Clive exposes the tension between the lines assigned to her and her wish to "proceed in my own female Strain" (pt. 2, 4: 610), and her extemporizing gestures in performance, about which we can only speculate, may have signaled her independent views. After Miller's *An Hospital for Fools* (1739), Clive voices her belief that the play had no plot. Similarly, in the epilogue to *The Fatal Retirement* (12 November 1739), expressing contempt for the play's lack of public-spirited satires and its unleavened tragedy, she charges that greater patriotic fervor would have improved it: "Well, Sirs, Your Judgment? Is it *wretched Stuff* / I think, and I'm a Judge, 'tis *well e-nough*" (pt. 2, 4: 70). In the epilogue to *Alfred, A Masque* (23 February 1751), Clive's magical wand empowers her speaker-character to charm the ladies, paralyze the critics by turning them to stone, and conjure up a pastoral scene (pt. 3, 5: 353). Other epilogues settled competitions between theatrical houses, companies, or actors; still others allowed Clive to advertise her writing skills. In epilogues across the several decades of her career, from the 1730s to the 1760s, the enchanting actress, singer, and playwright expressed critical opinions regarding the dramas, even though she ventriloquated these ideas. Empowering female spectators to develop their own aesthetic opinions, Clive's enacting these epilogues expanded the definition of an actress to include a thoroughly modern woman capable of publicly espousing her own views.

Caesar in Petticoats

In Clive's farewell epilogue on quitting the stage, 24 April 1769, the actress-character quipped that her fate in retirement would certainly not follow the tragic path of the beheaded King Charles. Though she still managed to continue to display "apt expression, and well-suited grace," as Clive approached retirement, "when past Meridian life," she grew large of size and old of face, according to the pseudonymous Sir Nicholas Nipclose, Baronet.[74] In order to sustain her career as she advanced into middle age, as her maturing soprano voice became less captivating, Clive turned to her paternal Irish origins to infuse her career with fresh vigor through the invention of new performative properties. Very few women playwrights produced theatrical material between 1740 and 1760,[75] and Clive is among a tiny number of actresses who wrote dramatic vehicles for themselves, venturing with originality and confidence into farce, burlesque, and pantomime that were not generally attractive to women writers.[76] Richard C. Frushell aptly praises her as "the best female writer of satiric drama in England at the mid-century."[77] Such farces, saturated with male infidelity and libertinism in both mainpiece and burletta, supposedly sparked illicit desire in the audience. One critic, for example, balked at the burletta's bawdy as unsuitable for women spectators: "These low exhibitions and mimes are calculated to arouse the passions, and lay asleep reason for other particular purposes; to the private rehearsal or public representation of which, I would not more suffer my wife, my daughter, or my sister to go, than I would to enter a brothel."[78]

In writing for the stage Clive combined farce with humours comedy, but perhaps most importantly she contributed to feminist parody in the afterpieces, *The Rehearsal; or, Bays in Petticoats* (1750), as well as *Every Woman in Her Humour* (1760, Larpent MS, LA 174) and *The Sketch of a Fine Lady's Return from a Rout* (1763, Larpent MS, LA 220), revised as *The Faithful Irish Woman* (1765, Larpent MS, LA 247).[79] The farce *The London 'Prentice* was performed at Drury Lane, 23 March 1743, at Clive's benefit. Though the afterpiece was first reported to have been written by Laetitia Pilkington, Clive insisted that it was her invention. Because it was also produced at her brother Jemmy Raftor's benefit, the family monopoly suggests that it was indeed her composition.[80] The highly topical afterpieces satirize her real-life identity as a learned lady, a self-assured professional, and a gambler; her dramatic writings are at once a celebration and a burlesque of herself as actress, playwright, and person. All focus on headstrong women characters who seek escape from men's rule and from the social expectations that required them to behave in a lady-like fashion.

Performed on Clive's benefit nights, the afterpieces characteristically provide strong dramatic roles for vibrant female characters, as well as lesser roles suitable for training novice actresses. Afterpieces were an actor's salvation in that they generated revenue in refreshing older plays; they also required little advance preparation. *Every Woman* is the best of Clive's small corpus, but the fact that the parodic *Rehearsal*, with its frequent allusion to the actress herself, was the most popular suggests that audiences doted on her self-references. Teasing the audience by interlacing intimate revelation with her public persona, she toyed with inventing and violating conventions of privacy, and she capitalized on that strategy to build audience demand.[81]

All the afterpieces were performed at Drury Lane, *The Rehearsal* more than a dozen times, *The Sketch* twice, and the other two plays once each. Clive's *Rehearsal; or, Bays in Petticoats* (1750), focusing on a woman professional, is a strikingly assertive adaptation that draws on the popularity of Buckingham's Restoration play, *The Rehearsal* (1664, rev. 1667).[82] Because Garrick had made the central role of Bayes his own, modernizing its satire by critiquing the antiquated ranting style and even specific actors, Clive's usurpation of the role in her play alludes yet again to the keen competition between actress and manager. Though Clive, like Mrs. Mountfort, had earlier acted Bayes as a travesty role, supplanting and parodying Garrick in Buckingham's *Rehearsal*, she was not terribly successful in the attempt. Plays about plays often took as their subject issues of petticoat government or female authorship,[83] and Clive obliged in putting the central character in petticoats—that is, she changed Bayes into a woman—not just a cross-dressed player—who shared many of the actress's traits. Just as Buckingham had satirized himself in the antiheroic character Bayes, in her *Rehearsal* Clive mocked herself in the role of author Mrs. Hazard who moves back and forth between dressing room and stage, suggesting the synthesis of Clive's public and private life. On 15 March 1750, Clive acted the lead in the farce and sang music composed by Dr. Boyce for her benefit following Garrick's acting in *Hamlet*. The afterpiece along with Garrick's epilogue, presented fourteen times between 1750 and 1762, was revised in 1753 with the addition of a final scene.[84]

Rehearsal plays were metadramatic vehicles that set up numerous opportunities to construct an actress's personality on stage. The protean nature of the script made the rehearsal play a reflection of theater practice itself, as audience and actors intermingled on stage, and actors sometimes added lines or scenes in rehearsal, or in an impromptu way during performance.[85] As a rehearsal about a rehearsal, Clive's afterpiece queries the authority, permanence, and status of the play itself. It is not in my judgment an antitheatrical piece but rather a cleverly ludic analysis of the theater's limitations and conventions.

Clive would have known the history of the rehearsal genre when it was earlier exploited to satirize women playwrights in *The Female Wits; or the Triumvirate of Poets at Rehearsal* (1704), a satire probably composed by a committee of actors at Drury Lane.[86] In that play, which also borrows from Buckingham's *Rehearsal*, Marsilia represents playwright Delarivier Manley (like Clive, famous for her quick temper) who is viciously attacked, along with other women dramatists Mary Pix and Catherine Trotter, whose mutual support in seeing plays through to production antagonized the men. Trotter had praised Manley in a poetic puff: "You were our Champion, and the Glory ours. / Well you've maintain'd our equal right in Fame, / To which vain Man had quite engrost the claim." Clive is clearly aware of the history of antagonism toward female playwrights in *Female Wits* with its allusion to Manley's treating the scribbling itch as sexual commerce, a linkage that the "Critick" had drawn in mocking Manley's play *The Lost Lover*: "I grant you the Poets call the Nine Muses by the Names of Women, but why so? Not because the Sex had any thing to do with Poetry, but because in the Sex they're much fitter for prostitution."[87] The Critick continues: "I hate these Petticoat-Authors; 'tis false Grammar, there's no Feminine for the *Latin* word, 'tis entirely of the Masculine Gender, and the Language won't bear such a thing as a She-Author" (27). Both *The Female Wits* and Buckingham's *Rehearsal* accuse women writers of appropriating men's ideas; both feature a play within a play and end with the actors' performance of a dance.[88] But in Clive's play, and most especially in the revisions, she distinguishes her play by successfully separating acting and playwriting from prostitution. Unlike *Female Wits*, the *Rehearsal* lampoons Clive as an actress and a woman dramatist while asserting her right to be both. It is this ongoing tradition of misogyny that Clive seems to be consciously countering.

In *The Rehearsal* Clive doubled in the principal parts of Mrs. Hazard, a widow playwright, and the pastoral maiden Marcella/Mrs. Hazard in the burletta (thus the only actor to play double parts). The imperious Mrs. Hazard flaunts her power in requesting "all your Side-Boxes and every first Row in the Front" for the prompter's benefit (2: 1). Made crotchety by her fear that the farce, which the servants accuse her of having plagiarized, will be hissed off the stage, the would-be lady insists that her assumed rank will protect her—"The Town never hiss any thing that is introduc'd to them, by a person of Consequence and Breeding" (1: 1)—though Clive is of course mocking the uncertain social standing of actresses as well.[89] Mrs. Hazard also voices Clive's fearlessness in the face of the Town's judgment. Ironically, though Mrs. Hazard threatens to tear up the script she has written, the characters judge it a successful performance.

There are significant differences between the manuscript of Clive's

Rehearsal and the published version.⁹⁰ Clive, commenting on the provisional nature of any script in rehearsal, introduced the Dublin edition of her afterpiece by indicating that "The last Scene was an Addition the Year after." That scene added to the printed version of the play, countering the misogyny in *The Female Wits*, is more explicitly feminist than has been previously noticed. In that final section, the woman-hating Sir Albany Odelove taunts the indignant Mrs. Hazard for lacking education and delivers a nasty warning to female playwrights: "If Men, who are properly graduated in Learning, who . . . are hand and glove with the Classics, if such Genius's as I'm describing, fail of Success in Dramatical Occurrences, or Performances, ('tis the same Sense in the Latin) what must a poor Lady expect, who is ignorant as the Dirt" (2: 1). He urges Mrs. Hazard to study the classical unities with gentlemen friends in order to conform to heroic tragedy conventions, the very conventions that Buckingham's original *Rehearsal* had burlesqued. Finally Sir Odelove encourages Hazard to use the ultimate female weapon—tears. Unlike the ladies in the boxes who in the 1690s found sentimentality appealing, Clive sarcastically remarks that her farce did not play well to the ladies in the audience who, allegedly, flounced off to a dance at its conclusion. Perhaps Clive was jesting, or perhaps she anticipated that there were limits to the support of "the ladies" for her unprecedented attitudes; but she repeatedly expresses her confidence in her patrons who must have been largely sympathetic.

Actress and playwright, public and private person, dizzyingly blend together from the opening scene of *The Rehearsal* set in Mrs. Hazard's dressing room on stage, allowing the audience to feel that they were intimately acquainted with character and player. Mrs. Hazard comically serves as the understudy who substitutes for Clive, the tardy actress who is, of course, already present on stage. Mrs. Hazard/Clive mentions other parallels that the audience would recognize—her substantial height, her actor brother, her quick temper, and her controversially large salary of £800 annually. The allusions include references to Clive's legendary singing role as Polly in *Beggar's Opera* and to the pug dog that she carried as Mrs. Riot, the fine lady, in Garrick's *Lethe*, of which she, like Clive, is purported to have been fonder than of her deceased husband. The play also refers to her willingness to tutor young actors. Throughout the play she mocks herself for her lack of education, most evident through her bad spelling; she satirizes her own tendency to stretch the truth, as well as her love of quadrille, piquet, and other card games, but she also brags about her commercial value: "*Her Wealth be boundless as her Charms*" (2: 1).

Demonstrating the arbitrary nature of an actor's relation to the company, Mrs. Hazard/Clive declares that the star actress shall have no benefit. Recalling *The Case of Mrs. Clive*, she remarks on "the slavish Life" of actors and then behaves like a slavemaster herself. Mrs. Hazard/Clive complains that acting conditions do not allow her to play more than three or four days per week, and about her near-constant need to struggle with Garrick in order to land the best parts.[91] Hazard smarts from Garrick's slight in refusing to assign choice parts to her, and she is late for "the rehearsal" because she must solicit ladies of quality to support her benefit. She characterizes Clive, the "absent" character in the play, as an arrogant actress who refuses instruction from the "author": Hazard/Clive says of Clive "for she's so conceited, and insolent, that she won't let me teach it her" (1: 1), and she affects to turn the actress over to Garrick for disciplining.

The afterpiece was surely inspired at least in part by Clive's jealous wish to rival Garrick with whom she energetically competed, hoping to surpass him in reputation. John Taylor rightly assesses her envy in noting that she deserved recognition well before Garrick debuted in 1737, having been a celebrated actress and star singer from 1728.[92] In the rehearsal play she wickedly mocks his short stature and whimsically weighs his superior education against her unparalleled singing talent: "oh! if that dear Garrick cou'd but sing" (1: 1). It annoyed Clive that her own education had been very slight, while Garrick—having been tutored by Gilbert Walmesly in Lichfield—knew Latin, French, and some Greek. In her public proclamations and dramatic writing, Clive relied on the Town to recognize the justice of her demands in spite of Garrick's arrogant reaction. Her fighting spirit persisted even as she spoke the epilogue to Elizabeth Griffith's *The School for Rakes* (1769): "You'll find, when once my passion is afloat, / The soul of *Cesar*, in a petticoat."[93]

The "Irish-English" Clive

Especially in the 1760s, London audiences welcomed plays by Irish playwrights including Isaac Bickerstaff, Arthur Murphy, Hugh Kelly, Richard Cumberland, and Oliver Goldsmith.[94] The relationship between Irish and English theater in the eighteenth century was arguably an asymmetric one negotiated by actors, performances, and theaters on both sides of the Irish Sea, though recent critics argue for a more reciprocal relationship than a colonial model might allow.[95] Such a transnational perspective subverts more traditional paradigms to emphasize instead the frequent traffic between the London and Dublin theaters.[96] The actual numbers of plays first produced in Dublin before premiering in London may be of less significance in gauging Irish influence than the longevity and success of particular works. In seeking new vehicles, Clive brazenly capitalized on the English audience's appetite for Irish fare that had been demonstrated in their taste for Thomas Sheridan's afterpiece *The Brave Irishman; or, Captain O'Blunder* (1743), as well as Charles Macklin's comedies *Love à la Mode* (1759) and *The True-Born Irishman* (1760) revised as *The Irish Fine Lady* (1767). The long-reigning assumption regarding the eighteenth-century Irish theaters in Smock Alley and Aungier Street has been that they were largely colonial institutions that merely fostered English loyalties, though this view has been vigorously contested to reveal a resistant native Irish counter-theater manifested especially in the seemingly extraneous matter surrounding the mainpiece (including prologues and epilogues).[97] The colonial theater in Dublin was certainly a venue through which Anglo-Irish views of themselves and their ambiguous position took shape. The London stage, too, was sometimes the site of ferment stirred by Irish actors and playwrights, and Clive's farcical afterpieces, staged first in London, like her epilogues, embodied this contestatory spirit.[98]

After her success with *The Rehearsal*, Kitty Clive made performative property of herself and her plays, and she ultimately carried them to Ireland. Writing in the tradition of Farquhar and Shadwell, Clive drew on an emergent motif of the sprightly Irish female aristocrat.[99] In the characters Clive created for Irish *women* on stage and on the page, she countered common prejudices that Ireland was merely "a rural backwater," a landscape populated by harmless, laughable Gaelic peasants, "where the English visitor could experience a welcome release from the pressures of modernity."[100] While the Irish working-class man was frequently portrayed as a blustering, ignorant buffoon, and the Irish maid as a lusty local, these stereotypes are complicated in Clive's dramatic pieces where Ireland becomes less a murky bog swarming with primitive rustics than a rich cultural resource for women to draw upon. At some level Clive also recognized that she was playing on English fears of what intermarriage between individuals—and, metaphorically, a union between the two countries—might bring; and she masks potentially serious political and social satire with self-deprecating humor.

Though reputed to have a rough Irish temper, Clive spent very little actual time in Ireland, acting in Dublin only in 1741 and again in the early 1760s. Spurred by Charles Churchill's mention of Clive in *The Rosciad* (1761), she was assaulted with Irish stereotypes in Hugh Kelly's *Thespis* (1766): "Formed for those coarse and vulgar scenes of life, / Where low-bred rudeness always breathes in strife; / When in some blessed union we find / The deadliest temper with the narrowest mind, / The boldest front that never knew a fear, / The flintiest eyes that never shed a tear,— / Then not an actress certainly alive / Can e'en dispute pre-eminence with CLIVE!"[101] She had, however, also been long identified with happier Irish associations, as when singing "Ellen-a-Roon," at her benefit 19 August 1741.[102]

The farce *Sketch of a Fine Lady's Return from a Rout* is among the few plays on Irish subjects written during this period, and perhaps the only one by a woman of Irish extraction.[103] It comically repeats the theme of conflict between a woman's real desires, whether serious or trivial, and her social and domestic obligations.[104] Produced for Clive's benefit night at Drury Lane (12 March 1763), *The Sketch* focuses on Lady Jenkings [sic], a new-minted lady of quality who insists on being addressed as "your Ladyship" rather than "Madam," and who shares Clive's passion for cardplaying. Lady Jenkings is uneasy about her Anglo-Irish ascendant status after her husband, the docile Sir Jeremy Jenkings, had recently been knighted.

The *Sketch* was performed at least once in Dublin, on 27 June 1763, during the time that Clive visited the city. When Clive revised it into the two-act afterpiece *The Faithful Irish Woman*, submitted to the Lord Chamberlain and signed by James Lacy (March 1765), she inserted an Irish plot into the earlier *Sketch* with would-be aristocrats. The uproarious farce good-humoredly defends Irish traditions and relegates vulgar characters to the lower social classes. Having acted Lady Jenkings in the *Sketch*, Clive switched roles and nationalities in its revision into *The Faithful Irish Woman* to act the lead, Mrs. Oconner, the good-natured Irish cousin of the gambling would-be fine Lady Jenkins (the "g" is dropped in the later farce). The play shares with Thomas Sheridan's *The Brave Irishman* (which debuted in Dublin before succeeding in London) a central character who, in spite of being Irish, displays manners that mark her as possessing more humane instincts than the English. Showing considerable pluck and not a few peculiarities, the uncouth, snuff-sniffing Mrs. Oconner nevertheless displays her enviable money-management skills and urges her cardplaying cousin Lady Jenkins to renounce her addictions and pretensions.

In this clever bit of performative property, Mrs. Oconner ironically instructs the English in improving their speech, and most significantly she defends "the Irish-English Language"—rather than "Anglo-Irish"—as the proper language of the upper classes in both countries. Clive and her character

Oconner intimately understand that a person's social standing could be significantly transformed through reforming their regional dialect or enunciation. Here Clive reflected an apparent shift in the status of the Irish language in the 1760s, for by some accounts, "the English language of Ireland was considered by its speakers to be superior to other variants."[105] Clive's faithful Irishwoman was unique in attempting to fix an *Irish-English* identity that displayed elements superior to English alone. Clive/Mrs. Oconner boldly hints that "Irish" takes precedence over "English," and that the English have much to learn from their neighbors. For example, Mrs. Oconner scoffs at the English superstition that Ireland teems with poisonous snakes, and that the Irish are toad-eaters: "'Tis an unaccountable thing what they get into their heads about Ireland." The Irishwoman twice tells her English cousin Lady Jenkins that sending her spoiled stepdaughter Miss Nancy to Ireland would "make her good for something" by marrying an Irish man. Social status also trumps country of origin in the play. The genteel Irish, Mrs. Oconner protests, speak without a brogue, although loutish people in both countries garble the language into nonsensical jargon: "But I'll tell you, if I was not worth a shilling in the World, I would Bett you 500£ that we speak truer English in the Castle of Dublin, than you do at your Almacks, and your Conneleys, and Allyns, grand Quality meeting houses; thats what I wou'd." Lady Jenkins replies, "Ha, ha, ha! Well said, Coz! Stand up for the Irish-English language."

There are significant textual indicators that Clive's views in *The Faithful Irish Woman* were not without controversy. The claim that the Dublin Castle inhabitants speak finer English than "is spoken in the circle at St. Jameses" is emended, in manuscript, as is Mrs. Oconner's remark that the Lord Lieutenant indicated that "English was spoken in the purest Manner in Dublin."[106] At the same time Mrs. Oconner boldly displays a lack of deference to the English: "We are civil to the English when they deserve it, and when they don't deserve it, why—." Still, Mrs. Oconner is describing a chronic problem at mid-century when emigrants with various dialects flocked to the metropole, all seeking a uniform pronunciation, a "language property so-called," that would earn them social mobility, and when language academies were being founded in Britain to help regularize speech.[107] Motley dialects were spoken, satirized, and negotiated in the later eighteenth-century theaters.[108]

The Faithful Irish Woman suggests that Clive herself, though an Irish patriot, had erased any sign of an Irish inflection, unlike some of her fellow Irish actors. Mrs. Oconner breaks character and speaks as actress and playwright when she says, "Well now I'll tell you a Story and it is very true ['in Dublin' crossed out] some years ago we invited an English Actress ['Actor' crossed out] to come over to Us; & upon my honour they were very civil to her [added above the line: '& she was very fond of us, well then she was invited about everywhere']. So one day she was Dining at a person of Quality's house, & there was no less a Person than my Lord Chancellor, & so he was complimenting her, & said he had never heard any Lady upon the Stage, speak the English so well; Well then, a gentleman in Company reply'd, Faith & my Lord, there is no great Wonder at that that she shou'd speak English well, for her Grandfather was a Irishman." If the "English Actress" was meant to be Clive, then the joke clearly turns Irishness into an asset and champions Clive the actress and character as the perfect blend of the two countries. Her writing and acting her own performative property allowed audiences to imagine her interiority as diplomatically encompassing sympathy for both countries.

In the short play Clive also ridicules the extremes to which the Irish will go to affect an English identity. Alluding to plots in popular Irish plays on the London stage, she remarks, "The English Ladies have sometimes done us the honour to shew a partiality for our Countrymen, & I am glad I have it in my power to return the Obligation by giving my fortune to an Englishman, who has behav'd nobly to his Kind & country, & preserv'd his affections to his Mistress." Like Clive, Mrs. Oconner ascends to become part of the Anglo-Irish—or Irish-English—elite, though she mocks those who attempt to hobnob above their rank. While Macklin's Irish Fine Lady signaled her affection for everything English (including "a new kind of London English" and the effeminate English fop Mushroom) by changing her name from O'Dogherty to Diggerty, Clive's Irishwoman takes pride in Irish values, and in the hybrid language that the Irish helped to create. Rather than debating the respective merits of being Irish and living as a Briton, a potentially combustible mixture, Clive resolves cultural difference through the romance of an Irishwoman and an Englishman, instead of the usual reverse pattern: she stands on its head the conventional plot of an Irishman marrying an Englishwoman.

In the second act of *The Faithful Irish Woman*, Mrs. Oconner receives word that her fiancé Truman, an English seacaptain, abruptly lost his fortune in a shipwreck. Mrs. Oconner/Clive reveals her nobility of spirit and *virtù*, her "Generosity and greatness of Soul," and shares her substantial fortune with him. Clive cleverly concludes the afterpiece with a satirical air from Gay's *Beggar's Opera*, playing on her winning the contested singing role as Polly and again bridging theatrical representation and her person: "And now I can sing to you with pretty Polly, Thus safe on Shore, I ask no more; / My All is in my Possession, Possession &c." Serving as a metaphor for her native land, she embodies a loyal Irishwoman who is willing to support both her husband and herself with money from property inherited from an Irish uncle. Clive, because of her husband's debts, was believed to have given her estranged English husband George Clive an allowance from her earnings yet, as we have noted, upon his death he left her nothing. In addition Clive, I suggest, signals through her characters onstage and off that although she willingly contributed her acting talent to England, England's trade inequalities vis-à-vis Ireland, its prejudices and misapprehensions about Ireland, and its extraction of Ireland's cultural and economic resources persist. Thus Ireland is personified as a wealthy, propertied independent woman who generously assumes the debts of a suddenly destitute Englishman and shares his identity in marriage.

Mrs. Oconner runs counter to more abject female figures, and Clive's interpretation in the afterpieces, written and produced in London, is highly original in her resistance to portraying the Irish, and particularly Irish women, as suffering mothers or even as fortune-hunters. Clive's comic heroines, like the actress herself, represent the antithesis of distressed femininity or anguished maternity. They are savvy, moneyed, high-spirited women with hearts of gold who speak "Irish-English" with true wit, who eschew traditional domestic duties, and who generally defend Ireland and its "civilized" culture—the very type of the celebrated actresses described throughout this book.

In short, Clive contributes to the formation of an Irish female identity that is distinct from the stereotypic native Irish servant or the blustering, drunken Teague figure. Rather than an Irish adventurer voraciously seeking a wealthy English wife, Clive's Englishman plans to endow a strong Irishwoman who ironically ends up supporting him, thus reversing the usual comic Irish plot. Traumatized by hailing from a country with a history of being dispossessed of one's land, Mrs. Oconner's "Irish-English" identity is bolstered by her being a landowner. She says, "I have Secret to tell you, I have got 2000£ in good firm Land that the Sea can't wash away." Just as Clive claimed a different sort of theatrical property in the parts she claimed as her own, her character, through its iteration in performative property, reclaims the real property from which many Irish had been dispossessed. In promoting this identity, Clive made available a social *and* a theatrical space that she could inhabit as a dispossessed Irish-English woman who was not anyone's possession, but who instead owned theatrical properties she claimed in her dramatic roles.

Clive's afterpieces highlighted the difficulty of negotiating a tenable relationship between unequal participants onstage and off because of national, religious, class, and gender affiliations and especially in trans-Irish Sea exchanges. As she invented a novel kind of Irish woman on stage, Irish and English were transformed in her equation. Clive, then, wrote women into the history of decolonization, as a group that was unassimilated to the state, and in a manner in which they might be perceived, if only partially, as participants in its conceptualization.[109] Clive's long career, like the extended dispute waged over the actors' rebellion, was symptomatic of the growing conflict between the patent theater as a collective entity and one that relied upon a celebrated individual's aggregate personality. Clive's loyalties to the broader theatrical community of actresses conflicted with her competitive instincts; her struggle throughout her career reflected a historic shift from the shared interests within a theater company to an individual actor's stake in fashioning a lucrative career based on personality. Though dispossessed of ordinary property as a woman, she was able to gather substantial economic power through her performative properties.

When Garrick asked her "how much she was worth" Clive replied self-assuredly, "as much as yourself."[110] She competed with Garrick and with other actors as a playwright, as a businesswoman, and as a celebrity, and her achievements rivaled those of any actress and many actors to this point in theater history. She remained dedicated to a craft that she believed merited respect, rights, and privileges. Kitty Clive, unparalleled in the eighteenth-century theater as a comedienne and singer, embodied a highly visible model of autonomy, compatible with an embryonic liberal feminism, which contributed to her particular brand of theatrical property. Clive came to personify the individualism on which modern feminism was founded (and has sometimes faltered as it has encountered critiques of its social class alignments); but, unlike a liberal self that preexists its actions, Clive's commercial identity took shape alongside and together with the dramatic characters she portrayed, and often on behalf of the other actors with whom she labored. On stage and in life she realigned virtue, property, and commerce to encompass aristocrat and commoner, lady and whore, English and Irish, and thus to personify eighteenth-century actresses' struggles as central to the cultures that spawned them.

CHAPTER 6

The Actress, Travesty, and Nation: Margaret Woffington

> You are tir'd of an Appendix to our Sex, that you can't so handsomly get rid of in Petticoats as if you were in Breeches."
> —Melinda to Sylvia in *The Recruiting Officer*

> In every Country, Decency requires, that the Sexes should be differenc'd by *Dress*, in order to prevent Multitudes of Irregularities, which would continually be occasion'd.
> —*Universal Spectator* (24 December 1728)

JOHN RICH REPORTEDLY found the actress Margaret Woffington (1720?–60) to be an impossibly beautiful woman. When the young Irish girl arrived in London in 1740 after taking Dublin by storm, she allegedly pestered Rich until he granted her a personal audience. The legendary scene of the dissolute Rich encountering the lovely wisp of a woman has been memorably captured in word and image: he met her while reclining "on a Couch, with one Leg lolling over the other, his left Hand holding a Play-Book, and his right a China Cup, out of which he was sipping some Tea. *Round* him, *upon* him, and *about* him, were seven-and-twenty Cats of different Sizes, Ages, and Complexions. Some were staring him in the Face, some eating the Toast and Butter out of his Mouth, some licking the Cream out of a cup, some frisking about, some lying down, some perched upon his Knee, some upon his Head, *&c.*

Figure 12. "Woffington's First Interview with Manager Rich." Edward Francis Finden, engraving after Frederick Smallfield. Harvard Theatre Collection, Houghton Library.

&c. &c. &c. &c. &c. &c. &c. &c. &c. &c. &c"[1] (Figure 12). Woffington's reaction to the manager surrounded by his virtual seraglio of felines is not recorded, but according to Sir Joshua Reynolds, only Rich's recollection of his marriage allowed him to maintain his composure when confronted with the enticing actress: "Had it been otherwise, I should have found it difficult to retain my equanimity enough to arrange business negotiations with that amalgamated Calypso, Circe and Armida who dazzled my eyes. A more fascinating daughter of Eve never presented herself to a manager in search of rare commodities. She was as majestic as Juno, as lovely as Venus, and as fresh and charming as Hebe"[2] (Figure 13). Rich hired her, but on many occasions Woffington found her negotiations with him difficult. She regularly quarreled with him over salary and other professional matters, including rivalries with other actresses. But it was Rich who eventually offered her the £800 per season that Thomas Sheridan had promised but reneged on when he fled Dublin after the Smock Alley affair.

It may be startling, then, to recall that this mesmerizingly feminine woman, Margaret "Peg" Woffington, performed most memorably as a man in cross-dressed and travesty parts, beginning her career as Macheath (December 1731), followed later by roles as Silvia in Farquhar's *The Recruiting Officer* (each season from 1740–41 to 1756–57 with one exception); the comic libertine Sir Harry Wildair in Farquhar's *The Constant Couple* (each season from 1740–41 to 1757); and the tragic libertine Lothario in Nicholas Rowe's *The Fair Penitent*. In addition, Woffington developed a cross-dressed persona in numerous epilogues, not infrequently as a female soldier. Woffington thus created an ambiguously gendered persona in a series of patriotic epilogues that promoted national loyalty but also implied a critique of that identity by exposing through sexual impersonation its constructed nature.[3]

Among the dramatic roles Woffington frequently acted in travesty were Sir Harry Wildair in *The Constant Couple* and Lothario in *The Fair Penitent*, both devil-may-care, womanizing libertines, like the rakish Captain Macheath in John Gay's *Beggar's Opera*, who might seem to be odd choices for a star actress. *The Constant Couple* comically addresses woman's plight—a theme which, along with its patriotic and anti-Papist sentiments, contributed significantly to the acceptance of Sir Harry Wildair as a credible travesty role. *The Fair Penitent*'s Lothario in Woffington's hands was judged by many to be confusingly ironic rather than powerfully tragic, and her interpretation appeared somewhat perverse to a London audience, though less so to Dublin viewers. Characters originally written for a male actor and performed by an actress, or vice versa, united the rake and his beautiful prey, the victimizer and the victim, in the

Figure 13. "Mrs. Margaret Woffington." Mezzotint by John Faber, Jr., after Jon Giles Eccardt (1745). © National Portrait Gallery, London.

female body to expose discomfiture regarding sexual difference at a time when it was linked with emergent ideas of the nation. As we will see later in the chapter, Woffington's Lothario represented to English theater-goers a retrograde masculinity that did not correspond easily with the performative potential of a progressive wo/manhood, yet the two were held together, however tentatively, through the actress' cross-dressing as a man. These travestied roles, I suggest, interestingly complicate rather than marginalize women's participation in the public sphere and their significance to the theaters of Rich and Garrick.

As earlier chapters have shown, the eighteenth-century actress in performance embodied a kind of "nodal point" encompassing a whole range of cultural contradictions. The female body, in Sue-Ellen Case's apt characterization, may be regarded as "a site where contesting discourses converge, rather than as a site for a shared identification as 'women'."[4] This is nowhere more complexly demonstrated than in the cross-dressed figure, which is, Marjorie Garber contends, "a mode of articulation, a way of describing a space of possibility" rather than a stable category.[5] The spectacle of transvestitism, of man and woman together, neither one alone, often points toward other kinds of contradictions located elsewhere in the culture. Breeches parts on the Restoration and eighteenth-century stage differed from Renaissance roles. Shakespeare's men dressed in female clothing for parts such as Rosalind in *As You Like It* (the final role of Woffington's career), who then appeared as doubly cross-dressed men when the plot demanded it. In contrast, women acting breeches roles in male clothing appeared in 89 of the 375 plays performed on the Restoration stage between 1660 and 1700.[6] John Harold Wilson locates at least 14 more plays during that period in which women in travesty played parts written for male actors. In breeches parts the female figure of the actress is seductively revealed before the conclusion, often affording a peek at her breast or ankle. No such unveiling takes place in travestied parts: the woman's body underneath the man's clothing remains disguised even at the end of the play. While men in skirts roles hark back to the Renaissance past, women adopting men's roles was an entirely new phenomenon on the Restoration and eighteenth-century stage. Women decked out in "small clothes" rather than hooped petticoats, then, paradoxically figured as a modern, avant-garde moment in contrast to the earlier single-sex theater. In the progress of the play there is often an attempt to recuperate the cross-dressed woman into a stricter regulation of gender, and thus nostalgically to evoke an earlier time, while actresses in travestied dress consistently resisted close association with outdated assumptions about women and became instead harbingers of freedoms yet to come. In this chapter I examine several of Woffington's cross-dressed and travesty parts to illuminate the way the performance of gender was uneasily tethered to concepts of nation and religion circulating at mid-century, especially during the years surrounding the Jacobite threat to the Hanoverian monarchy.

The London theater in which Woffington performed was a place where women (and men) of all social backgrounds could be tutored in becoming political subjects. Though nationhood is more commonly the subject of tragedy than comedy, both genres may reflect upon the issue of strong loyalty to one's country; and perhaps surprisingly women—especially actresses dressed as men—exercised a critical function in that formation of patriotism.[7] As is well known, women were conceptualized by Enlightenment philosophers and historians as trustworthy barometers of the level of civilization in a given culture. Less frequently recognized is the way the figure of woman may encompass the incompatibility between countries (in this case England, Ireland, Scotland, and France), systems (religious, political, and economic), and temporalities (past, present, and future).[8] We might, then, reevaluate historian Kathleen Wilson's belief that in the mid-eighteenth century "the feminine had no place in the political imaginary of the nation-state at this crucial moment in its development."[9] In her cross-dressed and travestied roles, Woffington represented an edgy temporality, an anxious accommodation to modernity, and gestured back to the past even while pressing on toward the future.

The eighteenth century, in fact, witnessed the inaugural moment of historiography when "modern Western history essentially begins with differentiation between the *present* and the *past*,"[10] as Michel de Certeau reminds us. The cross-dressed actress comes to embody such a shift toward modernity in the public forum. If women sometimes figure as the "atavistic and authentic body of national tradition (inert, backward-looking and natural), embodying nationalism's conservative principle of continuity," in contrast to men's representation of a progressive nationalism, as Anne McClintock has suggested,[11] eighteenth-century actresses impersonating men may, arguably, be seen not only to personify the nation's history but also to embody the tensions between the continuity of the past and the uncertainty of the future. The cross-dressed actress, then, represents a zone of temporal and cultural encounter and reflects a plethora of political, religious, and sexual confusions. In fact, for the Irish Woffington, nation proved to be not an essence but an amalgamation of characteristics, resembling in its variety and excess the travestied characters she played, which allowed her to become in performance an exceptional representative of England in spite of her Irish roots.

Cross-Dressed Women

Peg Woffington's biographical history reveals that her character onstage and in public life, projected as an interiority effect, involved a complicated web of referents. Her gendered identity was confusingly signaled through her anatomy, costuming, and sexual reputation, but also through her identity as a private individual whose activities were closely monitored in the periodical press. There was conflation not only between the actress onstage and off, but also between the dramatic character and the new freedoms she embodied. Cross-dressing enables dramatic characters to merge and diverge from their private personalities and actual bodies over the course of the play; playing a man, even fleetingly, allows them to exercise greater mobility than most women, something that was easily conflated with actual actresses' greater access to public space than previous generations had possessed.

The cross-dressed Woffington, resonating with a cluster of real gender disguises at mid-century, could be regarded as a signifier of both political and sexual liberty. Actresses and other women masquerading as soldiers were perceived to be simultaneously erotic and patriotic, for sexual freedom paralleled other kinds of dangerous independence. Among the many examples, actress Charlotte Charke achieved greater mobility when cross-dressed in real life as Mr. Brown who cohabited with her "wife" Mrs. Brown; Mary Hamilton masqueraded as "the female husband," Dr. Charles Hamilton, but came to trial in 1746 for having married Mary Price; and Hannah Snell published her story as the female soldier in 1750. Even David Garrick's wife-to-be, Viennese dancer Eva Maria Violette, disguised herself as a man to enable her to travel by sea from Holland to Harwich in 1746.[12]

Breeches roles in the theater, in addition to increasing nightly receipts because of the audience's wish to admire women's curves in pants, facilitated a variety of plot consequences in which the disguised heroine pursues her elusive lover whom she serves incognito; or she may act as liaison to a rival mistress. In other examples, a cross-dressed actress, tinged with homoerotic overtones, becomes the mistaken love object of another woman.[13] A third category of cross-dressed figure is immediately recognizable as a woman: she wears male dress while remaining openly female in order to take up an occupation, such as a military officer, from which she is ordinarily restricted. Cross-dressed or travestied roles heighten attention to the constructedness of gender categories in the real world. As Elin Diamond put it, "When gender is alienated or foregrounded, the spectator is enabled to see a sign system *as* a sign system. The gender lexicon becomes so many illusionistic trappings to be put on or shed at will."[14]

It is no surprise, then, that moral conservatives at the turn into the eighteenth century imagined cross-dressing onstage and off to be a threat to God-given sexual difference.[15] Jeremy Collier, a nonjuring Anglican clergyman who had refused to pledge allegiance to William and Mary, and who evidenced strong Jacobite sympathies, asserted that clothing must correspond to anatomy. In *The Conduct of the Stage Consider'd* (1721), for example, Collier argued that apparel should not be exchanged between the sexes, even for seemingly harmless amusement. He wrote, "Men *putting on womens Apparel, and Women Mens apparel, as they do in the Masquerades, is a Practice condemned by Revelation, and the Light of Nature.* The Holy Scriptures tell us, *The Women shall not wear that which pertains to the Man, neither shall a Man put on a Woman's Garment; for all that do so are an Abomination to the Lord*: Deut.22.5 . . . . Nature has made difference not only between the Sexes, but between the Apparel of Men and Women."[16] In short, the heterodox cross-dressed figure represented an artificial difference that competed with nature. It was, then, a clever ploy to use the character of a cross-dressed woman to call anti-Jacobites to arms later in the century, as Woffington did, and as late as 1745 swapping gender, even in costuming, was regarded with suspicion in some quarters. A letter in the *Daily Advertiser* urged Charlotte Charke—who flagrantly dressed as a man in private life and played Macheath, George Barnwell, Lord Foppington, and Lothario in travesty—to resume playing female characters so as to appear in "her proper Sphere" by "laying aside the Hero," which Charke had justified as occasioned by a scarcity of actors.[17] Charke's equivocal sexuality offstage invaded her stage persona and became troublingly real.

The eighteenth-century audience's pleasure in cross-dressed roles, as many critics have argued, was aroused partly through its recognition that the character was in camouflage, and that the woman's body beneath the disguise could readily be distinguished. Indeed, Stephen Orgel believes that the whole point of Renaissance boys pretending to be women was that the audience could easily see through the impersonation to admire their budding masculine anatomy.[18] Many critics have argued similarly that in the Restoration and the eighteenth century the delicious ambiguity of breeches evoked pleasure because the woman's figure beneath the male disguise was satisfyingly perceptible.[19] Considering breeches roles in the eighteenth century Dror Wahrman, drawing on and extending Kristina Straub's arguments, has maintained that penetrating the disguise to make out the female anatomy beneath the clothing signaled a larger historical shift from an ancien régime belief in a flexible, constructed identity to a fixed, essential gender identity as man or woman.[20] But the steady historical progression from an unstable to a fixed gender identity at the end of the century is perhaps not as straightforward as Wahrman suggests, and in travesty roles no unveiling occurs.

Contemporary observers, for example, were quite divided in their opinions about the extent to which Peg Woffington succeeded in fooling the public into believing she was a man. Commentators like Thomas Davies thought that Woffington acted male parts perfectly and without a hint of femininity, while other observers, such as her manager, costar, and sometime lover David Garrick, maintained that she was indeterminately gendered as a sexual impersonator. Still others thought her acting as a man was so convincing it could teach male spectators proper gentlemanly conduct. In her cross-dressed theatrical roles at mid-century, Woffington by many accounts behaved as if she were a virile, heterosexual man; her interpretation of male characters was applauded for avoiding the excesses of femininity labeled "effeminate," a term best understood as men's exaggerated rendering of conventionally feminine mannerisms that regularly provoked satirical responses to foppish characters.

When Woffington impersonated a man, her effortlessness in inhabiting the parts, described as uninhibited and free, catapulted her to the top of her profession and established her reputation. Robert Hitchcock noted her natural ease in assuming a male character, for Woffington offered an "elegant portrait of the Young Man of Fashion in a stile perhaps beyond the author's warmest ideas" (1: 108). James Quin compared Woffington's breeches roles to Ned Kynaston's impersonation of female characters but preferred her rendering to the Restoration actor's because she was happily "dispossessed . . . of that aukward stiffness and effeminacy which so commonly attend the fair sex in breeches." He continues, "It was a most nice point to decide between the gentlemen and ladies, whether she was the finest woman, or the prettiest fellow."[21] In Quin's view, the would-be opposites became indistinguishable from one another rather than antipodal, and the androgynous middle ground suggests a blending that made it difficult to discern the female form beneath the male costume. Francis Gentleman, too, remarked on her admirable blending of the sexes when he writes that her deportment in travesty as Sir Harry Wildair was "free and elegant, whose figure was so proportionate and delicate."[22]

The "*raison d'etre*" for the breeches role rested "in the *imperfect* masculinity of the performer" (Rogers, "Breeches Part," 257), but many of Woffington's contemporaries strongly praised instead how "well made" she was as a "model of [male] perfection" without differentiating between breeches and travesty roles: "Indeed when she assumes ye man there is such a *freedom* in her air, such a Disengagement from ye woman, with ye happiness of Being perfectly well made, that it is by no means surprising that she has been followed with uncommon & universal applause."[23] In short, to stage a convincing man whether in breeches or travesty meant, for many viewers, that Woffington separated herself completely from the gestures associated with female form and persuasively affected the style and manners of a gentleman; for others it involved combining the sexes in a harmonious fashion.

As we shall see with reference to specific travesty or cross-dressed parts, Woffington represented the tensions for eighteenth-century Dublin and London audiences that Diana Taylor has found to be characteristic of modern identity with its "entangled surplus subjectivity, full of tugs, pressures, and pleasures."[24] Woffington's popular characterizations in male dress also legislated against the idea that national identity rested on strict sexual difference, though her studied affectation of robust masculinity may have countered the nation's fears of contamination from French effeminacy. Yet while her transvestite impersonations and speeches rejected effeminacy, they also ambiguously incorporated women, of a certain sort, into the definition of nation: in her public performance as a man or a cross-dressed woman, Peg Woffington refuted both the idea that women should remain exclusively within the private domain and the belief that the female sex was entirely peripheral to the nation's interests.

Woffington's surplus of identities in performance might be described, then, as creating a kind of value-added onto the commodity that she had become. That is, the incremental increase in her value as a result of the very marketable identity-effect she produced could be converted into an economic surplus that resulted in higher net receipts for herself and the theater. In short, her simulated identity is the commodity that Woffington purveyed through the gaps and fissures exposed in her cross-dressed and travestied roles. That surplus of identities, created not only through reiterative performances but also through the varied sexual, religious, and national alignments they evoked, proves to be an index to modernity and key to the aspects of her interiority effect that produced her value.

The Irish Catholic Woffington

Woffington would at first glance seem to be a more appropriate national icon for Ireland than for England. Rising from humble Irish Catholic origins and probably the daughter of a journeyman bricklayer and washerwoman, Woffington, we are told by the eighteenth-century Irish theater historian Robert Hitchcock indicates, was transformed into a "peculiar ornament of the drama, and favourite of the graces." James Quin praised her as truly "an original in her way," excelling in both comedy and tragedy.[25] In spite of her low beginnings, no one since Anne Oldfield, remarked Theophilus Cibber admiringly, had "shewn themselves so equal to Characters of an elevated Rank."[26] Well known for her tempestuous and ill-fated affair with David Garrick, she was a renowned actress in her own right who circulated in the highest circles and was, Hitchcock reports, "able to set the fashions, prescribe laws to taste; and beyond any of her time, present us with a lively picture of the easy, well-bred woman of fashion."[27] Like the other high-salaried female players of her time, in real life she affected the manners of women of quality and the conspicuous consumption of a wealthy woman. Reputation attached itself to her modish clothing, and she dictated from the stage what was in vogue, having famously lent her fashionable gowns to the marriageable Gunning sisters in order to encourage their suitors. Because of her painstaking self-instruction in learning to imitate the mannerisms of a superior social standing when acting as would-be fine ladies such as Lady Modish or Lady Townly, Woffington was, like Oldfield and Clive, reputed to display "the Deportment of a Woman of Quality."[28] Her ability in this regard was so extraordinary that male actors playing roles as fine gentlemen were enjoined to mimic the actress's elevated bearing as a cross-dressed man.

Whether playing Sir Harry Wildair or fashionable ladies, Woffington conveyed the distinction to which she was not born, making her skills appear natural and easy, even though she had painstakingly instructed herself in the mannerisms of a superior social class. Theophilus Cibber wrote that "She manages her Voice with great Skill, which has not that Silver Tone some possess, who, notwithstanding that natural Advantage, frequently offend your Ear with uncouth Vulgarisms," and she managed to affect politeness, delicacy, and naturalness (*Romeo and Juliet*, 104). The few complaints against her shrill and dissonant voice may reflect English attitudes toward her possessing a slight Irish brogue or inflexion, though George Faulkner in the *Dublin*

Journal definitively found that "her correct pronunciation is accompanied by the most just and graceful action," along with ease, vivacity, nature, and art.[29] Ventriloquating a woman of quality meant consistently employing cultivated speech and refined gestures, and making fine distinctions over a wide range of characters. These real and imagined identities intermingled onstage and off.

Woffington's zest for the work of acting was legendary. Theater historians tell us that she performed six nights a week, acting even when ill in the numerous plays and benefits in which she starred. In addition, Woffington spoke the epilogues to several dozen plays, delivering some in her own person and others in boy's clothes, beginning from the 1742–43 season when she first recited Thomas Cooke's epilogue on Shakespeare's women characters and extending until she delivered her last epilogue in 1757 as she suffered death throes.[30] It was a clear mark of Woffington's favored stature and commercial drawing power, as it was for other featured actresses, that she was regularly assigned epilogues to recite, most of which were written especially for her. Because prologues and epilogues were "the most difficult Tasks of both Sexes on the Stage, it is to be remark'd but few besides the Capital Performers are trusted with them," according to William Chetwood.[31] These paratexts frequently drew explicit attention to sexual difference within the audience, as the actress called out in turn to the ladies or modern wives, and to young gentlemen or wandering husbands even when the speaker was cross-dressed.

While Woffington's remarkable dramatic talent when acting as a male or female character is uncontested, her political influence has been much disparaged by those who claim she was merely a convenient auditor and occasional mistress to those who wielded political power, especially in Ireland. In contrast to the native Irish Catholics, the Anglo-Irish were, as is well known, those English Protestants who emigrated to Ireland in search of improving their economic situation: together with the Irish who had converted from Catholicism, they were known as the Irish ascendancy—the landed gentry, military, clerical, and professional persons who ultimately formed the new Anglo-Irish aristocratic ruling party, dominating the Irish Catholic majority.[32] At the same time, however, the English who had not emigrated sometimes regarded their fellow countrymen in Ireland, the Anglo-Irish, with condescension, and theater manager Sheridan's loyalties reportedly favored the ruling Anglo-Irish ascendancy in Dublin Castle over the native Irish. Sheridan was widely believed to side with the Government to which he was indebted for his job, rather than the Nationalists,[33] and Woffington's purported sympathies for Sheridan's party made her the object of attack as well.

Woffington remained on good terms with the ruling Anglo-Irish Protestants, including the local authority, the Lord Lieutenant, Lionel Sackville, Duke of Dorset; a December 1751 poem capitalized on a rumored affair in suggesting that she should claim an annual kiss from him instead of a pension. A favorite of the Lord Lieutenant, Woffington was supposedly the only woman invited to the weekly Beefsteak Club dinners (founded in 1745) in Sheridan's home, where his leading actors could share close social contact with eminent patrons of the playhouse. In fact, the same gorgeous Woffington who had nearly paralyzed theater manager and harlequin actor Rich with her womanly beauty was regarded by Charles Macklin's biographer to be "*more like a man than a woman.*"[34] Woffington developed a reputation that embraced being both an elegant, fashionable woman and a lusty drinking companion: she possessed, Benjamin Victor underhandedly remarks, "captivating Charms, as a jovial, witty, Bottle-Companion, but very few remaining as a mere Female."[35] Woffington's heading the table made her, in this regard, both an honorary man—as if her Sir Harry Wildair persona could be taken to be real—and a kind of whorish mascot. Clubs of this nature also raised money for patriotic purposes, whether English or Anglo-Irish. According to Benjamin Victor (though his testimony is not altogether reliable), such clubs were fixtures of every theater.[36] Victor had hoped that they would serve as vetting bodies for theater performances but also might align themselves against the opposition in support of the theater manager. Sheridan's Dublin club was modeled after the "Sublime Society of Beefsteaks," founded in London by the same John Rich who had auditioned Woffington. Its purpose appears to have remained largely social, judging by James Boswell's proud testimony that in 1762 the London Beefsteak Club had met for thirty years in "a handsome room above the theatre" under the sign of "Beef and Liberty" to dine on bovine fare, and engage in raucous singing while drinking wine or punch.[37]

These gentlemen's clubs associated with the theaters gave prominent people an opportunity to socialize with select players and managers in an informal setting that was slightly more structured than the greenroom. Actors constituted important members of these groups that dined at the theater manager's expense, and as many as fifty or sixty authors and other notables, including members of Parliament, were invited guests (Victor, 1: 153–54). In addition to socializing at these meetings, Woffington would have been privy to debates concerning Irish politics even as she was the toast of Dublin's highest society.[38] These regular gatherings also would have afforded Woffington an informal education in political, economic, and military affairs.

The Irish Catholic members of the audience may well have been suspicious of Woffington's religious loyalties, a suspicion exacerbated by her close association with Sheridan.[39] As a young girl Woffington had been apprenticed to Mademoiselle Violante, an Italian gymnast and equilibrist, who "discovered" her at age twelve. Violante, both famous and feared, an "illustrious and dangerous female," was accused of being a Papist by the Dean of St. Patrick's, and Woffington was made guilty of papistry by association.[40] John O'Keeffe in his *Recollections* remembers her mother in Dublin as behaving in public as a social Catholic, and characterizes her as "a respectable looking old lady, in her short black velvet cloak with a deep rich fringe, a diamond ring, and small agate snuff-box." He continued, "She had got nothing to mind but going around the rounds of Catholic chapels and chatting with her neighbours."[41] Woffington supported her mother, who remained in Ireland, and arranged for her sister Mary (known as Polly) to be educated in a French convent school.

Woffington was, then, closely identified with Ireland, and theater advertisements exploited the connection between actress and country of origin as a commercial pull. For example, her character in *The Beggar's Opera* was billed as acted "After the Irish Manner"—the exact meaning of which we can only speculate. In her debut on the Irish stage around 1732 or 1733 she appeared as "the new Irish breeches sensation"; she first played Sir Harry Wildair in Irish Protestant Farquhar's *The Constant Couple* at Aungier Street in Dublin in April 1740. Woffington traveled back and forth across the Irish Sea on many occasions, and she successfully moved the transvestite role to London in November of the same year. Having convinced Rich to hire her, she performed the part at least fifteen times at Covent Garden. Acting on the London stage as Silvia in Farquhar's *The Recruiting Officer* on 6 November 1740, she returned to Dublin in 1742 with her lover Garrick for the summer season.

Especially in Catholic countries, women could be taken to be metonyms for the theater itself, and an England that was becoming more definitively Protestant and anti-Jacobite by the time of Woffington's London performances would have disdained the theatrical properties of Catholic ritual. Perhaps there played in the minds of English Protestants an association between Catholicism's theatricality and the conspicuous display of the female body in the playhouse and public arenas.[42] More than a century before actresses appeared on the legitimate stage in England, as we have seen, women had acted female roles in the theaters of the Catholic countries of France, Spain, and Italy. When Charles II, himself a Catholic, initiated in 1660 the practice of women playing in the theater, his importing actresses from France where they had mounted the stage from the early seventeenth century may have been evoked during the 1745 Jacobite threat as part of the nation's cultural memory. In any case, on the London stage the Irish Woffington, cross-dressing as an English soldier and articulating English sympathies, aimed her performance in several popular plays and especially a series of epilogues, toward distancing herself from Ireland, Catholicism, Jacobitism, *and* traditional femininity.[43] While her Irishness may have been a commercial asset at times, when the English theater became preoccupied with anti-Catholic plays around 1745, reflecting worries about the threat of Stuarts returning to the throne, Woffington's Catholicism may then have become somewhat problematic. Many of her characters in performance supported a Protestant Britain that was actively engaged in colonial wars, though she continued to be regarded by many as a native Catholic Irishwoman.

The linkage of Woffington to Catholicism in the popular imagination was made quite explicit in the racy, anonymous, and largely apocryphal *Memoirs of the Celebrated Mrs. Woffington* (1760), which positioned her as a beguiling celebrated personage, but a whore nevertheless. The memoir, reaching a second edition in the year of its first publication, charged the actress with loose sexual behavior, and an alleged avariciousness that resembled "a certain Church, who never refuses the Petitions of those who entreat Favours with a full Hand" (*Memoirs*, 54). A satire on the Catholic Church as well as the actress, it asserted that Woffington liberally granted clemency to those who worshipped in the playhouse. A country squire seeking her favors, enthralled by her performance on stage, had behaved as a worshipper would before an idol, and "threw the Wages of Love in her Lap . . . inspiring him with boldness, as he imagined that the Gold Supplicants it contained, would purchase Absolution" (54). At first rejecting the purse, like the corrupt Catholic Church the actress soon finds herself transported on hearing the chink of money, and she yields to the squire's seduction. The description of their liaison then becomes obscured by Shandean asterisks, punctuated with cryptic ellipses and euphoric ejaculations such as "Extatic Joys" and "Love's *Elysium*" (56). In short, the satirical biography portrays Woffington as a crass materialist and a whore of Babylon, but the narrative eventually evolves into a conversion narrative in which she reforms and turns her back on the stage. At the end of her life "she resolved to become a new Creature" (58) by leaving her lovers, attending church, and associating only with virtuous people. Finally, the memoir elaborates on her generosity to her family. At the end of her life she is described as Christian rather than Catholic, seeming to erase the connection of the theater with the papacy, and positioning her—in the tradition of other actresses' memoirs discussed earlier—as someone whose exceptional virtue, liberally interpreted, absolved her from an early reputation for sexual looseness.

Woffington's Catholicism was apparently not sufficiently ingrained to prevent a late, convenient conversion to the Church of Ireland when she allegedly recanted her Catholicism at Quilca, Sheridan's estate. There Woffington renounced "the Errors of the church of Rome" on 30 January 1753, according to the *Gray's Inn Journal*, which announced that professional reasons motivated Woffington's change of heart "in order to qualify herself to wear a Sword in the Characters of Sir *Harry Wildair* and *Lothario*; which she could not safely attempt as a Papist" for Catholics were forbidden to wear swords.[44] A more likely explanation is that she wished to qualify to receive a substantial sum left to her by Owen MacSwinny, former manager of the Haymarket Theatre, in a will dated 1 August 1752.[45] Her newfound Protestantism thus realigned her with Sheridan, and it was during this time that she was believed to have become president of the all-male Beefsteak Society in Dublin.

Woffington thus defied easy categorization by national, religious, and gender affiliation at the very time when the English Protestant nation was taking its modern shape, and she exemplified the complex private and public subjectivity that could accommodate these kinds of differences. Many of her acting parts during this period of time, just before and after the rebellion, aligned her with English rather than Irish interests, including her roles in *The Female Officer* and *The Recruiting Officer*, but the Irish Woffington would have seemed a somewhat surprising tool to arouse an apathetic and divided English populace against the Jacobites' advance from July to December 1745. Whether dressed as a man or acting in her own person, while scrambling the audiences' assumptions about gender, Woffington enticed the English nation to take up arms and incited various audiences to patriotic fervor, as if to reassure British audiences of the insignificance of religion in ensuring Irish loyalty to the crown.

The Actress as Nation

The role of the theater in the invention of a military and imperial nation and its emerging definition as "Protestant, commercial, maritime, and free" is only beginning to be told.[46] Peg Woffington came to the stage well after the earlier Stuart invasions in 1708 and 1715, but her activities in the theater figure very significantly in relation to the 1745 threat. Why was the English nation, a relatively new concept at mid-century, frequently represented in the figure of a comic cross-dressed woman? Why, when Anglican clergyman John Brown's *Estimate of the Manners and Principles of the Time* called England "a Nation which *resembles Women*," would theater audiences warm to Woffington's cross-dressed portrayal of a civilian recruit?[47] John Brown's comments linking England's weakness to effeminacy were, of course, unsympathetic to women, but at the same historical moment, the actress masquerading as a female volunteer enlisted women in patriotic acts and offered them potential agency.[48] At the same time that England's body politic was increasingly portrayed in popular pamphlets as corrupt and emasculated, the figure of a female soldier, most prominently represented in the person of Woffington, served as a rallying point for patriotism. Volunteers were widely recruited to defend the Hanoverian king against the Catholic pretender, and Woffington's performances responded to the urgent need for citizen volunteers to defend London against the encroaching Jacobites who were closely identified with the French and other foreign powers. Such petitions "were designed to show that the Hanoverian dynasty rested on the active consent of its subjects," according to Linda Colley (*Britons*, 81), though the reasons for citizens joining up may have had as much to do with regional loyalties and economic necessity as with national pride. The sexual ambiguity of the cross-dressed woman became closely aligned with the concept of a patriotic England that, united with Scotland in 1707, would become triumphant over Jacobitism and the contamination of Catholicism.

During the Jacobite crisis of the mid-1740s, Woffington recited several comic but unquestionably patriotic epilogues at Drury Lane that reinforced, with the apparent backing of the manager and the dramatists, her credentials as a legitimate spokesperson for the Hanoverians.[49] They included especially "The Female Volunteer "(c. February 1746), but she also recited epilogues that followed William Havard's *Regulus* (21 February 1744, written by Garrick), James Ralph's *The Astrologer* (3 April 1744, written by Garrick), *The Non-Juror* (22 October 1745); Macklin's *King Henry the VII; or, The Popish Imposter* (18 January 1746), Farquhar's *The Constant Couple* (12 December 1746[?]), an epilogue "in Man's clothes" delivered at least twice in 1747, and the prologue to Hill's adaptation of Shakespeare, *Harry the Fifth* (2 August 1744). Woffington's performances in these many epilogues raise the question as to whether the decision to portray herself as an English loyalist was principally hers, based on commercial interests, or whether her managers encouraged her to perform such roles to make less tidy and legible the political impact of her personal affiliations. Theater managers assigned epilogues to popular actresses who urged audiences to spread favorable reports of the play to their friends. As we have seen, the epilogues often spoke directly to contemporary affairs; they distinguished the current moment from the historical setting of the play and jokingly applied its "lessons" to the audience. Woffington, competing for the audience's favor with fellow actresses Clive, Cibber, and Pritchard, assured her listeners in various ways that she was a loyal patriot. Her specifically political epilogues came to an end when, in January 1749, speaking as Venturia at Covent Garden after James Thomson's *Coriolanus*, she disavowed politics and simultaneously chastised the male members of the audience for their attitudes toward women. In that epilogue she announced that she "will not interfere / in State-Affairs, nor undertake to steer / the Helm of Government," having returned "to my own Shape again" (Danchin, pt. 3, 5: 296).[50]

As a man-woman bursting with excess subjectivity, Woffington embodied a break with the past, a movement toward modern British nationhood, and a prefiguring of a nation that promised new opportunities for women as part of its proud self-definition. In her cross-dressed state Woffington pressed toward greater freedoms while calling to mind ancient values: she represented modernity's "double movement of . . . simultaneous promise and withholding," as Homi Bhabha characterized the narration of nation.[51] In her epilogue to the tragedy *Regulus*, for example, she chided the audience to emulate the eponymous classical hero who died for his country: "Our Patriots huff, 'tis true, and rant and roar, / And talk of this and that—but nothing more" (pt. 3, 5: 154). Beginning by mocking Roman women for their old-fashioned fidelity to roaming husbands and discouraging modern women from adopting such outdated values, the epilogue concludes by urging Britons to steadily practice Roman values of national loyalty in the now: "*Romans* at Sixty-three, as I'm alive, / Were better Men than ours at thirty-five" (155). In this jesting manner Woffington identified her speaking character and her own person more closely with British patriotism rather than with Irish insurrection, Jacobite rebellion, or a more generalized foreignness. Presenting herself as a kind of honorary Englishwoman in breeches, she obliterated Irish difference and aligned herself with freedom-loving female spectators in the theatrical present.

Similarly, in the anti-Papist epilogue to *King Henry the VII*, Irish playwright Charles Macklin brings the moment of performance into Britain's recent past to celebrate its liberties. Woffington, speaking as Lady Catherine Gordon, who possesses "a manly Heart" within a "female Form," announces that she wishes to be released from her Romish marriage vows to Prince Hal to seek a "British born" spouse: "That I my self, equip'd in Cap and Jerkin, / Am every whit as good a Prince as *Perkin*" (pt. 3, 5: 214). Similarly, in Garrick's epilogue to *The Astrologer* she diminishes the temporal distance of the play, that of Shakespeare and Jonson, from current history (pt. 3, 5: 159–60). Carrying over her role as Laetitia into the epilogue, Woffington adopts the patriot's voice in reinforcing British morals rather than French ones, to unite England and Ireland against a foreign power.

The contradictions made visible within these gender-bending, nationalist representations operate on several other levels as well. Woffington's reputed Irish Catholicism would surely have complicated the audience's reaction to her scolding the English forces for their weak-kneed response to attack. Speaking in her best-known part as "The Female Volunteer: Or An Attempt to make our Men *Stand*," Woffington claimed to defend "my Country's Cause" (pt. 3, 5: 215), meaning England, but the irony of an Irish Catholic woman speaking as an English Protestant in drag would have been palpable.[52] Adopting the role of a coquettish female in breeches who does not wish to confess her sins, she called for the formation of an army of truly patriotic women. Apparently speaking against her own beliefs, she complained that the present forces quivered while "We Women have strong Reason / To stop the Progress of this Popish Treason" (216). The epilogue is also a salacious call to women in the audience to "take the *Thing* in *hand*" (215) and cut loose from deserters. British beauties will salvage British rights and inspire men to their duties. Thus, in the epilogue, the Catholic Woffington, the "impudent Irish-faced girl" (as Henry Seymour Conway once described her to Walpole),[53] speaks as a patriotic Briton who calls English women to fight against the Jacobites.

The bawdy piece was probably spoken on 17 and 20 March 1746 after Beaumont and Fletcher's popular *The Scornful Lady*, in which Woffington played a female role, and on 22 March 1746 after *The Merchant of Venice*. It was also very likely delivered at Drury Lane after *The Lady's Last Stake*, 10 April 1746, "recommended the cause of Liberty to the Ladies of Great Britain."[54] As a woman in drag, Woffington represented a troublingly enticing sign of the future, yet her stage body evoked the most traditional of referents. The epilogue presents an account of the Jacobite victory at Falkirk, 17 January 1746, originally reported in the *Gazette*, against the king's forces led by Hawley. The Female Volunteer, a mercenary recruit, affects surprise and dismay that "our men," meaning the English soldiers, retreated before the Scots banditti. Having the cross-dressed Woffington speak these words would have heightened the erotic charge arising from the military victory of the Scots rebels, while mocking the impotence of the defeated English forces as part of a larger cultural scenario in which the virility of the English soldier was questioned.[55] Woffington's cross-dressed disguise combines both the "masculine" British culture and the "effeminate" French, as if to reassuringly incorporate yet quash the enemy within. Her performance implies that women may ironically perform masculinity better than men themselves.

The female soldier, then, became a patriotic English icon, even though the sentiments were recited by an Irish Catholic actress. The Female Volunteer was obviously a woman dressed in men's clothes, unlike the breeches or burlesque roles in which Woffington's femininity was purposely obscured, thus maintaining aspects of sexual difference even as they were called into question. Though a *female* volunteer, she claims that she accepts a man's duty to fight more readily than her fellow countrymen. The well-known engraving accompanying the printed epilogue of the Female Volunteer signifies manliness of a certain sort, though the female anatomy beneath can be discerned (Figure 14). As a "Kevenhuller'd Volunteer" she was jauntily clad in a waistcoat, a cravat, breeches, white stockings to the knees, and a cocked hat. The Covent Garden account book in the Folger Library indicates that a fashionable embroidered waistcoat costing £12 was designed for Woffington on 6 November 1740, the date she debuted as Silvia in *The Recruiting Officer* (Folger MS W.a.94). It is plausible that the waistcoat may have traveled from Silvia (1740) to Wildair (1740), on to the Female Volunteer epilogue (1746), and then to the heroine of the play, *The Female Officer* (1763), to further align her cross-dressed roles, this time through costuming, in the minds of the audience and to lock in the association of cross-dressing with Woffington's person. The outfit was regarded as thoroughly stylish in its first appearance: "The very suit which Peg Woffington wore as Sir Harry Wildair was some forty years after used to dress Foresight, the ridiculous judicial-astrologer, in Congreve's *Love for Love*. In its prime, Peg Woffington's costume was the height of modern elegance; while in its threadbare days, it was still retained as the contemporary garb of an out-of-date clown."[56] The costume would seem thus to store the theatrical memories within it and transmit them to a later generation of playgoers.

The waistcoat worn for the Female Volunteer epilogue is pictured as cutaway to reveal the thighs, but it is not as severely cropped as would become stylish later in the century; it is opened asymmetrically as if to avoid revealing the uncertain nature of the crotch. Woffington's hands are small and graceful, her expression alert and accessible, her hair gently framing her attractive face,

Figure 14. *The Female Volunteer: Or, an Attempt to Make Our Men Stand* (1746).

her breasts a little full, and her hips slightly wider than is manly. In one sense she represents an exemplary man, while in another she is almost a woman. The engraving also shows Woffington's sword traversing her back—representing perhaps a phallus manqué—pointing downward in the direction of the comic mask thrown on the stage floor along with the *Gazette*'s printed account of the battle tossed aside. The mask and frock hanging behind to the left emphasize the performative element of the soldier's clothing with Woffington's stays and hat cast aside nearby, a draped curtain at the corner and the hint of a proscenium just visible.

As the history of costuming makes clear, breeches onstage and off were increasingly exposed to view as the century progressed. From appearing "almost invisible at the beginning of the century," breeches "were gradually revealed by the shortening of the waistcoat and the backward movement of the coat and were cut high to meet the rising line of the waistcoat. With this emergence of the breeches from obscurity, a flap or fall-front was added to cover the vertical front fastening, sometimes made as a narrow central section, sometimes extending from seam to seam over the whole of the front."[57] One can clearly see this shift between the 1745 illustration of Woffington as the Female Volunteer and the 1777 picture of Ann Spranger Barry dressed in travesty as Sir Harry Wildair (Figure 15). Barry's stalwart stance is more typically masculine, and the shortened waistcoat is parted to reveal an apparent bulge in the crotch. Her breasts seem flattened, and she faces in the direction opposite to the full-length portrait of a woman standing behind, thus suggesting the self-aggrandizing convention of posing before one's own portrait.[58] The knees and thighs, however, are more fully revealed because the cutaway waistcoat and coat are flung back. Thus, the tension between Barry's femininity and masculinity is made external to her body to contrast her travestied character to the portrait of womanhood behind.

The Female Volunteer epilogue inspired a satirical response, *A Soldier's Letter to the Female Volunteer: Being an Earnest Request to Hang up the Hat, and Pull off the Breeches*,[59] that defends English soldiers against the Female Volunteer's jests at their masculinity. Women's claims to liberty, the soldier maintains, are merely shameless excuses to gain sexual freedom. As in the title to the engraving and the epilogue, "standing" army becomes a bawdy pun, and ribald allusions entreat the English soldiers to infect the homosexually inclined rebels with the clap as an act of patriotism. The pamphlet also, significantly, taunts Woffington for her disingenuous performance of arguments against popery. Women friendly to papistry are scoffingly told that they

Figure 15. "Mrs. Barry as Sir Harry Wildair." Frontispiece, *The Constant Couple* (1777), Act 2.2. Courtesy of Lewis Walpole Library, Yale University.

should be confined to a nunnery where they would be literally priest-ridden. The lurid conclusion urges the rebels to enter the "breach" of women where they will contract venereal disease. Finally, the *Letter* tells the female volunteer to abandon her breeches, for petticoats would afford a better barrier against "rebellious Members" (4). Woman's agency in battling Jacobitism is dismissed as potential sexual contamination rather than genuine patriotism. Instructed to re-feminize themselves by hanging up their hats and removing their trousers, they are being coaxed to return to more easily managed forms of docile femininity rather than continuing the destructive tactics of sabotage and seduction ascribed to them.

The trope of women transmitting sexual diseases was taken up again in *A Guide to the Stage* (1751) where the epithet applied to Woffington, "pretty Peggy Wildair," combined both sexes. Like the epilogue and the response it provoked, this later tract similarly maligns the actress by claiming that she, rather than the Jacobites, lures the audience "into a clap," and the double entendre implies that their applause exposes them to infection.[60] In short, in the patriotic epilogues at mid-century, Woffington created a doubly vexing gendered persona that advocated national interests but also implied a critique in exposing through sexual impersonation the nation's uncertain and vulnerable nature. Animating a repertoire of cultural practices that came to align her person with that nascent identity, Woffington—figured as a man-woman, Irish-English, Catholic-Protestant—performed the nation as a series of contradictions but called for unity in resisting the threats to its body politic.[61] Claiming patriotism, she pleaded for a unified country, yoking England to Scotland but further marginalizing Ireland.[62]

In yet another epilogue, probably spoken after *The Non-Juror* (22 October 1745 [?]), Woffington took on the character of Britannia, impersonating a united nation in spite of its civil division; with hair streaming from her helmet and carrying a spear, she again melded both sexes together. Rather than commissioning the extravagant £30 costume she preferred, Benjamin Victor had coached her to appear as feminine and to economize by wearing "a small pasteboard helmet, silvered, with a plume or feather, of what colour you please, the hair long and flowing, a large full silk robe, either white or red, and a spear for one hand, nothing in the other, because the speaker would appear ungraceful to have both hands encumbered."[63] As Britannia she exemplified English freedom in contrast to slavery in "fetter'd Europe" (pt. 3, 5: 200), thus pointing the finger most directly at the French. She adopts the English Protestant position against the Pretender whom she called "a vile Banditti [sic] from the Church of Rome" (200) to dissociate her Irish Catholicism from both Scottish and French Jacobitism. Her own Irish Catholicism thus rested uneasily in an antiPapist character that mocked the authority of Rome; she celebrated political union with Scotland but critiqued its festering Jacobitism; and mocked the (Catholic) "henpeck'd" (202) effeminate French while looking to France for the newest fashions.

In addition to the epilogues, Woffington extended her success in celebrated breeches roles in plays and afterpieces. In *The Female Officer, or the Humours of the Army*, revived in the 1740s in response to the Jacobite rebellion, the character Charlot dresses as a soldier, a "pretty pert young Fellow," to follow her beloved Wilmot who joined the English army fighting in Portugal because of her cruel rejection of him.[64] Sporting a soldier's uniform, Charlot affects masculinity with military airs, tough talk, chewing tobacco, and taking snuff. Her sword is lewdly compared to a phallus, for "the longest Sword must decide" (2.1) who is to be her commanding officer.[65] Charlot serves as the successful go-between for the Irish Major Buck and Victoria, but she is also re-anchored to femininity when she weds Wilmot after he is acquitted in a final-act court martial.

The anti-papist comedy plays off national stereotypes while claiming to foster British unity in the Female Officer who ultimately reveals herself to be a woman. Fighting the Spanish near Estremoz and Elvas, the British army intends "to support the *Portuguese* against Arbitrary Power and Popery, and to maintain them in Liberty and Property and so forth" (4.1). Though weak and cowardly, more interested in gossip and fashion than fighting, the soldiers regard themselves as morally superior to the Portuguese Catholics: "the honest *Englishman* makes a Friendship with all Mankind" (1.1). In the play, Britain's peace seems to rest upon the restitution of traditional sexual difference and marriage. Though Woffington's character in *The Female Officer* is situated on the boundaries between nations, regions, dialects, and sexes, the cross-dressed female—having ventured tentatively into a war, another country, another sex, and a future as a female officer—ultimately retreats into traditional values. Separated from home by war, she finally signifies a return to its domesticity and stability; the revolutionary potential of her disguise, although it is reiterated in her person and in subsequent performances, is nightly disarmed.

The Recruiting Officer

Woffington's role as the cross-dressed Silvia in Farquhar's *The Recruiting Officer*, just as in the epilogues and *The Female Officer*, drew together within her onstage body a union of England and Ireland, and we might linger over that play before turning to her travesty roles. The popular play first opened at Drury Lane, 8 April 1706, and from 1740–50 alone it saw well in excess of one hundred performances. In the plot when Silvia, because of her brother's assumed death, becomes heir to the family's fortune her father determines that her love interest, the recruiting officer Captain Plume, is insufficiently worthy. To win Plume's heart, she dons breeches to enlist as a recruit in his regiment and, cross-dressed, pleads her case before her father, Justice Balance. When Woffington first appeared in 1740 as Silvia in petticoats, the men in the audience were impassioned, while female spectators were enraged with jealousy. When she changed to breeches, the men were *envious* of her ability to combine "*the pretty fellow and the rake complete*," while the women fell in love with him/her.⁶⁶ This purportedly ambiguous response with both sexes doubly magnetized by her performance suggests, however, a division between them: men adored the woman in petticoats and envied the rake, while women were desirous of the "man" in breeches and jealous of the beautiful Sylvia. At the same time, both sexes' reactions hint at homoerotic desire as well, suggesting that men wished to emulate Sylvia in breeches and women were sexually aroused by someone of their own sex.

In *The Recruiting Officer* as in *The Constant Couple*, cross-dressing provides a contact zone where past and present as well as the sexes meet. The prologue, for example, speaks first of classical history when men—not women—cross-dressed for political reasons, and wars were fought to restore women to their rightful proprietors. The original recruiting officer, according to the prologue, was Ulysses; and his most famous recruit was Achilles who, enlisting in skirts in the Grecian cause to rescue Helen of Troy from the Trojans, aligns patriotism with cross-dressing.⁶⁷ The beautiful but whorish Helen, whose "*fatal Charms*" led to her abduction and "*Rous'd the contending Universe to Arms*" (2: 39), thus spawning the Trojan War, foreshadows the incompatibility between countries that Woffington as Sylvia in breeches represented.

The play evolves temporally from the prologue's ancient tales to the epilogue's timely appeal that the ladies in the audience should encourage volunteer soldiers to fight the Jacobites.⁶⁸ The classical past echoes throughout the play with its references to femmes fatales Helen and Cleopatra, but also to modern matrons such as Queen Anne whose face circulated on British currency.⁶⁹ *The Recruiting Officer* accompanies its allusions to recent Allied military victories against France in the War of Spanish Succession with the *Grenadier March*, the rousing tune especially appropriate to "the genius of the English" designed to attract recruits.⁷⁰ In contrast to the prologue's historical setting, the topical epilogue refers urges spectators to return to the play the following night.

The son of an Irish Protestant clergyman, playwright Farquhar had personally recruited Irish troops for service in the English wars, and there is critical disagreement about the extent to which *The Recruiting Officer* satirizes those wars or whether it more broadly derides violence. The War of Spanish Succession, like all wars, threatens the retention of body parts, and the play reveals that the toll on bodies may be severe. The very real prospect of amputation produces obscene jokes at several points in the play. Balance remarks that he would willingly have forfeited one of his "legs" to seduce a country gentleman's daughter. When enlisting a butcher, Kite disguised as a fortune-teller forecasts that his carving skills will prove to be handy in amputating an officer's leg in Flanders. Cupid on crutches and the disabled Vulcan, hobbled divine lovers, defy their disability through romance. Captain Plume glories in the fact that he had survived battles in Germany without having forfeited any limbs. In the final act of the play he congratulates himself on maintaining his corporeal integrity but ironically loses his bachelor freedom. In resigning his commission and marrying Silvia, Plume laments that he had "sav'd my Legs and Arms and lost my Liberty" (5.7.90–91).

Silvia's character similarly reflects tensions between the whole body, this time a womanly one, and its parts in love and war. War threatens to alter the flesh, but Silvia retains her womanly self; the play suggests that female anatomy is at risk in another way, whether she wears breeches or petticoats. Transforming herself into Captain Pinch to appear before her father Justice Balance, "a red Coat, a Sword, a Hat *bien troussee*, a Martial Twist in my Cravat, a fierce Knot in my Perriwig, a Cane upon my Button, Picket in my Head, and Dice in my Pocket" mark her masculinity (5.2.65–67). If recruited into war when dressed as a man, Silvia will metaphorically relinquish proper femininity, but far more significantly risk losing her life. If recruited into marriage, she will give up a body part, her hymen; and in surrendering her virginity, her freedom would be forfeited to her husband. In the final act, anatomy rather than clothing ultimately defines "woman," and like *The*

Female Officer, the play recoils from the potential modernity that it both threatens and promises to women.

Most importantly, Silvia complains that she is weary of the limitations that her sex imposes on her—a common complaint of eighteenth-century actresses that Woffington would have delivered forcefully. Silvia equates wearing petticoats, a useless accessory, with being worthless. Her cousin Melinda interprets her discomfort as a malady inherent in being a woman: "That is, you are tir'd of an Appendix to our Sex, that you can't so handsomly get rid of in Petticoats as if you were in Breeches—O' my Conscience, *Silvia*, hadst thou been a Man, thou hast been the greatest Rake in *Christendom*" (1.2.58–61), words that were interpreted as censurably risqué by at least one eighteenth-century commentator.[71] While an appendix is of course a nonessential body part, supplementary matter that is not essential, an "outgrowth or appendage attached as if hung on" (Oxford English Dictionary), it may also be an ornamental addition that resonates with the phallic. At the same time, the term "appendix" signifies for Melinda and Sylvia that a proper femininity depends upon wearing feminine apparel. By giving up this appendage, a woman paradoxically becomes a man, thus seeming to amputate an element of her social identity when she cross-dresses. The "appendix" may also signify women's sexual virtue or virginity itself, something that can be removed, broken, or lopped off rather than something integral to female anatomy or demeanor. "Appendix" thus refers to (sexual) anatomy, but it also refers to gendered behavior that can be put on or taken off along with articles of clothing.

Yet one more meaning of "appendix" may be relevant here. Samuel Johnson's definition in his *Dictionary* (1755) features a citation from *Hale's Civil Law of England* that describes Normandy as "an *appendix* to England, the nobler dominion." Thus, we might speculate that Silvia's tiring of being merely an adjunct to men rather than a man herself may also mirror Ireland's situation vis-à-vis England. Cross-dressing allows Silvia/Woffington to assume a more central role in the future of her nation, however compromised that role, or that nation, might be. In marrying Plume, she relinquishes a body part and her freedom as a woman, and she even hints at her subjugation as that country's representative. The play is, then, a somewhat bittersweet romantic comedy that, in Woffington's performance of its rich surplus of ambiguities, exposes through its cross-dressed female soldier, the restrictions imposed by sexual difference and the complicated relationship between England and Ireland. That role, like the epilogues designed for her, was perfectly suited to the national and sexual identities attached to Peg Woffington both as actress and as private person.

Travesty Roles: Sir Harry Wildair and Lothario

Woffington initiated the transformation of Sir Harry Wildair into a travesty role, though the lead part was first created for the Irish actor and manager Robert Wilks. Farquhar's *The Constant Couple; or, a Trip to the Jubilee* was almost certainly the most popular new play in the early eighteenth century until the *Beggar's Opera* in 1728. The comedy debuted on 28 November 1699 (perhaps a year after the playwright and actor arrived in London from Dublin) starring the Irish Wilks as the antihero and Susannah Verbruggen as Lady Lurewell.[72] Sir Harry Wildair's politics were believed to correspond to Wilks's Williamite sentiments, and the dedication to the play reiterates those political views. Posing in the preface to the reader as a stranger to England, Farquhar dedicates *The Constant Couple* to a Protestant "fine *English* Gentleman, with the noble Solidity of the antient *Britton*."[73] It played fity-three nights in its first London season, twenty-three in Dublin, and it was published on 11 December of the same year. A second revised edition (1 February 1700) offered a less sentimental resolution of the plot, followed by a third edition with a new prologue on 20 August, and a fourth edition in 1704. Farquhar himself acted in a benefit performance of the play in Dublin around March 1704.[74]

After triumphing as Wildair in Ireland (25 April 1740), Woffington performed the role on the London stage (6 November 1740) a few months after she had debuted as Silvia in the *Recruiting Officer* and following several early attempts at Lady Lurewell. The travesty role offered her the opportunity to play an incontrovertibly central character rather than being consigned to a secondary role because of competition from accomplished actresses in the company; the abundance of female talent may also explain her wish to take on the role of the seductive libertine Lothario in *The Fair Penitent*. Having performed in *The Constant Couple* for fourteen seasons and appeared in a total of seventy-three performances as Wildair (*Works*, ed. Kenny 1.127), she acted the part fifteen times at Covent Garden in 1740. She reappeared as Wildair in Dublin in 1742, playing the young rake thirteen times at Smock Alley from 1745 to 1753, including a record-smashing season in 1751–52; and reviving the part in 1755 (Kenny, 1: 129). It was Woffington's natural style of acting a male role that engaged appreciative playgoers: "The Ease, Manner of Address, Vivacity, and Figure of a young Man of Fashion was never more happily exhibited" (Victor, *History*, 3: 3).

According to a much-repeated and almost certainly apocryphal anecdote first mentioned by William Chetwood, after her performance as Wildair, Woffington allegedly exclaimed, "*In my conscience! I believe Half the Men in the House take me for one of their own Sex.* Another Actress reply'd, *It may be so; but, in my Conscience! the other Half can convince them to the contrary.*"[75] This teasing exchange clearly compromises Woffington's transvestite achievement by denigrating her dramatic victory as a sexual come-on. The anecdote erases her extraordinary acting talent to align the travesty role with prostitution; it limits her female libertinism to theatrics and, through a crude association of man-woman with a whore, demeans her stunningly successful performance.[76] Her legitimate acting talent is transmogrified into a prostitute's sexual energy assumed to unravel masculine authority.

These accusations of licentiousness continued to attach themselves to the star actress throughout her career. For example, the epigraph on the title page to Woffington's *Memoirs* compared her to Dryden's Cleopatra in *All for Love*, the most exotic of whores, a role she played in 1747: "She was so charming, Age budded at her Sight, / and so .... The holy Priests gaz'd on her when she smil'd, / And with Hands, forgetting Gravity, ... wanton eyes." According to the memoirist, men assumed "that so fine a Woman must be kept by somebody" (22). Even though she could successfully impersonate a man, she was imagined to be someone's "*Property*" (22), thus dispossessing Woffington of her right to possess her own theatrical properties. Similarly, *Woffington's Ghost: A Poem, in answer to the Meretriciad* (1761) again compared her to the Egyptian queen, "*the Queen of Love*," who "*Promiscuous Blessings to her Slaves assign'd ; / And shew'd the World that Beauty should be kind.*"[77] Though Woffington participated in unorthodox sexual arrangements and was mistress to prominent men, she was never a common prostitute, but shared the sexual casualness of the heroes she acted. She reportedly had an affair with a "noble lord" while living with David Garrick, who discovered her infidelity when an unexplained periwig appeared in their bedchamber. In the titillating story, she excused herself as needing the prop to rehearse the role of Sir Harry. The anecdote is surely bogus, but its linkage of loose sexuality with transvestite stage parts reiterates a persistent theme that followed the actress throughout her career. Though some have questioned whether Woffington was "to be admired for resembling a man in the role, or admired for not doing so,"[78] she was in fact esteemed *both* for her elegance as a fashionable gentleman rake *and* for her skill in conveying that a woman's body lurked beneath the masculine clothing. Yet the dialogue of Farquhar's play, I suggest, would have constantly interrogated an audience's naïve assumptions regarding sexual difference.

To return to the specific instance of Woffington's greatest success in travesty, *The Constant Couple*, wildly popular from its inception, deals with the 1699 disbanding of the army in England but not in Ireland. Though the play is set in London, the subtitle, "*A Trip to the Jubilee*," refers to the Papal Jubilee of 1700 that began on Christmas Eve 1699, when devout Catholics streamed to Rome. Most critics have maintained that the pope's Jubilee is tangential to the plot, but the play inspired publications such as "A True and Exact Account of all the Ceremonies observed by the Church of Rome, at the . . . Jubilee" (1699, reprinted 1750), which described the splendid spectacle of the pope and his cardinals during the holiday tourist attraction that resembled the Lord Mayor's Day.[79] The Jubilee emphasized the theatricality of Catholicism and connected it in Protestant minds with mystifying foreign display. In addition to its magnificent candlelight processions, the Jubilee boasted a carnivalesque element. Clincher Senior, a former apprentice to Smuggler, is the character most closely identified with the Jubilee. He longs to travel to the Jubilee, motivated not by religion but by a wish to imitate Wildair's modish fashions; his Jubilee clothing and pistols link Rome with magic, masquerade, and violence rather than piety. When Clincher Senior ends up in Newgate prison, Clincher Junior, believing his brother Senior is dead, determines to spend his much-anticipated inheritance by celebrating at the Jubilee in his stead.

The play, like the epilogues Woffington delivered as the Female Volunteer and *The Female Officer*, is peppered throughout with anti-Catholic sentiments, and Woffington's acting as the antipapist Sir Harry Wildair would have dissociated her from Catholicism's false piety and the selling of indulgences. In producing the play at mid-century, the theater manager thus appealed to patriotic sentiments, aligning the patent theater firmly on the side of the reigning English monarch, and calling to mind the recent squelching of the Jacobite rebellion.

Even more central than its focus on religious satire is *The Constant Couple*'s preoccupation with the concept of woman, a theme especially prominent when Sir Harry Wildair was played in travesty, and we might coin a new term, "she-comedy," to describe it. The preface and prologue look to women as moral repositories, and the opening lines boast about virtuous women, though the rakish Sir Harry Wildair is dedicated to demonstrating that "Inconstancy and Falshood are grounded in their Natures" (2.3.70–71). Sir Harry also jests regarding Catholic hypocrisy and claims to have raped six nuns in revenge against a French Catholic priest who denied his wife proper burial.[80] Sir Harry postpones his tour of Italy because, he protests, Lady Lurewell is more important to him than the Jubilee or the pope. Wronged as a young girl, Lurewell still longs for her first seducer, later revealed to be Standard. Lurewell's anger at men paradoxically propels her passion for him, but she takes vengeance on the sex by gathering charmed "captives" around her—Standard, Vizard, Clincher, Smuggler—and even Sir Harry who promises to duel in order to claim her. Her fury at the sex could be construed as the comic analogue to the tragic sentimental misery of a Jane Shore or a Millwood. Seduction and even rape are justified in the subplot (Standard-Lurewell) while they are eliminated in the main plot (Sir Harry-Angelica). Wildair, a "castrated" man when acted by a woman, embodies the female sex's antagonism toward men; but as an imitation man, s/he also would have defanged the misogyny of the play and called into question the stability of gender construction.

The heroine Angelica also bemoans the unhappy state of women, and bristles at the constraints on the sex's behavior: modesty is "a Chain to Enslave, [rather] than Bracelet to Adorn us—it shou'd show, when unmolested, easie and innocent as a Dove, but strong and vigorous as a Faulcon, when assaulted" (5.1.7–10). At the center of the play is Wildair's comic misunderstanding that Lady Darling, called the "whore of Babylon," lives in a bordello, thus extending the play's linkage of gentlewoman and prostitute. The womanizing Wildair, "a Scandal to the Name of Gentleman" (5.1.148–49), is branded as typical of his sex and s/he expresses thoughts antagonistic to women that confirm Lady Lurewell's embittered assumptions.

If, in fact, some audiences found "there was no trace of the woman" in Woffington's performance of Sir Harry Wildair in *The Constant Couple*, the remark reflects that for some members of the audience her impersonation of a man allowed for absolute suspension of belief. The play is enriched by Wildair's songs which would have been sung in Woffington's soprano voice, some in duet with Lurewell. In a particularly vulgar example, Woffington/Wildair lewdly calls attention to "his" anatomy when s/he sings, "*Behold the Goldfinches, tall al de rall, / And a Man of my Inches, tall al de rall, / You shall take um believe me, tall al de rall, / If you will give me, your tall al de rall*" (5.1.160–63). In the fourth act, s/he alternately adopts the voice of Damon and then Celia. In addition, other earthy airs enliven the play, as well as rondeaux, jigs, and country dances.

The transvestite Wildair's ardent lovemaking to Angelica would have been an appealing bit of comic stage business, especially when s/he offers to exchange money for her sexual services. When s/he, mocking the "value" of virtue, offers Angelica a hundred guineas as a whore, her tragic protestation resembles the matronly Statira's familiar heroic lines in Lee's *Rival Queens*. The freewheeling transvestite Wildair in performance would have undermined the play's notion that women lack liberty, for s/he draws a sword on Angelica's footmen and openly indulges in scandalous language. The gender-bending irony would have been underscored when the cross-dressed Wildair remarks, for example, that woman is a greater wonder than Amsterdam and Paris, the cities from which he has just returned. Angelica's ultimately forgiving Wildair, making him an exception in her condemnation of men, would also have made a kind of perverse sense when he was played by a woman.

Many of Wildair's speeches when imagined in the cross-dressed Woffington's voice become vulgar double entendres that heighten the paradox of his misogynist attitudes. For example, when taunted to fight over Lady Lurewell, heiress to £3,000 a year, Sir Harry insists to Standard that "A Man can never hear Reason with a Sword in his Hand. Sheath your Weapon; and then if I don't satisfie you, sheath it in my Body" (4.1.53–55). Sir Harry and Colonel Standard, both libertines, characterize Lurewell by her body parts—lips, tongue, pericranium, neck, breast, eyes, hand, foot—and Angelica fares little better because she is falsely assumed to be a whore. Lurewell, still reeling from her early mistreatment by men, raises the issue of fops' influence over women, made ironic when Wildair is played in travesty: "How easily is the vanity of Fops tickled by our Sex!" To which Standard responds: "Why, your Sex is the vanity of Fops" (1.2.21–22). Wildair's beating Smuggler would have presented yet another instance of "woman's" exercising power in the play and another satiric reversal of the play's antifeminism. To be a woman, or a man disguised as a woman, is to take one's sexual definition from being "in Petticoats" rather than from anatomy. But when Alderman Smuggler, Vizard's uncle, hides in Lurewell's closet disguised as her nurse, her maid Mrs. Parly outrageously fumbles for his private parts in the pleats of his gown. When Vizard later advances in the dark upon the cross-dressed Smuggler, s/he invokes the mysterious contradiction that is "woman": "I am very lovely and soft indeed, you shall find me much harder than you imagine, Friend" (4.2.143–44). The entire comedy, in other words, even in scenes in which Wildair/Woffington did not appear, offered new layers of meaning when it was played in travesty.

Like the other epilogues designed especially for her at mid-century, Woffington's epilogue to *The Constant Couple*, "*after her playing the part of Sir* Harry Wildair, *about the middle of* December *for the last time*," also addressed issues of sexual difference. In the satire on those effeminate men, "knights of the bloodless sword, and beardless face," who experience Wildair's blanching at war's horror, s/he claims to share the cowardice of men who flee the battlefield.[81] Like the fey Frenchmen, Wildair prefers the snuff box to the sword: "Be ours th'assembly, theirs the tented field; / Place we our pride in doing what we can, / And leave to men, to act the parts of man" (239). As Wildair, Woffington develops into a parodic symbol of war, the very antithesis of the ideal English soldier in her travesty that strengthens instead the masculinity of women.

Woffington's playing Harry Wildair encouraged talk of the actress's "double power to please" as "*both sexes* vanquished lie."[82] Though she was fully convincing in impersonating a man, numerous verses addressed to Woffington idealized her as the perfect *woman* in other roles: "In shapes as various as her Sexe's are—And all the woman seems comprised in her" (Daly, *Woffington*, 108). Whether acting as a man about town or a beautiful woman, Woffington was skilled in imitating the manners of people of quality: "To sum up all, while in petticoats, she shewed the woman of solid sense, and real fashion; when in breeches, the man of education, judgment and gentility" (Gentleman, *Dramatic Censor*, 1: 296).

In Dublin, Woffington extended her success as the worldly gentleman Sir Harry Wildair to the "haughty, gallant, gay" seducer Lothario, the villain of Nicholas Rowe's she-tragedy *The Fair Penitent* (1703), who was believed be the model for Samuel Richardson's Lovelace in the mid-century novel *Clarissa*. The she-tragedy had been extremely popular in both England and Dublin from its opening performance in March 1703 starring Elizabeth Barry as Calista and Anne Bracegirdle as Lavinia. Depicting Calista's sexual misstep with the irresistible Lothario, the play moves from heroic tragedy toward a sentimental interpretation of domestic misfortune. Rowe, taking his model in turn from Phillip Massinger's *Fatal Dowry* (1630), intensified the sympathy directed at the repentant heroine, although Samuel Johnson famously lamented that the character Calista regretted only her unenviable plight and the revelation, not the commission, of her sin. Betrothed to Altamont, Calista violates her solemn pledge. When Altamont kills the unrepentant offender Lothario, Calista stabs herself, but only after begging forgiveness from her father Sciolto and the man she has betrayed. Having taken a succession of lovers, Woffington might have more naturally stepped into the role of Calista (a part she had played only in 1748–49), the heroine who succumbs to the charming, unscrupulous Lothario and seems to be only ambivalently repentant. Calista's words spoken to Woffington as the inconstant cross-dressed Lothario might in fact have seemed to the audience applicable to the actress' conversion to Protestantism: "Villain! Monster! Base betrayer!"[83]

When she chose to act Lothario on 24 March 1757 as the last new part of her long career, Woffington was probably aware of the political and religious stage history of Rowe's *Fair Penitent*, including the disruption in Dublin over the play almost exactly a decade earlier. Susan Cannon Harris has argued that *The Fair Penitent* established solidarity between actresses and female spectators in the Dublin audience in their mutual resistance to masculine manipulation, whether sexual, marital, or paternal.[84] For Harris, though she does not mention Woffington's transvestite role as Lothario, Calista, a figure representing Ireland's subjugation to England, resembles the prototypical female victim subject to men who would assault or dispose of women. She finds the play to be both "the drama of Calista's betrayal, exposure, and destruction, and that of the little parliament of men struggling to hold itself together despite Lothario's interventions" (48). Harris interprets Lothario's omission from the billing for a benefit performance as making Horatio, Altamont's friend, the hero of the piece (50) rather than Calista or Lothario. Lothario as the "supposedly native Irish" may have been a figure for Kelly, the Catholic aristocratic marauder who captures the woman/actress in order to reclaim his property, and thus his elevated status. In Sheridan's benefit production, Horatio would have triumphed over Lothario/Kelly.[85] If Harris is right, then Woffington's performance as Lothario, in spite of her connection with the Anglo-Irish Lord Lieutenant, would have associated her in the minds of Dublin audiences with the native Catholic who justified rape or violence to repossess property that had been stolen.

Though Woffington apparently played Lothario to better reviews in Ireland than in England, audience reactions were still somewhat mixed. Why, we might ask, was Woffington mostly panned as Lothario when she was universally triumphant as Sir Harry Wildair in England and Dublin? As Davies wrote, "She tried her powers of acting a tragedy rake, for *Lothario* is certainly of that cast; but whether she was as greatly accomplished in the manly tread of the buskin'd libertine as she was in the genteel walk of the gay gentleman in comedy, I know not; but it is certain she did not meet with the same approbation in the part of *Lothario* as in that of *Wildair*."[86] When she bravely chose the part for her benefit, those who admired her as an actress praised her as triumphant in any role; but others, like her muckraking 1760 memoirist, carped "that both her Action and Elocution were highly improper, and her Conception of the Character quite erroneous. They alleged likewise, that though a Man may with great Propriety, in some particular Characters, personate a Woman, yet for a Woman . . . to personate that gay, perfidious Libertine" was "an absurd, an inconsistent and impotent Attempt," and added that "she was absolutely unfit for the Character, and played it with all the Impotence of mere Endeavour" (*Memoirs of Woffington*, 31). This peculiar combination of descriptors—"absurd," "inconsistent," and "impotent"—implies that her weak performance arose from her failing to possess the requisite male genitalia, something that would have been especially apparent in the high cut of the waistcoat of the time. Perhaps more relevant to the mixed response, her deficiency as a seducer would also have raised queer moments when s/he is described as satisfying her rapacious lust with a woman. These scenes may well have evoked the embarrassed titters peculiar to comedy rather than tragedy. Equally troubling would have been the female Lothario's protestation: "And with prevailing, youthful ardor pressed her, / Till with short sighs and murmuring reluctance / The yielding fair one gave me perfect happiness. / Ev'n all the livelong night we passed in bliss, / In ecstasies too fierce to last forever" (1.1.157–61). The "haughty, insolent" Lothario gloats about his easy "triumph o'er Calista," and offers the unconvincing excuse that he would not marry her because her father refused his request for her hand.

Bored with his victim's misery, Lothario remains unmoved when Calista turns accusatory, yet the condition of the female sex, when voiced in performance to a cross-dressed Lothario, would have turned amusingly ironic rather than tragically effective: "How hard is the condition of our sex, / Through ev'ry state of life the slaves of man! / In all the dear, delightful days of youth / A rigid father dictates to our wills, / And deals out pleasure with a scanty hand; / To his, the tyrant husband's reign succeeds" (3.1.39–44).

The confusing gendering of the betrothed pair was further complicated in Woffington's rendering by the need to counter a sexy, virile fe/male Lothario in drag with a soft Altamont who was as "kind as the softest virgin of our sex" (2.1.14). A more flaccid character than the libertine Lothario or the stoic Horatio, Altamont rather than Lothario might have been more convincingly cast as a woman. The hot-blooded Calista, resisting her father's infantilizing words, is haughty and fierce in contrast to Altamont's tender, if ineffectual, temperament. Further, when Calista attributes her succumbing to Lothario to the sex's weakness—"because I loved, and was a woman" (5.1.73)—it reads as both an excuse and a boast.

When a woman acts Lothario's part, it is not clear whether he is tamed and emasculated, or freed to transgress sexual boundaries. In addition, the sentiments and actions of "the personated *Lothario*" (31), as the *Memoir* described Woffington's performance, detracted from a certain immediacy of action. Voiced by a woman, the character's pale libertinism seemed ludicrous, and it was impossible to forget the female body beneath the rakish clothing. Perhaps Woffington's performance also heightened the characteristics Samuel Johnson found most disturbing: "Lothario, with gaiety which cannot be hated, and bravery which cannot be despised, retains too much of the spectator's kindness."[87] When Woffington ventriloquated libertine views, then the sympathy of the spectator might well have surged toward him/her. The concluding scene at the female Lothario's bier, as Calista's distracted reflections turn to madness, would have seemed more ridiculous than horrifying. Unlike Renaissance boy actors whose portrayal of Shakespeare's tragic heroines had been naturalized, Woffington's impersonation without the proper anatomy aroused laughter, although her portrayal of the comic Wildair had seemed relevant rather than strange. In short, travesty roles are especially difficult to sustain in tragedy because there appears to be something inherently amusing in a woman's daring to become a sexually aggressive man, while a serious female libertine coupling a feigned masculinity with sexual violence, disquieted the spectators. The uncomfortable audiences apparently found the tragic double standard combined with the sensuality of the play to be nearly insuperable obstacles. Travesty here troublingly defied a desire to reinstate absolute sexual difference and instead underlined the homoeroticism and homosociality central to tragic plays of this period. Finally, then, tragedy, especially she-tragedy, resisted the inclusion of travesty roles that worked to disrupt its nostalgic assertions, while she-comedies more easily absorbed the ambiguously gendered characters and excesses of identity that pointed toward modernity.

In sum, Woffington as a cross-dressed Silvia or female volunteer, or a travestied Wildair or Lothario, temporarily escaped the naturalized divisions of gender and unyielding national and religious affiliations. In playing the cross-dressed Irish/English, man/woman, Catholic/Protestant, Jacobite/Whig, Woffington gave reality to an unstable modernity, a modernity without a fundamental essence, embodied in celebrity actresses' lives and roles.[88] Plays such as *The Female Officer*, *The Constant Couple*, and *The Recruiting Officer* reclaimed Woffington for one or another identity when she revealed her womanly body beneath the disguise, but her travesty roles with their overabundance of interiority effects prevented limiting her to any one category. Fusing aspects of her personal life with her roles, Woffington performed the equivocal nature of these oppositions to display them spectacularly and, paradoxically, to become a figure through which a nation could unify itself. In representing a surplus of identities designed to advance her commercial appeal, Woffington became, for better and worse, an amalgamation of the new *British* citizen to come.

CHAPTER 7

The Actress and Material Femininity: Frances Abington

> I declare Mrs Abington may march through all my dominions at the head of as large a troop as she pleases—I do not say, as she can muster and command; for then I am sure my house would not hold them.
>
> —Horace Walpole, Strawberry Hill, 11 June 1780

FRANCES ABINGTON, NÉE Barton (1737–1815), was, according to Horace Walpole, equal to the first of her profession. "I do impartial justice to your merit," he exuberantly remarks, "and fairly allow it not only equal to that of any actress I have seen, but believe the present age will not be in the wrong, if they hereafter prefer it to those they may live to see."[1] Abington debuted as a principal on 29 October 1756 as Lady Pliant in *The Double Dealer*, along with her more experienced Drury Lane rivals Hannah Pritchard and Kitty Clive. Performing occasionally at Bath, Richmond, and the Haymarket, like many actors she sought more opportunity for work in Dublin at the Smock Alley Theatre where she successfully played Mrs. Sullen in Farquhar's *Beaux Stratagem* (11 December 1759), followed by triumphs as Shakespeare's Beatrice and Portia. During the same year she had married James Abington, a royal trumpeter and her music master, from whom she separated shortly after their move to Ireland. Abington negotiated between the two Dublin theaters, Smock Alley and Crow Street, to maximize her pay, and her remarkable achievements quickly aroused her husband's jealousy; he demanded that she pay him an annual pension. Her subsequent affair with Mr. Needham, a "Member of Parliament for Newry in the county of Down," ended when he met with ill health on their return to England, though he bequeathed her a considerable estate.[2] After Needham's death she became the mistress of William Petty, the first marquess of Lansdowne, and the addition of his estate to her considerable earnings made her a very wealthy woman.

Frances Abington rose rapidly to the status of stage goddess and fashion icon. As a magnificent "Priestess of Fashion," Abington functioned as a spiritual guide to a secular realm; her divine aura emanated from a combination of dazzling comic talent with haute couture. Sir Joshua Reynolds painted her as Thalia, "the first priestess of the Comic Muse in this country," echoing a description that Hugh Kelly had employed in the preface to *School for Wives* (1777).[3] Even in Paris, we are told, Mrs. Abington merited "the most flattering reception from the higher ranks of the Parisian Noblesse."[4] A commanding presence united with fashionable femininity, Abington transformed high style into the unlikely vehicle through which a woman's strength and independence could be articulated.[5] At the same time Abington lured her audiences into imbibing the curative power of consumption; she turned fashion into a religion of sorts, and the magic of capital into an aesthetic.

At the height of Abington's career in the 1770s, actresses achieving social mobility had developed a rather long history; by that time she was no longer an anomaly as an accomplished public woman. Paul Langford has pointed to the "full-blown revolution for women in the 1770s," paralleling the revolutionary spirit abroad, that turned in part on the expansion of women's presence in relation in print culture and the marketplace.[6] Peter Clark describes women's activities in the period as "fashionable sociability," a term that Gillian Russell usefully expanded into the concept of "domiciliary sociability" to define women's pervasive presence at operas, masquerades, lectures, concert halls, and exhibitions in the later eighteenth century.[7] The theatrical world nourished the large commercial enterprises that spilled out from private performances into the concert halls and entertainment centers of London and its environs. In order to impress friends with their intimacy with celebrities, hosts and hostesses invited star players willing to entertain guests at private events with recitation and song, and to grace social events with their charismatic presence. Star actresses—including Abington, Pritchard, Pope/Young, and Yates—attended the more austere Bluestocking assemblies where women's conversations reflected "polite, enlightened behavior as opposed to aristocratic decorum through their sociability";[8] they openly infiltrated gatherings at diverse venues such as Ranelagh and Vauxhall, and at Cornelys and Pantheon. Sarah Siddons, for example, was known to have undertaken public readings in the Argyll Rooms. Celebrated actresses, mingling in fashionable society, forecast the new freedoms for women later realized by Wollstonecraft and others in the 1790s who, though openly hostile to the frivolous consumption to which Abington gave license, shared the desire for economic independence and political influence.

Frances Abington's stature entitled her to choose her own costuming; her fashion expertise allowed her to upstage Garrick, who had difficulty competing for attention with "an actress of powerful talent, backed by half the women of fashion in the metropolis."[9] The dates of her active theatrical life (1754–98) correspond to an explosion in fashion accompanied by an increased audience demand for historically and geographically accurate stage costuming.[10] Reputed to have been a servant to a French milliner in Cockspur Street, she learned dressmaking and costume design in her youth, and these connections with millinery followed her in at least two ways. First, rumors of Abington having been a prostitute in her early years may have been a consequence of the customary linkage of "common Women of the Town" with millinery.[11] Apprentice milliners, in spite of being hard-working young women, were known to be the prey of unsavory men and regarded as morally suspect. *The London Tradesman*, for example, warned parents to avoid apprenticing their daughters to the trade because "The vast Resort of young Beaus and Rakes to Millinery Shops, exposes young Creatures to many Temptations, and insensibly debauches their Morals before they are capable of Vice" (208). The author of the tract reported that "nine out of ten of the young creatures that are obliged to serve in these Shops, are ruined and undone . . . debauched in their Houses" (209). Second, Abington's ability to influence style very likely evolved from her insider knowledge of the dressmaking trade. According to the treatise that described a plan to transform indigent and wayward girls into industrious seamstresses, a milliner's eye-popping list of products included "Smocks, Aprons, Tippits, Handerchiefs, Neckaties, Ruffles, Mobs, Caps, Dressed-Heads . . . Cloaks, Manteels, Mantelets, Cheens and Capucheens . . . Hats, Hoods and Caps . . . Gloves, Muffs, and Ribons" and more, all articles of clothing that Abington may well have known how to construct (208).

The most celebrated women players often commissioned the design of their own costumes and supervised the sewing (with the notable exceptions of handkerchiefs and slippers), and the purchase of elaborate costuming was a necessary expenditure for actresses who sought to maintain star status. At the height of her fame, Abington was annually granted the astronomical sum of £500 as her onstage costume allowance, but actresses were known to spend considerably more than allotted.[12] Actresses worked extremely closely with seamstresses but, less predictably, milliners served as their fashion advisors, designers, innovators, and even spies. Actress George Anne Bellamy mentions sponsoring a prospective young milliner going to France, "under the protection of the Mademoiselles Gressiers, in order to learn the art of making mantuas, robes, trimmings, and all the necessary appendages to dress."[13] According to the *London Tradesman*, a milliner "imports new Whims from *Paris* every Post, and puts the Ladies Heads in as many different Shapes in one Month as there are different Appearances of the Moon in that Space. The most noted of them keep an Agent at *Paris*, who have nothing else to do but to watch the Motions of the Fashions, and procure Intelligence of their Changes, which she signifies her Principals, with as much Zeal and secrecy as an Ambassador or Penipo would the important Discovery of some political Intrigue" (207–8). In spite of her humble origins, Abington possessed the requisite economic clout and insider's expertise to cultivate a signature style while employing others to carry out the labor she could knowledgeably supervise.

On her appearance at Covent Garden in 1782, Abington claimed to be a "noviciate" (in spite of being advanced in her career) to both fashion and a religious order when, dressed in a simple dark "Carmelite satin" with short white sleeves, her stage address reached from "the goddesses in the boxes to the gods in the upper regions" (*Life of Mrs. Abington*, 92). The newspapers lingered lovingly over the details of the Parisian fashion that combined elegance with religious overtones: "Mrs. Abington's dress was a *chef d'ouevre*, in point of taste and simple elegance: the body of her gown was of *Carmelite* satin, with white sleeves of silver-spotted muslin, tied near the middle of the arm, with a Carmelite ribbon, the bows of which were turned behind—The skirt of her dress was a white silver tissue, decorated with an *ostrich and silver trimming, studded with jewels*. Her apron was of silver-spotted muslin, with two flounces near the bottom, edged with a trimming of carmelite and white, below which appeared a rich embroidered petticoat fringe. Her head-dress contained no profusion of jewels, but was remarkably neat; the cap consisted of a few feathers, admirably disposed, and an artificial sprig, of carmelite colour, with white ribbons."[14] "Carmelite" is, of course, not only a warm golden brown color but also the name of an order of cloistered nuns, thus calling to the audience's mind her status as a heaven-sent intercessor who called them to consume.

Women's stage clothing in the Restoration period had been restricted to the theater, for one was not permitted to take away "feathers nor clothes nor ribbons nor any thing relating to the stage."[15] A defiant late seventeenth-century actress was warned, "Whereas by Experience Wee find our Cloathes Tarnished & Imperilled by frequent Weareing them out of the Playhouse It is thought fitt noe *Weoman* presume to goe out of the House with the Play House Cloathes or Properties upon Penalty of their Weekes pay."[16] But the boundaries of stage and theater became surprisingly more porous in the eighteenth century, and luxurious theatrical display thoroughly pervaded the London's social world that imitated it. One European observer who returned to England in the 1770s, for example, criticized the spectacular clothing worn as everyday dress as more suitable to masquerade costuming: "There is at present much more expence and taste in the trimmings of the Ladys Gowns than in the stuffs; they are full and in almost a theatrical style, but I think very handsome."[17]

Theatrical costumes were extremely expensive, amounting to an increasingly large percentage of the company's budget, and tempted lesser players to help themselves to stage clothing. Actress George Anne Bellamy describes in her memoirs the strange admixture of elegant, stained, and tattered clothing cobbled together for fellow actors in the tragic productions she witnessed: "Whilst the empresses and queens appeared in black velvet, and, upon extraordinary occasions, with the additional finery of an embroidered or tissue petticoat; and the younger part of the females, in cast[off] gowns of persons of quality, or altered habits rather soiled; the male part of the dramatis personae st[r]utted in tarnished laced coats and waistcoats, full bottom or tye wigs, and black worsted stockings."[18] Unlike the earlier decades when actresses often recycled cast-offs or dresses from ladies of quality through countless performances, Abington's high couture declared her newfound value. As a living mannequin dressed in high fashion, Abington advertised through her self-commodified person, and through democratizing exchanges with the audience, that being à la mode was newly accessible to them.

Though she was not the sole inventor of theatrical fashion-modeling, Abington turned à-la-mode clothing into her own idiosyncratic personal trademark and a sign of her value, thus paradoxically creating a material femininity through surface opulence but also producing an impression of a robust interiority. For better and for worse celebrity's effects, as Chris Rojek has neatly summarized them, operate "to articulate, and legitimate, various forms of subjectivity that enhance the value of individuality and personality."[19] Fashion afforded Abington a unique cultural authority that male actors, even as fops, would have found impossible to emulate. "Ladies of the first distinction," Charles Dibdin tells us, consulted "from a decided conviction of her judgment in blending what was beautiful with what was becoming."[20] Abington thus broke from the traditional generic costuming in the theater, which had included "black velvet and white satin dresses, point lace, and stomacher for the tragic line; pink, blue, and white satin dresses with feathers, fans, and veils for comedy; and scarlet or buff frocks with blue or green ribbons, crucifix pendant, and French head dress for melodrama."[21] Instead, Abington designed sumptuously beautiful clothing that was unique to particular performances and identified specifically with her, most especially the Francophile Lady Bab's magnificent costume in *Maid of the Oaks* in which she was immortalized in Thomas Hickey's painting[22] (Figure 16).

During her five-year sojourn in Dublin, Abington was fetishized as a highly prized commodity from her first performances as ingénue and fine lady in Ireland: "The whole circle were in surprise and rapture, each asking the other how such a treasure could have possibly been in Dublin, and almost in a state of obscurity; such a jewel was invaluable, and their own tastes and judgments they feared would justly be called in question, if this daughter of Thalia was not immediately taken by the hand, and distinguished as her certain and striking merit demanded."[23] Addressing epilogues to the ladies of quality seated in the boxes in Dublin "to lead the ton" in fashion, she soon developed the trademark "Abington cap," the mob cap she sported as Kitty in James Townley's two-act farce, *High Life below Stairs* (1760), which became "the prevailing rage" (2: 37). Attracting overflow audiences, Abington's triumph in the role was followed by critical acclaim for parts she was frequently to reprise: she played Lady Townly at Crow Street (22 May 1760), Lucy in *The Beggar's Opera* (Autumn 1760), and the fashionable Widow Bellmour in Murphy's *The Way to Keep Him* (27 November 1765). Other modish accessories, including the Abington bonnet and petticoat, were so closely linked with the actress's person that puchasing the accessory seemed to allow possession of a part of Abington herself: "There was not a milliner's shop window, great or small, but was adorned with it [the cap], and in large letters ABINGTON appeared to attract the passers by."[24] She reportedly supplemented her stage income by nearly £1500 annually in traveling around London as an advisor for elegant social events:

> She is consulted like a physician, and recompensed as if she were an artist. There never is a marriage or ball in which she is not consulted. A

Figure 16. "Frances Abington as Lady Bab Lardoon in The Maid of the Oaks." Thomas Hickey, oil on canvas (1775). The Garrick Club.

great number of people of fashion treat her in the most familiar manner, as if she were their equal. As she never appears on the stage but in the most elegant dress, her taste is sure to be copied by all the ladies who happen to be spectators. It is there that this priestess of the fashions displays all her art, being certain that she will be immediately copied with the most trivial exactness.[25]

From her early days as a flower vendor in Covent Garden where she was nicknamed "Nosegay Fan,"[26] Abington's identity was bound up with things for sale, but she was not alone in dictating fashion. "Catlified" women slavishly copied Anne Catley's hair worn low on the brow,[27] and Peg Woffington, too, was regarded as a fashionplate in Dublin and London. The *Dublin Gazette*, an arm of the Dublin Castle government, mocked the Town's susceptibility to Woffington's sartorial influence in "Verses wrote Extempore last Saturday on seeing A Lady Who Us'd to Rail at Mrs. Woffington dres't in imitation of her" (1753):

> *Folly* at *Reason* takes offence
> Yet apes the garb of common sense
> The Name of Thought her peace disturbs,
> Her choice prefers the dress of Words.
> Tho Mrs.—, With true theatric spirit
> Abuses Peg's Superior Merit,
> Neglects the Mind that marks her fame—
> But trims her Gown, exact the same.[28]

Other star actresses, known for their ties to the fashion business, were similarly consulted and imitated. Hannah Pritchard, daughter of a staymaker who may have supplied the theater, was an experienced dressmaker and designer who served as fashion consultant and dresser to Queen Charlotte, consort of King George III, for their wedding and for the coronation. Along with her husband, she established Pritchard's Warehouse to furnish theatrical costumes for the stage and for splendid social occasions.

Articles of clothing frequently transgressed public/private boundaries to take on semiotic agency independent of their wearers and, as we have seen, they could metonymically substitute for an actress, her dramatic character, or aspects of her private personality. In the thriving eighteenth-century culture of consumption, material objects assumed a value and agency usually restricted to human subjects. For example, *The Life of that Eminent Comedian Robert Wilks* (1733) lists for sale theatrical furniture that appears to possess an inherent celebrity, including Mrs. Oldfield's slippers, Mrs. Porter's petticoat, and the character Roxana's nightgown. Similarly, Susannah Cibber's handkerchief, a tragic prop she waved pervasively, was ridiculed for becoming an all-too-convenient proxy for real, heartfelt sentiment. Samuel Foote was among those who mocked the actress's dependence upon it: "I hope I shall have Mrs *Cibber's* Pardon, if I desire her (unless she has an absolute Occasion for it) to put the Handkerchief in her Pocket: and if she would not shake her Head quite so much, and pat her Hands together quite so often, she would infinitely oblige me, and many more of the Admirers."[29] *A Guide to the Stage* (1751) asserted that Cibber's accessory substituted for authentic emoting in Otway's *The Orphan*: "Monimia, taught by nature to lay every tumultuous passion, has the skill to attack the heart in the milder forms of pity, grief, and distress. But are these ever inexpressible without the handkerchief?"[30]

In addition to being linked with particular costumes and other theatrical properties, actresses were fetishized as miniatures, plaques, figurines, and medallions. When these nonhuman objects were transformed into active agents, they could be humanized, absorbed into actresses' identities to become the locus of diffuse longings brought to life through the celebrated actresses who wore or carried them, thus contributing to an audience's assumption of intimacy with them.[31] In this way material objects substituted for human beings; and although they did not literally speak, as they did in popular fictional "thing narratives" such as *The Adventures of a Rupee* (1783), they do seem to take on a life of their own. Unlike fictional characters, the actress animated in material form a self-fashioned representation integrated with being the treasure itself. Abington commodified her apparent interiority to personify accumulation and profit as she circulated in an aestheticized form that signified her value.

During the fashionable 1770s, familiar objects of everyday life gained magical properties on stage, thus possessing the double quality of being simultaneously ordinary and remarkable. Lynn M. Voskuil helpfully explicates this paradoxical doubleness of properties first articulated in Marx's *Capital*: "The talismanic properties of commodities, then, were precisely a function of their familiarity, their status as everyday, usable items. In the marketplace, triviality became fantastic when, in circulation, it was dislodged from its social and material context, lending commodities a hypostatic autonomy that appeared to be as objective as the wood that made up the table or the linen that went into the coat. In this way, the realistic and the fetishistic were closely related, their links embodied by objects that were at once familiar and strange."[32] Transformed into commodities like the charismatic Abington, these consumable objects took on mystical powers and potential agency, becoming attached to character and enmeshed with the identities of the human beings who wore them.

Theatrical fashion and accessories served as conduits for surprisingly intimate relations between actresses and women of elevated standing. When the New Theatre in Glasgow was set on fire by disgruntled Methodists, George Anne Bellamy's extensive wardrobe was incinerated: "I there beheld the ashes of all my finery, which had cost many, many hundreds of pounds . . . there being among them a complete set of garnets and pearls, from cap to stomacher" (*Apology*, 4: 69, 70). The ladies of the city and its environs, vividly demonstrating the interactivity between elite dress and theatrical fashion, promptly came to the rescue to loan the actress more than forty gowns, "some of these almost new, as well as very rich" (4: 71). Liberal numbers of social invitations for the actress followed, emanating from those who apparently sought to mingle their identities with Bellamy's celebrity through the public display of their borrowed clothing.

Spectacle and performance extended, of course, to the larger social theater that characterized eighteenth-century English society. Bellamy reports that high-ranking women consulted with her as they made their way to Court "to make their obeisance, and to shew their clothes" (3: 77). A patroness donated diamonds to ornament a dress of silver tissue, altered from clothing worn by the Princess of Wales, that her manager had purchased for Bellamy to wear as Cleopatra in Dryden's *All for Love*. A jealous rival queen Elizabeth Furnival stole the splendid gown to wear onstage as Octavia "without considering the impropriety of enrobing a Roman matron in the habiliments of the Egyptian Queen" (1: 145). Her seamstress, revealing the "fangs of [an] enraged Hibernian nymph" (146), fell on Mrs. Furnival tooth and nail to demand its return. But Bellamy as Cleopatra was forced to make do with wearing Octavia's unadorned white satin dress. In reporting the incident to manager Sheridan, she imperiously assumed her role as Cleopatra: "I had taken the advice Ventidius has sent me, by Alexis, and had parted with both my cloths and jewels to Antony's wife" (148). Bellamy was vindicated when—after the generous patroness cried from the audience, "Good Heaven, the woman has got on my diamonds!" (148–49)—the audience booed Furnival. As in the case of *The Rival Queens*, costumes and jewels, crossing the boundary between audience and stage, evolved into a form of hard currency that enhanced the actress's worth relative to other actresses and the female spectators whom they cultivated.

Epilogues and Things

Abington's promotion of conspicuous consumption capitalized upon her personal celebrity and mobilized the nation's fashion industry, while making her modish display appear to be a patriotic act, for she was a highly visible proponent of an industry that furthered the nation's prosperity. As we have seen in regard to other celebrity actresses, epilogues critically strengthened the appearance of an accessible, self-styled interiority; in Abington's case, the references often took material form. Abington's performance of popular roles and epilogues blended the milliner girl of her youth with the lady of quality she aspired to be. Parts written exclusively for her served as vehicles to unite dissimilar elements of fashion with expressions of women's rights. The persona that emerges from the epilogues, commercial add-on genres designed to coax the audience into returning for another night's performance, is often more unified than a given actress's dramatic roles, for the paratextual monologues reiterate aspects of the actress's "self" known to the audience. As Robert Weimann eloquently describes the contact zone the epilogue generates, "For one brief moment, before the illusion of the role vanishes and the world of the play finally surrenders to the world of existence, the arts of performance must confront and can playfully orchestrate the gulf between the two."[33] The actors sometimes remained on stage behind the epilogue speaker, making that speaker seem to be their proxy; their ad-lib gestures would have added layered nuance to the actress's words by underscoring or mocking them.

Though the writers of epilogues were overwhelmingly male, these authors apparently believed that the tactic of acknowledging women spectators, and sometimes inciting them to new freedoms through the person of the actress, would increase receipts. In Garrick's epilogue to Murphy's Oriental tragedy *Zenobia* (1768), in which Abington did not appear but only came onstage at the conclusion to add star power, she employs the convention of asking the audience to call her forth by approving the play. The epilogue figuratively traverses the liminal space between the stage and the audience while Abington literally bridges the gap to peep from behind the curtain before emerging to speak, vigorously cracking her fan to interrupt tragic emotion with comic gesture: "Some flippant hussey, like myself comes in; / Crack goes her fan, and with a giggling grin, / Hey! Presto! Pass!—all topsy turvy see, / For ho, ho, ho [tragic wailing]! Is chang'd to he, he he!"[34] While several epilogues incorporate flirtatious elements, allusions to Abington's chastity or lack of it are remarkably absent, as she asserted women's equality even when mocking women's stereotypical foibles.

In one of the most widely reprinted epilogues Garrick wrote for Abington to recite, the ornamental pins she ostentatiously displayed took on both a public and a private life. In reciting the popular piece that compares epilogues to pins, reprinted in *Town and Country Magazine* (March 1769) and elsewhere, Abington ironically chided the playwright for refusing to pen one: "You *must* write an epilogue to wake up the pit, box, and gallery," she insists, in the epilogue to John Home's *The Fatal Discovery* (1769):

> Our bard, a strange, unfashionable creature,
> As obstinate, as savage in his nature,
> Will have no Epilogue!—I told the brute—
> If Sir these trifles don't *your* genius suit;
> We have a working Prologue-smith within,
> Will strike one off, as if it were a pin.
> Nay, Epilogues are pins,—whose points, well plac'd,
> Will trick your muse out, in the tip-top taste![35]

In the epilogue, one of eleven Garrick wrote especially for her, pins possess intrinsic magical powers; they are talismans that replicate the function of epilogues. Just as they are essential for holding her costume together, epilogues bind the parts of the play together—plot, actors, costumes, props—and they make modern whatever they adorn or secure. Abington was particularly adept at employing a pin along with her characteristic fans, caps, hoops, and wigs, to speak volumes through her gestures and to reflect her interiority through stage accessories. John O'Keeffe tells us that she "had peculiar tricks in acting; one was turning her wrist, and seeming to stick a pin in the side of her waist; she was also very adroit in the use of her fan."[36]

Pins, essential for milliners, were reminders of Abington's personal origins in the sewing business. Costume making and the related trades of producing hats, gowns, petticoats, and mantuas were traditionally dominated by female labor, though there was increasing competition from male apprentices. As a spur to consumption and a growing economy, the clothing trades after mid-century offered a legitimate alternative to other less salubrious forms of female commerce. In her analysis of the kinds of redemptive labor in manufacturing and service that were encouraged for reformed prostitutes in Magdalen houses, Jennie Batchelor accurately describes the "emergence of the female laborer as a vital and active agent in the nation's moral and political economy."[37] In 1758 the author of *Observations on Mr. Fielding's Plan* proposed "pin-making" as a legitimate trade for deserted charity girls and former prostitutes seeking apprentice employment, in addition to embroidery, spinning, cookery, and housewifery.[38] The intricate assemblage of pins, according to Adam Smith's *The Wealth of Nations* (1766) provided an economic model for reforming the division of labor in order to increase national productivity. Instead of the usual practice in which a single pin-maker laboriously completed all the steps in its production, making only one pin in a day, Smith proposed a precursor to the modern assembly line, determining that ten persons working on separate tasks could produce 48,000 pins per day.[39]

The first definition of "pin" in Samuel Johnson's 1755 *Dictionary of the English Language* is "a short wire with a sharp point and round head, used by women to fasten their clothes." Pins, or "pines," were in great demand in order to dress and constituted an absolutely necessary expense that a woman of fashion regularly had to replenish. The diaries of actress, playwright, and novelist Elizabeth Inchbald—in addition to listing her many expenditures for hair dressing, washing silk stockings, and mending gowns, and for purchasing eyebrow powder, candles, gin, feathers, ribbons, and gloves—mention nearly every week an expenditure for pins, usually amounting to £0.0.2.[40] For example, in the month of January 1776 alone, she records purchasing pins on six different occasions, and on ten occasions in February of the same year. According to Aileen Ribeiro, "Pins were important in fastening the component parts of women's costume, mainly the bodice of the dress to the whaleboned stays, to pin decorative elements on the bodice and skirt of the dress, to pin hats to linen indoor coifs, to pin lace ruffles to sleeves, and so on . . . . They could be quite useful on the stage for costume changes, far quicker than lacing or unbuttoning/buttoning clothing/accessories."[41] In spite of being essential for dressing appropriately, pins had originally been considered to be luxury items, and wives often requested a separate allowance called "pin money" from their husbands in order to purchase such personal articles. By the late seventeenth century "pin money" became a more generic term to describe "one species of property that women could be said to own despite the coverture which under common law made the wife's property belong to her husband," as Susan Staves has shown.[42] Pin money allowed women to accumulate small amounts of capital that could be expended as discretionary funds and thus offered a measure of economic autonomy. As the pin-wearer rather than the pin-maker, and as part of the "authentic" interiority reflected in her performance, Abington called to mind both the successful rehabilitation of a miscreant (as in the case of Magdalen House reformed prostitutes), and the profitable display of Smith's exemplary economic model at work. As an inveterate consumer of pins, Abington stood onstage not as the pin-maker, but as the perfect union of the woman who, like her fellow actresses, required enormous numbers of pins both as ornaments and as functional fasteners for holding clothing in place, and the star who embodied the independence that money of one's own afforded.

Our current critical fascination with strange and wonderful objects often extracts them from the material conditions of their production, but it is instructive to reinsert the fashionable properties of Abington and other actresses into their historical context. Jonathan Gil Harris, following Walter Benjamin, points out that if an ordinary object is assigned marvelous properties, it may function effectively as a hinge between the opposing temporalities of timelessness and of long-forgotten histories encoded within it.[43] In this manner Abington's comic epilogue on pins after *The Fatal Discovery* would surely have reminded knowledgeable audiences of John Gay's earlier fable, *The Pin and the Needle* (Fable XVI), that traced the descent of a pin from a young woman's possession to the hands of a tailor, a beggar, and a miser, finally coming to be nearly lost in the merchandising center at Gresham Hall:

> A PIN who long had serv'd a Beauty,
> Proficient in the toilette's duty,
> Had form'd her sleeve, confin'd her hair,
> Or giv'n her knot a smarter air,
> Now nearest to her heart was plac'd
> Now in her manteau's tail disgrac'd;
> But could she partial fortune blame,
> Who saw her lovers serv'd the same?[44]

At the conclusion of the fable the haughty, manly needle confronts the feminine pin in a gendered encounter and boasts of the empires, far superior to a mere milliner's shop, that he commands: "'Tis I direct the pilot's hand / To shun the rocks and treacherous sand: / By me the distant world is known, / And either *India* is our own" (64).

Abington as "Priestess of Fashion" calls to mind another scene of worship at the altar of fashion, Belinda performing "sacred Rites of Pride" in Alexander Pope's *The Rape of the Lock*. The epilogue surely would have resonated with the audience's memory of Pope's alliterative lines describing Belinda's dazzling artifice at her boudoir altar: "Here files of Pins extend their shining Rows, / Puffs, Powders, Patches, Bibles, Billet-doux."[45] In the epilogue Abington pulls a pin from her side just as Belinda had done in the war between the sexes: "Now meet thy Fate, incens'd *Belinda* cry'd, / And drew a deadly *Bodkin* from her Side" (canto 5.87–88). Like the sprites with bodkin spears in Pope's poem, Abington, in boldly wielding the pin, arms herself with a fashionable instrument, an Amazonian weapon that expresses her forceful interiority. In the 1714 revision of the mock-heroic poem, Pope inserted a classical ancestry of the bodkin in which "the point of the pedigree is to compare a natural lineage with an artificial one," as Ralph Cohen cleverly described it.[46] In that supplementary passage Pope parodied Homer's history of Agamemnon's scepter that had served as a weapon as well as a reminder of patriarchal sovereignty. Its peculiar lineage implies the phallic nature of the bodkin as well as the venereal nature of the hairs in question: "A Bodkin grac'd her Mother's Hairs / which long she wore, and now Belinda wears" (canto 5.89–96). The lines also imply that male impotency is likely to accompany the war between the sexes that the misguided Belinda wages against the Baron—the kind of war Abington conducted against her manager Garrick.

The Rape of the Lock is, of course, a poem about women's hair—on the head and elsewhere—and one of bodkin's uses is to fasten hair, or to serve as an artificial ornament to it. Abington's hairs, like Belinda's, were the "envy of the world" and subject to a rakish suitor's theft: "Or any hairs but these!" There are further parallels between Abington and the *Rape of the Lock*, for the actress herself, like Belinda's bodkin, may have possessed an aristocratic pedigree: persistent rumors circulated that Abington's family descended from displaced quality, forcing the young girl to earn her living as a flower peddler and a milliner. The bodkin in *Rape of the Lock* originated as a sign of Belinda's patriarchal heritage; it began its "life" as her great-great-grandfather's seal rings used to solemnize bonds between noblemen until it was eventually transformed into an heirloom hair ornament, thus turning the patriarchal legacy into a maternal one: "Then in a *Bodkin* grac'd her Mother's Hairs,/Which long she wore, and now *Belinda* wears" (canto 5.96–97). Belinda defends her chastity in brandishing her weapon against the Baron, in a futile attempt to force him to return the lock.

Through Garrick's words in the epilogue, Abington embraces the warrior-woman interiority that her fashion accessory implies while dressed smartly à-la-mode. Abington, brasher than the fictional Belinda, speaks from a position of moral indignation directed at those who would forget to add an epilogue, frequently a feminist signature, to a tragedy. In Abington's speech the poet denies that the pins, or the epilogues they symbolize, possess any heroic heritage:

> "Pins, madam! (frown'd the bard) the Greeks us'd none,
> (Then mutt'ring Greek—something like this—went on)
> *Pinnos, painton, patcheros, no Graeco Modon.*"
> I coaxed, he swore—"That tie him to a stake,
> He'd suffer all for Decency's fair sake;
> No Bribery should make him change his plan." (Epilogue to *The Fatal Discovery*)

The pin seems to represent two compelling aspects of commerce at once: as a weapon it interrupted the moral order of society, destroying values and commodifying them, for self-interested purposes. On the other hand, as a tiny implement joining things together, it enhanced human bonds just as (women's) fashion contributed to sweet commerce.

Experienced actresses also employed parts of their costumes as agents of affect, of erotic desire, and of social class. Like bodkins, hoop skirts became weapons of authority, as they famously usurped social space. Women, no matter what their rank or social standing, Tate Wilkinson complained, asserted their territorial claim with their "large banging" hoops to inspire terror in any novice who dared set foot on those protected territories (*Memoirs*, 4: 90). Even onstage nuns wore hoops and powdered their hair.[47] "Strict propriety of habiliment" on stage, Wilkinson added, was seldom achieved because, whether playing a chambermaid or a farmer's daughter, a beautiful woman insisted on elaborate headdresses and satin shoes (90). Stage props and clothing were a means for actresses to assert personality and command authority in a manner that could be mimicked in everyday life.

In dexterous hands particular ornaments or clothing accessories similarly assumed the status of weapons in the war between the sexes, and Abington's epilogues elaborated on their potential martial effect.[48] A woman's fan could be employed like a pin or a bodkin as a threat. Pictures of actresses delivering epilogues frequently portrayed them gesturing flirtatiously with a fan that could also be employed in a more vehement way as a bludgeon or firing arm. *The Spectator* earlier in the century speaks of women transforming fans into weapons: "When the Fans are thus *discharged*, the Word of command in Course is to *ground their Fans*. This teaches a lady to quit her Fan gracefully when she throws it aside in order to take up a Pack of Cards, adjust a Curl of Hair, replace a falling Pin, or apply herself to any other Matter of Importance."[49] In her address delivered between the first and second acts of Frances Sheridan's *The Discovery* (29 November 1782),[50] Abington claims she will ward off Gorgons in the audience with her fan: "If such there be, who thus by measure scan, / Against his *Rule*—I parry with my fan— / An instrument, presented by the Graces, / To bear me harmless from such Gorgon faces" (*Life of Mrs. Abington*, 93). Andrew Sofer has illuminated the improvisational power of the fan to speak as a sexual semaphore in performance, and to counter the explicit message expressed in the text's words: "Trickier still to determine is to what extent an accomplished actress might have been able to twist the fan's message away from the patriarchal script set down by the playwrights."[51] He indicates, for example, that Abington's closed fan appears to extend her territorial domain in an engraving of her role as Aurelia in *The Twin Rivals* (1777) (Figure 17). According to James Boaden, Abington "took more entire possession of the stage, than any actress I have ever seen, there was however, no assumption in her dignity; she was a lawful and graceful sovereign, who exerted her full power and enjoyed her established prerogatives. The ladies of her day wore the hoop and its concomitants. The *Spectator*'s exercise of the fan was really a play of *fancy*. Shall I say that I have never seen it in a hand so dexterous as that of Mrs. Abington?"[52] In addition to serving as a weapon, the fan could also metamorphose into a fetishized reference to the actress's pubic area and mark the place of interest while seeming to shield it from view. The fan, open or shut, pointed or withheld, was thus a seductive accessory that could be used to mask, reveal, or simulate interiority, and to underscore or contest the words it punctuated.[53] These epilogues suggest that while Abington in performance would have reflected the feminine identity her dress or fashion or accessories intimated, she would also have resisted that trivialization in innovative ways through dexterous manipulation of pins, fans, and other costuming paraphernalia.

Not only were decorative ornaments such as the fan, the hoop, and the pin (meaning variously a pointed instrument, a sharp needle, or sometimes a hairpin with an ornamental head) instilled with various desires, but actresses themselves could mutate into semiotic weapons which enterprising wives

Figure 17. "Mrs. Abington in the Character of Aurelia" in George Farquhar's *The Twin Rivals* (1777). Private collection.

might then employ against patriarchal influence. One commentator found that Abington's style was especially self-assured in transferring this kind of power to women spectators: "In the same manner that the philosophical disciples of antiquity imposed silence on the inconsiderate scholars, by observing, *our master has said thus*; so it is sufficient for the beauties of London to observe Mrs. Abington has worn such a thing, to shut the mouths of their fathers and their husbands" (Boaden, *Life of Jordan*, 32). Aligned in the spectator's mind with pins, fans, and nosegays in her roles, her epilogues, and her portraits, Abington was idealized and aestheticized even while being reduced to the fetishized object of capital. In sum, Abington's onstage and offstage personae encouraged conspicuous consumption of fashionable dress as a material component of femininity that paradoxically organized women's desires toward possessing new freedoms. In an anecdote expressing his admiration, Horace Walpole applied military language to her model of fashionable femininity: "I declare Mrs. Abington may march through all my dominions at the head of as large a troop as she pleases—I do not say, as she can muster and command; for then I am sure my house would not hold them."[54] Abington did not surrender her identity to things but turned fashion and its instruments into a means to negotiate toward a modern feminism by energizing that commodification into a potential source of agency. Stoking women spectators' desire to consume, Abington's celebrity was imitated by her female audience through her brand-name style, hairdo, cap, fan, and other accessories linked to her idiosyncratic, strong-minded, virtual "self." These material properties, over which Abington might have exercised patents if they had existed, were elements that she engineered to assert her womanly command, a form of Amazonian femininity bolstered by the costuming and accessories that she manipulated. Rather than claiming her sexual power through anatomy—with heaving breasts and a finely turned ankle—Abington's manipulation of her accessories and of fashion *distracted* from her body parts to claim a voguish femininity paired with militancy that bolstered her performative identity and produced a mighty impact as a fashion deity who attested to women's worth.

Other Significant Roles and Epilogues

Given Abington's authority established through fashion and epilogues, it is not surprising that other vibrant, independent characters numbered among her favored parts. Abington triumphed as the Widow Bellmour, vexingly combining nostalgic femininity with modern feminism, in Arthur Murphy's *The Way to Keep Him* (1760), expanded to five acts with the addition of a more complicated subplot. Murphy came to define the play as Abington's performative property, flattering her that "your talents have made the Play your own" after twenty-five years of playing the role. He added, "It is the Performer that gives to the draught, however justly traced, a form, a spirit, a countenance, and a mind."[55] In the play Lovemore, pretending to be Lord Etheridge, courts Abington's character, the lovely young cosmopolitan Widow Bellmour. Mrs. Lovemore is allegedly responsible for her gamester husband's neglect because she has lost the will to dress elegantly to please him. Loosely based on Alexandre-Guillaume De Moissy's *Nouvelle école des femmes*, the English version was inspired by Jonathan Swift's scatological poem *Strephon and Chloe*, which combines antifeminist sentiments with a concluding injunction to the sexes to be companionate. The poem blames wives for their husbands' loss of interest but ultimately recommends that mutual esteem will sustain a marriage: "Let prudence with good nature strive,/To keep esteem and love alive."[56] Widow Bellmour cleverly convinces Mrs. Lovemore that, in forgetting to exercise her charms, she contributed to his philandering desires, but she also tutors Mrs. Lovemore in hatching a plot to make her husband jealous with the foppish Sir Brilliant Fashion.

Murphy's revisions to the original French play make the scenes in which Widow Bellmour schools Mrs. Lovemore in womanly wiles even more central to the plot. The learned Bellmour, whose library is prominently displayed, is discovered reading Pope's *Epistle to a Lady*, which, like Swift's satire, expresses ambivalence at best toward the portrait gallery of women who prefer pleasure and sway to moral integrity ("Most women have no characters at all"). In a 1787 illustration to the play, a buxom, handsomely dressed, and beautifully coiffured Abington is pictured reading at the door to her library, adjacent to her dressing table. The Widow / Abington recites Pope's couplets in praise of the ideal woman who "never shows she rules." The best woman, she continues, "Charms by accepting, by submitting sways, / Yet has her Humour most when she obeys," a lesson Widow Bellmour wants to teach Mrs. Lovemore. Just as Swift's and Pope's poems draw on a tradition of antifeminist satire to chide women into good sense, *The Way to Keep Him* uses the *Epistle* as a means to reinforce the stereotype that woman's "a contradiction still." Demonstrating feminine graces along with feminist sentiments, the Widow accompanies her singing with harpsichord playing, interrupting her musical performance to adjust her elaborate hairdo in the mirror. Attention to fashion is critical to woman's power, the play asserts, and Widow Bellmour convinces Mrs. Lovemore that stylish dress reflects an inner value: "Virtue alone cannot please the Taste of this Age.—It is *La Belle Nature*,—Nature embellish'd by the Advantages of Art, that the Men expect now-o'-days" (2: 1). Fashionable clothing is the visible sign of a feminine nature perfectly attune to its artful display, and the Widow/Abington inducts Mrs. Lovemore into the cult of fashion to restore domestic harmony.

Close observers of Abington were at pains to insist that her onstage transformations revealed true nature rather than artifice. In lines written about Abington's performance as Millamant in Congreve's *Way of the World*, a quarrel over the superiority of Beauty or Fashion, nature or art, is settled by declaring her to be deputy of both: "This treaty [between nature and art] no sooner was published aloud, / Than Abington! Abington! Echoed the crowd / And Taste, as High Priestess, confirmed the choice."[57] Similarly, she further personified this unity as Lady Bab in masquerade as the shepherdess Philly Nettletop, the Maid of the Oaks. This play, to which we now return, is indicative of Abington's ability to shape a definitive blend between a traditional femininity and an avant-garde feminism. According to the verses "On seeing Mrs. Abbington perform Lady Bab Lardoon, at the Request of her Grace the Duchess of Marlborough," as the high priestess of fashion, Abington united ideal nature with costumed elegance "in the very contrasted Characters of Lady Bab Lardoon and Philly Nettletop": "Nature and Fashion now no more/ Shall disagree as heretofore, / But both their force unite, / Convinc'd one female can display / Th'extended pow'rs of either's sway, / And variegate delight" (*Life of Mrs. Abington*, 114–15). Anti-commercial discourse, typified not least in Mary Wollstonecraft's contempt for the addiction of vain women to shopping, linked their consumption to corrupt femininity;[58] Abington contested this image of femininity as mere superficial display by commodifying it into a personal aesthetic.

The popular light comic entertainment *Maid of the Oaks* deserves more attention as central to Abington's dual representations as the locus of a material femininity. The play contrasted urban commercialism to the moral authority located in the bucolic English countryside. True Englishness, wrested away from the metropolitan center, reaches down to the laborers and artisans—the shepherds, gardeners, carpenters, chandlers—preparing for the nuptials that will unite representatives of ancient values. Maria, ironically played by the notorious courtesan Sophia Baddeley, personifies those rural virtues. The country scenes blend the robust stability of Oldworth, the landed older generation, with the youthful promise of Sir Harry Grovesby, "an honest country gentleman," whose nuptials to the maid of the oaks, "a plain English wife," are pending his father's approval. The traditional rural values he voices reaffirm England's strengths: "A contempt for old times may be fashionable, but I am pleas'd with every thing that brings them to my remembrance—I love an old oak at my heart . . . it is the emblem of British fortitude, and like the heroic spirits of the island, while it o'ertops, it protects the undergrowth—" (5: 1). Though Maria stands to inherit Oldworth's property and a substantial allowance, her song disingenuously idealizes the virtues of poverty: "lack of wealth is lack of woe." Similarly, the author in the preface voices what may be one of the first references to the widening social strata of the audience in noting that the play's democratizing appeal, merging English vigor with French sophistication, extends to "the middle class and the bulk of the assembly." After the inevitable impediments to the plot resolution are overcome, Celtic magic transpires in the oak forests when a druid waves his wand to reveal the "palace of celestial love." The fête champêtre masquerade (or rural wedding feast) in the final acts is peopled with cosmopolitans—Russians, Prussians, Dutchmen, and Turks.[59] In short, the country, the seat of English values, withstands attack from foreign influences—including French, Ottoman, and Indian—by absorbing them within.

Abington as Lady Bab, "the princess of dissipation," represents both elegance and excess. She might also be seen as an exotic curiosity whose foreignness is signaled through her affinity with the East as well as with France. The unusual admixture of the occasion of a country wedding and references to the East culminate in the huntress Actea appearing "with a tin crescent upon her head, big enough for a Turkish mosque" (4: 1), along with allusions to Cleopatra, the Grand Mogul, nabobs, and the seraglio.[60] "An epitome, or rather a caricature of what is call'd *very* fine life, and the first female gamester of the time" (1: 1), she is courted by the misogynist, foppish, and hypocritical coxcomb Charles Dupeley just returned from France. Abington in masquerade as a shepherdess, which she hopes will discomfit Dupeley, represents the height of rural fantasy: "the dress I am going to put on for the Fête will do admirably to impose upon him" (2: 1). Rural values engage in a genteel struggle within her person. Lady Bab in masquerade becomes the medium through which a fashionable femininity, juxtaposed against pastoral innocence and confusingly jumbled with the foreign, is absorbed into a modern notion of England that encompasses women's freedoms in the multiple identities of Lady Bab/Philly/Abington.

Abington made *Maid of the Oaks* a stunning success in spite of its slight and predictable plot, and because of its specific references to well-known aspects of Abington's actual person, including her penchant for playing cards.[61] Lady Bab, a precursor to Lady Teazle in Sheridan's *The School for Scandal*, delights in seeing her scandalous activities reported in the papers, including all-night gambling. In another self-reference, Abington calls to mind her youthful moniker as "Nosegay Fan" (also apparent in Hickey's portrait) when she "unpins" a nosegay, part of her masquerade as shepherdess Philly Nettletop, to hand it to her suitor Dupeley, whose foppishness merits *his* being called a nosegay. Alluding to her real-life status as displaced quality, Lady Bab/Abington remarks ironically, "You shall see what an excellent actress I should have made, if fortune had not unluckily brought me into the world an earl's daughter" (3: 1). Allusions to her as the favorite sultaness in "a rural seraglio" also reminded savvy audiences of her success in Bickerstaff's *The Sultan*, preferring "the Great Mogul at the back of a pack of cards" to Dupeley (3: 1). Lady Bab finally converts from the religion of artful fashion to the more traditional values represented by the young married couple, now Lord and Lady Groveby: "My mind has ever been on the side of reason, though the torrent in which I have lived has not allowed me time to practice, or even to contemplate it as I ought—but to follow fashion, where we feel shame, is surely the strongest of all hypocrisy, and from this moment I renounce it" (4: 1). Instead of revealing the magic of capital, in this rural fantasy "the magic lies in *truth of Love*."

Abington delivered a new concluding piece to *Maid of the Oaks* on 3 November 1774 in which she asked the audience to determine which persona they wished her to adopt: "Lady Bab, or Phill, or Abington? / For Mrs. Abington, her part I see, / Asks too much curt'sying and humility, / 'Twere tedious stuff, and let me never stir, / If I am perfect in her character." In Garrick's epilogue written specially for her, she confidently defends women's freedom and, as a catalyst for change, offers a prototype of the actress as a modern woman. Speaking directly to the female spectators, as she does in so many epilogues, Abington (comparing herself to a spy in the House of Parliament) authorizes women to vote on their aesthetic preferences—a privilege they can exercise only in the theater because they are disenfranchised in Parliament. Risking a charge of treason, she enjoins them to exercise their right to free speech: "I'll put the question—if you choose me speaker: / Suppose me now be-wigg'd, and seated here, / I call to order! You the chair! The chair! Is it your pleasure that this bill should pass—?"[62] Her forthright declarations strikingly contrast to the muddled moral of the play which promotes quaint English country values based on inherited wealth as antidotes to urban excess and empire's luxury. The comedy, then, unites the display of fashion with its renunciation in favor of the naturalness that the exquisitely coiffured and costumed Abington was alleged to embody; its songs idealizing poverty are performed in front of extravagant sets, and finish with a call for English women to openly express their approval for such lavish entertainments.

Frequently played as an afterpiece to *Maid in the Oaks*, *The Capricious Lady* in its eighteenth-century redaction acknowledges in its preface that Abington, "who combines an excellent understanding and great dramatic knowledge with her well-known theatrical talents," was single-handedly responsible for its success.[63] William Cooke revised Beaumont and Fletcher's *Scornful Lady* into *The Capricious Lady* at Abington's urging, for she correctly imagined that it would be a perfect vehicle for her comic talents. Abington transformed the title role, originally intended for a boy-actress, into a showpiece for a knowing femininity. Even in its Restoration production, Samuel Pepys had exulted in the improvement to the original when "done by a woman, which makes the play appear much better than ever it did to me" (*Diary*, 12 February 1660–61). Many of Abington's other roles update Renaissance comedies including the leads in *Rule a Wife and Have a Wife*, *The Sultan*, *The Way to Keep Him*, and *The Hypocrite*.

The Capricious Lady oddly yokes sentiments for and against female freedom. The Elder Loveless pursues the Lady/Abington, and he voices the play's satire against uppity women: "You are a woman, and the proudest that ever lov'd a coach; the scornfullest, absurdist, and most capricious woman; the greediest to be prais'd and never satisfied, though it be gross and open; [and] the most envious" (4: 1). The play uncovers the performative nature of sex roles, to question the essence of female nature: "O woman, woman! what are thou?" (5: 1). When the Lady finally becomes central to the play in the third act, she affects a righteous morality to scorn the men's dissipated behavior. Even though the lovers are equally duplicitous, the play defines fickleness as the particular province of women, and in spite of being embattled, the Lady ultimately controls the unfolding plot through her manipulations. She exacts revenge "by giving up a war, which, like many a potentate, I have got nothing by, but the disgrace of acting a part I am both heartily ashamed and tired of" (5: 1).

George Colman's timely epilogue to *The Capricious Lady* draws the Renaissance play into the actual occasion of its eighteenth-century production to provide an unexpectedly feminist response to a misogynist play. Modern women, the Lady/Abington charges, are more insolent and prideful, more frivolous and coquettish, than in the past; but their behavior is a legitimate reaction to modern men's infidelity in contrast to the knightly virtues of old. In the epilogue to Cumberland's sentimental comedy *The West Indian* (1771), also written by David Garrick, Abington parodies the catechism, turning it into a secular credo financed by colonial wealth. She celebrates the contemporary moment of frivolous pastimes as superior to Elizabethan restrictions to conclude, "You all rejoice with me, you're living now," thus epitomizing the modern moment for women. The epilogue to *The Capricious Lady* also recalls the martial imagery of weaponry familiar from Abington's other epilogues in contrasting prudish "starch'd ruff'd maidens of Queen Bess's reign" who slew knights to the freer modern maidens:

> In Fletcher's days it was the favorite plan
> Of Women, to dethrone the tyrant Man.
> Our modern fashions vary; yet their aim,
> Howe'er pursu'd, appears the very same.
> The starch'd ruff'd maidens of Queen *Bess's* reign,
> Were doomed a starch demeanor to maintain;
> Quill'd up like porcupines, they shot their darts,
> Slaughter'd whole rows of Knights, and wounded hearts:
> Their virtue nought could shake, no siege could alter;
> A rock impregnable as *Gibraltar*!
> In vain were signs, and tears, and idle flattery,
> Their red-hot balls la'd low each hostile battery;
> While they, bright stars, above all weak comparison,
> Shone forth the female Eliots of the garrison.[64]

The epilogue, like the play, demonstrates Abington's ability to move in and out of the coquetry of conventional femininity by alternating it with modern self-assertion. Her vigorous self-defense complicates and ultimately contests the play's hackneyed antagonisms.

On yet another occasion, Abington's stage weaponry doubles as fashion accessory. As Estifania in the updated Beaumont and Fletcher comedy, *Rule a Wife and Have a Wife* (1761), Abington, playing the Spanish "wild Young girl," dramatically illustrates women's ungovernable nature when she defends herself with a pistol[65] (Figure 18). She and her friend Margarita impersonate wealthy gentlewomen to swindle soldiers Perez and Juan out of their property

Figure 18. "Mrs. Abington as Estifania" in Beaumont and Fletcher, *Rule a Wife and Have a Wife* (1759–60) (Vet.A5 e. 3390). Bodleian Library, University of Oxford.

by duping them into marriage. When Estifania/Abington draws a pistol, her "husband" dissuades her from shooting him with bawdy wordplay: "Prithee let me see thy Gun, 'tis a very pretty one" (5: 1). In a phrase that would have resonated very differently on the same-sex Renaissance stage, Estifania responds, "No, no, Sir, you shall feel [it instead]," and she admits to having pawned his valuables. The pointed weapon substitutes both for a fan and for the body part missing from her female anatomy. The two women succumb to the rule of their husbands at play's end, but the picture of Abington holding a firearm reinforces the Amazonian courage of actress and character rather than feminine submission.

As an engine of fashion Abington, like other star actresses, continued to stimulate consumerism—thought to be in the best interests of the nation—and linked female sovereignty to voguish clothing when she spoke as Lady Rentless in Miles Peter Andrews's epilogue to his five-act comedy *Dissipation* (London, 1781): "Ladies, for us exert this darling passion / Do, ton it here, and make this play the fashion."[66] Fashion provides her sway, though she proclaims that sartorial splendor is a positive, leveling force: "All ranks alike adore my potent queen / From proud St. James's Square, to Bethnal-Green, / The titled dame not more her head can toss / Than the ship captain's wife, at Ratcliff-Cross." Finally and most tellingly, in *A Collection of . . . Prologues and Epilogues* (1779), although most of the illustrations depict men, the illustrations portraying opulently dressed actresses speaking prologues and epilogues are accompanied by dramatic lines that pointedly affirm the character's/actress's strength of mind. The excerpt from Miss Young's epilogue to *The Runaway* counsels, "Good Sense to Govern me;—and let me Govern him" (4: 241). Similarly, in reciting the prologue to *Polly Honeycombe*, Sarah Wilson declares, "Our Tongues will serve for Trumpet & for Drum, / I'll be your Leader—General Honeycombe" (3: 261). Mary Anne Yates delivering the epilogue to *The Earl of Warwick* adopts a dueling stance and points her fan boldly as if the accessory were an extension of her outstretched arm: "Now parry Margaret if you can" (4: 215). And resplendent in a gorgeous gown and plumed hat in the epilogue following *Zingis*, Abington incites women to declare their legitimate rights: "Oh that dear Sparta! / Their Women had a Noble Magna Charta" (4: 230) In other words, not only Abington, but other highly popular actresses, fashionably attired and calling attention to their own persons, assert women's authority in their most beloved prologues and epilogues (Figures 19–22).

Abington's debut in *Maid of Oaks* (1774) had anticipated by one year the initial performance of another favored role, Roxalana in *The Sultan, or, a Peep*

Figure 19. "Miss Young, Epilogue to *The Runaway*" (1780). From *A Collection of More than Eight Hundred Prologues and Epilogues . . . written by the late D. Garrick*, vol. 4 (PR1195.P7 C6*). William Andrews Clark Memorial Library, University of California, Los Angeles.

Figure 20. "Mrs. Wilson, Prologue to *Polly Honeycombe*" (1780). From *A Collection of More than Eight Hundred Prologues and Epilogues . . . written by the late D. Garrick*, vol. 3 (PR1195.P7 C6*). William Andrews Clark Memorial Library, University of California, Los Angeles.

Figure 21. "Mrs. Yates, Epilogue to *The Earl of Warwick*" (1779). From *A Collection of More than Eight Hundred Prologues and Epilogues . . . written by the late D. Garrick*, vol. 4 (PR1195.P7 C6*). William Andrews Clark Memorial Library, University of California, Los Angeles.

Figure 22. "Mrs. Abington, Epilogue to the *Tragedy of Zingis*" (1779). From *A Collection of More than Eight Hundred Prologues and Epilogues . . . written by the late D. Garrick*, vol. 4 (PR1195.P7 C6*). William Andrews Clark Memorial Library, University of California, Los Angeles.

into the Seraglio: A Farce on 12 December 1775 at Drury Lane; she reprised both parts throughout the 1780s. Continuing to take command of her professional career, Abington had inspired Isaac Bickerstaff to create the part for her: "The author has been pleased Publickly to declare that it was My Stile of acting, which first suggested to him the Idea of Bringing Roxalana upon the English Stage; and my friends are, one and all, particularly anxious to see me in the character."[67] As we have seen, Abington combined shepherdess with fashionplate in *Maid of the Oaks*, and outspoken woman with coquette in *Capricious Lady*. As Roxalana in *The Sultan* she blended English captive with Eastern harem woman so that the rural English fantasy of *Maid of the Oaks* was replaced by Orientalist romance, but both were enlisted in the cause of feminist sympathies.[68]

Like Lady Mary Wortley Montagu before her, Abington as Roxalana painted by Sir Joshua Reynolds in her rich Ottoman costume encoded Eastern alterity through dress. Abington is representative of the actress's plight, poised at the seraglio's/stage's edge.[69] Reynolds's portrait of Abington coyly peering from behind the curtain represented the character's—and by implication all actresses'—overthrow of despotic masculine rule, her claim to superiority, and her calculated intrusion into forbidden territory. Roxalana, the "quite ungovernable" Englishwoman and favorite captive of the Sultan, competes with the harem women (in part through singing) to become the adored object of the Sultan's affections. Osmyn the eunuch charges, "She is sure to do every thing she is forbid; she makes a joke of our threats, and answers our most serious admonitions with a laugh: besides, she is at variance with the rest of the women, and shows them such an example, that I cannot longer rule them" (1: 1).[70] Like the actress, the devilish and irreverent Roxalana exudes a puzzling "spirit of caprice and independence" (1: 1). Reversing the Sultan's authority, she turns the Muslim ruler into her pupil. Invading his forbidden territory and risking death, she offers unsolicited advice and urges him to disband his harem to allow the women to experience English liberty and companionate marriage. She boasts that she is "a free-born woman, prouder of that than all the pomp and splendour eastern monarchs can bestow" (1: 1) and demands to be treated as his equal and a rival to his power, "like the queen of the country" (2: 1). Forming a bond with the rejected sultana Elmira and the Persian slave Ismena while threatening to behead the eunuch Osymyn, she attempts to "civilize" the seraglio with English cutlery and "Christian" wine. Newly empowered, the harem women playfully pass the handkerchief, the marker of the drunken Sultan's favor and of female sexual subjection. Freeing Elmira and becoming the

Sultan's companionate partner, Roxalana reforms the seraglio, erases the erotic power of the tragic Eastern woman, and replaces it with comic female sway. Embodying the reigning stereotypes of Eastern women, Roxalana/Abington combined the seductive mystery of the Eastern woman with the liberal individualism alleged to be the Englishwoman's birthright.

The Oriental theme reappears in another Abington vehicle, Joseph Jekyll's epilogue to the three-act comedy, Baroness Elizabeth Craven's *Miniature Picture* (1781), originally intended as a closet drama. There she complains that Englishmen tyrannize, like Turks, over actresses, because they confine them to speaking "flippant" epilogues, while men monopolize the prologues. In one of her most forceful declarations, she contends that women's special abilities make them capable of steering the state: "Methinks, e'en how, I hear my sex's tongues, / The sweet, smart melody of female lungs! / The storm of Question, the Division calm, / With 'hear her! Hear her; Mrs. Speaker, Ma'am!'"[71] Satirizing foppish men, Abington describes a mock attack performed on Warley Common before the king (October 1778, painted by Philip de Loutherbourg and exhibited at the Royal Academy in 1779), and compares the female dramatist Craven to the Major's strong-minded wife. She specifically addresses the ladies in the audience as citizens: "Here should ye sign some patriot petition, / To men our 'constitutional' condition. / The men invade our rights." One of the men whom she felt invaded her rights was indeed David Garrick. Like Kitty Clive, Peg Woffington, and Hannah Pritchard, Abington was a worthy competitor to Garrick, in a competition spurred by his ambivalence toward her extraordinary commercial drawing power.

Competition with Garrick

Female playwrights flourished in writing almost two hundred plays between 1770 and 1800. Though Garrick's biographers maintain that the actor-manager greatly encouraged talented literary and creative women, and that he counted among his acquaintance public notables including Bluestocking Elizabeth Montagu, playwright Hannah More, and Lady Georgiana Spencer, his apparent generosity may have been a response to commercial demand rather than a genuine wish to support women.[72] While it is true that Garrick produced fifteen plays by women dramatists during his twenty-nine years as manager and provided many opportunities for actresses, as we have seen he often attempted to upstage and outwit the most successful women in his company including

Mrs. Pritchard, his costar in *Hamlet*, *Macbeth*, *Much Ado About Nothing*, and *The Jealous Wife*.[73]

In his difficult negotiations with Abington, many commentators, then and now, assign blame to the actress rather than the manager: for example, Garrick's modern biographers indicate that he "found her temperamental and at times unreasonable, especially in relation to contracts"[74]—though Abington, like Clive and Woffington before her, may have simply been insisting on her just deserts. They describe Abington as a "cross" that he had to bear (Stone and Kahrl, *Garrick*, 595); and Mary Knapp similarly charges that Abington was "dishonest, selfish, undependable, and a continual vexation to Garrick."[75] Garrick voiced his frustrations regarding the star actress in a letter to Peter Fountain: "That most Worthless Creature . . . she is below the thought of an honest Man or Woman—she is as *Silly*, as she is *false* & treacherous."[76] He mocked her attempt to play Ophelia as foundering "like a mackerel on a gravel walk";[77] and he became irate when she complained about his favoring actress Jane Pope. He further scolded Abington for unreasonably refusing to accept last-minute substitutions and insisting on a day's notice to play even so familiar a part as Charlotte Rusport in *The West Indian*.[78] Garrick's criticisms of Abington's alleged grandstanding were intense and the disputes ongoing. He complained frequently about what he perceived to be Abington's fantasies of injustice: "I never yet Saw Mrs Abington theatrically happy for a Week together, there is Such a continual working of a fancy'd Interest, such a Refinement of Importance, & Such imaginary good & Evil, continually arising in the Politicians Mind, that the only best Substantial Security of Public applause is neglected for these Shadows" (27 November 1772, Little and Kahrl, 3:830). Abington's rehearsal of a "Catalogue of Grievances" caused Garrick to inquire in frustration, "Why can't you ask a small favour without proving the infinite hardships you have suffer'd" (18 June [1774], 3:943). Dismissive of her complaints about the conditions of employment, Garrick launched a tirade of accusations in a letter to her:

> You mention *your great fatigue*: What is the Stage come to, if I must continually hear of your *hard labour*, when from the beginning of the season to this time, you have not play'd more than *twice* a Week? Mrs Oldfield perform'd Lady Townly for 29 Night[s] successively: let us now examine how just & genteel Your complaint is against me: I promis'd You, that I would procure a Character of consequence to be written on purpose for You, and that it should be Your own fault, if you were not on the

highest pinnacle of Yr profession—I have been at great pains, & you know it, to be as good as my word—I directed & assisted the Author to make a small Character, a very considerable one for You, I spar'd no Expence in dresses, Musick, scenes & decorations for the piece, & now the *fatigue of Acting* this Character, is very unjustly, as well [as] unkindly brought against me: had you play'd this part *40* times, instead of *20*, my gains would be less than by any other Successful play, I have produc'd in my Management—the greatest favour I can confer upon an Actress, is to give her the best Character in a favourite piece, & the longer it runs, the more Merit I have with her, & ought to receive her *thanks*, instead of *Complaints*. (28 January 1775, 3: 988)

In spite of Garrick's diatribe, however, Abington's a treatment by theater historians who recount them have been, I suggest, unduly partial to the theater manager. At least one eighteenth-century lampoon sided with the actress: "For managers will make th'absurdest laws; / But let them blunder—tho' we seldom view, / Yet, Abington must charm us when we do."[79] Early in her career Abington had protested that the roles of Beatrice, Mrs. Sullen, Clarinda, and the like were considered to be the sacrosanct performative property of the senior actresses in the company, and she sought Garrick's help in obtaining new roles. When he turned a deaf ear to her requests for more substantial parts, she demanded that Garrick put her "on such a respectable footing with the public, and of course, with authors, that I should be thought not unequal to, nor be ill received in such light and easy characters of comedy as my talents confine me to."[80] She rudely reminded him of her professional superiority to his wife: "Perhaps you do not know that Mrs. Garrick had £300 per annum given to her upon the fresh Establishment, only for Dancing two years; and I have been Dancing, and Playing the Fool for more than 20 [sic] years, to the great divertion of his Majesties good and faithful Subjects."[81] When Garrick announced his retirement in 1775, Abington too pretended that she would promptly retire and insisted that the two actors should share a "final" mutual benefit performance. Each celebrity felt misunderstood by the other—Garrick demanding that the actress give credence to the challenges he faced as a theater manager, and Abington insisting that he grant her greater respect, recognition, and more favorable working conditions.

Further demanding her right to star billing, Abington quarreled with Anne Barry over the lead role Lady Bell in Arthur Murphy's *Know Your own Mind* (1778). When she claimed that Garrick had mistreated not only herself but also his friend Murphy, Garrick worried that the actress was spreading malignant rumors. At other times Abington felt insulted in being called to perform to a nearly empty house. When she insisted on her legitimate right to choose the first benefit night and quarreled over being assigned Miss Younge's rejected date, the dispute led to a legal consultation. Abington solicited an additional £200 pay per annum to be awarded to her in the event that George Colman's death (he died on 1 April 1790) would bring a grant to the theater. But in spite of their fraught relationship, Garrick sporadically offered reluctant admiration for his lead actress: "Yours very truly, when You are not *unruly*." He collaborated with Abington on the choice of "what to speak, & what to reject" in the epilogues he wrote for her to recite including John Burgoyne's *The Maid of the Oaks* and Hugh Kelly's *School for Wives* (18 December [1773], 2.910)—epilogues like those of other star actresses which, in Garrick's words, reinforced her personal authority.[82]

Sir Joshua Reynolds's alluring picture of Abington (1771) as the coquettish country girl Miss Prue in Congreve's *Love for Love* suggests further evidence that Garrick's envy was common knowledge. The charmingly seductive portrait resonates with Angelica Kauffman's 1764 painting of David Garrick in which he, positioned similarly to Abington, is seated with the chairback facing the viewer in a visual reference to the boundary between stage and audience (Figures 23, 24). If this paired contrast between actor and actress was intended, then the images implicitly reflect the tension between the rivals. Garrick's short, stocky stature, especially in relation to the company's statuesque actresses, may well have led Reynolds to pose him as seated. He is attired in street clothing rather than a costume, sporting a cocky look through the half-shadow crossing his face; his hands gesture as if signaling a stage direction, making him appear to be more the manager-director than the actor. Abington's portrait, however, inserts the actress's private personality into the stage role; it portrays "Miss Prue playing Mrs. Abington" rather than the reverse.[83] Characteristically overdressed for the part of a chambermaid, she wears elegant pink satin, while her fluffy white lapdog peers appealingly through the chair's curved filigreed back. Her thumb provocatively parts her lips, and her white apron on which the dog is perched is arranged in folds suggestive of the sitter's genitalia. Each of the portrait sitters, actor and actress, flirtatiously engages with an imagined audience, Garrick with knowing authority and Abington with seductive confidence.

In short, their very public quarrels reveal active professional jealousy but also grudging admiration in spite of their competing concerns—Garrick's

Figure 23. "Mrs. Abington as Miss Prue in *William Congreve's Love for Love*." Sir Joshua Reynolds (1771), oil on canvas. Paul Mellon Collection, Yale Center for British Art.

wish to protect his own reputation and the health of the company, and Abington's desire to increase her wages and professional status by manipulating the economics of the system. Abington keenly resisted being mistreated in a sustained effort to serve her own best interests, thus laying claim to being a rival queen not only because of her spectacular talent but also because of her skill as a venerable guide to fashionable consumption.

Material Femininity: Frances Abington 263

Figure 24. "David Garrick." Angelica Kauffman (1771), oil on canvas. Burghley House Collection, Stamford, England.

Weaving a consistent thread throughout the roles and epilogues designed for her—including especially Lady Bab, the Capricious Lady, and Roxalana—Abington embodied the highly independent spirit of the successful professional actress. She fought for equal status with a reluctant Garrick; she managed her career, even commissioning her own portrait impersonating the Comic

Muse;[84] she encouraged playwrights to adapt plays especially suited to her talents; and with the assistance of fashionable properties, she developed an authoritative epilogue-persona that conveyed the effect of a forceful interiority. Whether costumed as a shepherdess, a sultana, or coquettish ingénue, she cultivated sartorial exchange between theater and society. The fashion trade and its culture of consumption, so important to the nation's economic growth, flourished as Abington personified the values of commerce: she shaped her identity to navigate the notions of the actress as a commodity and as an *objet d'art*, to turn fashion into a career path that allowed her to resist becoming *merely* public property. As an iconic actress, Abington refined the nation's aesthetic. Inspiring women to become arbiters of a nation's taste in fashion *and* in drama, she made available a coveted identity that female spectators could share, not just vicariously, but materially. Infusing her properties with "life" histories that were not confined to the stage, she exploited her interiority effect with props and things, to transform material femininity into a feminist weapon. A locus for the debates about commercial culture, Abington stood on the threshold between nostalgia for a past sustained by a conventional, virtuous femininity, and the potential that the future held for women who challenged its terms and embodied revolutionary change.

Epilogue: Contracted Virtue

> How long have *Females* merited our scorn?
> *They* have pow'rs superior to perform
> Than *Men,* and why not *Females* equal share
> The just reward of Fame, the envied *Chair?*
> —James Leigh, *The New Rosciad* (1785)

> It is not a little remarkable, that the drama was uncommonly productive, the theatre more than usually attended, during that season when the principal dramatic characters were performed by women under the age of twenty. Among these were Miss Farren (now Lady Derby), Miss Walpole (now Mrs. Arkins), Miss P. Hopkins (now Mrs. John Kemble), and myself.
> —Mary Robinson, *Memoirs of the Late Mrs. Robinson* (1801)

NEAR CENTURY'S END a canon of plays emerged with the publication of the twenty-one- volume *Bell's British Theatre* (1776–81) and later the twenty-five-volume edition of *The British Theatre* (1808) accompanied by Elizabeth Inchbald's remarkable critical prefaces.[1] Each volume in the first edition of *Bell's British Theatre* consisted of five comedies or five tragedies, the volumes alternating evenhandedly between the two genres to convey a sense of their equivalence. In his advertisement to a similar set of *British Poets,* John Bell wrote that the little volumes were designed to "form a truly elegant ornamental appearance, in the drawing-room, dressing-room, or study, and may be cased so to render them a portable and complete traveling poetical, biographical, and critical library."[2] The theater volumes resembled the extraordinary poetry editions in their compactness: one could seem to master the whole of English drama, or of English poetry, by reading through the sets.

Appealing to both men and women readers, the selected plays and engraved illustrations in the much-reprinted and later expanded *Bell's British Theatre* reveal the absolute centrality of actresses and their dramatic parts by the late 1770s. Each of the images portrays a heightened subjective state or a climactic moment in the plot that draws the reader into an active engagement with the visual representation and the line of text accompanying the picture. Among the actresses pictured in the engravings—with feet planted firmly, arms gesturing emphatically, reflecting in their static pose the rules for posture and gesture and pointing assertively while delivering their forceful lines—are, for example, "Miss Younge in the Character of Hermione" in Ambrose Phillips's *The Distrest Mother* who cries, "I'll hurl Destruction like a Whirlwind round me" (vol. 1); "Mrs. Yates in the Character of Calista" in Nicholas Rowe's *The Fair Penitent* who taunts, "Strike home, & I will bless thee for the blow" (vol. 3); "Miss Younge in the Character of Artemis[i]a" in Rowe's *The Ambitious Step-Mother* who bravely challenges her foes, "Let them come on, I cannot fear" (vol. 10) ; and "Mrs. Lessingham [Lessing] in the Character of Oriana" in George Farquhar's *The Inconstant or The Way to Win Him* who declares, "Sir, I am proud of my power and am resolved to use it" (vol. 13). The pictures devoid of accompanying scenery emphasize the actress as much as the part and reinforce the impression of her commanding authority. More than half of the illustrations in this first edition of *Bell's* feature female characters, occasionally paired with male costars, in high dramatic focus, thus confirming the theater's thoroughgoing dependence upon actresses and even their slight predominance in both genres in the emerging canon of plays (Figures 25–28).

The pattern continues in Bell's 1795–96 edition, where the portraits of Mary Ann Yates and Sarah Siddons (twelve each) outnumber those of Garrick (ten), and those of Frances Abington, Elizabeth Pope, and Ann Barry (nine each) outnumber John Philip Kemble (seven).[3] Actresses provided the most visible signs of cultural change regarding the role of women in the thriving commercial society of the 1770s and 1780s. These queens of the theater, having proved their indispensability to it, rivaled their managers, their fellow actors, and other women players to memorialize what surely may be called an age of the actress.

If Sir Joshua Reynolds's magnificent painting of Sarah Siddons as *The Tragic Muse* (1783–84) significantly enhanced the status of the actress near the end of the century, then that ascent rests not only on her theatrical genius but also on the myriad talents that celebrity actresses exhibited throughout the earlier decades.[4] The continual public presence of this select but influential

Figure 25. "Miss Younge in the Character of Hermione." Engraver J. Roberts (?), artist J. Roberts. In Ambrose Phillips, *The Distrest Mother*, Act 5: 2, *Bell's British Theatre*, vol. 1.

Figure 26. "Mrs. Yates in the Character of Calista." Engraver J. Thornthwaite, artist J. Roberts. In Nicholas Rowe, *The Fair Penitent*, Act 4: 4, *Bell's British Theatre*, vol. 3.

Figure 27. "Miss Younge in the Character of Artemis[i]a." Engraver J. Thornthwaite, artist J. Roberts. In Nicholas Rowe, *The Ambitious Step-Mother*, Act 5: 1, in *Bell's British Theatre*, vol. 10.

Figure 28. "Mrs. Lessingham in the Character of Oriana." Engraver J. Thornthwaite, artist J. Roberts. In George Farquhar, *The Inconstant or The Way to Win Him*, Act 2: 2, *Bell's British Theatre*, vol. 13.

group, I have argued, animated the stage with regular reminders of women's right to claim a public presence. Attuned to a narrative of progress, they became proponents of the freedoms they embodied as they explored ways to emancipate themselves from the restraints assumed to have been characteristic of the modern female subject. They crafted public, performative identities that meshed in varying degrees with intimations of their putatively private personalities. These women players maneuvered within designated dramatic roles to base star power on the theatrical properties that were guarantors of a recognizable personhood whether in adaptations of Renaissance plays, comedies of manners, sentimental comedies, heroic dramas, she-tragedies, or bourgeois tragedies. This active pursuit of a publicly recognized interiority reflected on stage was compatible with what Deborah Heller has described, in another context, as "the salient aspect of modern subjectivity: namely, an interiority that can elude the identities constructed for it by discourse or culture."[5]

Celebrity actresses, adjudicating among genres and systems of patronage and commerce, made new configurations of feminine subjectivities available to be imagined and even realized. As we have seen, numerous Restoration and eighteenth-century plays were preoccupied with the definition of "woman," often introducing female characters who pushed at the boundaries of sexual difference to appear to be "more than a woman." Throughout the century, but especially during the 1770s and 1780s, actresses embodied the kinds of options available to women in an increasingly commercial society, consistent with an "exceptional" virtue that helped them locate a viable place within its contradictions. Actresses were not simply exceptions who proved the rule of domestic retreat: they were constitutive of alternatives to conventional femininity in the public sphere, for they embodied the private-in-the-public even as they commodified a simulacrum of intimacy. In sum, the most ambitious and successful actresses penetrated bourgeois life, fashionable society, and the court to stimulate the aesthetic, commercial, professional, and personal desires of women from apprentice milliners to city wives to ladies of quality.

The theater, as we have seen, encouraged the formation of mutually engaged female communities, uniting actress and female spectator even as early as the turn into the eighteenth century, and encouraging the emergence of women's shared political consciousness.[6] The theater tolerated social exchange that was often freer and less class-bound than more private assemblies; and thus the differences among political factions, in spite of the Licensing Act and subsequent legal restrictions, could often be heard in Drury Lane or Covent Garden. Elite women, resembling the earlier Shakespeare Ladies Club that the Countess of Shaftesbury had organized around 1736 because of their shared interest in drama, were also participants in the larger political culture, at least in an informal way. Women such as Lady Pembroke, Mrs. Fitzroy, Mrs. Meynel, Lady Molyneux, Miss Pelham, and Miss Lloyd, members of the Ladies Club or Coterie, according to Horace Walpole, combined theatrical with political interests and encouraged anti-ministerial Whiggish sentiments.[7] In addition to aristocratic ladies, professional women including the Bluestockings also established linkages, though more obliquely, with the emergence of a feminist political voice near the end of the century. While recent studies have shown that the theater was extensively involved in contemporary politics of the day, little attention has been given to actresses' participation, a tendency I have attempted to remedy, especially in the chapters on Kitty Clive and Peg Woffington.[8] Actresses such as these, alert to the theater's potential for contesting the status quo, edged toward proclaiming a politics compatible with women's greater independence through their dramatic roles and writings. In the decades preceding the radical 1790s, assertive and sometimes strident heroines were central to the commercial success of the theater, and many actresses' proto-feminism in various performative venues was not only tolerated but often assumed. At the same time, these rival queens' competition for their share of the market often interfered with their inclination to develop close relationships with other actresses. Their economic independence, social mobility, sexual liberty, and self-reflexivity anticipated modern forms of female identity, the price of which was their reliance upon exploiting a free-market, possessive individualism with all its imperfections that would inspire, but also plague, an emerging liberal feminism.

When the Pantheon opened in 1771–72, actresses mixed easily in polite company and in semiprivate social gatherings as they had done earlier at masquerades. The theater's influence on these fashionable entertainments included the mixing of social classes, the subscription to events by ticket, the active solicitation of purchasers for the coveted vouchers, and the practice of favoritism in allowing certain people to participate or subscribe.[9] It follows that actresses, often regarded as evading the limitations placed on ordinary women, rather than being located in one world or limited to one sexual identity alone, could be imagined as a legitimate driving force that facilitated the movement between worlds and identities. Actresses such as Sophia Baddeley, for example, sometimes supplemented their income by appearing at Ranelagh while performing in the same season at Drury Lane, thus moving easily between the theater and fashionable entertainments to join the two public places together in the minds of those who frequented both. Few actresses could compete for social status with the intellectual and artistic women who circulated in the cosmopolitan centers of Europe. Yet, as we have seen, star women players—including Barry, Clive, Pritchard, Abington, Yates, and of course Sarah Siddons—openly infiltrated the private gatherings, concerts, and fashionable soirees given by ladies and gentlemen of quality, and their activities were widely reported in the periodical press.

New assumptions regarding public, rational exchange between the sexes prevailed in the woman-centered fashionable society that the very different worlds of actresses and Bluestockings shared. The Blues, invested in a particular kind of decorous, learned feminism, served as a counterforce and a rebuttal to actresses' questionable definitions of virtue and their associations with commerce.[10] Exclusive gatherings at the homes of Bluestockings such as Elizabeth Montagu, Elizabeth Vesey, and Hester Thrale during these later decades differed from the Cornelys Society, the Coterie, Almack's, and Carlisle House in that no cardplaying or similarly frivolous activities were allowed, and they did not sell tickets to their events (though Mrs. Thrale was chided in the popular press for cardplaying). During the decades following the 1770s, expectations of exemplary virtue persisted and even tightened, as educated women, singers, painters, and moral writers of a certain caliber were idealized as icons of the British nation. As respectable and not-so-respectable women intermingled in public, Hester Thrale knowingly described a "contracted" virtue—in many ways opposite to the exceptional virtue actresses could claim—possessed by her large social circle. In July 1778 she commented in *Thraliana*, her journal of gossipy personal anecdotes, on these kinds of moral expectations that determined one's friendships. Thrale assigned numerical rankings to her acquaintances, codings that resemble those we have noted were assigned to actors in the periodical press: "Now for the Women; as they must possess *Virtue* in the contracted Sense, or one wd not keep em Company, so that is not thought about, & would not be contracted about Beauty neither; it is general Appearance rather than Beauty that is meant by Person Mien & Manner the useful Knowledge we can all comprehend."[11] The friends that she rated include intellectual and artistic women, among whom several were regarded as Bluestockings.

When Hester Thrale tallied up her friends' comparative merits and demerits in her journal, she graded men and women separately, and the categories differed for each sex. The rankings for women ignored scholarship, religion, and morality—categories she used to assess the men—but not surprisingly she focused instead on women's sociable characteristics. These traits included "worth of heart," conversational powers, manner and mien, good humor, and two kinds of knowledge, useful and ornamental.[12] In Thrale's scale she ranked herself second only to Bluestocking Elizabeth Montagu, who reigned supreme over the forty-five women among her acquaintance. Thrale tied with Lady Burgoyne, closely followed by Mrs. Byron. Among the Bluestockings, Mrs. Boscawen, Mrs. Crewe, Frances Reynolds, Mrs. Carter, Mrs. Chapone, Frances Burney, and Hannah More figured highest near the top of her rankings. The Bluestockings clearly established the moral norm against whom other women were to be judged. Thrale later thumbed her nose at these rigid strictures when in 1784 she scandalized her friends and disappointed Samuel Johnson by marrying Gabriel Piozzi, her social inferior and the object of her enduring passion, after the death of her first husband three years earlier.

The theater increasingly encroached upon the assemblies that learned women such as Montagu, Vesey, and Thrale sponsored, and the drama figured importantly in their correspondence and social interchanges. Dr. Campbell, a Scottish parson visiting London for the first time, confirmed that his dinner engagement on 8 April 1777 included Frances Abington before they joined a party at Henry and Hester Thrale's home: "Lady --, Miss Jeffries, one of the Maids of Honour, Sir Joshua Reynolds, & c., at Mrs. Abingdon's. He said Sir C. Thompson, and some others who were there, spoke like people who had seen good company, and so did Mrs. Abingdon herself," defining "good company" as "company of rank and fashion." Adding a caveat he apparently intended to heighten Abington's stature, Campbell remarked that she "shows a certain dignity of soul which despises all vulgar means of attracting the applause of the crowd."[13] Thrale came finally to prefer exceptional virtue, comprised of personal integrity and dignity of soul, to the contracted virtue valued among her social circle.

Surprising as it might seem, given the alleged prejudice against actresses, theatrical women intruded into Richard Samuel's well-known group picture, *Portraits in the Characters of the Muses in the Temple of Apollo* (1778)—popularly known as *The Nine Living Muses of Great Britain*—which derived from an earlier sketch and print[14] (Figure 29). The staging of literary and artistic women grouped companionably together before the temple of Apollo included Elizabeth Carter, Anna Laetitia (Aikin) Barbauld, Elizabeth Linley Sheridan, Charlotte Lennox, Catharine Macaulay, Hannah More, Elizabeth Montagu, and Elizabeth Griffith. The women, posing as the classical muses draped in soft Grecian robes, hold objects representing their intellectual or creative

Figure 29. "Portraits in the Character of the Muses in the Temple of Apollo." Richard Samuel (1778), oil on canvas. © National Portrait Gallery, London.

achievements, including a scroll, goblet, tablet, lyre, palette, and a stringed instrument. Each is apparently intended to impersonate a specific muse, though the correlation between any individual lady and her muse is not readily apparent. Samuel did not paint from live models, and the unindividuated women are represented as if they were, as Kate Davies has accurately observed, "one indeterminate classical figure divided into nine cultural activities."[15]

Apparently the Bluestockings pictured in the painting were not immune to the wish for public fame that permeated the society of the period, as much as they worried over celebrity's compromise of virtue. Though they seldom admitted to the pleasures of gaining public attention, Elizabeth Carter and Elizabeth Montagu allowed themselves a certain smug satisfaction in the public notoriety that Samuel's painting brought them. Seeming to compete with popular actresses, they joked that, in spite of the ladies being indistinguishable from each another, *Nine Living Muses* would afford them a fleeting celebrity, and they seemed surprisingly amenable to enjoying the briefest whiff of fame. Carter wrote to Montagu on 23 November 1777, "O Dear, O dear, how pretty we look and what brave things has Mr. Johnson said of us! Indeed, my dear friend, I am just as sensible to present fame as can be. Your Virgils and your Horaces may talk what they will of posterity, but I think it is much better to be celebrated by the men, women, and children among whom one is actually living and looking."[16] Montagu responds, "I think it extraordinary felicity even to enjoy a little brief celebrity, & contracted fame."[17] The lure and contagion of celebrity touched even the most proper of Bluestockings.

Actresses, especially star actresses, as we have seen throughout this book, were instrumental in making it possible for the British populace, and most especially British women across the ranks, to envision the kind of female public presence celebrated in Samuel's picture and to create a powerful dynamic relationship between the theater and the larger culture.[18] Perhaps benefiting from the concept of exceptional virtue, several theatrical women were enfolded into Samuel's feminotopic image of exemplary British women and its evocative image of refined, cohesive, polite sociability and patriotism in the late 1770s. The intellectual ladies of the Bluestocking semipublic assemblies, who are usually assumed to have kept themselves completely apart from actresses, if not from the actor-managers David Garrick and Richard Sheridan, frequented their sociable gatherings at mid-century and beyond. But located at the center of *Nine Living Muses* is Elizabeth Linley, well-known singer and performer in the concert rooms of Bath. Drawing attention to the theatrical and performative nature of the picture's setting, she prominently offers up her song to Apollo's statue, and she fixes the spectator's view. Linley had sung and acted on the stage briefly before eloping with Richard Brinsley Sheridan (after refusing her family's choice of an aged country squire and rejecting the advances of Captain Thomas Matthews, a married man), behavior that would have disqualified Linley as unequivocally representative of exemplary virtue in its most constricted sense. Her story had been very publicly retold in Samuel Foote's *The Maid of Bath*, a sentimental drama produced in June 1771 that satirized Linley's plight.[19] Yet another woman featured in Samuel's picture, Charlotte Lennox, was much involved in the theater. After an attempt at acting, Lennox turned to writing novels such as the popular *Female Quixote* (1752) in order to seek a greater profit; but she also wrote two plays: *The Sister*, performed once at Covent Garden in 1769, and *Old City Manners*, produced at Drury Lane in 1775. In addition, Hannah More, author of the successful tragedy *Percy* (1777) and later *The Fatal Falsehood* (1779), stands just to the right of the statue of Apollo. Among the women, More's figure is most explicitly linked with the theater through the stone goblet she raises to the god of music and poetry, for it is an object traditionally associated with Melpomene, the muse of tragedy. The dramatic mask, the conventional sign of tragedy or comedy, is, however, noticeably absent from the picture: masquerade or disguise was not part of Bluestocking assemblies that valued instead the authentic opinions of those gathered for conversational exchange.

Samuel's picture is also indicative of the fact that female playwrights came to prominence at the end of the eighteenth century. The Welshwoman Elizabeth Griffith, seated while studying a tablet, was most closely identified with the stage because she had acted and written for the theater, especially during the decade just preceding the exhibition of *Nine Living Muses*, with her comedies *The Platonic Wife* (1765), *The Double Mistake* (1766), *The School for Rakes* (1769), *The Wife in the Right* (1772), and *The Times* (1779). From 1775 until the end of the century, other women playwrights including Hannah Cowley, Frances Brooke, Sophia Lee, Elizabeth Inchbald, Frances Burney, and Joanna Baillie were able to see their plays successfully produced.[20] As I have argued, the theater of the 1770s often served as a platform for women's independence, especially in comic epilogues, thus bringing to fruition attitudes that star actresses had boldly forwarded earlier in the century. In a journal letter to her sister Susanna on 3 September 1778, Frances Burney related Hester Thrale had urged her to become a playwright: "Because You have proved what are your own real resources, she said, and now,—you have nothing to do but to write a *Play*, and both Fame and Profit will attend you." The letter continues, "Hannah More, added she [Thrale], got near 400 pounds for her foolish play, [*Percy*] and I am sure *that* would be real pleasure to you."[21] Some critics have claimed that Drury Lane and Covent Garden offered preferential treatment to women writers because of Garrick's altruistic wish to grant women opportunities in the theater, but, as we have seen, the choice to feature female playwrights was more likely a commercial decision propelled by public interest, and the urgent need for new scripts (especially in the 1760s).[22] Garrick did, however, reject some scripts by women, including one by Frances Brooke who consequently satirized him for cronyism in her novel *The Excursion* (1777). Garrick turned the incident into a case of sexual politics when he wrote dismissingly of Brooke's request a decade later: "She once wrote a play, which I did not like, & would not act, for which heinous offence, she vented her female Spite upon Me, in a paper she publish'd call'd ye [the periodical] *Old Maid*."[23] When in

1773 Brooke and actress Mary Anne Yates became joint managers of the King's Theatre (known as the Haymarket Opera House), which was a competitor with Garrick's Drury Lane Theatre, and which they eventually sold to Richard Sheridan and Thomas Harris, there is some evidence that Garrick actively sought to interfere with their being granted a license.

In short, associations with the theater clearly did not automatically taint a woman's virtue beyond repair in the 1770s and, as *The Nine Living Muses* testifies, women playwrights and performers were forwarded as appropriate models for the classical muses. They, like Garrick and his carefully crafted promotion of Shakespeare as the national bard, could be featured as unambiguously representative of the intellectual and creative strength of England, for thespians Linley, Lennox, More, and Griffith appear as embodiments of British national pride. *The Nine Living Muses* gives evidence that women of the theater had by this time been assimilated into definitions of national identity, the state, and its conceptualization, paving the way for "the Siddons."

The "contracted" virtue Thrale refers to in *Thraliana* should be clearly distinguished from the exceptional virtue characteristic of the memoirs vindicating celebrated actresses' missteps discussed in Chapter 4, though both seem to require being "more than a woman." In the later decades of the century, this kind of constriction on women's behavior was exemplified most publicly in Thrale's friend, Sarah Siddons, who held to a firm, patriotic standard in shielding the country from revolutionary ideas that threatened it. After being schooled in the provinces, Siddons had debuted at Drury Lane in 1782–83, and she later shared an intimate relationship with Thrale, whom she befriended when the Bluestockings excluded her from their circle because of her marriage to Piozzi. The alleged sexual transgression of the celebrated actress (though probably specious), supposed to have taken place after her separation from her husband, paired with her ambition, violated her onstage self-fashioning as loyal wife and mother, and may help explain the two women's forming a fast friendship after Thrale had been vilified in the press for leaving her daughters to join Piozzi in Italy. In fact, Siddons had named her daughter (born in August 1794) after Hester's daughter, Cecilia Thrale. Both women, portrayed as inappropriately passionate in midlife, were accused of being insufficiently attentive mothers, in spite of Siddons's reputation for being devoted to her children. Thrale writes with admiration of the actress, "Charming Siddons has spent some Weeks with me, I think mighty well of her Virtue, & am amazed at the Cultivated State in which I have found her Mind: —She is a fine Creature Body & Soul, & has a very distinguish'd Superiority over other

Mortals—High Breeding too . . . & all her Grace has dignity: that She loves *me* I am not so sure, but I love her exceedingly" (*Thraliana* 2: 769). The mutual admiration was indeed strong: Thrale Piozzi identified with her friend's travails and sympathized with her because Siddons's insatiable fans (like everyone in Thrale Piozzi's family) ingratiated themselves to seek favors from the star actress. Having experienced a less than happy first marriage herself, Thrale Piozzi believed that Mr. Siddons mistreated his wife, and she charged him with cowardice: "that odious Husband of hers never coming forward to protect her" (2: 1052).[24] Both women also shared considerable ambition, Thrale Piozzi having inaugurated her writing career after her second marriage with *The Anecdotes of the Late Samuel Johnson* (1786), followed by prolific publication.

Several critics have argued that Siddons found a mixed-gender agency, bonding maternal femininity with masculinity, through sentimentality, in the 1790s, and that she represented to the British public an "equivocal [sexual] being."[25] Thrale Piozzi thoroughly admired the actress's manly power which James Boaden, Siddons's first biographer, described as "a male dignity in the understanding . . . that raised her above the helpless timidity of other women."[26] At the same time Boaden claimed that women in particular showed "a strongly marked *sensibility*, derived from the enjoyment of this fascinating actress" (1: 301). This remarkable emotional strength allowed Siddons to exceed the restrictions placed upon her sex but, as we have seen, similar characterizations of star actresses had surfaced earlier in the century as well. Siddons became the very personification of Thrale's notion of contracted virtue, and she dignified her portrayals of regal tragic heroines with her own reputation for moral worth, but—like rival queens such as Elizabeth Barry, Susannah Cibber, and Hannah Pritchard before her—she also made them central to the plays in unprecedented ways.[27]

Rather than modernizing the stage—which I have argued that Oldfield, Clive, Woffington, and others achieved in integrating an interior life into comic parts, updated adaptations, topical afterpieces, and timely epilogues to tragic plays—Siddons most notably represented a tragic persona with a dignified stage presence that called to mind the classical and the timeless rather than the ephemeral. She evoked the majestic power of a Greek goddess or Roman matron, an exemplary mother of the British nation, a position only strengthened by the Reynolds portrait. Siddons's reign on the stage in the characters of Octavia, Statira, and their dramatic sisters seemed to signal that they, rather than their more seductive sisters, had won the dramatic rivalry, at least throughout Siddons's career, between her reassuring stability and the actresses who threatened moral certainty with a corrupt femininity. Siddons became, according to Boaden's *Memoirs of Mrs. Siddons*, the mirror "in which our noble youth did dress themselves." He added, "Those who frequented her exhibitions, became *related* to her look, to her deportment and her utterance; the lowest point of imitation, that of the dress, was early and wisely too adopted; for it was at all times the praise of Mrs. Siddons to be exquisitely chaste and dignified in her exterior—SIMPLEX MUNDITIIS" (1: 301). Her public and private performances revealed that the theater, after having relaxed the tensions between the proper lady and the actress, redrew that division at the end of the century. Siddons came to personify and symbolize a domestic respectability combined with an unparalleled regal grandeur, never before witnessed in the public arena outside of elite social circles, that allowed her to rise above the distraction of personal scandal. Siddons in her person relieved the strain between acting and sexuality that had plagued Restoration and eighteenth-century actresses, building her career on a solid culturally sanctioned base of domesticity, maternity, and virtue, managing to keep at bay rumors of more than one affair, and fighting to block the invasion of privacy that earlier actresses had traded on.

Siddons is often assumed to be an exception to earlier Restoration and eighteenth-century actresses because of her enormous earnings, unparalleled celebrity, and much proclaimed chastity: the consummate thespian, Siddons is credited by many as constituting a class of her own, as an author of herself constructing a morally upright and dignified persona,[28] but unlike Oldfield or Clive, she was able to draw upon more than a century of female performance models to mold that inimitable public self. It is doubtful that Siddons (whose difficulties with managers extended from Garrick to Colman and Sheridan) would have dared to assert herself so vigorously without the precedents of Bracegirdle, Oldfield, Clive, Woffington, Bellamy, Abington, Cibber, and Pritchard. Siddons transformed herself from an object of spectacle into a powerful speaking subject;[29] but, as we have seen, even after audiences were banned from the stage, numerous eighteenth-century actresses retorted to audiences through extempore ejaculations, as well as in conversational epilogues, or interacted informally with them in interludes and afterpieces. Nor did Siddons invent from whole cloth her ability to combine traditionally feminine traits with masculine strength on stage.[30] Pat Rogers is among those critics who have suggested that Siddons broadened the concept of femininity and stressed her masculine vigor, but again, this gender-blending is something that actresses from Oldfield to Abington had thoroughly exploited.[31] As we have seen, Peg

Woffington in travesty was outrageously successful as Sir Harry Wildair in *The Constant Couple*, and other actresses had performed breeches and travesty roles to critical acclaim from the Restoration on.

Siddons in the representation of dramatic characters arguably projected an interiority that affected a mode more authentic than theatrical. Siddons's achievement, Lisa Freeman argues, brought "a new standard of performative realism to the London stage";[32] but it was, we might argue, a kind of "realism" that allowed the actress to avoid exposing personal foibles, to remain relatively aloof from her admirers, and to heavily subordinate her private identity to her public persona. In short, she exploited a new theatrical style that differed from her predecessors; she conveyed a consistent self-contained manner in public *and* private, even as she built upon their talents and professional accomplishments. At the height of Siddons's reign, there is evidence that she remained fully absorbed in the character she portrayed, her focus seldom wandering, even as the theater's increasing size produced greater distance from the audience. In inventing herself as a rather different kind of public commodity—one less dependent on projecting a recognizable interiority associated with her actual person, exemplary in its self-presentation, and drawn instead from investing in the intense emotion and deep subjectivity of the tragic characters she played—Siddons, by repudiating the practice of incorporating a competing self-presence on stage as earlier actresses had done, may well have interrupted a certain line of thespian possibility. With the notable exception of famously bringing her children onstage after *The Distress'd Mother* in a move regarded by some as stage trickery, she largely withdrew her own person from the audience's scrutiny to merge with the dramatic character and to evoke for her audience a cathartic experience leading, ideally, to a morally inspirational performance.[33]

The life histories of several noteworthy female players performing in the last two decades of the century contrast strongly with Siddons. Those more notorious women offered fuller accounts of their lives than earlier actresses had risked, some written in first-person while others appeared in letters and memoirs, including Sophia Baddeley (1742–80), Mary Robinson (1758–1800), and Dora Jordan (1762–1816). These biographical and autobiographical writings of unconventional lives tellingly contrast to that of the formidable paragon Siddons. Women such as actress Mary Robinson did not, of course, qualify for Thrale's definition of contracted virtue, having conducted affairs with Banastre Tarleton, Charles James Fox, and the Prince of Wales. Robinson's *Memoirs* offered an unusual combination of first- and third-person accounts in which protestations regarding "chastity" remained quite important in spite of the public behavior that contradicted its strict definition. In the first volume, and in a short portion of the second written in first-person, Robinson (popularly known as "Perdita" from her role in Shakespeare's *The Winter's Tale*), believing herself to have been a social victim in her youth, reveled in the independence that acting afforded. Indulging her romantic fantasies with the Prince of Wales ("Florizel," Perdita's lover), whose mistress she became, she interrupted her acting career and brought the tale of her life story to an abrupt halt. The *Memoirs* insist that in spite of their affair, Robinson nevertheless remained a good mother, a generous daughter, and a faithful wife. Declaring exceptional virtue, "the purity of my soul" (1: 109), she protests that she considered "chastity as the brightest ornament, that could embellish the female mind" (1: 79–80), to which her sonnet "Temple of Chastity" (1796) later testifies: "Pale vestals kneel the Goddess to adore, / While Love, his arrows broke, retires forlorn." But Robinson's troubled and embarrassing relationship with the royal prince obviously excluded her from the realization of her fantasy of national grandeur.

Following the conventional pattern of earlier biographies that assigned exceptional virtue to their subjects, the author of Ann Catley's scandalous 1789 biography, Miss E. Ambross, reproves the actress's parents for their willing collusion in encouraging the young actress to exchange sexual services for meat, drink, and clothing: "The loss of that bright and illustrious jewel chastity, gave no material uneasiness to Mr. or Mrs. Catley."[34] In spite of Catley's blatant prostitution necessary for her survival, female spectators at the theater, according to the memoirist, absolved her of responsibility for her sexual looseness. Like the readers of earlier memoirs, the audience was reputed to have excused her lack of ordinary virtue: "She was perhaps the only woman of easy virtue that ever received countenance on the stage from the modest women of Ireland; but they looked upon her as an eccentric character, making proper allowance for her early habits, and imputed her failings more to early misfortune than to vice" (Ambross, 41). As we have seen, this cultural wink was the exception that proved the rule: British theatergoers frequently pardoned talented actresses for their sexual misbehavior as inevitable compromises required because of difficult circumstances, or as lapses that were forgivable because of their generosity to family and friends.

Similarly, the popular comic actress who rivaled the most frequently tragic Siddons was Dorothy Jordan, mistress to William IV, duke of Clarence, who followed in the train of scandalous women players. Ladies of elevated standing cultivated her celebrity with uneasiness, for she was balanced on the margins of social legitimacy and associated with the political opposition. She, unlike Siddons, seemed entirely herself on stage, establishing few boundaries between her private subjectivity and her public persona. Boaden writes that her comic performances "sunk the actress in the woman; she seemed only to exhibit herself, and her own wild fancies, and utter the impromptus of the moment"—but he concludes that this impression was actually misleading, for her natural character was in truth sad and melancholic.[35]

Siddons, then, in contrast to Jordan, was original in crafting a performative identity on stage, exemplary and chaste, that she carried nobly into the private realm instead of the opposite. Reversing the pattern of other eighteenth-century actresses who traded on manipulating allusions to their personal lives, she limited hints of her private subjectivity to being a British matron, as if to counter or at least to balance the power which accrued to her in the theater: "Siddons herself wrote in a letter that she *performed* at home, attempting to appear cheerful through the illness of her daughter, and expressed her heart-felt maternal grief on stage" (Rosenthal, "Sublime," 59). Rather than employing the public revelation of private sentiments as many of her talented predecessors had done, the reserved Siddons largely aimed to keep her personal life out of the public realm and to maintain a virtuous reputation clear of any impurities, even while drawing on her real-life experiences of emotion. In part as a reaction to these several actresses' public affairs late in the century and beyond, Siddons during most of her career combined legendary public virtue with an ideal domesticity, and she did not require the exemption that exceptional virtue would have provided. Appearing in sympathetic parts that inspired orthodox ideas of femininity such as Constance in *King John*, Queen Katherine in *Henry VIII*, and even Lady Macbeth, she (re)instituted a crucial separation between her private person and the characters she played, refusing to reveal her inner distresses as her own, or to trade on the public circulation of gossip or scandal to enhance her salary. In favoring the chaste and maternal Siddons over the playful, talented, but scandalous Jordan who excelled in comedy, the Shakespearean canon that David Garrick so lovingly nurtured was profoundly shaped by the theatrical success of one eighteenth-century actress over another.[36] Unlike Jordan, Robinson, Baddeley, Catley, or the celebrated actresses discussed earlier, Siddons attempted to project a kind of transcendence over personal misfortune through exercising her remarkable talents while still managing to accrue the wealth of commercial success. Virtue for her, like virtue for Richardson's Pamela, was rewarded, and Siddons's special brand of interiority remained submerged within her dramatic characters rather than emerging as an effect of publicity. In evading allusions to her private persona, the very celebrated Siddons curiously seems to offer us a kind of retrenchment into the idealized domesticity and maternity many readers had come to expect from the eighteenth-century novel.

To the extent that Siddons's private life intruded onto the stage, it involved maternity rather than the sexuality, politics, ethnic allusions, fashion, or personality foibles that earlier star actresses had found so productive for their careers. Bolstered by dramatic roles in Shakespearean plays that were captured for nationalist purposes, even costumed on occasion as Britannia, Siddons reassured apprehensive audiences that the nation would remain safe in the face of foreign and revolutionary threats because women such as she strengthened its moral fiber. Without flaunting fashion or femininity, she masterfully married respectability and elegance to commercial viability to become a national symbol of virtuous commerce. Supplementing her salary with the profits from an unprecedented two-benefit season, Siddons earned "more money than was ever acquired in the same period, by any stage performer, from the time of Roscius, the great Roman actor, to the present hour" (Boaden, *Memoirs*, 1: 301). As such, she represented the culmination of the audience's century-long struggle to legitimize their fascination with the actress. Though "the Siddons" may not have readily acknowledged her indebtedness to actresses who came before her, the pedestal on which she stood rested solidly on the foundation of rival queens, current and long dead, whose extraordinary achievements made possible her reign.

NOTES

INTRODUCTION: AT STAGE'S EDGE

1. *A Critical Balance of the Performers at Drury-Lane Theatre. For the last season 1765* (London, 1765).
2. *The Theatrical Review: For the Year 1757, and Beginning of 1758* (London, 1758), 45–46. My thanks to Ilias Chrissochoidis for drawing my attention to the tables reproduced in Figures 1–3.
3. *Thraliana: The Diary of Mrs. Hester Lynch Thrale (Later Mrs. Piozzi), 1776–1809*, ed. Katharine C. Balderston, 2 vols. (Oxford: Clarendon Press, 1951), 2: 725.
4. George Anne Bellamy, *An Apology for the Life of George Anne Bellamy*, 6 vols., 3rd ed. (London, 1785), 2: 157.
5. James Boaden, *Memoirs of Mrs. Siddons. Interspersed with Anecdotes of Authors and Actors*, 2 vols. (London: Henry Colburn, 1827), 1: 156.
6. Allardyce Nicoll, *A History of Early Eighteenth Century Drama 1700–1750* (Cambridge: Cambridge University Press, 1929), 39. All theater historians are deeply indebted to the monumental achievements of Allardyce Nicoll and, more recently, of Robert Hume and Judith Milhous.
7. Chris Rojek, *Celebrity* (London: Reaktion Books, 2001) discusses these Shakespearean actors as the first celebrities, 113.
8. Lenard R. Belanstein, *Daughters of Eve: A Cultural History of French Theater Women from the Old Regime to the Fin de Siècle* (Cambridge, Mass.: Harvard University Press, 2001), 30. The actresses' pay could be supplemented by gratuities or command performances. See also Rosamond Gilder, *Enter the Actress: The First Women in the Theater* (Boston: Houghton Mifflin, 1931), 57–81.
9. Sophie Tomlinson, *Women on Stage in Stuart Drama* (Cambridge: Cambridge University Press, 2005), 156.
10. *The Playhouse Pocket-Companion, or Theatrical Vade Medum* (London, 1779), 37.
11. John Harold Wilson, *All the King's Ladies: Actresses of the Restoration* (Chicago: University of Chicago Press, 1958), 105–6.
12. Jacky Bratton, *New Readings in Theatre History* (Cambridge: Cambridge University Press, 2003), 15, rightly observes, "Research today constantly turns up women whose

contribution to theatre was substantial, innovative and decisive, but whose stories were not remembered or were inaccurately recorded."

13. Cindy McCreery, *The Satirical Gaze: Prints of Women in Late Eighteenth-Century England* (Oxford: Clarendon Press, 2004) carefully distinguishes among courtesans, scandalous actresses, and common prostitutes. See also Laura Rosenthal's nuanced approach in *Infamous Commerce: Prostitution in Eighteenth-Century British Literature and Culture* (Ithaca, N.Y.: Cornell University Press, 2006); and Kirsten Pullen, *Actresses and Whores: On Stage and in Society* (Cambridge: Cambridge University Press, 2005).

14. Diana Taylor, *The Archive and the Repertoire: Performing Cultural Memory in the Americas* (Durham, N.C.: Duke University Press, 2003), 26–27, contends that "part of what performance and performance studies allow us to *do*, then, is take seriously the repertoire of embodied practices as an important system of knowing and transmitting knowledge" to free us from the "dominance of the text"; but such a process is difficult, if not impossible, when describing an eighteenth-century theater that predates replicating technologies.

15. Katherine E. Maus, "'Playhouse Flesh and Blood': Sexual Ideology and the Restoration Actress," *ELH* 46, 4 (Winter 1979): 597–617; Gilli Bush-Bailey, *Treading the Bawds: Actresses and Playwrights on the Late-Stuart Stage* (Manchester: Manchester University Press, 2007). Jean I. Marsden, *Fatal Desire: Women, Sexuality, and the English Stage, 1660–1720* (Ithaca, N.Y.: Cornell University Press, 2007) discusses women's roles but not actresses or female playwrights.

16. Ellen Donkin, *Getting into the Act: Women Playwrights in London 1776–1829* (London: Routledge, 1995); and David Mann and Susan Garland Mann, *Women Playwrights in England, Ireland, and Scotland, 1660–1823* (Bloomington: Indiana University Press, 1996).

17. See Allardyce Nicoll, *A History of Early Eighteenth Century Drama*.

18. Kristina Straub, *Sexual Suspects: Eighteenth-Century Players and Sexual Ideology* (Princeton, N.J.: Princeton University Press, 1992); Elizabeth Howe, *The First English Actresses: Women and Drama, 1660–1700* (Cambridge: Cambridge University Press, 1992).I locate the rapid ascent of the actress somewhat earlier in the century than Sandra Richards, *The Rise of the English Actress* (New York: St. Martin's Press, 1993). *The Cambridge Companion to the Actress*, ed. Maggie B. Gale and John Stokes (Cambridge: Cambridge University Press, 2007) includes only three essays that touch on this period. Tracy Davis's *Actresses as Working Women: Their Social Identity in Victorian Culture* (London: Routledge, 1991) treats a later period. Several fine recent biographies of actresses include Kathryn Shevelow, *Charlotte: Being a True Account of an Actress's Flamboyant Adventures* (New York: Holt, 2005), Paula Byrne, *Perdita: The Life of Mary Robinson* (London: HarperCollins, 2004), and Deirdre David, *Fanny Kemble: A Performed Life* (Philadelphia: University of Pennsylvania Press, 2007).

19. Lisa Freeman, *Character's Theater: Genre and Identity on the Eighteenth-Century English Stage* (Philadelphia: University of Pennsylvania Press, 2002) and Bridget Orr, *Empire on the English Stage, 1660–1714* (Cambridge: Cambridge University Press, 2001).

20. For example, for the arrest of Charlotte Charke as a vagrant under the Licensing Act, see Shevelow, *Charlotte*, 331–32.

21. Stella Tillyard, "Celebrity in 18th-Century London," *History Today* 55 (June 2005): 20–27, argues that the cult of celebrity fades after the 1790s, and only arises in its modern form at the end of the nineteenth century, and I have drawn on her arguments here.

22. Harriet Guest, *Small Change: Women, Learning, Patriotism, 1750–1810* (Chicago: University of Chicago Press, 2000) notes, "Domesticity gains in value as a result of its continuity with the social or the public, and not only as a result of its asocial exclusion," 15. See also Amanda Vickery, "Golden Age to Separate Spheres? A Review of the Categories and Chronology of English Women's History," *Historical Journal* 36, 2 (1993): 383–414.

23. John Brewer, "This, That and the Other: Public, Social and Private in the Seventeenth and Eighteenth Centuries," in *Shifting the Boundaries: Transformation of the Languages of Public and Private in the Eighteenth Century*, ed. Dario Castiglione and Lesley Sharpe (Exeter: University of Exeter Press, 1995), 1–21, 17.

24. Jürgen Habermas, *The Structural Transformation of the Public Sphere: An Inquiry into a Category of Bourgeois Society*, 1962, trans. Thomas Burger (Cambridge: Polity Press, 1989).

25. Lawrence E. Klein, "Gender and the Public/Private Distinction in the Eighteenth Century: Some Questions About Evidence and Analytic Procedure," *Eighteenth-Century Studies* 29, 1 (1996): 97–109, who describes "an associative public sphere of social, discursive, and cultural production"; and Elizabeth Eger, Charlotte Grant, Clíona Ó Gallchoir, and Penny Warburton, "Introduction: Women, Writing, and Representation," to *Women, Writing and the Public Sphere, 1700–1830*, ed. Elizabeth Eger, Charlotte Grant, Clíona Ó Gallchoir, and Penny Warburton (Cambridge: Cambridge University Press, 2001), 7–10.

26. For a lucid analysis of recent approaches to Habermas's terms, see Guest, *Small Change*, 1–18. Barrell, Brewer, and Klein provide other examples.

27. John Barrell, "Coffee-House Politicians," *Journal of British Studies* 43 (2004): 206–32.

28. J. A. Downie, "Public and Private: The Myth of the Bourgeois Public Sphere," in *A Concise Companion to the Restoration and Eighteenth Century*, ed. Cynthia Wall (Malden, Mass.: Blackwell, 2005), 58–79.

29. Though he cites several feminist historians (Amy Erickson, Norma Landau, Joan Landes), and political theorist Carole Pateman, Downie largely ignores the work of feminist literary scholars over the past several decades, mentioning only Markman Ellis.

30. As Tillyard puts it, celebrity "had, and still has a more feminine face than fame, because private life, and the kind of virtue around which reputations could pivot, were both seen to reside in femininity and in women" ("Celebrity," 25). See E. J. Clery, *The Feminization Debate in Eighteenth-Century England: Literature, Commerce, and Luxury* (Basingstoke: Palgrave Macmillan, 2004).

31. Tracy C. Davis and Thomas Postlewait, eds., *Theatricality* (Cambridge: Cambridge University Press, 2003), 17.

32. C. B. Macpherson, *The Political Theory of Possessive Individualism: Hobbes to Locke* (1962; Oxford: Oxford University Press, 1990), 3. Jody Greene sounds these themes re-

garding authorship and print culture in *The Trouble with Ownership: Literary Property and Authorial Liability in England, 1660–1730* (Philadelphia: University of Pennsylvania Press, 2005).

33. Joseph Roach speaks of "public intimacy" in "Celebrity Erotics: Pepys, Performance, and Painted Ladies," *Yale Journal of Criticism* 16, 1 (2003): 211–30, and also in *It* (Ann Arbor: University of Michigan Press, 2007). Peter Holland, *The Ornament of Action: Text and Performance in Restoration Comedy* (Cambridge: Cambridge University Press, 1979), first called attention to this mediating effect. *It* offers a romp of a read through the "deep eighteenth century," a phrase meant to describe the ghostly afterimages that persist as Enlightenment's unfinished project.

34. Gentlemen spectators regularly violated bans against fraternizing with actresses at stage's edge or in the greenroom until late in the century. For example, in the Dublin theater (1742) a spectator, moved by Woffington's Cordelia nursing Garrick's Lear in the final act of Tate's version, threw himself onstage to stroke her.

35. Carla Hesse, *The Other Enlightenment: How French Women Became Modern* (Princeton, N.J.: Princeton University Press, 2001), xii.

36. Catherine Gallagher, *Nobody's Story: The Vanishing Acts of Women Writers in the Marketplace* (Berkeley: University of California Press, 1995), 202.

37. See Catherine Gallagher's influential claim that the professional woman writer found her radical and productive identity as "a newfangled whore" in "Who Was That Masked Woman? The Prostitute and the Playwright in the Comedies of Aphra Behn," *Women's Studies* 15 (1988): 41.

38. See especially James Thompson, *Models of Value: Eighteenth-Century Political Economy and the Novel* (Durham, N.C.: Duke University Press, 1996), 16.

39. Deirdre Shauna Lynch, *The Economy of Character: Novels, Market Culture, and the Business of Inner Meaning* (Chicago: University of Chicago Press, 1998) focuses on print-based and print-related concepts of character.

40. The dominant version of such a model for eighteenth-century fiction was forwarded by Nancy Armstrong, *Desire and Domestic Fiction: A Political History of the Novel* (New York: Oxford University Press, 1987). Catherine Gallagher, *Nobody's Story*, describes woman writers' self-presentation as evolving from self-promoting prostitute to decorous femininity. In contrast, Harriet Guest contests "the thesis that middle-class women were in the second half of the eighteenth century increasingly confined to domesticity and the demands of propriety" (*Small Change*, 15).

41. Freeman writes, "Any attempt to establish a proprietary claim on dramatic character would be frustrated not only by confusion over which aspect of 'character' ought to be given priority in establishing value, but also over which aspects of 'character' were 'authentic' and which were 'assumed'" (*Character's Theater*, 19). Freeman emphasizes the contrast between dramatic and fictional characters while I focus in addition on the importance of real women, principally celebrity actresses, as inhabiting dramatic characters with recognizable yet virtual interiorities that they project onstage.

42. Wai Chee Dimock, "Introduction: Genres as Fields of Knowledge," in *Special*

Topic: Remapping Genre, PMLA 122, 5 (2007): 1377. She defines genre as "an unscripted effect" of any taxonomy and "of what they [genres] could be at any given moment" (1379).

43. Tiffany Stern, *Rehearsal from Shakespeare to Sheridan* (Oxford: Clarendon Press, 2000), notes, "Shared stage and auditorium lighting, and the close proximity of the stage, boxes, and pit, meant that there was less imaginary 'distance' imposed between audience and actor than now," 149.

44. For examples, see the epilogues to *Comus*, 4 March 1738, in Pierre Danchin, ed., *The Prologues and Epilogues of the Eighteenth Century: A Complete Edition*, 6 vols. (Nancy: Presses Universitaires de Nancy, 1997), pt. 3, 5: 34; and *Britons Strike Home*, 31 December 1739 (ibid., pt. 3, 5: 78).

45. Tiffany Stern, *Rehearsal from Shakespeare to Sheridan*, 282–83, indicates that epilogues were regularly dropped after the third night: "Indeed, when Mrs. Clive was [25 October 1750], unusually, made by the audience to speak her epilogue every evening, the prompter still saw that it was 'left out of ye bills after ye 6th Night,' presumably because a billed epilogue would give a wrong message about the play itself."

46. Robert Weimann, *Author's Pen and Actor's Voice: Playing and Writing in Shakespeare's Theatre*, ed. Helen Higbee and William West (Cambridge: Cambridge University Press, 2000), 221.

47. James Boswell, "Remarks on the Profession of a Player," *London Magazine* 39 (August-October 1770): 469.

48. Joseph Roach, *The Player's Passion: Studies in the Science of Acting* (Newark: University of Delaware Press, 1985), and Marvin Carlson, *Theories of the Theatre: A Historical and Critical Survey from the Greeks to the Present* (Ithaca, N.Y.: Cornell University Press, 1984), consider the extent to which an actor in performance may be said to exercise an independent will that emanates from a stable, autonomous subjectivity.

49. See Cheryl Wanko's important book, *Roles of Authority: Thespian Biography and Celebrity in Eighteenth-Century Britain* (Lubbock: Texas Tech University Press, 2003).

50. Sarah Prescott, *Women, Authorship, and Literary Culture, 1690–1740* (Basingstoke: Palgrave Macmillan, 2003), 206.

51. See Betty Schellenberg, *The Professionalization of Women Writers in Eighteenth-Century Britain* (Cambridge: Cambridge University Press, 2005).

52. John Locke, *Two Treatises of Government*, ed. Peter Laslett (Cambridge: Cambridge University Press, 1988), 287; and Carole Pateman, *The Sexual Contract* (Stanford, Calif.: Stanford University Press, 1988).

53. Diana Taylor, "Remapping Genre through Performance: From 'American' to 'Hemispheric' Studies," in *Special Topic: Remapping Genre, PMLA* 122, 5 (October 2007): 1419.

54. Richard Schechner, *Performance Theory*, rev. ed. (London: Routledge, 2003), 79, defines theater as "the event enacted by a specific group of performers," and performance as "the whole constellation of events, most of them passing unnoticed, that take place in/among both performers and audience from the time the first spectator enters the field of performance . . . to the time the last spectator leaves."

55. Gillian Russell, *Women, Sociability, and the Theatre in Georgian London* (Cambridge: Cambridge University Press, 2007), 10 and 15.

56. Shannon Jackson, "Theatricality's Proper Objects: Genealogies of Performance and Gender Theory," in *Theatricality*, ed. Davis and Postlewait, 186–213, 193.

57. See the now classic works of Judith Butler, *Gender Trouble: Feminism and the Subversion of Identity* (London: Routledge, 1990) and *Bodies That Matter: On the Discursive Limits of Sex* (London: Routledge, 1993); Sue-Ellen Case, "Toward a Butch-Femme Aesthetic," in *Making a Spectacle*, ed. Lynda Hart (Ann Arbor: University of Michigan Press, 1989), 282–99 and *The Domain Matrix: Performing Lesbian at the End of Print Culture* (Bloomington: Indiana University Press, 1996); Elin Diamond, "Brechtian Theory/Feminist Theory: Toward a Gestic Feminist Criticism," *Drama Review* 32, 1 (1988): 82–94 and *Unmaking Mimesis: Essays on Feminism and Theatre* (New York: Routledge, 1997). Jackson, "Theatricality's Proper Objects," provides an evenhanded analysis of the controversies.

58. Jackson prefers the term "flexible essentialism" to the more familiar "strategic essentialism" in "Theatricality's Proper Objects," 189.

59. Judith Butler, "Performative Acts and Gender Constitution: An Essay in Phenomenology and Feminist Theory," in *Performing Feminisms: Feminist Critical Theory and Theatre*, ed. Sue-Ellen Case (Baltimore: Johns Hopkins University Press, 1990), 282, uses the phrase "modernity without foundationalism." Case has critiqued Butler to reinstate the subject's gendered identity and autonomous agency, albeit in a nuanced way, in the face of postmodernism's repudiation.

60. Butler, *Bodies That Matter*, 144.

61. Elizabeth Griffith, *The Delicate Distress: A Novel in Letters* (1769), ed. Cynthia Booth Ricciardi and Susan Staves (Lexington: University Press of Kentucky, 1997), 166–67.

62. Laura Mandell, *Misogynous Economies: The Business of Literature in Eighteenth-Century Britain* (Lexington: University Press of Kentucky, 1999), 39, describes eighteenth-century women's shift from hereditary rights to gaining purchasing power.

63. Laura Brown, *English Dramatic Form 1660–1760: An Essay in Generic History* (New Haven, Conn.: Yale University Press, 1981), 19.

CHAPTER 1. THE ECONOMICS OF CELEBRITY

1. Edward Young, *Love of Fame, the Universal Passion. In Seven Characteristical Satires*, in *Poetical Works of Edward Young* (1833; Westport, Conn.: Greenwood Press, 1970), 113.

2. This contradiction appears in the entry for "actress" in *Encyclopaedia Britannica; or, a Dictionary of Arts, Sciences, and Miscellaneous Literature*, 3rd ed., 18 vols. (Edinburgh, 1797), 1: 103.

3. *The Diary of Samuel Pepys*, ed. Robert Latham and William Matthews, 11 vols., 18 August 1660, (London: G. Bell and Sons, 1970), 1: 224. References to Pepys (given subsequently by date) are from this edition.

4. Nokes also acted women's roles in *Maid in the Mill* at Salisbury (29 January 1661) in Stapylton's *The Slighted Maid* (23 February 1663), in D'Urfey's *The Banditti* (7 January 1686), and perhaps as the Nurse in *Romeo and Juliet* (1 March 1662). Charles Hart is reported to have acted as the Duchess in *The Cardinal* (23 August 1662). Kynaston played Olympia, the Duke's sister, in Fletcher's *The Loyal Subject* (18 August 1660), and Pepys reports an all-male cast in Beaumont and Fletcher's *The Beggar's Bush* (10 November 1660), though women probably did not appear until December 1660.

5. Thomas Campbell, *Life of Mrs. Siddons* (New York: Harper and Brothers, 1834), 47.

6. Michael Shapiro, "The Introduction of Actresses in England: Delay or Defensiveness?" in *Enacting Gender on the English Renaissance Stage*, ed. Viviana Comensoli and Anne Russell (Urbana: University of Illinois Press, 1999), 185, counters Stephen Orgel's claim in *Impersonations: The Performance of Gender in Shakespeare's England* (Cambridge: Cambridge University Press, 1996) that women came late to the English stage because of men's fear of female sexuality.

7. See Rosamond Gilder, *Enter the Actress: The First Women in the Theater* (Boston: Houghton Mifflin, 1931), 86, who cites the 1468 performance of *Mystère de Sainte Catherine* as the first public appearance of an actress in a religious drama.

8. Abbé Hedelin, *The Whole Art of the Stage* (London, 1657, trans. 1684), 173.

9. William Egerton [Edmund Curll], *Memoirs of the Life, Amours, and Performances of That Justly Celebrated, and Most Eminent Actress of Her Time, Mrs. Anne Oldfield* (London, 1731), 76.

10. William Rufus Chetwood, *A General History of the Stage, from its origin in Greece down to the present time . . . collected and digested by W. R. Chetwood* (London, 1749), 127; and *The London Stage 1660–1800*, pt. 4, *1747–1776*, ed. George Winchester Stone, Jr. (Carbondale: Southern Illinois University Press, 1962), 342.

11. Robert Barrie, "Elizabethan Play-Boys in the Adult London Companies," *SEL* 48, 2 (Spring 2008): 237–57, distinguishes the Elizabethan and early Stuart drama companies' recruitment of playboys from those of the London guild companies. Barrie speculates that the degree to which playboys owned their own labor differed depending on the class of theater company apprentices into which they fell: guild apprentices not permanently bound, covenant servants paid an annual wage and bound for a year or two, or apprentices ostensibly enslaved with little hope of release.

12. See also Scott McMillin, "The Sharer and His Boy: Rehearsing Shakespeare's Women," in *From Script to Stage in Early Modern England*, ed. Peter Holland and Stephen Orgel (Basingstoke: Palgrave Macmillan, 2004), 231–45. Actor training was contracted at an earlier age than trade apprenticeships.

13. Paul Langford, *A Polite and Commercial People, England 1727–1783* (Oxford: Oxford University Press, 1998), 180, states that guilds declined after the Revolution of 1688. With the demise of apprenticeship laws around 1770, the years of being bound shortened from seven to five.

14. See Lucinda Cole, "*The London Merchant* and the Institution of Apprentice-

ship," *Criticism* 37, 1 (Winter 1995): 57–84. Lisa Freeman, "The Cultural Politics of Anti-Theatricality: The Case of John Home's *Douglas*," *Eighteenth Century: Theory and Interpretation* 43 (2002): 210–35, argues that a positive effect of apprentices' distraction from labor was increased theatrical and national economic prosperity.

15. Gilli Bush-Bailey, "Revolution, Legislation and Autonomy," in *The Cambridge Companion to the Actress*, ed. Maggie B. Gale and John Stokes (Cambridge: Cambridge University Press, 2007), 15–32.

16. John Harold Wilson, *All the King's Ladies: Actresses of the Restoration* (Chicago: University of Chicago Press, 1958), 10.

17. Guy Miège, *The Present State of Great Britain. In Two Parts . . .* 2 vols. (London, 1707), 1: 290.

18. Katherine Romack, "Striking the Posture of a Whore: The Bawdy House Riots and the 'Antitheatrical Prejudice,'" unpublished essay.

19. "Tristram Shandy," *Miss C---y's Cabinet of Curiosities; or, the Green-Room Broke Open* (London, 1765).

20. *Chiron: or, the mental optician*, 2 vols. (London, 1758), 2: 100.

21. State Papers (Domestic) 44/15, 117–19, cited in Robert D. Freeburn, "Charles II, The Theatre Patentees and the Actor's Nursery," *Theatre Notebook* 48, 3 (1994): 150.

22. Elizabeth Howe, *The First English Actresses: Women and Drama, 1660–1700* (Cambridge: Cambridge University Press, 1992), 26.

23. Tiffany Stern, *Rehearsal from Shakespeare to Sheridan* (Oxford: Clarendon Press, 2000), 161, 146. Stern shows that actors often paid little attention to the play as a whole and thus increased the autonomy of individual actors.

24. Allardyce Nicoll, *A History of Restoration Drama, 1660–1700*, 4th ed. (Cambridge: Cambridge University Press, 1952), 324.

25. Clive writes: "I have never envyd you your equipage . . . I have had but a very small share of the publick money, you give Mrs Cibber 600 pounds for playing Sixty Nights, and three to me for playing a hundred and eighty [nights] . . . I hope you need not want to take anything from it," Folger MS 1083 Y.c.552(4). The Folger Library collection of letters from Clive to her protegée Jane Pope is in the hand of James Winston.

26. *The History of the Stage. In which is included the Theatrical Character of the most celebrated Actors* (London, 1742), 63.

27. 18 October 1750, *The Letters of David Garrick*, ed. David M. Little and George M. Karhl, 3 vols. (Cambridge, Mass.: Belknap Press of Harvard University Press, 1963), 1: 158.

28. George Anne Bellamy, *An Apology for the Life of George Anne Bellamy*, 5 vols. (London, 1786), 4: 58.

29. William Maitland, *The History of London from its Foundation by the Romans to the Present Time* (London, 1739), 160.

30. Declaration of the Justices of the Peace for Whitechapel, appended to Arthur Bedford, *A Sermon Preached in the Parish-Church of St. Butolph's Aldgate* (London, 1730), cited in Samuel Richardson, *The Apprentice's Vade Mecum*, (1734), intro. Alan Dugald McKillop,

Augustan Reprint Society 169–70 (Los Angeles: William Andrews Clark Memorial Library, 1975), vii.

31. Cited in Samuel Richardson, *Vade Mecum*, ii; repr. in *London Magazine* 4 (March 1735): 117–18.

32. Mary E. Knapp, *Prologues and Epilogues of the Eighteenth Century* (New Haven, Conn.: Yale University Press, 1961), 139.

33. Tate Wilkinson, "The Mirror; or, Actor's Tablet" in *Memoirs of His Own Life*, 4 vols. (York 1790), 4: 114.

34. See Theodora Jankowski, "The Development of Middle-Class Identity and the 'Problem' of the 'Gentle' Apprentice," *Proceedings of the Eleventh Annual Northern Plains Conference on Early British Literature*, ed. Michelle M. Sauer (Minot, N.D.: Minot State University Printing Services, 2003), 1–15.

35. Arthur Murphy, *The Apprentice*, 2nd ed. (London, 1756), 39.

36. K. D. M. Snell, *Annals of the Labouring Poor: Social Change and Agrarian England, 1660–1900* (Cambridge: Cambridge University Press, 1985), provides statistics for female apprentices, 270–319.

37. "Nobody" was the generic nomenclature sometimes given to the black-draped character who spoke the prologue or epilogue. See Pierre Danchin, *The Prologues and Epilogues of the Restoration, 1660–1700: A Complete Edition*, 4 vols. in 7 (Nancy: Presses Universitaires de Nancy II, 1981–), pt. 1, *1660–1676*, 1: xxxvii.

38. Epilogue to Arthur Murphy, *The Apprentice* (London, 1756), in Pierre Danchin, ed., *The Prologues and Epilogues of the Eighteenth Century: A Complete Edition*, 6 vols. (Nancy: Presses Universitaires de Nancy, 1993), pt. 3, *1737–1760*, 6: 546–47. The author's performance dressed in the traditional black of the character "Prologue" ("Trickt out in Black thus Actors try their Art, / To melt that *Rock* of *Rocks*,—the Critic's Heart,") may have reminded spectators of Oroonoko's corked blackness in the mainpiece.

39. Theophilus Cibber, *A Serio-Comic Apology for Part of the Life of Mr. Theophilus Cibber, Comedian* (Dublin, 1748), 12.

40. Charlotte Charke, *A Narrative of the Life of Mrs. Charlotte Charke*, ed. Robert Rehder (London: Pickering and Chatto, 1999), 91.

41. Patrick J. Crean, "The Life and Times of Kitty Clive" (Dissertation, University of London, 1933), 292.

42. Howe, *First English Actresses*, describes the Restoration actress as prostitute, 32–36. See also Wilson, *All the King's Ladies*, who claims that actresses helped playwrights "heap the steaming ordure of the stage," 107.

43. Laura Rosenthal, '"Counterfeit Scrubbado': Women Actors in the Restoration," *The Eighteenth Century: Theory and Interpretation* 34 (1993): 3–22, helpfully suggested that "this tension between an actress's own social position and the position of the characters she played . . . brought the actress as whore sign into play," 8, though I am claiming that actresses' upward mobility is not wholly illusory. Deborah C. Payne finds that the actress is a supplicating intermediary rather than a sexual object in "Reified Object or Emergent Professional? Retheorizing the Restoration Actress," in *Cultural Readings of Restoration and*

Eighteenth-Century Theater, ed. J. Douglas Canfield and Deborah Payne (Athens: University of Georgia Press, 1995), 13–38.

44. Philip H. Highfill, Jr., Kalman Burnim, and Edward Langhans, *A Biographical Dictionary of Actors, Actresses . . . & other stage personnel in London*, 16 vols. (Carbondale: Southern Illinois University Press, 1973–93), 16: 217.

45. *The Servants Calling; with Some Advice to the Apprentice* (London, 1725), 21.

46. Joseph Roach, *It* (Ann Arbor: University of Michigan Press, 2007) suggests that actors became modern equivalents to royalty.

47. Thomas A. King, "'As If (She) Were Made on Purpose to Put the Whole World into Good Humour': Reconstructing the First English Actresses," *Drama Review* 36, 3 (Fall 1992): 78–102.

48. Joseph Roach, "Celebrity Erotics: Pepys, Performance, and Painted Ladies," *Yale Journal of Criticism* 16, 1 (2003): 213, sardonically remarks that public intimacy is "the sexy version of the worthy but stolid bourgeois public sphere described by Jürgen Habermas." See also Diana Taylor, *The Archive and the Repertoire: Performing Cultural Memory in the Americas* (Durham, N.C.: Duke University Press, 2003), 30.

49. Howe, *The First English Actresses*, 27, 31.

50. See Cheryl Wanko's fine study, *Roles of Authority: Thespian Biography and Celebrity in Eighteenth-Century Britain* (Lubbock: Texas Tech University Press, 2003) to which I am indebted. See also Kristina Straub, *Sexual Suspects: Eighteenth-Century Players and Sexual Ideology* (Princeton, N.J.: Princeton University Press, 1992); and James Thompson, *Models of Value: Eighteenth-Century Political Economy and the Novel* (Durham, N.C.: Duke University Press, 1996).

51. Colley Cibber, *An Apology for the Life of Colley Cibber, Written by Himself*, 1740, ed. Robert W. Lowe, 2 vols. (London: John C. Nimmo, 1889), 1: 135–36.

52. Thomas Davies, *Memoirs of the Life of David Garrick, Esq. Interspersed with characters and anecdotes of his theatrical contemporaries*, new ed. (London, 1780), 2: 191.

53. The details are listed in Egerton [Edmund Curll], *Faithful Memoirs*, 209–12, and the will appears as Appendix 2. The original is in the Public Record Office, Principal Probate Registry, 12.100, f. 312.

54. Kimberly Crouch, "The Public Life of Actresses: Prostitutes or Ladies?" in *Gender in Eighteenth-Century England: Roles, Representations and Responsibilities*, ed. Hannah Barker and Elaine Chalus (London: Longman, 1997), 71, notes that Woffington bought a home in Teddington for herself and her sister Polly. Pritchard purchased "Ragman's Castle" in Twickenham; Oldfield bequeathed a house on Grosvenor Street to her son; and Frances Abington, after leasing a Hammersmith house near the Thames, sold it to fellow actress Sophia Baddeley. Horace Walpole gave Kitty Clive a small house dubbed "Clive's-den" at Strawberry Hill that she occupied from around 1753.

55. *The History of the English Stage from the Restauration to the Present Time. By Dr. Thomas Betterton. Written really by Edmund Curll* (London, 1741), 14. For more reliable evidence, see Elizabeth Barry's letter to Lady Lisburne, 5 January 1698/9 in M. A. Shaaber, "A Letter from Mrs. Barry," *The Library Chronicle* 16, 2 (Summer 1950): 46–49.

56. Terry Castle, *Masquerade and Civilization: The Carnivalesque in Eighteenth-Century English Culture and Fiction* (Stanford, Calif.: Stanford University Press, 1986); Jessica Munns and Penny Richards, "Introduction," in *The Clothes That Wear Us: Essays on Dressing and Transgressing in Eighteenth-Century Culture* (Newark: University of Delaware Press, 1999), 9–36; and Cynthia Lowenthal, *Performing Identities on the Restoration Stage* (Carbondale: Southern Illinois University Press, 2003), discuss the class instability triggered by actresses emulating aristocrats on stage. I am arguing that actresses actually were in reality socially mobile, and that the aristocracy also emulated *them*.

57. William Cooke, *Memoirs of Charles Macklin, Comedian* (London: James Asperne, 1804); New York: B. Blom, 1972), 41–42.

58. Mr. Neither-Side [Charles Fleetwood], *An Impartial Examen of the Present Contests between the Town and the Manager of the Theatre with Some Proposals for accommodating the present Misunderstandings between the Town and the Manager* (London, 1744), 9. For the rivalry between Garrick and Cibber, see for example Mary Nash, *The Provoked Wife: The Life and Times of Susannah Cibber* (Boston: Little, Brown, 1977). The salary figures may be overinflated, but my point is that actresses were reputed to make great sums of money. Mrs. Cibber's income "exceeded fourfold her pre-Dublin revenue, and set a record for London's theatrical annals," outstripping Garrick who had earned £1130 in his Dublin debut. Ilias Chrissochoidis has generously shared this assessment, based on *The Tryals of Two Causes, between Theophilus Cibber . . . and William Sloper* (London, 1740), 9n., and *London Daily Post and General Advertiser*, 15 October 1743 [2].

59. Francis Truelove, *The Comforts of Matrimony; Exemplified in the Memorable Case and Trial. . . . brought by Theo-s C-r against ---, Esq.*, 6th ed. (London, 1739), 12.

60. Claire Tomalin, *Mrs. Jordan's Profession: The Story of a Great Actress and a Future King* (London: Viking, 1994), 166.

61. Many women dramatists apparently shared a similar aversion to sharing their profits. David Roberts, *The Ladies: Female Patronage of Restoration Drama 1660–1700* (Oxford: Clarendon Press, Oxford 1989), 7 n.9, notes, "Aphra Behn wrote as a widow; Katherine Phillips as a 'Platonick'; Catherine Trotter married after completing her last play; and Mary Manley enjoyed casual relationships and one bigamous marriage. Mary Pix apart, only the aristocrats, the Duchess of Newcastle and the Countess of Winchelsea, wrote during wedlock." Roberts's study extends only to 1700, the date of Susanna Centlivre's first play, *The Perjur'd Husband*, when her husband at the time complained about her lack of profit from writing. On Centlivre's contest with Cibber over literary property, see Laura Rosenthal, *Playwrights and Plagiarists in Early Modern England: Gender, Authorship, Literary Property* (Ithaca, N.Y.: Cornell University Press, 1996), 218–42.

62. *Theatrical Correspondence in Death. An Epistle from Mrs Oldfield, in the Shades to Mrs Br---ceg---dle, upon Earth* (London, 1743), 7, 12.

63. Examples include Charlotte Butler, Frances Abington, Elizabeth Boutell, Kitty Clive, and Mary (Davies) Sumbel. Elizabeth Barry was probably raised in the home of Lady Davenant. See Sandra Richards, *The Rise of the English Actress* (London: St. Martin's Press, 1993).

64. Henry Fielding, *The Covent Garden Journal*, in *The Works of Henry Fielding, Esq., in Twelve Volumes, with the Life of the Author*, 12 vols. (London, 1775), 12: 119–20, may be exaggerating, but his figures are indicative of a general perception: "The stage at present promises a much better provision than any of the professions . . . The income of an actor of any rank is from six to twelve hundred a year; whereas, that of two-thirds of the gentlemen of the army is considerably under one hundred; the income of nine-tenths of the clergy is less than fifty pounds a year; and the profits in the law, to ninety-nine in the hundred, amount not to a single shilling."

65. Cheryl Wanko, "Contracts for Two Drury Lane Actresses in 1822," *Harvard Library Bulletin* ser. 2, 5 (1994), 53–67. Some salary lists divide players into four ranks, according to Edward A. Langhans in "Tough Actresses to Follow," in *Curtain Calls: British and American Women and the Theater, 1660–1820*, ed. Mary Anne Schofield and Cecilia Macheski (Athens: Ohio University Press, 1991), 4. Percy Fitzgerald, *A New History of the English Stage*, 2 vols. (London: Tinsley Brothers, 1882), 2: 445, cites an agreement regarding actors' benefits that divides them into those making £4, £2.10, and £2 per week respectively. The better-paid actor managers may have constituted a fourth category.

66. Judith Milhous, "United Company Finances, 1682–1692," *Theatre Research International* 7, 1 (Winter 1981/82): 45–50, notes that actors earned more than most people in the trades, and more than actresses. Nevertheless, a few celebrated and influential actresses earned more than most men. Milhous deciphered a five-step salary scale ranging from 12s. to 60s. per week. Robert Hume states that 30 to 40s. per week was a typical actress's wage in "The Origins of the Actor Benefit in London," *Theatre Research International* 9, 2 (1984): 99–111.

67. A common laborer earned about £25 per year, a curate about £40, while £400 per year allowed a family and household supporting two servants to attain a genteel life in the 1790s, according to Edward Copeland, *Women Writing About Money: Women's Fiction in England, 1790–1820* (Cambridge: Cambridge University Press, 1995), 29.

68. Cheryl Turner, *Living by the Pen: Women Writers in the Eighteenth Century* (London: Routledge, 1992), 111–16.

69. I have relied on Robert Hume, "The Economics of Culture in London, 1660–1740," *Huntington Library Quarterly* 69, 4 (2006): 487–533, 503, for information in this paragraph.

70. Ellen Donkin, *Getting into the Act: Women Playwrights in London 1776–1829* (London: Routledge, 1995), 130, notes that Inchbald's fortune upon her death amounted to £6000.

71. See Angela Smallwood, "Women and the Theatre," in *Women and Literature in Britain 1700–1800*, ed. Vivien Jones (Cambridge: Cambridge University Press, 2000), 238–62.

72. Judith Milhous and Robert D. Hume, "Playwrights' Remuneration in Eighteenth-Century London," *Harvard Library Bulletin* 10, 2–3 (1999): 3–90.

73. Elizabeth Inchbald letter to William Godwin, 3 November 1792, Bodleian Library, Abinger collection, Dep c509. My thanks to Harriet Guest for calling my attention to this reference.

74. Copeland, *Women Writing About Money*, cited in Wanko, *Roles of Authority*, 166–67. This wage would be typical for actors performing near the time of the 1737 Licensing Act. For the salary range at Covent Garden, see Robert Hume and Judith Milhous, "John Rich's Covent Garden Account Books for 1735–36," *Theatre Survey* 31 (November 1990): 200–241.

75. Joanne Lafler, *The Celebrated Mrs. Oldfield: The Life and Art of an Augustan Actress* (Carbondale: Southern Illinois University Press, 1989), 51, provides statistics for the Haymarket.

76. Cooke, *Memoirs of Charles Macklin*, 129.

77. George Winchester Stone, Jr., and George M. Kahrl, *David Garrick: A Critical Biography* (Carbondale: Southern Illinois University Press, 1979), 593. The figure for Pritchard appears in a satire, *A Letter to a Certain Patentee: In Which the Conduct of Managers is Impartially Considered; and a few Periods bestowed on those Darlings of the Publick, Mr. G---k, Mr. F---e, Mrs. P--d, &c.* (London [1747]), 16, and may, of course, be inflated.

78. Langhans, "Tough Actresses to Follow," 3; S. Richards, *Rise of the English Actress*, 56, 78; and Highfill, et al., *Biographical Dictionary*, 14: 22–23.

79. For example, Elizabeth Barry loaned Alexander Davenant £400 in exchange for a share in the United Company, and Samuel Johnson's *Life of Savage* (1744) indicates that Anne Oldfield settled an annuity of £50 per year on the poet Richard Savage, but see Lafler's skepticism regarding the account, *Celebrated Mrs. Oldfield*, 150–53.

80. Langhans, 5; Highfill et al., 3; Richards, 44. Joanne Lafler, "Theatre and the Female Presence," in *The Cambridge History of British Theatre, 1660–1895*, ed. Joseph Donohue, 3 vols. (Cambridge: Cambridge University Press, 2004), 2: 79, notes "The privilege of sharing in company management and profits was denied to female performers except for the brief period 1695–1705, when eight senior actors from the United Company, including Elizabeth Barry, Anne Bracegirdle and Elinor Leigh, established a rival company at Lincoln's Inn Fields, in which they shared managerial responsibilities and profits." Susannah Cibber unsuccessfully sought to share executive authority in Garrick's theater; and Frances Brooke and Mary Anne Yates briefly managed the King's Theatre late in the century.

81. Hume, "Origins of the Actor Benefit" concludes that the actor benefit, drawing from the earlier practice of allowing a third-night benefit for playwrights, began at Drury Lane in 1696.

82. James Boaden, *Life of Mrs. Jordan, Including Original Private Correspondence, and Numerous Anecdotes of her Contemporaries*, 2 vols. (London: Edward Bull, 1831), 1: 179.

83. *Dublin Gazette*, 9–13 April 1728, cited in John C. Greene and Gladys L. H. Clark, *The Dublin Stage, 1720–1745: A Calendar of Plays, Entertainments, and Afterpieces* (Bethlehem, Pa.: Lehigh University Press, 1993), 112–13.

84. Miss E. Ambross, *The Life and Memoirs of the Late Miss Ann Catley, the Celebrated Actress* (London, [1789]), 55.

85. Matthew J. Kinservik, "Benefit Play Selection at Drury Lane in 1729–1769: The Cases of Mrs Cibber, Mrs Clive, and Mrs Pritchard," *Theatre Notebook* 50 (1996): 17, has helpful statistics.

86. David Edward McKenty, "The Benefit System in Augustan Drama" (Dissertation, University of Pennsylvania, 1966).

87. Harry William Pedicord, *The Theatrical Public in the Time of Garrick* (Carbondale: Southern Illinois University Press, 1966).

88. Aaron Hill and William Popple, *The Prompter: A Theatrical Paper (1734–1736)*, selected and ed. William W. Appleton and Kalman A. Burnim (New York: B. Blom, 1966), 55.

89. St Vincent Troubridge, *The Benefit System in the British Theatre* (London: Society for Theatre Research, 1967), 39, 41, 51.

90. The salary figures derive from the account books and are tabulated in Kinservik, "Benefit Play Selection."

91. S. W. Ryley, *The Itinerant, or, Memoirs of an Actor* 9 vols. (London: Sherwood, Neely and Jones, 1816–27), 1: 255.

92. Anthony Aston, *A Brief Supplement to Colley Cibber, Esq.; his lives of the late famous actors and actresses* [London, 1747], 10. *The Life of Lavinia Beswick, alias Fenton, alias Polly Peachum* (London, 1728), title page.

93. Henry Fielding, "An Epistle to Mrs. Clive," in Henry Fielding and Jean Françoise Regnard, *The Intriguing Chambermaid. A Comedy of Two Acts* (London, 1734), 3.

94. See Charles E. Pearce, *Polly Peachum: Being the Story of Lavinia Fenton . . . and "The Beggar's Opera"* (New York: Brentano's, 1913).

95. Dedication, *Authentick Memoirs of the Life of that celebrated Actress Mrs. Ann Oldfield* (London, 1730), vii.

96. See Iain Mackintosh assisted by Geoffrey Ashton, *The Georgian Playhouse: Actors, Artists, Audiences, and Architecture, 1730–1830* (London: Arts Council of Great Britain, 1975), entry 112.

97. Aileen Ribeiro, "Costuming the Part: A Discourse of Fashion and Fiction in the Image of the Actress in England, 1776–1812," in *Notorious Muse: The Actress in British Art and Culture, 1776–1812*, ed. Robyn Asleson (New Haven, Conn.: Yale University Press, 2003), 122.

98. Ambross, *Life and Memoirs of the Late Miss Ann Catley*, 51.

99. Letter from Sarah Siddons to Mrs. FitzHugh, 12 July 1819, in Campbell, *Life of Mrs. Siddons*, 2: 366.

100. Folger MSS Y.D. 23 (170?), Folger Shakespeare Library, Washington, DC.

101. Clive later fought with Peg Woffington which sparked the creation of an unpublished play, "The Green-Room Scuffle: Or Drury-Lane in an Uproar." I have been unable to locate further information about this play mentioned in Crean, "The Life and Times of Kitty Clive."

102. Attributed to Henry Fielding as "Theo" without source by Fitzgerald, *Life of Mrs. Catherine Clive* (1888; New York: B. Blom, 1971), 19.

103. Mr. Lun, Junior [Henry Woodward], "Prologue" to *The Beggar's Pantomime; Or, the Contending Columbines . . . Dedicated to Mrs. Clive and Mrs. Cibber*, 3rd ed. (London, 1736).

104. William Chetwood, *Dramatic Congress: A Short State of the Stage under the present management. Concluding with a dialogue . . . between the illustrious Bashas of Dr—ry Lane and Co—nt Garden* (London, 1743), 21.

105. On Cross, see Judith Milhous and Robert Hume, "Theatrical Politics at Drury Lane: New Light on Letitia Cross, Jane Rogers, and Anne Oldfield," *Bulletin of Research in the Humanities* 85 (Winter 1982): 412–29.

CHAPTER 2. "REAL, BEAUTIFUL WOMEN": RIVAL QUEENS

1. Colley Cibber, *An Apology for the Life of Colley Cibber, Written by Himself* (1740), ed. Robert W. Lowe, 2 vols. (London: John C. Nimmo, 1889), 1: 90–91. This edition is cited throughout the chapter.

2. John Downes compliments the performance of *Theodosius, or the Force of Love*, adding "especially the Ladies, by their daily charming presence, gave it great Encouragement," in *Roscius Anglicanus, or a Historical Review of the Stage from 1660 to 1706*, ed. Judith Milhous and Robert D. Hume (London: Society for Theatre Research, 1987), 80.

3. Diana Taylor, *The Archive and the Repertoire: Performing Cultural Memory in the Americas* (Durham, N.C.: Duke University Press, 2003), 31, speaks of the transformative power of performative repetition.

4. Susan Staves, "Tragedy," in *The Cambridge Companion to British Theatre, 1730–1830*, ed. Jane Moody and Daniel O'Quinn (Cambridge: Cambridge University Press, 2007), 87–102.

5. Wendy Brown remarks in *Edgework: Critical Essays on Knowledge and Politics* (Princeton, N.J.: Princeton University Press, 2005), "Untimeliness deployed as an effective intellectual and political strategy, far from being a gesture of indifference to time, is a bid to reset time," 4.

6. Jean-Christophe Agnew, *Worlds Apart: The Market and the Theater in Anglo-American Thought, 1550–1750* (New York: Cambridge University Press, 1986); David Marshall, *The Figure of Theater: Shaftesbury, Defoe, Adam Smith and George Eliot* (New York: Columbia University Press, 1986); and Richard Sennett, *Authority* (New York: Knopf, 1980).

7. Natasha Korda, "Labours Lost: Women's Work and Early Modern Theatrical Commerce," in *From Script to Stage in Early Modern England*, ed. Peter Holland and Stephen Orgel (Basingstoke: Palgrave Macmillan, 2004), 195–230, especially 196.

8. See Nancy Armstrong, *Desire and Domestic Fiction: A Political History of the Novel* (New York and Oxford: Oxford University Press, 1987), 8. Harriet Guest, *Small Change: Women, Learning, Patriotism, 1750–1810* (Chicago: University of Chicago Press, 2000) defines women's critical role as a civilizing force in shaping modern civil society. For actresses' memoirs, see Cheryl Wanko, *Roles of Authority: Thespian Biography and Celebrity in Eighteenth-Century Britain* (Lubbock: Texas Tech University Press, 2003).

9. Peggy Phelan, *Unmarked: The Politics of Performance* (London: Routledge, 1993), 152.

10. Frances Burney, *Evelina; or the History of a Young Lady's Entrance into the World*, ed. Edward A. Bloom with Vivien Jones (Oxford: Oxford University Press, 2002), 198.

11. Relevant here is Catherine Gallagher's well-known distinction between a "nobody" and a "somebody" in *Nobody's Story: The Vanishing Acts of Women Writers in the Marketplace 1670–1820* (Berkeley: University of California Press, 1994), though I am employing these terms in ways Gallagher did not suggest.

12. Cheryl Wanko, "Colley Cibber's *The Rival Queans*: A New Consideration," *Restoration and Eighteenth-Century Theatre Research* 2nd ser. 3, 2 (1988): 38–52, writes that "the wide-open conditions for new plays and playwrights . . . that had existed in the period 1697–1701 simply evaporated by 1702," 38. Robert Hume, "Drama and Theatre in the Mid and Later Eighteenth Century," *The Cambridge History of English Literature, 1660–1780*, ed. John Richetti (Cambridge: Cambridge University Press, 2005), observes that from 1730 to 1790 "about 85 percent of the mainpiece performances in London were of old plays," 316. See also Nancy Eloise Lewis, "Nathaniel Lee's *The Rival Queens*: A Study of Dramatic Taste and Technique in the Restoration" (Dissertation, Ohio State University, 1957).

13. Jean I. Marsden, *Fatal Desire: Women, Sexuality and the English Stage, 1660–1720* (Ithaca, N.Y.: Cornell University Press, 2006) suggests that woman-centered tragedy gives way to male-centered plays in the 1730s, but this claim should be moderated in relation to revivals of *The Rival Queens* as well as the extraordinary popularity of she-tragedies throughout the century.

14. Aaron Hill and William Popple, *The Prompter: A Theatrical Paper (1734–1736)*, selectd and ed. William W. Appleton and Kalman A. Burnim (New York: B. Blom, 1966), 120.

15. Nathaniel Lee, *The Rival Queens*, ed. P. F. Vernon (Lincoln: University of Nebraska Press, 1970), xvii. I am much indebted throughout to Vernon's fine introduction. Subsequent references to the play are cited parenthetically from this edition.

16. Richard Schechner, *Between Theater & Anthropology* (Philadelphia: University of Pennsylvania Press, 1985), 36–37.

17. The prologue for the performance of *The Rival Queens* in Dublin, 14 October 1685, the birthday of James II, spoke to the occasion, changing the names from the original allusions to Charles II. See Pierre Danchin, ed., *The Prologues and Epilogues of the Restoration 1660–1700*, 4 vols. in 7 (Nancy: Presses Universitaires de Nancy II, 1981–88), pt. 2, *1677–1690*, 4: 593.

18. Joseph Roach, *It* (Ann Arbor: University of Michigan Press, 2007), 36.

19. Terry Castle in "The Gothic Novel," in *The Cambridge History of English Literature, 1660–1780*, ed. John Richetti (Cambridge: Cambridge University Press, 2005), suggests that the Gothic novel was "the first full-blown effort to reanimate, artificially, an extinct historical style for the purposes of mass entertainment" (678), yet we might note that the productions of the heroic tragedy antedate the Gothic novel.

20. Hill and Popple, *The Prompter*, no. 105, Tuesday, 11 November 1735, 121.

21. Thomas Davies, *Dramatic Miscellanies*, 3 vols. (London, 1785), 3: 272.

22. Robert Hume, *The Development of English Drama in the Late Seventeenth Century* (Oxford: Clarendon Press, 1976), 204.

23. Other actresses who later adopted the role of Statira included Mrs. Spiller, Mrs. Bullock, Mrs. Gifford, Mrs. Giffard, Mrs. Horton, Mrs. Cibber, Mrs. Mills, Mrs. Palmer, Mrs. Ward, Mrs. Mattocks, Mrs. W. Barry, Mrs. Yates, Miss Mansell, Mrs. Hartley, Mrs. Baddeley, Mrs. Robinson, Mrs. Bulkley, Mrs. Whitfield, Miss Moore, Mrs. Robinson, Mrs. Ward, Miss Farren, Mrs. Yates, Miss Satchell, Miss Kemble, Miss Younge, Mrs. Wells, Miss Brunton, Mrs. Merry, Mrs. Twistleton, Mrs. Powell; and as Roxana Mrs. Kent, Mrs. Seymour, Mrs. Knight, Mrs. Parker, Mrs. Berrman, Mrs. Hallam, Mrs. Thurmond, Mrs. Roberts, Mrs. Woodward, Mrs. Baker, Mrs. Pritchard, Mrs. Hopkins, Mrs. Yates, Mrs. Burden, Mrs. Thompson in the 1770 burlesque, Mrs. Miller, Miss Younge, Mrs. Melmoth, Mrs. Hunter, Mrs. Ward, Miss Sherry, Mrs. Jackson, Mrs. Crawford, Mrs. Pope, Miss Morris, Miss Betterton, and Mrs. Siddons on 23 November 1795 in Drury Lane. I am very grateful to Regulus Allen for her scrupulous tracking of the stage performances of *The Rival Queens*, derived largely from William Van Lennep, Emmett L. Avery, Arthur H. Scouten, George Winchester Stone, Jr., and Charles Beecher Hogan, eds., *The London Stage, 1660–1800*, 5 pts. in 11 vols. (Carbondale: Southern Illinois University Press, 1960–68).

24. Elizabeth Howe, *The First English Actresses: Women and Drama* (Cambridge: Cambridge University Press, 1992). For other descriptions of parts that lent themselves to actresses' rivalries, see Sandra Richards, *The Rise of the English Actress* (London: St. Martin's Press, 1993), 57–60.

25. John Genest, *Some Account of the English Stage from the Restoration in 1660 to 1830*, 10 vols. (Bath, 1832; New York: B. Franklin, 1965): 10: 444–45. Mrs. Palmer and Mrs. Pritchard acted as Statira and Roxana. Mrs. Dancer acted on 15 March 1768 opposite her lover and husband-to-be Spranger Barry as Alexander. In 1771 Mrs. Yates acted as Statira.

26. Sophie Tomlinson, *Women on Stage in Stuart Drama* (Cambridge: Cambridge University Press, 2005), 158.

27. Banks's plays "led to the invention of the 'she-tragedy,' moving toward the farthest reaches of pathos" in renouncing exotic language, settings, and the explicitly masculine, according to Eric Rothstein, *Restoration Tragedy: Form and the Process of Change* (Madison: University of Wisconsin Press, 1967), 110.

28. Laura Brown, "The Defenseless Woman and the Development of English Tragedy," *SEL* 22, 3 (Summer 1982): 429–43, 441. Bridget Orr, *Empire on the English Stage, 1660–1714* (Cambridge: Cambridge University Press, 2001), 126–27, notes that Restoration plays about Persia frequently feature powerful heroines.

29. Lisa Freeman, *Character's Theater: Genre and Identity on the Eighteenth-Century English Stage* (Philadelphia: University of Pennsylvania Press, 2002), 98. Laura Rosenthal discusses Freeman's views on tragedy in "Entertaining Women: The Actress in the Eighteenth-Century British Theatre and Culture," in *The Cambridge Companion to the British Theatre, 1730–1830*, ed. Jane Moody and Daniel O'Quinn (Cambridge: Cambridge University Press, 2007), 159–74. Laura Brown in *English Dramatic Form 1660–1760: An Essay in Generic History* (New Haven, Conn.: Yale University Press, 1981), 74–79, finds that the "evaluative chaos" and "particular incoherence" between pathos and tyranny, the "absolutely irreconcilable [elements] of Alexander's story," are indicative of a formal tran-

sition; and that *Lucius Junius Brutus* successfully binds together pathos with republican heroism.

30. Diana Solomon, "Tragic Play, Bawdy Epilogue?" in *Prologues, Epilogues, Curtain-Raisers, and Afterpieces: The Rest of the Eighteenth-Century London Stage*, ed. Daniel J. Ennis and Judith B. Slagle (Newark: University of Delaware Press, 2007), 155–78, has helpfully applied Danchin's findings to Restoration plays.

31. See the introduction by Danchin in *The Prologues and Epilogues of the Restoration*, pt. 1, *1660–1676*, 1: xxxviii. The identity of the speaker of the original epilogue to the 1677 production is not certain; but because the topic addresses actresses as "our women," the evidence points to the actor who played Lysimachus, whose rivalry for Parisatis's love against Hephestion parallels but reverses Alexander's dilemma.

32. Colley Cibber took this threat literally in writing and producing the cross-dressed *The Rival Queans*, in *The Plays of Colley Cibber*, ed. Timothy J. Viator and William Burling (Madison, N.J.: Fairleigh Dickinson University Press, 2001), 419–77; citations are from this edition unless otherwise indicated.

33. Tate Wilkinson, *The Wandering Patentee*, 4 vols. in 2 (York, 1795; repr. London: Scolar Press, 1973), 1: 128, refers to "Queen Woffington" versus her rival Mrs. Hamilton: "And could we have supposed the two rival queens to have had a pitched battle, the Lord have mercy upon poor Woofy, for Hamilton would have plunged her dagger and hurled her devoted victim to the avenging gods." Cited in Richards, *The Rise of the English Actress*, 31. On 23 March 1762 Mrs. Hamilton recited another new epilogue. Mrs. Ward spoke in character with a new epilogue on 26 March 1765, as did Mrs. Fitzhenry (formerly Mrs Gregory) on 9 April 1766; George Anne Bellamy repeated it on 23 March 1767, and Miss Younge spoke it "with alterations" on 30 March 1778. See Danchin, *The Prologues and Epilogues of the Eighteenth Century*, pt. 3.

34. Epilogue to *Alexander the Great, a Tragedy; with Alterations, as it is now performed at the Theatres-Royal in Drury-Lane and Covent Garden* (London, 1772).

35. Regarding the rival queens episode and Charles II's presentation of his mistress to the queen, see P. F. Vernon, "Introduction," *The Rival Queens*, xx.

36. Mary Beth Rose, *The Expense of Spirit: Love and Sexuality in English Renaissance Drama* (Ithaca, N.Y.: Cornell University Press, 1988), 182.

37. Vivian Davis in "Colley Cibber and the Laughter of Tragedy," an unpublished paper, suggests that the parody *Rival Queans* cannily interrupts the original play's seriousness to question the merit of evoking pity and fear. She shows that Cibber questions the idealization of the pathetic heroine familiar from she-tragedy and demonstrates how the nation's idealized masculinity depends upon strong heroines. I am grateful to her and to the UCLA graduate seminar (Spring 2005) for many shared insights.

38. Colley Cibber, *The Rival Queans, with the Humours of Alexander the Great*, ed. William M. Peterson, Lake Erie College Studies 5 (Painesville, Ohio: Lake Erie College Press, 1965), xi.

39. Pierre Danchin, *The Prologues and Epilogues of the Eighteenth Century: A Complete Edition*, 6 vols. (Nancy: Presses Universitaires de Nancy, 1990–), pt. 1, *1701–1720*, 1: 283.

40. "A Letter to Mrs. *CLIVE*, from an humble Admirer. *Nonpareil of the Age*," *Daily Advertiser*, no. 3166, Saturday 14 March 1741, [1]. My thanks to Ilias Chrissochoidis for forwarding this reference.

41. Appleton and Burnim's edition of *The Prompter* omits the original bawdy reference to "*Fig's Champions*," an allusion to the actresses' genitalia and sexual prowess. The omitted phrase appears in Hill and Popple, *The Prompter*, 11 November 1735.

42. Thomas Betterton [E. Curll], *The History of the English Stage* (London, 1741), 19–20.

43. P. F. Vernon argues that the audience's sympathetic imagination for Statira's plight combined with Alexander's heroism in decline contributed substantially to the play's longevity, "Introduction," xix.

44. Joel Fineman writes, "The anecdote produces the effect of the real, the occurrence of contingency, by establishing an event as an event within and yet without the framing context of historical successivity" in "The History of the Anecdote," in *The New Historicism*, ed. H. Aram Veeser (New York: Routledge, 1989), 61.

45. Philip H. Highfill, Jr., Kalman A. Burnim, and Edward A. Langhans, *A Biographical Dictionary of Actors, Actresses . . . and Other Stage Personnel in London, 1660–1800*, 16 vols. (Carbondale: Southern Illinois University Press, 1973–93).

46. Colley Cibber, *An Apology for the Life*, 1: 108. The incident is recounted in the entry for Bracegirdl in Highfill et al., *A Biographical Dictionary*, 2: 269–81.

47. Betterton [E. Curll], *History of the English Stage*, 19–20. See also the entry for Elizabeth Barry in Highfill et al., *Biographical Dictionary*, 1: 313–25.

48. Herbert Blau probably originated the term for repressed theatrical memory in *Take Up the Bodies: Theater of the Vanishing Point* (Urbana: University of Illinois Press, 1982). Marvin Carlson, *The Haunted Stage: The Theatre as Memory Machine* (Ann Arbor: University of Michigan Press, 2001), and Joseph Roach, *Cities of the Dead: Circum-Atlantic Performance* (New York: Columbia University, 1996) enrich its meanings.

49. George Anne Bellamy, *An Apology for the Life of George Anne Bellamy*, 5 vols., 4th ed. (London, 1786),. All subsequent references to this edition are cited parenthetically in the text.

50. The dispute was immortalized in a lost theater piece attributed to Samuel Foote, *Green-room Squabble, or a Battle-Royal between the Queen of Babylon and the Daughter of Darius*. The poet characterizes Woffington and Clive as "artful Nymphs, red-Fac'd B--ch," "Prostitute," "Hell's Duchess," and "Old Stage Goat." See Timothy Silence, *The Foundling Hospital for Wit* (London, 1746), 18.

51. For the various versions, see Allardyce Nicoll, *The History of English Drama, 1660–1900*, 3: 271, 318; D. E. Baker et al., *Biographia Dramatica* 3 vols. in 4 (London, 1812), 2: 14; and William van Lennep, "The Life and Works of Nathaniel Lee . . . A Study of Sources" (Dissertation, Harvard University, 1933), 669. Cited in P. F. Vernon, xvii nn. 23, 24.

52. See Wanko, "Colley Cibber's *The Rival Queans*."

53. Cibber, *The Rival Queans*.

54. Peter Stallybrass, "Transvestism and the 'Body Beneath': Speculating on the Boy Actor," in *Erotic Politics: Desire on the Renaisssance Stage*, ed. Susan Zimmerman (New York: Routledge, 1992), 77.

55. Wanko, "Colley Cibber's *The Rival Queans*," notes that an all-male production occurred on 19 April 1765 at Drury Lane. Both men and women actors appeared on 19 and 20 April 1780 at Covent Garden. Cibber never acknowledged the play as his own.

56. "Dialogue III. *Between* Nat. Lee *the Tragedian and* Colly C---r *the Plagiary*," *Visits from the Shades: or, Dialogues Serious, Comical, and Political. Calculated for these Times* (London, 1704–5), 22.

57. Special thanks to Bridget Orr for her suggestions. See her *Empire on the English Stage, 1660–1714*, 2. For an illuminating discussion of the play's Oriental context, see 19–124. Orr interprets Clytus's manly Greek values as a critique of Alexander's effeminate dissipation and corruption (signified by his wearing a Persian vest), and thus of the Carolean court. See also Ros Ballaster, *Fabulous Orients: Fictions of the East in England, 1662–1785* (Oxford: Oxford University Press, 2005).

58. Mary Robinson played Roxana in a Persian costume and ornamental sandals, but sans hoop or hairpowder, *Memoirs of the Late Mrs. Robinson*, 4 vols. (London: R. Phillips, 1801), 2.5.

59. *The Contre Temps; or, Rival Queans: A Small Farce* (1777) is reproduced in *The Dramatic Works of Colley Cibber, Esq. in Five Volumes, Volume the Fourth* . . . (London, 1777), 373–81, but assigning it to Cibber is a joke perhaps perpetrated by George Stevens. See Viator and Burling in *Plays of Colley Cibber*, 424–25.

60. Colley Cibber continues, "Does not this prove, that there is very near as much Enchantment in the well-govern'd Voice of an Actor as in the sweet Pipe of an Eunuch?" *Apology*, 1: 106.

61. See Danchin, *Prologues and Epilogues of the Eighteenth Century*, pt. 2, *1721–1737*, 1: 233–34.

62. The queenly divas are sometimes distinguished as Queen Cuzzoni and Princess Faustina.

63. George Alexander Stevens, *The Court of Alexander. An Opera, in Two Acts. As it is performed at the Theatre Royal in Covent-Garden* (London [1770]).

64. The legendary courtesan Thais incited Alexander to burn down the palace of Persopolis after a drinking party.

65. See my *The Limits of the Human: Fictions of Anomaly, Race, and Gender in the Long Eighteenth Century* (Cambridge: Cambridge University Press, 2003), chap. 8.

CHAPTER 3. ACTRESSES' MEMOIRS: EXCEPTIONAL VIRTUE

1. Samuel Richardson, *Pamela; or, Virtue Rewarded*, ed. Thomas Keymer and Alice Wakeley (New York: Oxford University Press, 2001), 15.

2. Jocelyn Harris, introduction, in *Samuel Richardson's Published Commentary on "Clarissa," 1747–65*, ed. Thomas Keymer, 3 vols. (London: Pickering and Chatto, 1998), 1: lxxii–lxxvi.

3. For an assessment of the erosion of privacy for eighteenth-century men, see John Barrell, "Coffee-House Politicians," *Journal of British Studies* 43 (2004): 225.

4. John Brewer, "This, That and the Other: Public, Social and Private in the Seventeenth and Eighteenth Centuries," in *Shifting the Boundaries: Transformation of the Languages of Public and Private in the Eighteenth Century*, ed. Dario Castiglione and Lesley Sharpe (Exeter: University of Exeter Press, 1995), 17.

5. For classical concepts of *virtù*, see J. G. A. Pocock, *The Machiavellian Moment: Florentine Political Thought and the Atlantic Republican Tradition* (Princeton, N.J.: Princeton University Press, 1975); and in relation to the Irish theater, Desmond Slowey, *The Radicalization of Irish Drama, 1600–1900: The Rise and Fall of the Ascendancy Theatre* (Dublin: Irish Academic Press, 2008), 58, 96.

6. Colin Nicolson, *Writing and The Rise of Finance: Capital Satires of the Early Eighteenth Century* (Cambridge: Cambridge University Press, 1994), 7, has linked the rise of credit to fractured selves: "The emergence of classes whose property consisted not of lands or goods or even bullion, but of paper promises to repay in an undefined future, was seen as entailing the emergence of new types of personality, unprecedentedly dangerous and unstable." See Cheryl Wanko, *Roles of Authority: Thespian Biography and Celebrity in Eighteenth-Century Britain* (Lubbock: Texas Tech University Press, 2003), 163.

7. John Dryden, *Tyrannick Love, or the Royal Martyr. A Tragedy. As it is acted by His Majesties servants, at the Theatre Royal* (1669; London, 1670).

8. Edward Copeland, *Women Writing About Money: Women's Fiction in England, 1790–1820* (Cambridge: Cambridge University Press, 1995), 29.

9. My argument differs somewhat from that forwarded by Wanko who finds that *The Life of Fenton* presents the actress as a "gold digger" (*Roles of Authority*, 62), and that the memoir "denies her public achievement and condemns her path of upward mobility" (60).

10. Edmund Curll, *The Life of that Eminent Comedian Robert Wilks, Esq.* (London, 1733), 28. Curll is unreliable regarding factual information, but his impressions may well reflect popular assumptions.

11. Laura Rosenthal, "'Counterfeit Scrubbado': Women Actors in the Restoration," *Eighteenth Century: Theory and Interpretation* 34 (1993): 3–22, writes, "As long as the actress could not claim virtue, she could not parley her professionalized seductiveness into class mobility" (20), but the nature of that claim to "virtue," I am arguing, was much in dispute.

12. I am citing the first edition (1730) unless otherwise noted.

13. Curll, *Life of Robert Wilks*; Benjamin Victor, *Memoirs of the Life of Barton Booth, Esq.* (London, 1733); and Colley Cibber, *An Apology for the Life of Colley Cibber, Written by Himself* (1740), ed. Robert W. Lowe, 2 vols. (London: John C. Nimmo, 1889), 1: 5.

14. Sarah Prescott, *Women, Authorship, and Literary Culture, 1690–1740* (Basingstoke: Palgrave Macmillan: 2003), 108–9.

15. Mary E. Knapp, *Prologues and Epilogues of the Eighteenth Century* (New Haven, Conn.: Yale University Press, 1961) provides an excellent study regarding the performance of these forms.

16. Samuel Richardson, *Pamela; or, Virtue Rewarded*, 4 vols. (London, 1742), 4: 98–99.

17. *The Spectator*, no. 341, Tuesday, 1 April 1712, entered the controversy in a paper ascribed to Budgell by asserting that Mrs. Oldfield was no longer Andromache when she spoke the "facetious Epilogue" after the end of the play: "Every one knows that on the *British S*tage they are distinct Performances by themselves, Pieces intirely detached from the play, and no way essential to it," *The Spectator*, ed. Donald F. Bond, 5 vols. (Oxford: Clarendon Press, 1965), 3: 266–67. See also Knapp, 296–97.

18. William Chetwood, *A General History of the Stage, from its origin in Greece down to the Present Time* (London, 1749), 201–2; and Joanne Lafler, *The Celebrated Mrs. Oldfield: The Life and Art of an Augustan Actress* (Carbondale: Southern Illinois University Press, 1989), 146–48.

19. Thomas Davies, *Dramatic Miscellanies: Consisting of Critical Observations on Several Plays of Shakespeare*, 3 vols., new ed. (London, 1785), 3: 462.

20. See William W. Appleton's introduction to Colley Cibber, *The Careless Husband* (Lincoln: University of Nebraska Press, 1966), ix–xvi.

21. Joanne Lafler reports that the Earl and Countess of Bristol and their son John, Lord Hervey, were among Oldfield's aristocratic friends who welcomed her into their home, 123.

22. William Cooke, *Memoirs of Charles Macklin, Comedian*, 23.

23. Colley Cibber, preface to Sir John Vanbrugh and Colley Cibber, *The Provoked Husband* [1728], ed. Peter Dixon (Lincoln: University of Nebraska Press, 1973), 9. Capitalization is modernized in this edition.

24. *Authentick Memoirs of the Life of that celebrated Actress Mrs. Ann Oldfield. Containing a Genuine Account of her Transactions from her Infancy to the Time of her Decease* (London, 1730), 38.

25. *Life of Lavinia Beswick, alias Fenton, alias Polly Peachum* (London, 1728), 42.

26. Jane Rogers, *The Memorial of Jane Rogers Humbly Submitted to the Town* (London, 1712); and Catherine Clive, *The Case of Mrs. Clive Submitted to the Publick* (London, 1744).

27. Thomas Postlewait, "Autobiography and Theatre History," in *Interpreting the Theatrical Past: Essays in the Historiography of Performance*, ed. Postlewait and Bruce A. McConachie (Iowa City: University of Iowa Press, 1989), 251.

28. George Ballard, *Memoirs of Several Ladies of Great Britain* (1752), ed. Ruth Perry

(Detroit: Wayne State University Press, 1985), 28. See also Harriet Guest's important study of Bluestockings as Roman matrons in *Small Change: Women, Learning, Patriotism, 1750–1810* (Chicago: University of Chicago Press, 2000).

29. Charlotte Charke, *A Narrative of the Life of Mrs. Charlotte Charke*, ed. Robert Rehder (London: Pickering and Chatto, 1999), 73. For further discussion of Charke, see Felicity Nussbaum, *The Autobiographical Subject: Gender and Ideology in Eighteenth-Century England* (Baltimore: Johns Hopkins University Press, 1989), 195–98.

30. George Anne Bellamy, *An Apology for the Life of George Anne Bellamy*, 5 vols., 4th ed. (London, 1786).

31. Kristina Straub, *Sexual Suspects: Eighteenth-Century Players and Sexual Ideology* (Princeton, N.J.: Princeton University Press, 1992), 109–26. Wanko also describes Bellamy as characterizing herself as a victim, 152.

32. Quotations are from reviews in *English Review* (February 1785) and *Westminster Magazine* (March 1785), included as puffs in the final volume of Bellamy's *An Apology for the Life of George Anne Bellamy, Late of Covent-Garden Theatre*, 6 vols. (London, 1785), 6: 173, 177.

33. Elizabeth Griffith, *The Delicate Distress, A Novel in Letters* (1769), ed. Cynthia Booth Ricciardi and Susan Staves (Lexington: University Press of Kentucky, 1997), 166–67.

34. James Boaden, *Memoirs of Mrs. Siddons*, 2 vols. (London: Henry Colburn, 1827), 1: 15.

CHAPTER 4. ACTRESSES AND PATRONS: THE THEATRICAL CONTRACT

1. Richard Steele, *The Theatre*, ed. John Loftis, no. 1, Saturday, 2 January 1720 (Oxford: Clarendon Press, 1962), 3. Sir John Edgar resembles Sir John Bevil, the central character in Steele's *The Conscious Lovers*.

2. The phrase appears in Jupiter's speech in John Crowne, *Calisto, or, the Chaste Nimph; the Late Masque at Court* (London, 1675), 5: 2.

3. Jeremy Collier, *A Short View of the Immorality and Profaneness of the English Stage*, 3rd ed. (London, 1698), 13.

4. Nathaniel Lee, *The Rival Queens*, ed. Paul Frank Vernon (Lincoln: University of Nebraska Press, 1970), 11.

5. Arthur Murphy, *The Gray's Inn Journal*, no. 74, 2 vols. (Dublin [1756]), 2: 125.

6. Robert Weimann, *Author's Pen and Actor's Voice: Playing and Writing in Shakespeare's Theatre*, ed. Helen Higbee and William West (Cambridge: Cambridge University Press, 2000), 225, speaks of "an exchange, almost, of roles."

7. *The London Stage* indicates that a popular play with a similar name, Charles Johnson's *The Wife's Relief; or, the Husband's Cure*, played on 5 October 1736 at Lincoln's Inn Fields, continuing on 13 and 15 October. Though performed at Drury Lane on 18 and 20 October, and 10 November, it was not staged again at Lincoln's Inn Fields until 11 February 1737.

8. *Gentleman's Magazine* 6 (October 1736): [617]–618.

9. The passage appears in Robert Palfrey Utter and Gwendolyn Bridges Needham, *Pamela's Daughters* (New York: Macmillan, 1936). See also John Ashton, *Social Life in the Reign of Queen Anne* (London: Chatto and Windus, 1883), 315; and *Gentleman's Magazine* 6 (1736): 487, 617. Ironically, the remarkable Mrs. Mapp died so impoverished that the parish paid for her burial, *Gentleman's Magazine* 7 (1737): 767.

10. Letter signed "Churchillus," *Volunteer Manager*, 24 April 1763.

11. Charles Gildon, *Life of Mr. Thomas Betterton* (London, 1710), 37.

12. David Garrick to the Countess of Burlington, 13 October 1750, in *The Letters of David Garrick*, ed. David M. Little and George M. Kahrl, 3 vols. (Cambridge, Mass.: Harvard University Press, 1963), 1: 156.

13. Tiffany Stern, *Rehearsal from Shakespeare to Sheridan* (Oxford: Clarendon Press, 2000), 13; and regarding actors' extemporization, 183–94.

14. See Mary E. Knapp, *Prologues and Epilogues of the Eighteenth Century* (New Haven, Conn.: Yale University Press, 1961); and Deborah C. Payne, "Reified Object or Emergent Professional? Retheorizing the Restoration Actress," in *Cultural Readings of Restoration and Eighteenth-Century Theater*, ed. J. Douglas Canfield and Deborah Payne Fisk (Athens: University of Georgia Press, 1995): 13–38.

15. Thomas Davies, *Dramatic Miscellanies: Consisting of Critical Observations on Several Plays of Shakspeare*, 3 vols., new ed. (London, 1785), 3: 467.

16. Cited in Patrick J. Crean, "The Life and Times of Kitty Clive" (Dissertation, University of London, 1933), 158.

17. Epilogue, "The Author Written by a Lady Spoken by Mrs. Clive," in *The Theatrical Bouquet: Containing an Alphabetical Arrangement of the Prologues and Epilogues, Which have been Published by Distinguished Wits, from the Time that Colley Cibber first came on the Stage, to the present Year* (London, 1778), 278–79.

18. John Macky, *A Journey through England. In Familiar Letters from a Gentleman Here, to His Friend Abroad* (London, 1714), 110. *A Seasonable Rebuke to the Playhouse Rioters... To which is prefixed, a Petitionary Dedication to the Fair Members of the Shakespear-Club* (London, 1740), 16, specifically solicits the attendance of the Ladies as critical in making possible "*a well fill'd Theatre ... in a Nation remarkable for a beautiful Race of Women.*"

19. Alice LeFanu, *Memoirs of the Life and Writings of Mrs. Frances Sheridan* (London: G. and W.B. Whittaker, 1824), 26.

20. Christopher Morash, *A History of Irish Theatre, 1601–2000* (Cambridge: Cambridge University Press, 2002), 35.

21. John Macky testified that "on the first row of *Boxes* sit all the Ladies of Quality; in the second the Citizens Wives & Daughters ... so that between the Acts you may be diverted by viewing the Beauties of the Audience, as while they act with the Subject of the Play" (*Journey through England*, 110).

22. Susan Cannon Harris, "Outside the Box: The Female Spectator, *The Fair Penitent*, and the Kelly Riots of 1747," *Theatre Journal* 57, 1 (2005): 44. David Roberts, *The Ladies: Female Patronage of Restoration Drama, 1660–1700* (Oxford: Clarendon Press, 1989), 165,

anticipated Harris in describing "a female audience united . . . by a developing awareness of its insecurity in the modern world."

23. *Dublin Gazette*, 25–29 January 1743, cited in Esther K. Sheldon, *Thomas Sheridan of Smock Alley* (Princeton, N.J.: Princeton University Press, 1967), 3.

24. Tate Wilkinson, *Memoirs of His Own Life*, 4 vols. (York, 1790), 4: 110–11.

25. *The Life of Lavinia Beswick, alias Fenton, alias Polly Peachum* (London, 1728), 36.

26. Kristina Straub, *Sexual Suspects: Eighteenth-Century Players and Sexual Ideology* (Princeton, N.J.: Princeton University Press, 1992). Jean I. Marsden, *Fatal Desire: Women, Sexuality, and the English Stage, 1660–1720* (Ithaca, N.Y.: Cornell University Press, 2006), among other scholars, emphasizes actresses as objects of the desiring male gaze. Marsden usefully revives interest in the agency of female playwrights but largely overlooks the actresses' own economic and performative power.

27. If, in fact, kneeling or baring one's backside occurred when the audience scourged an actor, as Straub indicates, then whipping or caning would have involved at least proxy representation of the audience on stage. I have found no other references to this practice.

28. P. David Marshall, *Celebrity and Power: Fame in Contemporary Culture* (Minneapolis: University of Minnesota Press, 1997), xiii, writes, "The concept of the 'audience-subject' is developed to express the simultaneous construction of celebrity power through its intense development of the individual personality's power and its dependence on collective configurations for the maintenance of its public representation of power." Lisa Freeman, *Character's Theater: Genre and Identity on the Eighteenth-Century English Stage* (Philadelphia: University of Pennsylvania Press, 2002), 5, also mentions a "theater of interaction," though she does not pursue the implications of this valuable insight.

29. Robert Weimann, *Shakespeare and the Popular Tradition in the Theater: Studies in the Social Dimension of Dramatic Form and Function* (Baltimore: Johns Hopkins University Press, 1987), 7, contends that the bond between audience and stage was largely limited to those who shared the same social class.

30. Willmar Sauter, *The Theatrical Event: Dynamics of Performance and Perception* (Iowa City: University of Iowa Press, 2000), 50–72. See also Thomas Postlewait and Tracy C. Davis, "Theatricality: An Introduction," in *Theatricality*, ed. Tracy C. Davis and Thomas Postlewait (Cambridge: Cambridge University Press, 2003), 23.

31. The model of a more interactive stage was dominant among critics of earlier decades, though the particular role of women has not been sufficiently analyzed. See especially Harry William Pedicord, *The Theatrical Public in the Time of Garrick* (Carbondale: Southern Illinois University Press, 1966); Leo Hughes, *Drama's Patrons: A Study of the Eighteenth-Century London Audience* (Austin: University of Texas Press, 1971); Judith Milhous, *Thomas Betterton and the Management of Lincoln's Inn Fields, 1695–1708* (Carbondale: Southern Illinois University Press, 1979).

32. Theophilus Cibber, "Preface to the Town," *An Epistle from Theophilus Cibber, to David Garrick, Esq.* (London, 1755), 2.

33. Steele, *The Theatre*, no. 2 (Tuesday, 5 January 1720), 5.

34. Colley Cibber, *An Apology for the Life of Colley Cibber, Written by Himself* (1740), ed. Robert W. Lowe, 2 vols. (London: John C. Nimmo, 1889), 1: 323–24.

35. James Ralph, *The Touch-Stone: or, Historical, Critical, Political, Philosophical, and Theological Essays on the Reigning Diversions of the Town* (London, 1728), 145.

36. *The Public Advertiser* 12, 3 (1763) and 23, 3 (1764) notes that the "Nuisance of Building on the Stage" was removed from both theaters. Cited in Crean, "Life and Times of Kitty Clive," 337.

37. Benjamin Victor, *The History of the Theatres of London and Dublin*, 3 vols. (London 1761), 1: 127–28.

38. Cited in John Alexander Kelly, *German Visitors to English Theaters in the Eighteenth Century* (Princeton, N.J.: Princeton University Press, 1936), 55.

39. Johann Wilhelm Von Archenholz, *A Picture of England*, 2 vols. (London, 1789), 2: 166.

40. See Marc Baer, *Theatre and Disorder in Late Georgian London* (Oxford: Clarendon Press, 1992), 14, 189.

41. Jean-Christophe Agnew, *Worlds Apart: The Market and the Theater in Anglo-American Thought, 1550–1750* (New York: Cambridge University Press, 1986), 7, 11.

42. Sophie Tomlinson, *Women on Stage in Stuart Drama* (Cambridge: Cambridge University Press, 2005), 204.

43. Roberts, *The Ladies,* concludes that "any idea of a 'ladies' faction' depends entirely on a literal reading of worn-out evidence" (136, 139). For various views, see John Harrington Smith, "Shadwell, the Ladies, and the Change in Comedy," *Modern Philology* 46 (1948): 22–33; and Robert D. Hume and A. H. Scouten, "'Restoration Comedy' and Its Audiences, 1660–1776," in Robert D. Hume, *The Rakish Stage: Studies in English Drama, 1660–1800* (Carbondale: Southern Illinois University Press, 1983), 46–82; Peter Holland, *The Ornament of Action: Text and Performance in Restoration Comedy* (Cambridge: Cambridge University Press, 1979), 15–16; Allan Richard Botica, "Audience, Playhouse and Play in Restoration Theatre, 1660–1710" (Dissertation, Oxford University, 1985), 106–8, 186; and John Harley, *Music in Purcell's London: The Social Background* (London: Dobson, 1968), 120–21.

44. Hume and Scouten, "'Restoration Comedy,' and its Audiences, 1660–1776," 62–64, argue this point. Roberts, *The Ladies*, shows that no one faction dominated and gives evidence that women from different ranks expressed varied preferences, 135–36.

45. Janet Todd, *The Secret Life of Aphra Behn* (New Brunswick, N.J.: Rutgers University Press, 1997), 360.

46. Collier, *A Short View of Immorality* (London, 1698), 7.

47. Prologue to *The Constant Couple*, *The Works of George Farquhar*, ed. Shirley Strum Kenny, 2 vols. (Oxford: Clarendon Press, 1988), 1: 151–52.

48. Macky, *A Journey through England*, 133.

49. Desmond Slowey, *The Radicalization of Irish Drama, 1600–1900: The Rise and Fall of the Ascendancy Theatre* (Dublin: Irish Academic Press, 2008), notes that from 1715 to 1720 women "were constantly appealed to in the prologues and epilogues to Shadwell to use their charms on behalf of the playwright and theatre," 73.

50. See William Van Lennep, Emmett L. Avery, Arthur H. Scouten, George Winchester Stone, Jr., and Charles Beecher Hogan, eds., *The London Stage 1660–1800: A Calendar of Plays, Entertainments and Afterpieces*, 5 parts in 11 vols. (Carbondale: Southern Illinois University Press, 1960–68).

51. Robert D. Hume, *The Development of English Drama in the Late Seventeenth Century* (Oxford: Clarendon Press, 1976), 488.

52. Agnew, *Worlds Apart*, 102, notes, "The state had its vicegerents, the church had its vicars, but only the theater projected a whole world of vicarious relations."

53. John Dennis, *Original Letters Familiar, Moral, and Critical*, 2 vols. (London, 1721), 1: 63–64.

54. Jonathan Swift, "Thoughts on Various Subjects," in Alexander Pope, *The Works of Alexander Pope*, ed. Whitwell Elwin and William John Courthope, 10 vols. (New York: Gordian Press, 1967), 10: 560.

55. John C. Greene and Gladys L. H. Clark, *The Dublin Stage, 1720–1745: A Calendar of Plays, Entertainments, and Afterpieces* (Bethlehem, Pa.: Lehigh University Press, 1993), 93–402; and Morash, *History of Irish Theatre*, 35–36.

56. Judith Milhous, "Reading Theatre History for Account Books," in *Players, Playwrights, Playhouses: Investigating Performance 1660–1800*, ed. Peter Holland and Michael Cordner (Basingstoke: Palgrave Macmillan, 2007), has shown that the few extant account books provide critical information regarding exact attendance and the profits garnered from each segment of the audience.

57. The manuscript regarding Hannah Pritchard is Folger MS W.Bb.11 Y.d.100, Folger Shakespeare Library, Washington, D.C.

58. Susanna Centlivre, *The Wonder: A Woman Keeps a Secret*, ed. John O'Brien (Peterborough, Ont.: Broadview Press, 2004).

59. I am very grateful to Regulus Allen for her careful work in compiling data regarding productions staged at the desire of the ladies of quality.

60. See especially Fiona Ritchie, "The Influence of the Female Audience on the Shakespeare Revival of 1736–1738: The Case of the Shakespeare Ladies Club," in *Shakespeare and the Eighteenth Century*, ed. Peter Sabor and Paul Yachnin (Aldershot: Ashgate, 2008), 57–69. We share similar conclusions regarding the importance of the Club.

61. See Emmett L. Avery, "The Shakespeare Ladies' Club," *Shakespeare Quarterly* (Spring 1956): 152–58; and Michael Dobson, *The Making of the National Poet: Shakespeare, Adaptation and Authorship, 1660–1769* (Oxford: Clarendon Press, 1992), 146–84, who reprints in full Mary Cowper's "On the Revival of Shakespear's Plays by the Ladies in 1738." Garrick praised the women for restoring Shakespeare to the stage, though he was later to take credit for the revival himself.

62. "To the Ladies of the Shakespear's Club," *A Collection of Miscellany Poems, never before publish'd* (London, 1737), 178. Among the subscribers to the collection were Theophilus Cibber, Kitty Clive, and Mr. Cibber, Senior.

63. Francis Hawling, *A Miscellany of Original Poems on Various Subjects*, pt.1 (London 1751), 112.

64. Greene and Clark provide a full listing in *The Dublin Stage*.

65. *Universal Advertiser*, 9 May 1758, cited in La Tourette Stockwell, *Dublin Theatres and Theatre Customs, 1637–1820* (Kingsport, Tenn.: Kingsport Press, 1938), 185.

66. Elizabeth Steele, *The Memoirs of Mrs. Sophia Baddeley, late of Drury Lane Theatre*, 6 vols. (Clerkenwell, 1787), 1: 58.

67. Letter from Elizabeth Carter to Mrs. Underdown, 10 April 1742, Canterbury, in *Elizabeth Carter, 1717–1806: An Edition of Some Unpublished Letters*, ed. Gwen Hampshire (Newark: University of Delaware Press, 2005).

68. George Anne Bellamy, *An Apology for the Life of George Anne Bellamy*, 5 vols., 4th ed. (London, 1786), 3: 183.

69. Daniel O'Quinn, "Introduction to Wallace's *The Ton*: "The Sport of a Theatrical Damnation," *British Women Playwrights Around 1800*, http://www.etang.umontreal.ca/bwp1800/essays/oquinn_ton_intro.html., has argued that the audience disorder provoked by anger at the privileged ranks effectively kept social violence from spreading beyond the space of the English theater. O'Quinn interprets the reviews and audience reactions to Lady Wallace's *The Ton* as public shaming of the dissolute aristocracy whose moral and aesthetic standards faced near-constant critique from the bourgeois classes.

70. Mary Robinson, *Walsingham, or, The Pupil of Nature* (1797), ed. Julie Shaffer (Toronto: Broadview, 2003), 218–20, 342–43. I am grateful to Harriet Guest for this reference.

71. See Margaret J. M. Ezell, *Social Authorship and the Advent of Print* (Baltimore: Johns Hopkins University Press, 1999). Sarah Prescott, *Women, Authorship and Literary Culture, 1690–1740* (Basingstoke: Palgrave Macmillan, 2003), 125, describes the literary market of print culture in this manner but does not include the theater.

72. Dustin Griffin, *Literary Patronage in England, 1650–1800* (Cambridge: Cambridge University Press, 1996), 10, 16–17.

73. Victor Turner, *The Forest of Symbols: Aspects of Ndembu Ritual* (Ithaca, N.Y.: Cornell University Press, 1967), 97.

74. Josette Féral, "Foreword," *SubStance*, special issue on Theatricality 31, 2/3 (2002): 9.

75. George Raymond, *Life and Enterprises of Robert William Elliston, Comedian* (London: Routledge, 1857), 166–67.

76. Victor, *History of the Theatres of London and Dublin*, 3: 261.

77. Thomas Betterton [Edmund Curll], *The History of the English Stage* (London, 1741), 17.

78. Mary Nash, *The Provoked Wife: The Life and Times of Susannah Cibber* (Boston: Little, Brown, 1977), 97, cites the notice printed by Theophilus Cibber in the *Daily Advertiser* (April 1736).

CHAPTER 5. THE ACTRESS AND PERFORMATIVE PROPERTY:
CATHERINE CLIVE

1. For a fine discussion of the 1710 Statute of Anne, see Jody Greene, *The Trouble with Ownership: Literary Property and Authorial Liability in England, 1660–1730* (Philadelphia: University of Pennsylvania Press, 2005), which traces the 1680 persecution of Elizabeth Cellier for being "guilty of valuing herself, and of valuing herself specifically as an author" (95). See also Mark Rose, *Authors and Owners: The Invention of Copyright* (Cambridge, Mass.: Harvard University Press, 1993).

2. See, for example, Harriet Guest, *Small Change: Women, Learning, Patriotism, 1750–1810* (Chicago: University of Chicago Press, 2000); and Emma Clery, *The Feminization Debate in Eighteenth-Century England: Literature, Commerce, and Luxury* (Basingstoke: Palgrave Macmillan, 2004).

3. *The Life of Mr. James Quin, Comedian. With the History of the Stage from his commencing Actor to his Retreat to Bath* (London, 1766), 70–71. When Quin accosted her with "coarse and indelicate" talk, Clive complained to the manager.

4. Letter from Catherine Clive to Garrick, 14 April 1769, *The Harcourt Papers*, ed. E. W. Harcourt, 13 vols. (Oxford, Parker, 1880–1905), 8: 171.

5. Tate Wilkinson, *Memoirs of His Own Life*, 4 vols. (York, 1790), 3: 42–43.

6. The anecdote is recounted by W. R. Chetwood, *A General History of the Stage, from its origin in Greece down to the Present Time* (London, 1749), 127.

7. *The Comedian, or Philosophical Enquirer*, 7 October 1732, 37–42, 39. I am grateful to Ilias Chrissochoidis for this reference.

8. Berta Joncus, "Handel at Drury Lane: Ballad Opera and the Production of Kitty Clive," *Journal of the Royal Musical Association* 131, 2 (2006): 179–226, expertly traces the evolution of Clive's relationship to Handel and his music from initially being an avid proponent (1728–33), then a harsh critic (1733), turning to marketing and popularizing his songs as native (late 1730s), and finally, their becoming "cultural intimates" in 1740. Joncus's full-length study of Clive's career is eagerly awaited.

9. *Life of Mr. James Quin, Comedian*, 69. Berta Joncus, "'His Spirit is in Action Seen': Milton, Mrs. Clive and the Simulacra of the Pastoral in *Comus*," *Eighteenth-Century Music* 2, 1 (2005): 7–40, describes aspects of Clive's manipulation of social codes through the masque form. While Joncus focuses on Clive's singing career, rather than her acting, we have independently arrived at similar conclusions regarding her public persona.

10. Sandra Richards, *The Rise of the English Actress* (London: St. Martin's Press, 1993), 24.

11. Joncus, "Handel at Drury Lane," argues that Clive's Patriot sympathies were voiced openly in the music for James Miller, *The Coffee House* (1737), and Edward Phillips, *Britons Strike Home* (1739), though she does not discuss the important epilogues. She interprets Clive's performance as Dalila in the libretto to Handel's *Samson* (1744) as overt self-mockery of her Patriot sympathies. Clive concurs with pit and stage in demanding an epilogue to follow *Britons Strike Home*.

12. Thomas Davies, *Memoirs of the Life of David Garrick, Esq. Interspersed with characters and Anecdotes of His Theatrical Contemporaries*, 2 vols., 4th ed. (London, 1784), 2: 196.

13. James Boswell, *The Life of Johnson*, ed. George Birkbeck Hill, rev. L. F. Powell, 6 vols. (Oxford: Clarendon Press, 1934–50), 4: 243.

14. Oliver Goldsmith, *The Bee; Being Essays on the Most Interesting Subjects*, no. 5 (London, 1759), 156.

15. Kitty Clive to Garrick, 27 November 1768, in *Letters of David Garrick*, ed. David Little and George Kahrl, 3 vols. (Cambridge, Mass.: Belknap Press of Harvard University Press, 1963), 2: 628.

16. James Boaden, *Memoirs of Mrs. Siddons*, 2 vols. (London: Henry Colburn, 1827), 1: 191.

17. J. G. A. Pocock, *Virtue, Commerce, and History: Essays on Political Thought, Chiefly in the Eighteenth Century* (New York: Cambridge University Press, 1985), 103.

18. J. G. A. Pocock, *The Machiavellian Moment: Florentine Political Thought and the Atlantic Republican Tradition* (Princeton, N.J.: Princeton University Press, 1975), 464.

19. See Carole Pateman, *The Sexual Contract* (Stanford, Calif.: Stanford University Press, 1988); and John Locke, *Two Treatises of Government*, ed. Peter Laslett (Cambridge: Cambridge University Press, 1988), 287, 290.

20. Etienne Balibar, "My *Self* and My Own: One and the Same?" in *Accelerating Possession: Global Futures of Prosperity and Personhood*, ed. Bill Maurer and Gabriele Schwab (New York: Columbia University Press, 2006), 24, helpfully queries the linguistic and philosophical relationship between Locke's use of "self" and "own" in "Of Identity and Diversity," *Essay Concerning Human Understanding* (1690), 2: 27.

21. Catherine Clive, *The Case of Mrs. Clive* (1744), intro. Richard C. Frushell, Augustan Reprint Society 159 (Los Angeles: William Andrews Clark Memorial Library, UCLA, 1973). I am very grateful to Lisa Freeman for the stimulating exchange that helped me to formulate these ideas, though she is not, of course, responsible for my interpretation.

22. The intricacies involved in property arrangements of contracts and wills, of personal property and land, were vital components of many popular Restoration dramatic plots. On women's property rights, see Amy Louise Erickson, *Women and Property in Early Modern England* (London: Routledge, 1993); and "Coverture and Capitalism," *History Workshop Journal* 59, 1 (2005): 1–16; Susan Staves, *Married Women's Separate Property in England, 1660–1833* (Cambridge, Mass.: Harvard University Press, 1990); and Tracy Davis, *Actresses as Working Women: Their Social Identity in Victorian Culture* (London: Routledge, 1991), 3–35.

23. Davies, *Memoirs of the Life of David Garrick*, 2: 324–25.

24. *The Disputes between the Director of D--y, and the Pit Potentates: Being a Letter to a Friend, Concerning the Behaviour of the Melancholly Manager of the Suff'ring Theatre* (London, 1744), 19.

25. See Erickson, *Women and Property*, 19. Nicola Phillips, *Women in Business, 1700–1850* (Woodbridge: Boydell Press, 2006), finds, however, that married women could defend their property in court, and that the law was not consistently applied.

26. George Anne Bellamy, *An Apology for the Life*, 1: 108, offers this explanation of her defection to Dublin to act for Sheridan rather than remaining in London with manager Rich.

27. Ruth Perry, *Novel Relations: The Transformation of Kinship in English Literature and Culture, 1748–1818* (Cambridge: Cambridge University Press, 2004), 76, writes, "What *Clarissa* enacts . . . is the dispossession of daughters in the new capitalist dispensation, and the daughters' difficulty in finding a place in the world to belong to once this dispossession has taken effect."

28. Richards, *Rise of the English Actress*, provides a telling example: Anne Crawford's "third marriage demonstrates how actresses of this period could work their economic independence even in wedlock. Upon marrying an Irish barrister turned actor named Thomas Crawford in July 1778, she retained 'to herself by law the Crow-street theatre properties' Spranger Barry left her. She rented the Dublin theater to her new husband who acted as manager, with the agreement that she should play one night a week," 63.

29. Staves, *Married Women's Separate Property*, shows that in the early nineteenth century, contracts between a husband and a wife's trustees were substituted for contracts between spouses, and the legal status of women, especially married women, declined.

30. Greene, *The Trouble with Ownership*, has re-centered women's individual authorship in this period as exerting "identifiable intention and an originative agency" (9). Greene notes that "for a woman to [claim to] own anything at all, especially a book, creates . . . a disturbance in the emergent norms that link originative agency with proprietorship as essential attributes of modern authorship" (102). In contrast, see Paula McDowell's emphasis in *Women of Grub Street: Press, Politics, and Gender in the London Literary Marketplace, 1678–1730* (Oxford: Clarendon Press, 1998) on women's collective activity as writers in the Grub Street book trade, and Catherine Gallagher's discussion in *Nobody's Story: The Vanishing Acts of Women Writers in the Marketplace* (Berkeley: University of California Press, 1995) of women writers' exploitation of their vulnerabilities while disavowing authorship.

31. Her antagonism to Mrs. Cibber may have been enflamed by her close attachment to Theophilus Cibber's first wife. See Mary Nash, *The Provoked Wife: The Life and Times of Susannah Cibber* (Boston: Little, Brown, 1977), 57–59.

32. Letter to the *London Daily Post and General Advertiser*, 19 November 1736.

33. Henry Woodward, *The Beggar's Pantomime; or, the Contending Colombines: A New Comic Interlude*, 3rd ed. (London, 1736), 21.

34. Kathryn Shevelow, *Charlotte: Being a True Account of an Actress's Flamboyant Adventures in Eighteenth-Century London's Wild and Wicked Theatrical World* (New York: Henry Holt, 2005), provides a lively account, 224–37.

35. Frushell offers this explanation in the introduction to *The Case of Mrs. Clive*, i–xiii, to which I am indebted.

36. *The Complete Works of Henry Fielding, Esq.*, ed. William Ernest Henley, 16 vols. (New York: Croscup and Sterling, 1902; repr. Barnes and Noble, 1967), 10: 277–78.

37. See *Queries upon Queries; to be Answer'd by the Male-Content Players* (London, [1743?]).

38. Richards, *Rise of the English Actress*, 266–67 n. 26, summarizes the situation as "a conspiracy of the two patent houses to retain [Clive's] services at a gradually reduced salary by agreed price-fixing."

39. Though Garrick too was involved in attempting to form a rebel company at the Opera House, Clive, the "*Sing-Song* Girl" was singled out as the main culprit in the satirical *Theatrical Correspondence in Death. An Epistle from Mrs. Oldfield, in the Shades, to Mrs. Br--ceg—dle upon Earth* (London, 1743): "Notwithstanding her Sex, I believe we may justly say, she is one of the chiefs of these *State Revolters—Dux Foemina facti*," 2–3.

40. The paper war included *The Case Between the Managers of the Two Theatres, and their Principal Actors* (1743, misdated 1713); *Queries to be Answered by the Manager of Drury Lane* (1743); *Queries upon Queries* [1743?]; *A Full answer to Queries upon Queries* (1743); and *An Impartial Examen* (1744).

41. [Samuel Richardson?], *A Seasonable Examination of the Pleas and Pretensions of the Proprietors of, and Subscribers to, Playhouses erected in defiance of the Royal Licence* (London, 1735), 6.

42. *Rosalind: or, an Apology for the History of a Theatrical Lady* (Dublin, 1759), xiii–xiv.

43. Mr. Neither-Side, *An Impartial Examen of the Present Contests between the Town and the Manager of the Theatre with Some Proposals for accommodating the present Misunderstandings between the Town and the Manager* (London, 1744), 21–22.

44. See Patrick J. Crean, "The Life and Times of Kitty Clive" (Dissertation, University of London, 1933), 244 ff., for the most accurate biography. Percy Fitzgerald's entertaining *The Life of Catherine Clive* (1888; New York: B. Blom, 1971) is less reliable.

45. As an indication of the contracts actresses were later able to negotiate, in 1822 Frances Maria (Fanny) Kelly demanded the following: "For three seasons . . . with liberty for Miss Kelly to absent herself during the six weeks in Lent; to have the exclusive use of her dresses. Salary to be 20*l* [£] a week, but to be raised to equal any other actress who may be engaged. To have the most desirable dressing-room, with not more than one other lady, of the highest rank and respectability; the liberty to decline any new part or character, and also such parts in old pieces, as she does not consider adapted to her powers; to enjoy all privileges and indulgences granted to the most favoured performer; to be exempted from the condition of the sick clause, whenever sickness, &c., shall arise out of the exercise of her profession, or any consequence thereof." Cited in Cheryl Wanko, "Contracts for Two Drury Lane Actresses in 1822," *Harvard Library Bulletin* ser. 2, 5 (1994): 65.

46. Letter from Catherine Clive to David Garrick, 14 October 1765, Folger MS 1083 Y.c.552(4), Folger Shakespeare Library, Washington, D.C..

47. *The Plays of David Garrick*, ed. Harry William Pedicord and Fredrick Louis Bergmann, 7 vols. (Carbondale: Southern Illinois University Press, 1980), 1: 377–84. I have drawn on the commentary and notes to this edition.

48. *Lethe Rehears'd; or, A Critical Discussion of the Beauties & Blemishes of that Performance, etc.* (London, 1749), 21.

49. "Epilogue" to *Lethe*, from the surreptitious edition printed by J. Cooke (London, 1745), *The Plays of David Garrick*, 1: 34.

50. Samuel Foote, *The Roman and English Comedy Consider'd and Compar'd . . . And an Examen into the Merit of the Present Comic Actors* (London, 1747), 42–43.

51. John Doran, "Their Majesties' Servants," *Annals of the English Stage, from Thomas Betterton to Edmund Kean*, 2 vols. (London: W.H. Allen, 1864), 2: 112.

52. John Fyvie, *Comedy Queens of the Georgian Era* (London: Constable, 1906), 98.

53. JoAllen Bradham, "A Good Country Gentlewoman: Catherine Clive's Epistolary Autobiography," *Biography* 19, 3 (Summer 1996): 259–82, claims the gentlewoman's role was unavailable to Clive on stage; but in fact, she played Millamant in Congreve's *Way of the World*.

54. David Garrick, *The Clandestine Marriage*, in *Plays of David Garrick*, 1: 253–336.

55. Tiffany Stern, *Rehearsal from Shakespeare to Sheridan* (Oxford: Clarendon Press, 2000), 203.

56. The first burletta was performed at the Haymarket in 1748. Kathryn Shevelow succinctly defines the form: "Burlettas were joke-based, fast-paced, high-spirited, light-hearted, sexually suggestive, highly physical entertainments that delighted their audiences with frenetic foolery, absurd lyrics, and elaborate finales," *Charlotte*, 372.

57. Phyllis T. Dircks, "Garrick's Fail-Safe Musical Venture, *A Peep Behind the Curtain*, an English Burletta," in *The Stage and the Page: London's "Whole Show" in the Eighteenth-Century Theatre*, ed. George Winchester Stone, Jr. (Berkeley: University of California Press, 1981), 144–45.

58. David Garrick, *A Peep Behind the Curtain*, in *Plays of David Garrick*, 2: 331 n.19.

59. Peter de Bolla, "'A Submission, Sir!' Who Has the Right to Person in Eighteenth-Century Britain?" in *Land, Nation and Culture, 1740–1840: Thinking the Republic of Taste*, ed. Peter de Bolla, Nigel Leask, and David Simpson (Basingstoke: Palgrave Macmillan, 2005), 155, remarks that the title page of published plays advertises actors as servants of the king.

60. Benjamin Victor, *Original Letters, Dramatic Pieces and Poems*, 3 vols. (London 1776), 1: 127. Peter de Bolla, "A Submission, Sir!" 152, cites this passage.

61. Clive was not successful in the tragic roles of Ophelia in *Hamlet* and Zara in *The Mourning Bride*.

62. Francis Gentleman, *The Dramatic Censor; or, Critical Companion*, 2 vols. (1770), 1: 297. See also Judith Fisher, "'The Quality of Mercy' in the Eighteenth Century; or, Kitty Clive's Portia," *Restoration and Eighteenth Century Theatre Research*, 2nd ser. 14, 1 (Summer 1999): 19–42.

63. Diana Solomon, "Tragic Play, Bawdy Epilogue?" in *Prologues, Epilogues, Curtain-Raisers, and Afterpieces: The Rest of the Eighteenth-Century London Stage*, ed. Daniel J. Ennis and Judith B. Slagle (Newark: University of Delaware Press, 2007), 155–78, discusses Anne Bracegirdle's transformation of "high tragedy" into "low comedy" through its epilogue.

64. *The Spouter's Companion; or, Theatrical Remembrancer. Containing a Select Collection of the most esteemed Prologues and Epilogues, Which Have Been Spoken by the most Celebrated Performers of both Sexes* (London [1770?]), 9.

65. *The Prologues and Epilogues of the Eighteenth Century: A Complete Edition*, ed. Pierre Danchin, 6 vols. (Nancy: Presses Universitaires de Nancy, 1997), pt. 3, *1737–1760*, 5: 188–89.

66. Mary E. Knapp, *Prologues and Epilogues of the Eighteenth Century* (New Haven, Conn.: Yale University Press, 1961), 68.

67. Henry Fielding, *The Lottery. A Farce*, 2nd ed. (London, 1732), n.p.

68. Epilogue to Aaron Hill, *The Tragedy of Zara* (London, 1736), in Danchin, *The Prologues and Epilogues of the Eighteenth Century*, pt. 2, *1721–1737*, 4: 717.

69. James Worsdale, *A Cure for A Scold* (Dublin, 1738), 40.

70. The epilogue to *The Dupe* appears in *The Theatrical Bouquet: Containing an Alphabetical Arrangement of the Prologues and Epilogues, Which have been Published by Distinguished Wits, from the Time that Colley Cibber first came on the Stage, to the present Year* (London, 1778), 132.

71. Danchin, *Eighteenth Century*, pt. 3, *1737–1760*, 5: 366.

72. See *Theatrical Bouquet*, 188; and especially Matthew J. Kinservik, "Garrick's Unpublished Epilogue for Catherine Clive's *The Rehearsal: or, Bays in Petticoats* (1750)," *Études Anglaises* 49, 3 (1996): 320–26, who suggests that the feminist sentiments are contained by the misogyny. Rather than determine whether the ridicule of female dramatists is directed at Clive or her character Hazard, I suggest that it is directed at both, and deflected by both as well.

73. The epilogue to *Covent Garden Tragedy* and Clive's farewell epilogue appear in Horace Walpole, *The Works of Horatio Walpole, Earl of Orford*, 5 vols. (London, 1798), 4: 397–99. The highly topical farewell epilogue, also printed in *The Public Advertiser*, 25 April 1769, and *St. James Chronicle*, 22–25 June 1769, alludes to the publication of William Robertson's *History of Charles the Fifth* (1769).

74. Francis Gentleman, *The Theatres: A Poetical Dissection. By Sir Nicholas Nipclose, Baronet* (London, 1772), 57.

75. For statistics, see Judith Phillips Stanton, "'This New-Found Path Attempting': Women Dramatists in England, 1660–1800," in *Curtain Calls: British and American Women and the Theater, 1660–1820*, ed. Mary Anne Schofield and Cecilia Macheski (Athens: Ohio University Press, 1991), 325–54.

76. Joanne Lafler, "Theatre and the Female Presence," in *The Cambridge History of British Theatre, 1660–1895*, ed. Joseph Donohue, 3 vols. (Cambridge: Cambridge University Press, 2004), 2: 83, remarks that "Philippina Burton, Jane Egleton and Jane Pope wrote plays as vehicles for themselves, to be performed only once at their annual benefits." Actresses Charlotte Charke, Eliza Haywood, and Susannah Cibber were also dramatists.

77. Richard C. Frushell, "Kitty Clive as Dramatist," *Durham University Journal* n.s. 32, 2 (March 1971): 126. Kinservik, "Garrick's Unpublished Epilogue," 321, remarks sardonically that competition for that accolade was not keen.

78. *The Theatrical Monitor* 14 (27 February 1768). Speaking of Elizabeth Barry, *The Female Tatler*, ed. Fidelis Morgan (London: J.M. Dent, 1992), 94, had similarly cautioned that "no Woman ever yet turn'd *Poetess*, but lost her *Reputation* by appearing at *Rehearsals*, and *Conversing with Imoinda, Desdemonda, and a Maidenhead Amintor.*"

79. The manuscripts of the afterpieces, including those of doubtful attribution, are in the Larpent Collection, Henry E. Huntington Library, San Marino, California.

80. P. J. Crean, "The London 'Prentice," *Notes and Queries* 163, 20 (12 November 1932): 346–47, makes this argument.

81. Jean-Christophe Agnew, *Worlds Apart: The Market and the Theater in Anglo-American Thought, 1550–1750* (New York: Cambridge University Press, 1986), 190, finds this strategy characteristic of Defoe's novels, though he does not apply it to drama.

82. In *British Dramatists from Dryden to Sheridan*, ed. George H. Nettleton and Arthur E. Case, rev. George Winchester Stone, Jr., 2nd ed. (Boston: Houghton Mifflin, 1969), 39–40. *The Rehearsal*'s mockery of heroic drama was updated in the 1739 revival with a parade of hobbyhorses. When the original *Rehearsal* was revived at mid-century, Theophilus Cibber acted as its pretentious hero.

83. For other examples, see Lisa Freeman, *Character's Theater: Genre and Identity on the Eighteenth-Century English Stage* (Philadelphia: University of Pennsylvania Press, 2002), 66–76.

84. Richard C. Frushell has provided an edition of *The Rehearsal* in "An Edition of the Afterpieces of Kitty Clive" (Dissertation, Duquesne University, 1968), to which I am indebted.

85. Stern, *Rehearsal from Shakespeare to Sheridan*, 183–94, remarks that the ongoing revision in production was typical of eighteenth-century rehearsals.

86. Lucyle Hook, ed., *The Female Wits*, Augustan Reprint Society 124 (Los Angeles: William Andrews Clark Memorial Library, UCLA, 1967), xii.

87. *A Comparison between the Two Stages* (London, 1702), 26–27.

88. For examples of plagiarism charges against women, see Laura J. Rosenthal, *Playwrights and Plagiarists in Early Modern England: Gender, Authorship, Literary Property* (Ithaca, N.Y.: Cornell University Press, 1996); Nancy Cotton, *Women Playwrights in England, c. 1363 to 1750* (Lewisburg, Pa.: Bucknell University Press, 1980); and Freeman, *Character's Theater*, 66–76.

89. The reference to Hazard's plagiarism may derive from Mary Pix having accused George Powell, an actor in *The Female Wits*, of drawing without attribution on one of her plays.

90. Mrs. [Catherine] Clive, *The Rehearsal: Or, Bays in Petticoats* (Dublin, 1753). The changes include a shift to Gatty in the published version from Nelly in manuscript, and the addition of Sir Albany Odelove. See Frushell, "An Edition of the Afterpieces of Kitty Clive," 45 n. 539.

91. Frushell isolates several of Clive's satiric objects in "Kitty Clive as Dramatist," 125–32.

92. John Taylor, *Records of My Life*, 2 vols. (London: Edward Bull, 1832), 1: 346: "As his blaze of excellence threw all others into comparative insignificance, she never forgave him, and took every opportunity of venting her spleen. She was coarse, rude, and violent in her temper, and spared nobody. One night, as Garrick was performing 'King Lear,' she stood behind the scenes to observe him, and in spite of the roughness of her nature, was so deeply

affected that she sobbed one minute and abused him the next, and at length, overcome by his pathetic touches, she hurried from the place with the following extraordinary tribute to the universality of his powers: 'D—n him! I believe he could act a *gridiron*'."

93. Henry James Pye, "Epilogue" to Elizabeth Griffith, *The School for Rakes: A Comedy* (London, 1769), 93.

94. Christopher Morash, *A History of Irish Theatre 1601–2000* (Cambridge: Cambridge University Press, 2002), 51, notes the trend toward highlighting the uncertain identity of the Anglo-Irish aristocracy, and toward producing Irish comedies in the 1760s London theater.

95. See, for example, Susan Cannon Harris, "Mixed Marriage: Sheridan, Macklin, and the Hybrid Audience," in *Players, Playwrights, Playhouses: Investigating Performance, 1660–1800*, ed. Michael Cordner and Peter Holland (Basingstoke: Palgrave Macmillan, 2007), 189–212, who builds on Mary Louise Pratt's concept of the "contact zone" in *Imperial Eyes: Studies in Travel Writing and Transculturation* (London: Routledge, 1992).

96. See Stuart Hall, "Thinking the Diaspora: Home-Thoughts from Abroad" in *Postcolonialisms: An Anthology of Cultural Theory*, ed. Gaurav Desai and Supriya Nair (New Brunswick, N.J.: Rutgers University Press, 2005), 543–60.

97. Helen M. Burke, *Riotous Performances: The Struggle for Hegemony in the Irish Theater, 1712–1784* (Notre Dame, Ind.: University of Notre Dame Press, 2003).

98. Helen Burke, "Acting in the Periphery: The Irish Theatre," in *The Cambridge Companion To British Theatre, 1730–1830*, ed. Jane Moody and Danny O'Quinn (Cambridge: Cambridge University Press, 2007), 219–32, indicates that British theater was most often exported to Ireland; but Irish plays were also imported into England, exerting perhaps more influence than she suggests. John C. Greene and Gladys L. H. Clark, in *The Dublin Stage, 1720–1745: A Calendar of Plays, Entertainments, and Afterpieces* (Bethlehem, Pa.: Lehigh University Press, 1993), 72, find that from 1720 to 1745 only 26 of 175 original plays on the Dublin stage did not first premier in London.

99. See Desmond Slowey, *The Radicalization of Irish Drama, 1600–1900: The Rise and Fall of the Ascendancy Theatre* (Dublin: Irish Academic Press, 2008), 97, though he does not mention Clive's contributions.

100. Helen Burke, "Eighteenth-Century Theatrical Touring and Irish Popular Culture," in *Irish Theatre on Tour*, ed. Nicholas Grene and Christopher Morash (Dublin: Carysfort Press, 2005), 88, describes English stereotypes of the Irish in this way.

101. Hugh Kelly, *Thespis: or, a Critical Examination into the Merits of all the Principal Performers Belonging to Drury-Lane Theatre* (London, 1766), 33.

102. Benefit of Mrs. Clive in *The Miser*, DNL 4-8.8 in Dublin music calendar. "Ellen-a-Roon" was first performed in Charles Coffey's ballad opera, *The Beggar's Wedding*, 1729.

103. Greene and Clark write, "Few distinctly Irish plays were staged in our period" in *The Dublin Stage*, 89. *The London 'Prentice* (1754) and a translation, *The Island of Slaves* (1761), have been attributed to Clive but are much less certainly her creations.

104. All the manuscript afterpieces in the Huntington Library Larpent collection are unpaginated.

105. Slowey, *Radicalization of Irish Drama*, 139.

106. Richard C. Frushell, "The Textual Relationship and Biographical Significance of Two Petite Pieces by Mrs. Catherine (Kitty) Clive," *Restoration and Eighteenth Century Theatre Research* 9, 1 (May 1970): 51–58, carefully collates the afterpieces to argue that the changes to *Irish Woman* were probably made in rehearsal with Clive's approval, but the emendations in manuscript might instead indicate the censor's wishes.

107. John Barrell, *English Literature in History, 1730–80: An Equal, Wide Survey* (London: Hutchinson, 1983), 110–75, describes the unifying force of a standardized language in mid-century Britain.

108. Michael Ragussis, "Jews and Other 'Outlandish Englishmen': Ethnic Performance and the Invention of British Identity Under the Georges," *Critical Inquiry* 26 (Summer 2000): 773–97, shows that the Georgian playhouse played a critical role in the invention of a theatricalized national identity in which the native voice is both legitimized and contradicted by characters who fail to pass as authentic English persons. Ragussis does not consider the third possibility of happy hybridity that Clive proposes.

109. David Lloyd, *Ireland After History* (Cork: Cork University Press, 1999), 77–78, describes popular and non-élite history as revealing examples of deliberate and "persistent inassimilability to the state."

110. Davies, *Memoirs of the Life of David Garrick*, 2: 195.

CHAPTER 6. THE ACTRESS, TRAVESTY, AND NATION:
MARGARET WOFFINGTON

1. *Memoirs of the celebrated Mrs. Woffington, interspersed with several Theatrical Anecdotes; The Amours of many Persons of the First Rank; and some interesting Characters drawn from real Life*, 2nd ed. (London, [1760]), 20. The anachronistic nineteenth-century engraving (Fig. 12), based on the eighteenth-century account, offers a compelling afterimage of manager-actor and actress.

2. Reynolds painted Woffington's portrait. Rich's comment is cited in *A Biographical Dictionary of Actors, Actresses, Musicians, Dancers, Managers, and Other Stage Personnel in London, 1660–1800*, ed. Philip H. Highfill, Jr., Kalman A. Burnim, and Edward A. Langhans, 16 vols. (Carbondale: Southern Illinois University Press, 1973–93), 16: 201. Among the more than one hundred roles Woffington performed at mid-century were Mrs. Sullen in Farquhar's *The Beaux Stratagem* (a dozen seasons beginning in 1741–42); and Mrs. Ruth in Sir Robert Howard's *The Committee; or, The Faithful Irishman* (eleven seasons beginning in 1741–42).

3. Diana Taylor, "Remapping Genre through Performance: From 'American' to 'Hemispheric' Studies," *PMLA* 122, 5 (October 2007): 1416–30, conceptualizes the nation as a repertoire of cultural practices rather than a fixed entity or known place.

4. Sue-Ellen Case, "Feminism and Performance: A Post-Disciplinary Couple," *Theatre Research International* 26, 2 (2001): 150. Jill Susan Dolan, *The Feminist Spectator as Critic*

(Ann Arbor, Mich.: UMI Research Press, 1988), 42, notes that postmodern theorists have convincingly shown "that character can no longer act as a stable referent, and that narrative can no longer be assumed to be a coherent, linear system that delivers a single, authoritative meaning."

5. Marjorie Garber, *Vested Interests: Cross-Dressing and Cultural Anxiety* (New York: Routledge, 1992), 11.

6. John Harold Wilson, *All the King's Ladies: Actresses of the Restoration* (Chicago: University of Chicago Press, 1958), 73.

7. Lisa Freeman, *Character's Theater: Genre and Identity on the Eighteenth-Century English Stage* (Philadelphia: University of Pennsylvania Press, 2002), 98, argues that tragedy in the period tends to push women to its periphery in defining national identity.

8. See Betty Joseph, "Gendering Time in Globalization: The Belatedness of the Other Woman and Jamaica Kincaid's *Lucy*," *Tulsa Studies in Women's Literature* 21, 1 (Spring 2002): 67–84, to which I am much indebted.

9. Kathleen Wilson, *The Sense of the People: Politics, Culture and Imperialism in England 1715–1785* (New York: Cambridge University Press, 1998), 203. Wilson writes, "Britain's imperial rivalry with France thus produced anti-Jacobitism as a rallying point for the consolidation of a loyalism that had a distinctly imperialist hue," 174, performed musically as "God Save the King" and "Rule Britannia," 164–65.

10. Michel de Certeau, *The Writing of History*, trans. Tom Conley (New York: Columbia University Press, 1988), 2.

11. Anne McClintock, *Imperial Leather: Race, Gender and Sexuality in the Colonial Context* (London: Routledge, 1995), 358–59, suggests, in a view that differs somewhat from the one I am arguing, that *men* serve as the "progressive agent of national modernity (forward-thrusting, potent and historic), embodying nationalism's progressive, or revolutionary principle of discontinuity."

12. George Winchester Stone, Jr., and George M. Kahrl, *David Garrick: A Critical Biography* (Carbondale: Southern Illinois University Press, 1979), 405.

13. See Beth H. Friedman-Romell, "Breaking the Code: Toward a Reception Theory of Theatrical Cross-Dressing in Eighteenth-Century London," *Theatre Journal* 47 (1995): 459–79, for a helpful discussion.

14. Elin Diamond, "Brechtian Theory/Feminist Theory: Toward a Gestic Feminist Criticism," *Drama Review* 32, 1 (1988): 85.

15. Farquhar had attacked Jacobite Jeremy Collier in the epilogue to his earlier play, the often vulgar *Love in a Bottle*.

16. *The Conduct of the Stage Consider'd. Being A Short Historical Account of its Original, Progress, various Aspects, and Treatment in the Pagan, Jewish and Christian World* (London, 1721), 40. Charles Macklin and others later echo this sentiment.

17. Letters from "Q.Z." and from Charlotte Charke in the *Daily Advertiser*, 27–28 February 1745. My thanks to Ilias Chrissochoidis for sharing this reference.

18. Stephen Orgel, *Impersonations: The Performance of Gender in Shakespeare's England* (Cambridge: Cambridge University Press, 1996), 19.

19. See Cynthia Lowenthal, *Performing Identities on the Restoration Stage* (Carbondale: Southern Illinois University Press, 2003), 229; Laura Mandell, *Misogynous Economies: The Business of Literature in Eighteenth-Century Britain* (Lexington: University Press of Kentucky, 1999), 77; Pat Rogers, "The Breeches Part" in *Sexuality in Eighteenth-Century Britain*, ed. Paul-Gabriel Boucé (Manchester: Manchester University Press, 1982): 244–58; Kristina Straub, *Sexual Suspects: Eighteenth-Century Players and Sexual Ideology* (Princeton, N.J.: Princeton University Press, 1992); and Frances M. Kavenik, "Aphra Behn: The Playwright as 'Breeches Part'," in *Curtain Calls: British and American Women and the Theater, 1660–1820*, ed. Mary Anne Schofield and Cecilia Macheski (Athens: Ohio University Press, 1991), 177–92.

20. Dror Wahrman, *The Making of the Modern Self: Identity and Culture in Eighteenth-Century England* (New Haven, Conn.: Yale University Press, 2004), 48–58 and passim, argues that a delay until 1780 in the theater in portraying rigid distinctions between the sexes indicates resistance to a broader cultural conservatism. He initially separates roles that require unveiling from those that do not (48), but there is slippage in the term "breeches roles" for both (337n.8). According to this argument, the Romantic period would seem to revert to the Renaissance model Orgel suggests.

21. Robert Hitchcock, *An Historical View of the Irish Stage; from the Earliest Period Down to the Close of the Season, 1788*, 2 vols. (Dublin, 1788), 1: 108; and *The Life of Mr. James Quin, Comedian. With the History of the Stage from his Commencing Actor to his Retreat to Bath* (London, 1766), 67–68.

22. Francis Gentleman, *The Dramatic Censor; or, Critical Companion*, 2 vols. (London, 1770), 1: 296.

23. Manuscript bequeathed to the Garrick Club by Mr. Dame, author unknown, cited in Augustin Daly, *Woffington: A Tribute to the Actress and the Woman*, 2nd ed. (Troy, N.Y.: Nims and Knight, 1891), 105.

24. Diana Taylor, *The Archive and the Repertoire: Performing Cultural Memory in the Americas* (Durham, N.C.: Duke University Press, 2003), xv, employs these terms. Philip B. Zarilli writes that an actor's "complex subjectivity is never settled or fixed within a present or a body, but rather is continually in a process of its own play with the 'to's' and 'from's' which are characteristic of each mode of embodiment," in "Toward a Phenomenological Model of the Actor's Embodied Modes of Experience," special issue *Theorizing the Performer, Theatre Journal* 56, 4 (December 2004), 66.

25. Robert Hitchcock, *An Historical View of the Irish Stage*, 1: 50; and *The Life of Mr. James Quin*, 67. Woffington's 1743 purchase of an estate at Teddington early in her career indicates her considerable economic success.

26. Theophilus Cibber, *Romeo and Juliet, a Tragedy, Revis'd, and Alter'd from Shakespear, ... to which is added, A Serio-Comic Apology for Part of the Life of Mr. Theophilus Cibber, Comedian* (London, [1748]), 104.

27. Hitchcock, *An Historical View*, 1: 48. Tate Wilkinson in *Memoirs of His Own Life*, 4 vols. (York, 1790), 1: 33, believes that Woffington left Garrick because he proved false to her. Garrick and she allegedly divided living expenses, in spite of his earning considerably more

than she. Perhaps Woffington realized that it was to her economic advantage to remain a single, celebrated actress rather than Garrick's wife.

28. T. Cibber, *Romeo and Juliet, a Tragedy*, 103.

29. See Richard Allen Cave, "Woffington," *Oxford Dictionary of National Biography*, 60 vols. (Oxford: Oxfrod University Press, 2004), 59: 942.

30. Allardyce Nicoll, *A History of Early Eighteenth Century Drama 1700–1750* (Cambridge: Cambridge University Press, 1929), 49. Examples of epilogues delivered in boy's clothes at Drury Lane include Mrs. Spiller "in Man's Cloaths" at the conclusion to Moore's *Mangora* (1717); Mrs. Bradshaw's epilogue to Charles Johnson's *The Generous Husband* (1711); Miss Robinson to Breval's *The Strolers* (1723) and Mallet's *Eurydice* (1731). Nicoll also provides examples of women's roles performed in boy's garments, 50.

31. William Rufus Chetwood, *A General History of the Stage; From its Origin in Greece down to the Present Time* (London, 1749), 254.

32. Desmond Slowey, *The Radicalization of Irish Drama, 1600–1900: The Rise and Fall of the Ascendancy Theatre* (Dublin: Irish Academic Press, 2008), helps clarify these relationships.

33. For a full account, see Helen M. Burke, *Riotous Performances: The Struggle for Hegemony in the Irish Theatre, 1712–1784* (Notre Dame, Ind.: University of Notre Dame Press, 2003), 229–40. In the 2 February 1754 performance of *Mahomet*, Sheridan instructed West Digges to make his own decision whether to respond to the audience's demand for a speech that was interpreted as supporting the Nationalists. When Sheridan declined to appear and withdrew to his home, Woffington was called upon to calm the audience. After Digges refused to perform an encore, the theater was demolished. In acting the role of Zaphna in the play, Woffington may have been associated with Sheridan's waffling sympathies. Sheridan subsequently left Ireland after apologizing to the audience for offending them.

34. James Thomas Kirkman, *Memoirs of the Life of Charles Macklin*, 2 vols. (London, 1799), 1: 316. Woffington joined in a short-lived triumvirate partnership with Charles Macklin and David Garrick.

35. Benjamin Victor, *History of the Theatres of London and Dublin from the Year 1730 to the Present Time, To which is added, an Annual Register of All the Plays*, 3 vols. (London, 1761), 1: 55. Woffington was also rumored to have engaged in a sexual liaison with Sheridan.

36. See Victor, *History of the Theatres* 1: 153–54.

37. James Boswell, *The London Journal, 1762–63*, ed. Frederick A. Pottle (New York: McGraw-Hill, 1950), 51.

38. La Tourette Stockwell, *Dublin Theatres and Theatre Customs, 1637–1820* (Kingsport, Tenn.: Kingsport Press, 1938), 110–11.

39. Highfill et al., *Biographical Dictionary* (16: 212) maintains Woffington developed close relationships with Dublin Castle.

40. See The *Vindications of Lord Carteret* (London, 1730).

41. John O'Keeffe, *Recollections of the Life*, 2 vols. (London, 1826), 1: 30.

42. Orgel, *Impersonations*, 11, makes this suggestion regarding the Renaissance theater.

43. Slowey, *Radicalization of Irish Drama*, 129, notes that at mid-century "the leaders of the Catholic interest hastened to assure the authorities of their unswerving loyalty to the Hanoverian dynasty." He adds, "The resurgence of the native Irish gentry . . . provoked a hostile response from the Protestant Establishment."

44. No. 15, 27 January 1753 in Arthur Murphy, *The Gray's Inn Journal*, 2 vols. (London, 1756), 1: 90. My thanks to Nush Powell for forwarding this reference.

45. See Victor, *The History of the Theatres*, 1: 156–57. *The Oxford Dictionary of National Biography* entry by Cave, 59: 942, estimates she received over £1,100 monthly as a result of the bequest.

46. David Armitage, *The Ideological Origins of the British Empire* (New York: Cambridge University Press, 2000), 195; See also Linda Colley, *Britons: Forging the Nation 1707–1837* (New Haven, Conn.: Yale University Press, 1992), 81; and Kathleen Wilson, "Rowe's *Fair Penitent* as Global History: Or, A Diversionary Voyage to New South Wales," *Eighteenth-Century Studies* 41, 2 (2008): 231–51.

47. John Brown, *An Estimate of the Manners and Principles of the Times*, 2 vols. (London 1757), 2: 40. See also Kathleen Wilson, *The Sense of the People*, 185–205.

48. Perhaps the satirical responses to Woffington's appearance as The Female Volunteer accusing her of Popish sympathies also encouraged her later conversion to Protestantism.

49. According to Robert Hume, *Henry Fielding and the London Theatre, 1728–1737* (Oxford: Clarendon Press, 1988), 110 and passim, Drury Lane was a Whig stronghold from the early decades of the century.

50. The epilogues appear in Pierre Danchin, ed., *The Prologues and Epilogues of the Eighteenth Century: A Complete Edition*, 6 vols. (Nancy: Presses Universitaires de Nancy, 1997), pt. 3, *1737–1760*, vol. 5. Citations to this edition are given parenthetically in the text.

51. Homi Bhabha, *Nation and Narration* (New York: Routledge, 1990).

52. Widely reprinted in popular publications including Timothy Silence, *The Foundling Hospital for Wit* (1746), *A Banquet of the Muses* (1746), *The London Magazine* (February 1746), and *The Theatrical Bouquet* (1778), the printed version of "The Female Volunteer" in the *General Advertiser* (26 February 1746) and elsewhere (pt. 3, 5: 215) may not have had identical wording.

53. Letter from H. S. Conway to Horace Walpole, 26 October 1741, *The Yale Edition of Horace Walpole's Correspondence*, 48 vols. in 49 (New Haven, Conn.: Yale University Press, 1937–83), 37: 113.

54. *The London Stage, 1660–1800; A Calendar of Plays, Entertainments and Afterpieces*, 5 pt. in 11 (Carbondale: Southern Illinois University Press, 1960–68), pt. 3, *1729–1747*, ed. A. H. Scouten, 2 vols. (1961), 3: 1231.

55. Dianne Dugaw, *Warrior Women and Popular Balladry, 1650–1850* (Cambridge: Cambridge University Press, 1989) documents the "widespread presence of women in the military," and the comparative nonchalance with which women donned soldier's garb, 129. She argues that "this conventional Female Warrior was not the obscure curiosity that she is today," 147. See also Felicity Nussbaum, *The Limits of the Human: Fictions of Anomaly*,

Race, and Gender in the Long Eighteenth Century (Cambridge: Cambridge University Press, 2003), 58–83.

56. George Farquhar, *The Complete Works of George Farquhar*, ed. Charles Stonehill, 2 vols. (London: Nonesuch Press, 1930), 1: 84, cites Richard Cumberland who chastises Mrs. Goodall for taking such a licentious part as Sir Harry. He adds that Farquhar's plays "were considered as being entirely 'modern,' and were performed in 'modern' dress." Anthony Pasquin, *The Pin Basket to the Children of Thespis* (London, 1797), 50n. writes, "The suit of brown which is worn by Mr. Suett in the character of *Foresight*, in Love for Love, was made for the late Mrs. Woffington, who wore it in the character of *Sir Harry Wildair!*"

57. Anne Buck, *Dress in Eighteenth-Century England* (London: Batsford, 1979), 31, notes, "An elegant leg in a white silk stocking was an important part of fashionable appearance; after the 1770s the breeches, closely moulding the leg above the knee, extended this display." Laura Rosenthal, "'Counterfeit Scrubbado': Women Actors in the Restoration," *The Eighteenth Century: Theory and Interpretation* 34, 1 (1993): 3–22, 14, remarks that while breeches costuming "admittedly would reveal customarily unseen body parts, at the same time it would cover her shoulders, arms and breasts," 14.

58. Angela Rosenthal indicates that actors and actresses performed their subjectivity even in the artist's studio: "At the Royal Academy performatively inclined personalities would even pose under their portraits on display at the summer exhibition" (private correspondence).

59. Will Wattle, *A Soldier's Letter to the Female Volunteer: Being an Earnest Request to Hang up the Hat, and Pull off the Breeches. With a Persuasive against False Appearances* (London, [1750?]).

60. *A Guide to the Stage; or, Select Instructions and Precedents from the Best Authorities Towards Forming a Polite Audience* (London, 1751), 14.

61. Taylor, "Remapping Genre Through Performance," conceptualizes nation as a repertoire of cultural practices rather than a fixed entity or known place.

62. Christopher Morash, *A History of Irish Theatre, 1601–2000* (Cambridge: Cambridge University Press, 2002), 34, notes that for Irish Catholics, "the monarch's claim to be a defender of liberty" was tenuous. Economic incentives convinced Scotland's Parliament to accept the Act of Union with England and Wales effective on 16 January 1707. Because England feared the Scots would side with France, the Scottish parliament was dissolved, though England and Scotland remained legally and religiously distinct. England became sovereign over coinage, taxing, trade, and the flag; they were, as Robert Burns reputedly intoned, "bought and sold for English gold." Ireland did not follow until 1801.

63. Quoted in Danchin, *The Eighteenth Century*, pt. 3, 5: 200, from Benjamin Victor, *Original Letters, Dramatic Pieces, and Poems*, 3 vols. (London, 1776), 1: 119–20.

64. John Philip Kemble, *The Female Officer, or the Humours of the Army, A Comedy, Altered from Shadwell* (Dublin, 1763).

65. The vulgar joke is something of a commonplace, occurring also in *The Recruiting Officer* when Brazen indicates that the longest sword will win Melinda.

66. "To Miss Woffington on her Playing the Part of Silvia," *London Daily Post and General Advertiser*, cited in Highfill et al., *Biographical Dictionary*, 16: 202.

67. Recruiting actors to the stage was compared to seeking army recruits. When Lacy was manager of Drury Lane, a commercial advertisement sought "to raise a Regiment of actors in defense of his Majesty's person against the young Pretender." See Esther K. Sheldon, *Thomas Sheridan of Smock-Alley* (Princeton, N.J.: Princeton University Press, 1967), 57–58.

68. A volunteer against the Jacobites, Farquhar who favored the Protestant William and Mary, had fought at the Battle of the Boyne and mourned the Protestant Duke of Schomberg in a Pindaric ode. Farquhar's father was an Anglican clergyman from northern Ireland, and the family had been burned out in the siege against Londonderry. See the introduction to George Farquhar, *The Recruiting Officer*, ed. Peter Dixon (Manchester: University of Manchester Press, 1986), 1–51.

69. In serving her country for love rather than money, Silvia removes herself from the economy of coinage and currency.

70. The play operates within the backdrop of the War of Spanish Succession, an attempt to bring about the union of France and Spain by appointing the French Philip of Anjou to the throne of Spain. The Peace of Utrecht occurred when Archduke Charles became king over Austria and France after the death of Emperor Joseph.

71. Gentleman, *The Dramatic Censor*, 1: 63.

72. The role of Wildair was later played by Dorothy Jordan, Anne Spranger Barry, and Charlotte Goodall.

73. *The Works of George Farquhar*, ed. Shirley Strum Kenny, 2 vols. (Oxford: Clarendon Press, 1988), 1: 149.

74. See the helpful introduction in ibid., 1: 115–44, esp. 125–26.

75. Chetwood, *A General History of the Stage*, 252. The anecdote is repeated in *Memoirs of . . . Woffington*, 32; and *The Life of Mr. James Quin*, 68. A variation appears in Tate Wilkinson's *Memoirs of His Own Life*, 4 vols. (York, 1790), 1: 34: When she was alleged to have boasted that "one half of the audience took her for a man," a respondent (whose identity varies in the accounts) jibed, "do not be uneasy, as you are satisfied the other half know the contrary."

76. On the whore as ambiguously gendered, see Felicity Nussbaum, *Torrid Zones: Maternity, Sexuality, and Empire in Eighteenth-Century English Narrative* (Baltimore: Johns Hopkins University Press, 1995, rpt. 2005). Laura Rosenthal helpfully suggests that actresses negotiated a third position between the extreme possibilities of female reputation in "Entertaining Women" in *The Cambridge Companion to British Theatre, 1730–1830*, ed. Jane Moody and Daniel O'Quinn (Cambridge: Cambridge University Press, 2007), 163.

77. *Woffington's Ghost: A Poem. In Answer to the Meretriciad* (London, 1761).

78. Rogers, "The Breeches Part," 248.

79. In her edition of *The Works of George Farquhar*, Kenny remarks that "the Pope remained anathema to Englishmen, but the Jubilee proved a fashionable jaunt to see the sights of the Continent, particularly Rome," 1: 607.

80. Eric Rothstein, *George Farquhar* (New York: Twayne, 1967) describes Wildair as

the "last of the gay extravagant libertine-rakes," 39–49. Morash, *A History of Irish Theatre*, 37, finds in Sir Harry a new kind of *libertarian* hero whose loyalty to his king arises not from aristocratic heritage but from "a contract of reciprocal rights in a marketplace whose freedoms depend upon the exclusion of . . . Frenchmen, Catholics, and anyone associated with the old regime."

81. "Epilogue for *The Constant Couple*" (12 December 1748?) in Danchin, *The Eighteenth Century*, pt. 3, 5: 239.

82. Robert Hitchcock, *An Historical View of the Irish Stage*, 2 vols. (Dublin, 1788–84), 1: 107.

83. Nicholas Rowe, *The Fair Penitent*, ed. Malcolm Goldstein (Lincoln: University of Nebraska Press, 1969), 1.1.204.

84. Susan Cannon Harris, "Outside the Box: The Female Spectator, *The Fair Penitent*, and the Kelly Riots of 1747," *Theatre Journal* 57, 1 (2005): 33–55, draws an analogy between the plot of the tragedy and Ireland's position vis-à-vis England, reflected in the Kelly riots (called "The Gentleman's Quarrel between Sheridan and Kelly"). Calista's resistance to her father's choice, Horatio (Sheridan), "show[s] that once a lady begins to conceive of Empire in patriarchal terms, her other identity positions—class, nationality, ethnicity—threaten to dissolve," 53.

85. For a somewhat different approach, see Peter de Bolla, "'A Submission, Sir!' Who has the Right to Person in Eighteenth-Century Britain?" in *Land, Nation and Culture, 1740–1840: Thinking the Republic of Taste*, ed. Peter de Bolla, Nigel Leask, and David Simpson (Basingstoke: Palgrave Macmillan, 2005), 148–68.

86. Thomas Davies, *Memoirs of the Life of David Garrick*, 2 vols. (London, 1780), 1: 307.

87. Samuel Johnson, "The Life of Rowe," in *The Lives of the Most Eminent English Poets*, ed. Roger Lonsdale, 4 vols. (Oxford: Clarendon Press, 2006), 2: 200.

88. Judith Butler, "Performative Acts and Gender Constitution: An Essay in Phenomenology and Feminist Theory," in *Performing Feminisms: Feminist Critical Theory and Theatre*, ed. Sue-Ellen Case (Baltimore: Johns Hopkins University Press, 1990), 270–82, uses the phrase "modernity without foundationalism."

CHAPTER 7. THE ACTRESS AND MATERIAL FEMININITY: FRANCES ABINGTON

1. Horace Walpole's flattering letter to Abington, 1 September 1771, *The Yale Edition of Horace Walpole's Correspondence*, ed. W. S. Lewis, 48 vols. (New Haven, Conn.: Yale University Press, 1937–83), 41: 216.

2. *The Life of Mrs. Abington (formerly Miss Barton) Celebrated Comic Actress, by the editor of the "Life of Quinn"* (London: Reader, 1888), 38. This compilation offers an entertaining, if not always reliable, biography.

3. Hugh Kelly, "Preface" to *The School for Wives. A Comedy*, 3rd ed. (London, 1774), vi.

4. Handwritten note, 21 October 1783, in "A Biography of the Actress Frances Abington with Printed Memoirs and Press Notices," National Library of Ireland MS 8263 (4).

5. Angela Smallwood argues that Abington's fashion display as Lady Teazle disarmed "female assertiveness by reducing it to style, a superficial fashion accessory, even (as in Sir Peter's eyes) an adornment," in "Woman and the Theatre," in *Women and Literature in Britain, 1700–1800*, ed. Vivien Jones (Cambridge: Cambridge University Press), 246, while I stress Abington's redefinition of femininity as cultural authority.

6. Paul Langford, *A Polite and Commercial People: England 1727–1783* (Oxford: Oxford University Press, 1998), 603. See also E.J. Clery, "Bluestocking 'Feminism' and the Fame Game," *British Journal for Eighteenth-Century Studies* 28 (2005): 280.

7. Peter Clark, *British Clubs and Societies: The Origins of an Associational World* (Oxford: Oxford University Press, 2000), 39, 192, 451, cited in Gillian Russell, *Women, Sociability, and the Theatre in Georgian London* (Cambridge: Cambridge University Press, 2007), 10–11, to which I am indebted.

8. Harriet Guest, "Bluestocking Feminism," in *Reconsidering the Bluestockings*, ed. Nicole Pohl and Betty A. Schellenberg (San Marino, Calif.: Huntington Library, 2003), 74. Clarissa Campbell-Orr, "Countesses and Courtesans," *History Workshop Journal* 62, 1 (2006): 289, reminds us that "the [scandalous] behaviour of the aristocracy was one factor provoking debate on the nature of female political power."

9. The editor of the Garrick correspondence finds her insistence that the manager should supply an audience inexplicable, given Abington's sway over her female audience: "The Power of a manager indeed!" cited in *Life of Mrs. Abington*, 77.

10. Aileen Ribeiro, "Costuming the Part: A Discourse of Fashion and Fiction in the Image of the Actress in England, 1776–1812," in *Notorious Muse: The Actress in British Art and Culture, 1776–1812*, ed. Robyn Asleson (New Haven, Conn.: Yale University Press, 2003), 118, indicates that "the publication in 1757 of the first two volumes of Jeffreys's *Collection of the Dresses of Different Nations Ancient and Modern* was, in this respect, a seminal event." Thomas Wilkes [Samuel Derrick] in his *General View of the Stage* (London, 1759) urged actors to read Jeffreys's book in the hope that they might be "habited according to the fashion of the country where their scene was," 1430.

11. R. Campbell, *The London Tradesman. Being a Compendious View of All the Trades, Professions, Arts, both Liberal and Mechanic, Now practised in the Cities of London and Westminster* (London, 1747), 208, remarks generally on the connection between millinery and prostitution.

12. *The Gentleman's Magazine* 13 (November 1743), 609.

13. George Anne Bellamy, *An Apology for the Life of George Anne Bellamy*, 5 vols., 4th ed. (London, 1786), 5: 90.

14. *The Public Advertiser*, 29 November 1782, on Abington as Lady Flutter in Frances Sheridan's *The Discovery*.

15. Rosamond Gilder, *Enter the Actress: The First Women in the Theater* (Boston: Houghton Mifflin, 1931) cites a 1675 agreement.

16. Footnote to "Articles of Agreement for Better Regulateing theire Majesties Ser-

vants, 1674/65," 10. Reprinted in Allardyce Nicoll, *A History of Early Eighteenth Century Drama, 1700–1750* (Cambridge: Cambridge University Press, 1929), 291.

17. Anne Buck, *Dress in Eighteenth-Century England* (London: Batsford, 1979), 39. After a year in England, Frederick Robinson continued to find everyday clothing resembled masquerade costuming.

18. Bellamy, *An Apology for the Life*, 1: 58.

19. Chris Rojek, *Celebrity* (London: Reaktion Books, 2001), 37. See also P. David Marshall, *Celebrity and Power: Fame in Contemporary Culture* (Minneapolis: University of Minnesota Press, 1997).

20. Charles Dibdin, *A Complete History of the English Stage*, 5 vols. (London, 1800), 5: 359. See also Lynn Festa, "Cosmetic Differences, or the Changing Faces of England and France," *Studies in Eighteenth-Century Culture* 34 (Spring 2005): 25–54.

21. Leman Thomas Rede, *The Road to the Stage* (London: J. Onwhyn, 1836), 25–28; and Tracy Davis, *Actresses as Working Women: Their Social Identity in Victorian Culture* (London: Routledge, 1991), 109.

22. John Burgoyne, *Maid of the Oaks* (London, 1774).

23. Robert Hitchcock, *An Historical View of the Irish Stage; from the Earliest Period Down to the Close of the Season 1788*, 2 vols. (Dublin 1788–79), 2: 30–31.

24. Tate Wilkinson, *Memoirs of His Own Life*, 4 vols. (York, 1790), 2: 183.

25. Johann Wilhelm von Archenholz, *A Picture of England: Containing a Description of the Laws, Customs, and Manners of England*, trans. from French, 2 vols. in 1 (London, 1789), 110.

26. See, for example, Philip H. Highfill, Jr., Kalman A. Burnim, and Edward A. Langhans, *A Biographical Dictionary of Actors, Actresses, Musicians, Dancers, Managers, and Other Stage Personnel in London, 1660–1800*, 16 vols. (Carbondale: Southern Illinois University Press, 1973–93), 1: 12. "Fan" or "Fanny" was, of course, a common nickname for Frances. Jonathan Gil Harris and Natasha Korda, *Staged Properties in Early Modern English Drama* (Ithaca, N.Y.: Cornell University Press, 2002), show how stage objects and accessories introduce a plurality of meanings to the refractory social lives of things. See also Arjun Appadurai's influential *The Social Life of Things: Commodities in Cultural Perspective* (Cambridge: Cambridge University Press, 1986).

27. *The Life of Miss Anne Catley* (London, 1888), 63.

28. Cited in Augustin Daly, *Woffington: A Tribute to the Actress and Woman*, 2nd ed. (Troy, N.Y.: Nims and Knight, 1891), 134.

29. Samuel Foote, *The Roman and English Comedy Consider'd and Compar'd* (London, 1747), 36–37.

30. *A Guide to the Stage: Or, Select Instructions and Precedents from the Best Authorities Toward Forming a Polite Audience* (London, 1751), 27.

31. Rojek, *Celebrity*, 189, remarks that celebrity culture mobilizes abstract desire by embodying it within "an animate object, which allows for deeper levels of attachment and identification than with inanimate commodities . . . . In a word, [celebrities] *humanize* desire."

32. Lynn M. Voskuil, *Acting Naturally: Victorian Theatricality and Authenticity* (Charlottesville: University of Virginia Press, 2004), 78–79. See Karl Marx, *Capital: A Critique of Political Economy*, vol .1 of *A Critical Analysis of Capitalist Production*, ed. Frederick Engels (1887; repr. New York: International Publishers, 1967).

33. Robert Weimann, *Author's Pen and Actor's Voice: Playing and Writing in Shakespeare's Theatre*, ed. Helen Higbee and William West (Cambridge: Cambridge University Press, 2000), 221.

34. David Garrick, Epilogue to Arthur Murphy, *Zenobia: A Tragedy* (Dublin, 1784). Nicoll, *A History of Early Eighteenth Century Drama*, 28–29, notes, "No doubt the curtain was employed on some occasions, as in Restoration times [to distinguish between scenes], but the scantiness of reference to its use makes us believe that, when it was so employed, it was for very special and ornate effects." It is unclear whether the curtain fell at the conclusion of the play, or after the epilogue.

35. David Garrick, Epilogue to John Home, *The Fatal Discovery* (London, 1769).

36. *Recollections of the Life of John O'Keeffe, Written by Himself*, 2 vols. (London: H. Colburn, 1826), 1: 48.

37. Jennie Batchelor, "'Industry in Distress': Reconfiguring Femininity and Labor in the Magdalen House," *Eighteenth-Century Life* 28, 1 (2004): 3.

38. [Mr. Marchant], *Observations on Mr. Fielding's Plan for a Preservatory and Reformatory* (London, 1758), 7. Jennie Batchelor observes that this pamphlet expanded the appropriate trades in which charity girls could participate.

39. Adam Smith, *An Inquiry into the Nature and Causes of the Wealth of Nations*, 3 vols., 8th ed. (London, 1796), 1: 7–13.

40. *The Diaries of Elizabeth Inchbald*, ed. Ben P. Robertson, 3 vols. (London: Pickering and Chatto, 2007).

41. I am grateful to Aileen Ribeiro for private correspondence regarding this matter, and to Judith Milhous for her suggestions.

42. Susan Staves, *Married Women's Separate Property in England, 1660–1833* (Cambridge, Mass.: Harvard University Press, 1990), 133.

43. Jonathan Gil Harris draws his example from the "old" new historicism in Stephen Greenblatt's *Shakespearean Negotiations: The Circulation of Social Energy in Renaissance England* (Berkeley: University of California Press, 1988). In "The New New Historicism's *Wunderkammer* of Objects," *European Journal of English Studies* 4, 2 (2000): 113, Harris suggests that the newest new historicism focuses on everyday objects and practices rather than elite sites of religious and political authority, but that it is evacuated of its original emphasis on material culture to center on miraculous aspects, as if to place the objects in a Wunderkammer. See also Patricia Fumerton, "Introduction: A New New Historicism," in *Renaissance Culture and the Everyday*, ed. Patricia Fumerton and Simon Hunt (Philadelphia: University of Pennsylvania Press, 1999), 1–17.

44. John Gay, *Fables*, 2nd ed. (London, 1728), 61–62.

45. Alexander Pope, "The Rape of the Lock," in *The Rape of the Lock and Other Poems*, ed. Geoffrey Tillotson, *Twickenham Edition of the Poems of Alexander Pope*, gen.

ed. John Butt, 11 vols. (London: Routledge, 1993), vol. 2, canto 1. All references are to this edition.

46. Ralph Cohen, "Transformation in the *Rape of the Lock*," *Eighteenth-Century Studies* 2, 3 (1989): 220. In a metamorphic mock-epic tumble, the rings were melted down into a decorative buckle adorning a widow's gown, followed by a bathetic conversion into a grandchild's toy.

47. John Fyvie, *Comedy Queens of the Georgian Era* (London: Archibald Constable, 1906), 177.

48. The epilogue to Arthur Murphy, *The Orphan of China* (1759) mentions "the pleasure of seeing Mrs. Yates flirt with her fan," in *A Collection of More than Eight Hundred Prologues and Epilogues, from the following Authors: Shakespeare, Beaumont and Fletcher, Massinger . . . Together with all the Prologues and Epilogues Written by the Late D. Garrick*, 4 vols. (London, 1779).

49. *The Spectator*, ed. Donald F. Bond, 5 vols. (Oxford: Clarendon Press, 1965), 1: 427.

50. Frances Sheridan, *The Discovery* (1763) in *The Plays of Frances Sheridan*, ed. Robert Hogan and Jerry C. Beasley (Newark: University of Delaware Press, 1984).

51. Andrew Sofer, *The Stage Life of Props* (Ann Arbor: University of Michigan Press, 2003), 130.

52. James Boaden, *The Life of Mrs. Jordan* (London: Edward Bull, 1831), 16–18. As Sofer, *Stage Life of Props*, 164, points out, "The prop strives to demonstrate female agency and control; yet . . . the prop always risks congealing into the symbol of female helplessness and panic."

53. Angela Rosenthal, "Unfolding Gender: Women and the 'Secret' Sign Language of Fans in Hogarth's Work," in *The Other Hogarth: Aesthetics of Difference*, ed. Bernadette Fort and Angela Rosenthal (Princeton, N.J.: Princeton University Press, 2001), 122–23, describes the fan as a "gestural prosthetic."

54. Horace Walpole, 11 June 1780, *Yale Edition*, 41: 413.

55. Arthur Murphy, "Dedication," *The Way to Keep Him: A Comedy* (London, 1787), iii.

56. *Jonathan Swift: The Complete Poems*, ed. Pat Rogers (London: Penguin, 1983), 463.

57. "Impromptu on seeing Mrs. Abington in the character of Millamant," cited in *Life of Mrs. Abington*, 87.

58. Harriet Guest, *Small Change: Women, Learning, Patriotism, 1750–1810* (Chicago: University of Chicago Press, 2000), 284.

59. De Loutherbourg's scenery, reported to have cost £1500, vied with the fabulous costumes for the audience's rapt attention.

60. Similarly the Elder Groveby insists that in the rural retreat he "will have no Nabobs nor Nabobesses in my family" (4: 1), recalling a similar sentiment in Kitty Clive's Irish plays.

61. "A Biography of the Actress Frances Abington with Printed Memoirs and Press

Notices," National Library of Ireland MS 8263 (1–6): MS. 8263 (4). The following notation appears in manuscript hand: "Mrs Abington lost between 20&30 thousand pounds at the gaming Tables of [Lord?] and Lady Buckinghamshire now she has not money to lose, they do not know her." 9 Oct is crossed out and replaced by 9 November.

62. *A Collection of More Than Eight Hundred Prologues and Epilogues*, 4: 235.

63. William Cooke, *The Capricious Lady: A Comedy (altered from Beaumont and Fletcher)* (Dublin, 1783).

64. George Colman, Epilogue to *The Capricious Lady*. Abington followed in the footsteps of Mrs. Oldfield, a famous clotheshorse, as the Capricious Lady, and both actresses performed as Lady Townley. "Eliots" refers to General Roger Elliott and his son General Granville Elliott, both war heroes and governors of Gibraltar.

65. Francis Beaumont, *Rule a Wife and Have a Wife* (Dublin, 1761).

66. Miles Peter Andrews, Epilogue to his *Dissipation* in *A Collection of More Than Eight Hundred Prologues and Epilogues* (London, 1781), 4: 235.

67. Frances Abington to David Garrick (14 June 1774), cited in *The Letters of David Garrick*, ed. David M. Little and George M. Kahrl, 3 vols. (Cambridge, Mass.: Belknap Press of Harvard University Press, 1963), 3: 943n.4.

68. Isaac Bickerstaff, *The Sultan, or a Peep into the Seraglio: A Farce* (London, 1787). Taken from Marmontel, the play was originally produced in 1775; Abington delivered her epilogue in 1778.

69. Angela Rosenthal, *Angelica Kauffmann: Art and Sensibility* (New Haven, Conn.: Yale University Press, 2006), 146, aptly regards Sir Joshua Reynolds' painting, *Frances Abington as Roxalana* (1782, private collection), as representing the actress as blurring "the boundaries separating that private realm [of the harem] and the space of public, theatrical spectacle." I suggest that the stakes are even higher because Abington and her fellow celebrity actresses insisted on professional equality.

70. When playing in *The Sultan*, Abington requested Garrick's advice regarding the dinner scene and her song. The Sultana was a common masquerade costume, and the Oriental cloak was termed a "sultane" by the French. See *The Modes: Or, A Conversation Upon the Fashions of all Nations. Made English from the French of L'Abbe Bellegarde* (London, 1735), 41.

71. Mr. Jekyll, Epilogue to Baroness Elizabeth Craven, *The Miniature Picture* (London, 1781).

72. George Winchester Stone, Jr., and George M. Kahrl, *David Garrick: A Critical Biography* (Carbondale: Southern Illinois University Press, 1979), 403–46.

73. Hester Thrale Piozzi, *Thraliana: The Diary of Mrs. Hester Lynch Thrale (Later Mrs. Piozzi), 1776–1809*, ed. Katharine C. Balderston, 2 vols. 2nd ed. (Oxford: Clarendon Press, 1951), 2: 725. See Ellen Donkin, *Getting into the Act: Women Playwrights in London 1776–1829* (New York: Routledge, 1995), 30 and passim on the difficulties women dramatists encountered.

74. *Letters of David Garrick*, 2: 599 n.3.

75. Mary E. Knapp, *Prologues and Epilogues of the Eighteenth Century* (New Haven, Conn.: Yale University Press, 1961), 77.

76. Garrick to Peter Fountain, 31 July 1776, *Letters of David Garrick*, 3: 1122.
77. John Taylor, *Records of My Life*, 2 vols. (London: Edward Bull, 1832), 2: 417n.
78. Garrick to Abington, 7 March [1775], *The Letters of David Garrick*, 3: 990.
79. [Francis Gentleman], *The Theatres: A Poetical Dissection: By Sir Nicholas Nipclose, Baronet*, (London, 1772), 61.
80. Abington to Garrick, 26 November 1775, cited in *Life of Mrs. Abington*, 73.
81. The manuscript letter is Folger Y.c.7(8), Folger Shakespeare Library, Washington, DC.
82. Garrick's epilogue to Kelly's *School for Wives* mocks women's ambition ("We've caps, and gowns; nay, bands too, if you please, / Cornelly's, and Almack's, our universities!") and warns husbands against unruly wives who visit Mrs. Cornelly's masquerade hall or Almack's assembly room, ruled by the Lady Patronesses.
83. Angela Rosenthal brilliantly analyzes Reynolds's portrait of Abington in *Angelica Kauffmann: Art and Sensibility*, 74, and suggests the parallel to Garrick's portrait.
84. See Gill Perry, *Spectacular Flirtations: Viewing the Actress in British Art and Theatre, 1768–1820* (New Haven, Conn.: Yale University Press, 2007).

EPILOGUE: CONTRACTED VIRTUE

1. [John Bell, ed.], *Bell's British Theatre: Consisting of the most esteemed English plays*, 21 vols. (London, 1776–81, 1780–81); 90 vols. (1793); 140 vols. (1790–97); and Elizabeth Inchbald, ed., *The British Theatre, or, A Collection of Plays . . . with biographical and critical remarks*, 25 vols. (London, 1808). Appearing every Saturday, each volume in Bell's series cost 6d.
2. Byrne R. S. Fone, "Preface" to John Bell, *Bell's British Theatre, 1776–1781*, 21 vols. (New York: AMS Press, 1977). Advertisement to *The Poets of Great Britain*, vol. 1 (London, 1778), cited in John Brewer, *The Pleasures of the Imagination: English Culture in the Eighteenth Century* (Chicago: University of Chicago Press, 1997), 484–88.
3. Without noting the predominance of actresses, Kalman A. Burnim and Philip H. Highfill, Jr., remark in *John Bell, Patron of British Theatrical Portraiture: A Catalog of the Theatrical Portraits in His Editions of Bell's Shakespeare and Bell's British Theatre* (Carbondale: Southern Illinois University Press, 1998), that "Whatever the reasons for the choices, the primacy of the actor in Bell's calculated plan for stimulating the sale of these editions is obvious—the actor, not the play or the role," 24.
4. Sandra Richards, *The Rise of the English Actress* (London: St. Martin's Press, 1993), writes that Reynolds's *Sarah Siddons as the Tragic Muse* (1784), now at the Huntington, San Marino, CA, "raised the status of the actress in one of the greatest portraits ever painted of a woman," 86.
5. Deborah Heller, "Subjectivity Unbound: Elizabeth Vesey as the Sylph in Bluestocking Correspondence," in *Reconsidering the Bluestockings*, ed. Nicole Pohl and Betty A. Schellenberg (San Marino, Calif.: Huntington Library, 2003), 218.

6. Harriet Guest, "Bluestocking Feminism," in *Reconsidering the Bluestockings*, 69, notes, "It seems to be this consciousness of a gendered group identity, and of their capacity to represent its interests, that informs the powerful sense of their duty or obligation to be socially and publicly useful."

7. Gillian Russell, *Women, Sociability, and the Theatre in Georgian London* (Cambridge: Cambridge University Press, 2007), 68. Founded in 1770 by fourteen women, the Ladies Club or Coterie grew to two hundred members of both sexes.

8. Peter Thomson mentions the lack of attention to the tight relationship between politics and theater in "Acting and Actors from Garrick to Kean," in *The Cambridge Companion to British Theatre, 1730–1830*, ed. Jane Moody and Daniel O'Quinn (Cambridge: Cambridge University Press, 2007), 17, without noting women's political investments. He writes, "On 19 April 1787, the House of Commons postponed a debate on the national budget because it was the opening night of the Richmond House theatricals. The audience of the play—Arthur Murphy's *The Way to Keep Him*—included both Pitt and Fox, inveterate political enemies, as well as the Prince of Wales, the Duke and Duchess of Cumberland, General Burgoyne (who had composed the epilogue) and such theatrical luminaries as the Sheridans, Mrs Garrick and John Philip Kemble."

9. In her otherwise impressive book *Women, Sociability, and the Theatre*, Gillian Russell seems to reinscribe the dichotomy between public and the private that actresses clearly undermined. She contrasts the "manly industry" of the commercial theater and the homosocial male connections in coffeehouses and clubs to the "feminized space" of the pleasure gardens attended by elite women. This configuration understates, I think, the mixed-sex nature of many private assemblies in London, Bath, and elsewhere.

10. E. J. Clery, "Bluestocking 'Feminism' and the Fame Game," *British Journal for Eighteenth-Century Studies* 28 (2005): 276.

11. *Thraliana: The Diary of Mrs. Hester Lynch Thrale (Later Mrs. Piozzi), 1776–1809*, ed. Katharine C. Balderston, 2 vols. (Oxford: Clarendon Press, 1951), 2: 330.

12. These numerical scales are typical of an Enlightenment fascination with quantifying social behavior.

13. Thomas Taylor, *The Great Actors of 1775* [s.l. 1863], 87. Sophia Baddeley famously frequented Ranelagh and Vauxhall.

14. Miriam Lerenbaum, "The Nine Living Muses of Great Britain," *Proceedings of the American Society for Eighteenth-Century Studies* (Carbondale: Southern Illinois University Press, 1979), offers an evaluative history of the earlier print and the painting.

15. Kate Davies, *Catherine Macaulay and Mercy Otis Warren: The Revolutionary Atlantic and the Politics of Gender* (Oxford: Oxford University Press, 2005), 78, 80. See also Elizabeth Eger, "Representing Culture: *The Nine Living Muses of Great Britain* (1779)," in *Women, Writing and the Public Sphere, 1700–1830*, ed. Elizabeth Eger, Charlotte Grant, Clíona Ó Gallchoir, and Penny Warburton (Cambridge: Cambridge University Press, 2001), 104–32.

16. Elizabeth Carter to Elizabeth Montagu, 23 November [1777], Huntington Library, San Marino, California, mo3434.

17. Elizabeth Montagu to Elizabeth Carter, 24 November 1777, Huntington Library, San Marino, California, MO 3435.

18. Angela Smallwood, "Women and the Theatre," in *Women and Literature in Britain, 1700–1800*, ed. Vivien Jones (Cambridge: Cambridge University Press), 257, writes that late in the century "a combination of cultural and theatrical dynamics came into play, within which negotiations of female identity must have been a palpable presence."

19. Gill Perry, *Spectacular Flirtations: Viewing the Actress in British Art and Theatre, 1768–1820* (New Haven, Conn.: Yale University Press, 2007), 147–58, discusses pictures of Linley in some detail but does not consider *The Nine Living Muses*.

20. Ellen Donkin, *Getting into the Act: Women Playwrights in London, 1776–1829* (New York: Routledge, 1995), counts 28 playwrights in this period, but more women writers' works did not reach the stage.

21. Frances Burney, *The Witlings and the Woman-Hater*, ed. Peter Sabor and Geoffrey Sill (Peterborough, Ont.: Broadview, 2002), Appendix B, 294–95.

22. See Ellen Donkin, "The Paper War of Hannah Cowley and Hannah More," in *Curtain Calls: British and American Women and the Theater, 1660–1820*, ed. Mary Anne Schofield and Cecilia Macheski (Athens: Ohio University Press, 1991), 143–62, believes that a paternal Garrick mentored Cowley and More, offering editorial advice. I interpret her account, however, to support my claim that pitting women playwrights as rivals was part of Garrick's strategy.

23. The entire exchange is considered in Betty A. Schellenberg, *The Professionalization of Women Writers in Eighteenth-Century Britain* (Cambridge: Cambridge University Press, 2005), 49–50. Garrick defends himself vis-à-vis women playwrights in a letter to Frances Cadogan, *The Letters of David Garrick*, ed. David M. Little and George M. Kahrl, 3 vols. (Cambridge, Mass.: Harvard University Press, 1963), 3: 1172 See also Kevin Berland, "Frances Brooke and David Garrick," *Studies in Eighteenth-Century Culture* 20 (1990): 217–30.

24. Siddons amicably separated from her husband at age forty-seven. An affair was rumored with the artist Sir Thomas Lawrence who painted her picture.

25. Laura Rosenthal, "The Sublime, the Beautiful, 'The Siddons,'" in *The Clothes That Wear Us: Essays on Dressing and Transgressing in Eighteenth-Century Culture*, ed. Jessica Munns and Penny Richards (Newark: University of Delaware Press, 1999), 59. See also Claudia Johnson, *Equivocal Beings: Politics, Gender, and Sentimentality in the 1790s* (Chicago: University of Chicago Press, 1995).

26. James Boaden, *Memoirs of Mrs. Siddons*, 2 vols. (London: Henry Colburn, 1827), 1: 312; 2: 116.

27. This was especially true of Siddons's Lady Macbeth, as numerous commentators then and now have shown. See, for example, Julie Carlson, *In the Theatre of Romanticism: Coleridge, Nationalism, Women* (Cambridge: Cambridge University Press, 1994).

28. Nina A. Kennard, *Mrs. Siddons* (Boston: Robert Brothers, 1887), 5, mentions her "untarnished private character."

29. Ellen Donkin, "Mrs. Siddons Looks Back in Anger: Feminist Historiography for

Eighteenth-Century British Theater," in *Critical Theory and Performance*, ed. Janelle G. Reinelt and Joseph R. Roach (Ann Arbor: University of Michigan Press, 1992), 276–90.

30. According to Laura Rosenthal, "The Sublime, the Beautiful, 'The Siddons'," 70, Siddons was successful "in her skillful manipulation of her categories of gender and her capacity to perform *both* masculinity *and* femininity in a way that allowed her to escape, for the most part, sexual suspicion" and "balanced her masculine sublime with a specifically *maternal* beauty."

31. Pat Rogers, "'Towering Beyond Her Sex': Stature and Sublimity in the Achievement of Sarah Siddons," in *Curtain Calls*, ed. Schofield and Macheski, 50. Siddons also acted Hamlet as a travesty role.

32. See Lisa Freeman, "Introduction," *Sarah Siddons*, ed. Lisa Freeman, *Lives of Shakespearian Actors: Edmund Kean, Sarah Siddons, and Harriet Smithson by Their Contemporaries*, 3 vols. (London: Pickering and Chatto, 2009), 2: xxii; and Michael S. Wilson, "The 'Incomparable' Siddons as Reynolds's Muse: Art and Ideology on the British Stage," in *So Rich a Tapestry: The Sister Arts and Cultural Studies*, ed. Ann Hurley and Kate Greenspan (Lewisburg, Pa.: Bucknell University Press, 1995), 116–50.

33. Shearer West, "The Public and Private Roles of Sarah Siddons," in *A Passion for Performance: Sarah Siddons and her Portraitists*, ed. Robyn Asleson (Los Angeles: J. Paul Getty Museum, 1999), 1–39, cites especially the impassioned responses of women spectators to Siddons's highly emotional performances.

34. Miss E. Ambross, *The Life and Memoirs of the Late Miss Ann Catley, the Celebrated Actress* (London, [1789]), 12.

35. James Boaden, *The Life of Mrs. Jordan*, vol. 2, pt. 1, ed. Sharon Setzer, in *Women's Theatrical Memoirs*, general editor Jennie Batchelor, 5 vols. (London: Pickering and Chatto, 2007), 1: 20.

36. See Jonathan Bate, "Shakespeare and the Rival Muses: Siddons Versus Jordan," in *Notorious Muse: The Actress in British Act and Culture, 1776–1812*, ed. Robyn Asleson (New Haven, Conn.: Yale University Press, 2003), 81–103.

BIBLIOGRAPHY

PRIMARY SOURCES

The Comedian, or, Philosophical Enquirer
Critical Review, or, Annals of Literature
The Daily Advertiser
The Dublin Gazette
The English Review
The Gentleman's Magazine
The Grub-Street Journal
The London Daily Post and General Advertiser
The London Magazine
The Morning Chronicle and London Advertiser
The Public Advertiser
St. James Chronicle
The Theatrical Monitor
The Volunteer Manager
Westminster Magazine

Alexander the Great, A Tragedy; with Alterations, as it is now performed at the Theatres-Royal in Drury-Lane and Covent Garden. London, 1772.
Ambross, Miss E. *The Life and Memoirs of the Late Miss Ann Catley, the Celebrated Actress.* London [1789].
Andrews, Miles Peter. *Dissipation. A Comedy, in Five Acts.* London, 1781.
Aston, Anthony. *A Brief Supplement to Colley Cibber, Esq. his Lives of the late famous actors and actresses.* [London, 1747?].
Aubignac, François-Hédelin. *The Whole Art of the Stage.* London, 1684.
Authentick Memoirs of the Life of that celebrated Actress Mrs. Ann Oldfield. Containing a Genuine Account of her Transactions from her Infancy to the Time of her Decease. 1st ed. and 6th ed. London, 1730.
Baker, David Erskine, Stephen Jones, and Isaac Reed. *Biographia Dramatica; or, a Companion to the Playhouse: Containing Historical and Critical Memoirs, and Original Anecdotes,*

of British and Irish Dramatic Writers from the Commencement of Our Theatrical Exhibitions. 3 vols. in 4. London: Longman, Hurst, Rees, Orme, and Brown [etc.], 1812.

A Banquet of the Muses: or, the Miscellany of Miscellanies. London, 1746.

Beaumont, Francis. *Rule a Wife and Have a Wife. A Comedy*. Dublin, 1761.

Bedford, Arthur. *A Sermon Preached in the Parish-Church of St. Butolph's Aldgate*. London, 1730.

[Bell, John, ed.] *Bell's British Theatre: Consisting of the most esteemed English plays*, 21 vols. London, 1776–81, 1780–81; 90 vols. London, 1793; 140 vols. 1790–97.

Bellamy, George Anne. *An Apology for the Life of George Anne Bellamy*. 6 vols. London, 1785; 4th ed. 5 vols. London, 1786.

Betterton, Thomas [Edmund Curll]. *The History of the English Stage from the Restauration to the Present Time*. London, 1741.

Bickerstaff, Isaac. *The Sultan, or a Peep into the Seraglio. A Farce*. London, 1787.

A Biography of the Actress Frances Abington with Printed Memoirs and Press Notices. National Library of Ireland MS 8263.

Boaden, James. *Memoirs of Mrs. Siddons. Interspersed with Anecdotes of Authors and Actors*. 2 vols. London: Henry Colburn, 1827.

———. *The Life of Mrs. Jordan; Including Original Private Correspondence, and Numerous Anecdotes of Her Contemporaries*. 2 vols. London: Edward Bull, 1831.

Boswell, James. "Remarks on the Profession of a Player." *London Magazine* 39, Aug.–Oct. 1770.

Brown, John. *An Estimate of the Manners and Principles of the Times*. 2 vols. London, 1757.

Burgoyne, John. *Maid of the Oaks. A New Dramatic Entertainment*. London, 1774.

Campbell, R. *The London Tradesman. Being a Compendious View of all the Trades, Professions, Arts, both Liberal and Mechanic, now practised in the Cities of London and Westminster*. London, 1747.

Campbell, Thomas. *Life of Mrs. Siddons*. New York: Harper, 1834.

Caraccioli, Charles. *Chiron: or, the Mental Optician*. 2 vols. in one. London, 1758.

The Case Between the Managers of the Two Theatres, and their Principal Actors. London, 1743 [misdated 1713].

Chetwood, William Rufus. *Dramatic Congress. A Short State of the Stage under the present management. Concluding with a dialogue . . . between the illustrious Bashas of Dr-ry Lane and Co--nt Garden*. London, 1743.

———. *A General History of the Stage, from its origin in Greece down to the Present Time . . .* collected and digested by W. R. Chetwood. London, 1749.

Cibber, Colley. *The Dramatic Works of Colley Cibber. Esq. in Five Volumes*. London, 1777.

———. *The Rival Queens, With the Humours of Alexander the Great*. Dublin, 1729.

Cibber, Theophilus. *An Epistle from Mr. Theophilus Cibber, to David Garrick, Esq; to Which Are Prefixed, Some Occasional Verses, Petitions, &c*. London, 1755.

———. *Romeo and Juliet, a Tragedy, Revis'd, and Alter'd from Shakespear, First Reviv'd (in September, 1744, . . . To which Is added, a Serio-Comic Apology, for Part of the Life of*

Mr. Theophilus Cibber, Comedian. Written by Himself. Interspersed with Memoirs and Anecdotes. London, [1748].
———. A Serio-Comic Apology for Part of the Life of Mr. Theophilus Cibber, Comedian. Dublin, 1748.
Clive, Catherine Raftor. The Rehearsal: Or, Bays in Petticoats. A Comedy in Two Acts. London, 1753.
A Collection of Miscellany Poems, never before Publish'd. London, 1737
A Collection of More than Eight Hundred Prologues and Epilogues from the Following Authors: Shakespeare, Beaumont and Fletcher, Massinger . . . Together with all the Prologues and Epilogues Written by the Late D. Garrick. 4 vols. London, 1779.
Collier, Jeremy. A Short View of the Immorality and Profaneness of the English Stage, Together with the Sense of Antiquity Upon This Argument. 3rd ed. London, 1698.
A Comparison Between the Two Stages. London, 1702.
The Conduct of the Stage Consider'd. Being a Short Historical Account of Its Original, Progress, various Aspects, and Treatment in the Pagan, Jewish and Christian World. London, 1721.
Cooke, William. The Capricious Lady: A Comedy (Altered from Beaumont and Fletcher). Dublin, 1783.
The Court of Alexander. An Opera, in Two Acts. As it is performed at the Theatre Royal in Covent-Garden. London, [1770].
Craven, Baroness Elizabeth. The Miniature Picture; A Comedy in Three Acts. London, 1781.
A Critical Balance of the Performers at Drury-Lane Theatre. For the last season 1765. London, [1766?].
Crowne, John. Calisto. or, the Chaste Nimph; the Late Masque at Court. London, 1675.
———. Crowne's Plays. [London, 1671–1698].
Curll, Edmund. The Life of That Eminent Comedian Robert Wilks, Esq. London, 1733.
———. See also Betterton; Egerton.
Davies, Thomas. Memoirs of the Life of David Garrick, Esq., Interspersed with Characters and Anecdotes of His Theatrical Contemporaries. 2 vols. 4th ed. London, 1784.
———. Dramatic Miscellanies: Consisting of Critical Observations on Several Plays of Shakspeare: With a Review of His Principal Characters, and Those of Various Eminent Writers. 3 vols. New ed. London, 1784.
Dennis, John. Original Letters Familiar, Moral, and Critical. 2 vols. London, 1721.
Dibdin, Charles. A Complete History of the English Stage. 5 vols. London, 1800.
The Disputes between the Director of D—Y, and the Pit Potentates: Being a Letter to a Friend, Concerning the Behaviour of the Melancholly Manager of the Suff'ring Theatre. London, 1744.
Doran, John. Their Majesties' Servants. Annals of the English Stage, from Thomas Betterton to Edmund Kean. 2 vols. London: W.H. Allen, 1864.
Downes, John. Roscius Anglicanus, or, an Historical Review of the Stage. Ed. Judith Milhous and Robert D. Hume. London: The Society for Theatre Research, 1987.
Dryden, John. Tyrannick Love, or the Royal Martyr. A Tragedy. London, 1670.

Egerton, William [Edmund Curll]. *Faithful Memoirs of the Life, Amours, and Performances of That Justly Celebrated, and Most Eminent Actress of her Time, Mrs. Anne Oldfield.* London, 1731.
Encyclopaedia Britannica; or, a Dictionary of Arts, Sciences, and Miscellaneous Literature. Ed. Colin MacFarquhar and George Gleig. 18 vols. 3rd ed. Edinburgh, 1797.
An Epistle from Mrs. Oldfield in the Shades, to Mrs. Br--ceg--dle on Earth. London, 1743.
Fielding, Henry. *The Complete Works of Henry Fielding, Esq., with an Essay on the Life, Genius, and Achievement of the Author.* Ed. William Henley. 16 vols. New York: Croscup and Sterling [1902]; repr. Barnes and Noble, 1967.
———. *The Intriguing Chambermaid. A Comedy of Two Acts. Taken from the French of Regnard.* London, 1734.
———. *The Lottery. A Farce.* 2nd ed. London, 1732.
———. *The Works of Henry Fielding . . . With a Life of the Author.* 12 vols. London, 1776.
Foote, Samuel. *The Roman and English Comedy Consider'd and Compar'd . . . and an Examen into the Merit of the Present Comic Actors.* London, 1747.
A Full Answer to Queries upon Queries. London, 1743.
Gay, John. *Fables.* 2nd ed. London, 1728.
Genest, John. *Some Account of the English Stage from the Restoration in 1660 to 1830.* 10 vols. Bath, 1832; repr. New York: B. Franklin, 1965.
Gentleman, Francis. *The Dramatic Censor; or, Critical Companion.* 2 vols. London, 1770.
———. *The Theatres: A Poetical Dissection. By Sir Nicholas Nipclose, Baronet.* London, 1772.
Gildon, Charles. *The Life of Mr. Thomas Betterton, the Late Eminent Tragedian . . . With the Judgment Of . . . Monsieur De St. Evremond, . . . To Which Is Added, the Amorous Widow, or the Wanton Wife. A Comedy.* London, 1710.
Goldsmith, Oliver. *The Bee; Being Essays on the Most Interesting Subjects.* London, 1759.
Griffith, Elizabeth. *The School for Rakes. A Comedy.* London, 1769.
A Guide to the Stage; or, Select Instructions and Precedents from the Best Authorities Towards Forming a Polite Audience. London, 1751.
Harcourt, E. W., ed. *The Harcourt Papers.* 13 vols. Oxford: Parker Press, 1880–1905.
Hawling, Francis. *A Miscellany of Original Poems on Various Subjects.* London, 1751.
Hedelin, Abbé. *The Whole Art of the Stage.* London, 1657, trans. 1684.
Hill, Aaron. *The Tragedy of Zara.* [An adaptation of Voltaire's *Zaïre*]. London, 1736.
The History of the Stage. In which is included, the Theatrical Characters of the most celebrated Actors. London, 1742.
Hitchcock, Robert. *An Historical View of the Irish Stage; from the Earliest Period Down to the Close of the Season 1788.* 2 vols. Dublin, 1788–94.
Home, John. *The Fatal Discovery. A Tragedy.* London, 1769.
An Impartial Examen. See Mr. Neither-Side.
Inchbald, Elizabeth, ed. *The British Theatre, or, a Collection of Plays . . . with biographical and critical remarks.* 25 vols. London, 1808.
Johnson, Charles. *The Generous Husband, or, the Coffeehouse Politician. A Comedy.* London, 1711.

Kelly, Hugh. *The School for Wives. A Comedy.* 3rd ed. London, 1774.

———. *Thespis: Or, a Critical Examination into the Merits of all the Principal Performers Belonging to Drury-Lane Theatre.* London, 1766.

Kemble, John Philip. *The Female Officer, or the Humours of the Army, a Comedy, Altered from Shadwell.* Dublin, 1763.

Kirkman, James Thomas. *Memoirs of the Life of Charles Macklin.* 2 vols. London, 1799.

LeFanu, Alice. *Memoirs of the Life and Writings of Mrs. Frances Sheridan.* London: G. and W.B. Whittaker, 1824.

Lethe Rehears'd; or, a Critical Discussion of the Beauties & Blemishes of That Performance, etc. London, 1749.

A Letter to a Certain Patentee: In Which the Conduct of Managers Is Impartially Considered; and a few Periods Bestowed on those Darlings of the Publick, Mr. G--K, Mr. F--E, Mrs. P--D, &c. London, [1747].

The Life of Lavinia Beswick, alias Fenton, alias Polly Peachum: Containing, Her Birth and Education. . . . The Whole interspers'd with convincing Proofs of Her Ingenuity, Wit, and Smart Repartees. And concluding with some remarkable Instances of her Humanity to the Distressed. London, 1728.

The Life of Mr. James Quin, Comedian. With the History of the Stage from his commencing Actor to his Retreat to Bath. London, 1766.

Lun, Junior, Mr. [Henry Woodward]. *The Beggar's Pantomime ; Or, The Contending Columbines . . . Dedicated to Mrs. Clive and Mrs. Cibber.* 3rd ed. London, 1736.

MacFarquhar, Colin, and George Gleig, ed. *Encyclopædia Britannica: Or, a Dictionary of Arts, Sciences, and Miscellaneous Literature: Constructed on a Plan, by Which the Different Sciences and Arts Are Digested into the Form of Distinct Treatises or Systems.* 3rd ed. 18 vols. Edinburgh, 1797.

Macky, John. *A Journey through England. In Familiar Letters from a Gentleman Here, to His Friend Abroad.* London, 1714.

Maitland, William. *The History of London: From its Foundation by the Romans, to the Present Time . . . .in Nine Books.* London, 1739.

Marchant, Mr. *Observations on Mr. Fielding's Plan for a Preservatory and Reformatory.* London, 1758.

Memoirs of the celebrated Mrs. Woffington, interspersed with several Theatrical Anecdotes; the Amours of many Persons of the First Rank; and some interesting Characters drawn from real Life. 2nd ed. London, 1760.

Miège, Guy. *The present state of Great Britain. In two parts . . . Containing an Accurate and Impartial Account of this great and famous Island.* 2 vols. London, 1707.

The Modes: Or, a Conversation Upon the Fashions of all Nations. Made English from the French of L'Abbe Bellegarde. London, 1735.

Murphy, Arthur. *The Apprentice. A Farce in Two Acts.* London, 1756.

———. *The Gray's Inn Journal.* 2 vols. London, 1756.

———. *Zenobia. A Tragedy.* Dublin, 1768.

———. *The Way to Keep Him: A Comedy.* London, 1787.

Neither-Side, Mr. [Charles Fleetwood]. *An Impartial Examen of the Present Contests between the Town and the Manager of the Theatre with Some Proposals for accommodating the present Misunderstandings between the Town and the Manager.* London, 1744.
O'Keeffe, John. *Recollections of the Life of John O'Keeffe, written by Himself.* 2 vols. London: H. Colburn, 1826.
Oldfield, Anne. See *Authentick Memoirs*.
Oldys, William. *Memoirs of Mrs. Anne Oldfield.* London, 1741.
Pasquin, Anthony. [John Williams]. *The Pin Basket. To the Children of Thespis.* London, 1797.
Pepys, Samuel. *The Diary of Samuel Pepys.* Ed. Robert Latham and William Matthews. 11 vols. London: G. Bell and Sons, 1970.
Phillips, Edward. *Britons Strike Home: or, the Sailor's Rehearsal. A Farce.* London, 1739.
The Playhouse Pocket-Companion, or Theatrical Vade Mecum. London, 1779.
Queries upon Queries; to be Answer'd by the Male-content Players. London [1743?].
Ralph, James. *The Touch-Stone: or, Historical, Critical, Political, Philosophical, and Theological Essays on the Reigning Diversions of the Town.* London, 1728.
Raymond, George. *The Life and Enterprises of Robert William Elliston, Comedian.* London, Routledge, 1857.
Rede, Leman Thomas. *The Road to the Stage; or, the Performer's Preceptor.* London: J. Onwhyn, 1836.
Richardson, Samuel. *Pamela; or, Virtue Rewarded.* 4 vols. London, 1742.
[Richardson, Samuel?]. *A Seasonable Examination of the Pleas and Pretensions of the Proprietors of, and Subscribers to, Playhouses erected in defiance of the Royal Licence.* London, 1735.
Robinson, Mary. *Memoirs of the Late Mrs. Robinson.* 4 vols. London: R. Phillips, 1801.
Rogers, Jane. *The Memorial of Jane Rogers Humbly Submitted to the Town.* London, 1712.
Rosalind: Or, an Apology for the History of a Theatrical Lady. Dublin, 1759.
Ryley, S. W. *The Itinerant; or, Memoirs of an Actor.* 9 vols. London: Sherwood, Neely and Jones, 1816–1827.
A Seasonable Rebuke to the Playhouse Rioters . . . to which is prefixed, a Petitionary Dedication to the Fair Members of the Shakespear-Club. London, 1740.
The Servants Calling; with Some Advice to the Apprentice. London, 1725.
Shandy, Tristram. *Miss C--y's Cabinet of Curiosities; or, the Green-Room Broke Open.* London, 1765.
Silence, Timothy. *The Foundling Hospital for Wit.* London, 1746.
Smith, Adam. *An Inquiry into the Nature and Causes of the Wealth of Nations.* 3 vols., 8th ed. London, 1796.
The Spouter's Companion; or, Theatrical Remembrancer. Containing a Select Collection of the most esteemed Prologues and Epilogues, Which Have Been Spoken by the most celebrated Performers of both Sexes. London [1770?].
Steele, Elizabeth. *The Memoirs of Mrs. Sophia Baddeley, late of Drury Lane Theatre.* 6 vols. Clerkenwell, 1787.

Stevens, George Alexander. *The Court of Alexander. An Opera, in Two Acts.* 2d ed. London, 1770.
Taylor, John. *Records of My Life.* 2 vols. London: Edward Bull, 1832.
The Theatrical Bouquet: Containing an Alphabetical Arrangement of the Prologues and Epilogues, Which have been Published by Distinguished Wits, from the Time that Colley Cibber first came on the Stage, to the present Year. London, 1778.
Theatrical Correspondence in Death. An Epistle from Mrs Oldfield, in the Shades to Mrs Br--ceg---dle, upon Earth. London, 1743.
The Theatrical Review: For the Year 1757, and Beginning of 1758. London, 1758.
Truelove, Francis. *The Comforts of Matrimony; Exemplified in the Memorable Case and Trial Upon an Action Brought by Theo--s C--R against –S--r, Esq.* 6th ed. London, 1739.
The Tryals of Two Causes, between Theophilus Cibber . . . and William Sloper. London, 1740.
Victor, Benjamin. *The History of the Theatres of London and Dublin, from the Year 1730 to the present Time, To which is added, an Annual Register of all the Plays, &c., performed at the Theatres-Royal in London, from the Year 1712. With Occasional Notes and Anecdotes.* 2 vols. London, 1761; vol. 3, London, 1771.
———. *Memoirs of the Life of Barton Booth Esq:; with his Character: To which are added Several Poetical Pieces, Written by Himself.* London, 1733.
———. *Original Letters, Dramatic Pieces and Poems.* 3 vols. London, 1776.
The Vindications of Lord Carteret. London, 1730.
Visits from the Shades: or, dialogues serious, comical, and political. Calculated for these Times. London, 1704–05.
Von Archenholz, Johann Wilhelm. *A Picture of England. Containing a Description of the Laws, Customs, and Manners of England.* Trans. from the French. 2 vols. London, 1789.
Walpole, Horace. *The Works of Horatio Walpole, Earl of Orford.* 5 vols. London, 1798.
Wattle, Will. *A Soldier's Letter to the Female Volunteer: Being an Earnest Request to Hang up the Hat, and Pull off the Breeches. With a Persuasive against False Appearances.* London, [1750?].
Wilkes, Thomas [Samuel Derrick]. *A General View of the Stage.* London, 1759.
Wilkinson, Tate. *Memoirs of His Own Life.* 4 vols. York, 1790.
———. *The Wandering Patentee; or, a History of the Yorkshire Theatres, from 1770 to the Present Time: Interspersed with Anecdotes Respecting Most of the Performers in the Three Kingdoms, from 1765 to 1795.* 4 vols. in 2. York, 1795. Repr. London: Scolar Press, 1973.
Woffington's Ghost: A Poem. In answer to the Meretriciad. London, 1761.
[Woodward, Henry]. Lun , Jr., Mr. *The Beggar's Pantomime; or, The Contending Colombines: A New Comic Interlude.* 3rd ed. London, 1736.
Worsdale, James. *A Cure for a Scold.* Dublin, 1738.

SECONDARY SOURCES

Agnew, Jean-Christophe. *Worlds Apart: The Market and the Theater in Anglo-American Thought, 1550–1750.* Cambridge: Cambridge University Press, 1986.

Appadurai, Arjun. *The Social Life of Things: Commodities in Cultural Perspective*. Cambridge: Cambridge University Press, 1986.
Armitage, David. *The Ideological Origins of the British Empire*. Ideas in Context. Cambridge: Cambridge University Press, 2000.
Armstrong, Nancy. *Desire and Domestic Fiction: A Political History of the Novel*. Oxford: Oxford University Press, 1987.
Ashton, John. *Social Life in the Reign of Queen Anne, Taken from Original Sources*. New ed. London: Chatto & Windus, 1883.
———. "The Shakespeare Ladies' Club." *Shakespeare Quarterly* 7, 2 (Spring 1956): 153–58.
Baer, Marc. *Theatre and Disorder in Late Georgian London*. Oxford: Clarendon Press, 1992.
Balderston, Katharine C., ed. *Thraliana: The Diary of Mrs. Hester Lynch Thrale (Later Mrs. Piozzi), 1776–1809*. 2 vols. 2nd ed. Oxford: Clarendon Press, 1951.
Balibar, Etienne. "My *Self* and My *Own*: One and the Same?" In *Accelerating Possession: Global Futures of Prosperity and Personhood*, ed. Bill Maurer and Gabriele Schwab. New York: Columbia University Press, 2006. 21–44.
Ballard, George. *Memoirs of Several Ladies of Great Britain: Who Have Been Celebrated for Their Writings or Skill in the Learned Languages, Arts, and Sciences*. Ed Ruth Perry. Detroit: Wayne State University Press, 1985.
Ballaster, Rosalind. *Fabulous Orients: Fictions of the East in England, 1662–1785*. Oxford: Oxford University Press, 2005.
Barrell, John. "Coffee-House Politicians." *Journal of British Studies* 43 (April 2004): 206–32.
———. *English Literature in History, 1730–80: An Equal, Wide Survey*. London: Hutchinson, 1983.
Barrie, Robert. "Elizabethan Play-Boys in the Adult London Companies." *SEL* 48, 2 (Spring 2008): 237–57.
Batchelor, Jennie. "'Industry in Distress': Reconfiguring Femininity and Labor in the Magdalen House." *Eighteenth-Century Life* 28, 1 (2004): 1–20.
Bate, Jonathan. "Shakespeare and the Rival Muses: Siddons Versus Jordan." In *Notorious Muse: The Actress in British Act and Culture, 1776–1812*, ed. Robyn Asleson. New Haven, Conn.: Yale University Press, 2003. 81–103.
Behn, Aphra. *The Rover; the Feigned Courtesans; the Lucky Chance; the Emperor of the Moon*. Ed. Jane Spencer. Oxford: Oxford University Press, 1995.
Belanstein, Lenard R. *Daughters of Eve: A Cultural History of French Theater Women from the Old Regime to the Fin de Siècle*. Cambridge, Mass.: Harvard University Press, 2001.
Berland, Kevin. "Frances Brooke and David Garrick." *Studies in Eighteenth-Century Culture* 20 (1990): 217–30.
Bhabha, Homi. *Nation and Narration*. New York: Routledge, 1990.
Blau, Herbert. *Take Up the Bodies: Theater at the Vanishing Point*. Urbana: University of Illinois Press, 1982.
Boaden, James. *The Life of Mrs. Jordan*. Ed. Sharon Setzer. In *Women's Theatrical Memoirs*. General editor Jennie Batchelor. 5 vols. London: Pickering and Chatto, 2007.

de Bolla, Peter. "'A Submission, Sir!' Who Has the Right to Person in Eighteenth-Century Britain?" In *Land, Nation and Culture, 1740–1840: Thinking the Republic of Taste*, ed. Peter de Bolla, Nigel Leask, and David Simpson. Basingstoke: Palgrave Macmillan, 2005. 148–68.

Boswell, James. *The Life of Johnson*. Ed. George Birkbeck Hill, rev. L. F. Powell. 6 vols. Oxford: Clarendon Press, 1934–50.

———. *The London Journal, 1762–63*. Ed. Frederick A. Pottle. New York: McGraw-Hill, 1950.

Botica, Allan Richard. "Audience, Playhouse and Play in Restoration Theatre, 1660–1710." Dissertation, Oxford University, 1985.

Boucé, Paul-Gabriel. *Sexuality in Eighteenth-Century Britain*. Manchester: Manchester University Press, 1982.

Bradham, JoAllen. "A Good Country Gentlewoman: Catherine Clive's Epistolary Autobiography." *Biography* 19, 2 (Summer 1996): 259–82.

Bratton, Jacky. *New Readings in Theatre History*. Cambridge: Cambridge University Press, 2003.

Brewer, John. *The Pleasures of the Imagination: English Culture in the Eighteenth Century*. Chicago: University of Chicago Press, 1997.

———. "This, That and the Other: Public, Social and Private in the Seventeenth and Eighteenth Centuries." In *Shifting the Boundaries: Transformation of the Languages of Public and Private in the Eighteenth Century*, ed. Dario Castiglione and Lesley Sharpe. Exeter: University of Exeter Press, 1995. 1–21.

Brown, Laura. "The Defenseless Woman and the Development of English Tragedy." *Studies in English Literature, 1500–1900* 22, 3 (Summer 1982): 429–43.

———. *English Dramatic Form, 1660–1760: An Essay in Generic History*. New Haven, Conn.: Yale University Press, 1981.

Brown, Wendy. *Edgework: Critical Essays on Knowledge and Politics*. Princeton, N.J.: Princeton University Press, 2005.

Buck, Anne. *Dress in Eighteenth-Century England*. London: Batsford, 1979.

Burke, Helen M. "Acting in the Periphery: The Irish Theatre." In *The Cambridge Companion to British Theatre, 1730–1830*, ed. Jane Moody and Danny O'Quinn. Cambridge: Cambridge University Press, 2007, 219–32.

———. "Eighteenth-Century Theatrical Touring and Irish Popular Culture." In *Irish Theatre on Tour*, ed. Nicholas Grene and Christopher Morash. Dublin: Carysfort Press, 2005, 86–107.

———. *Riotous Performances: The Struggle for Hegemony in the Irish Theater, 1712–1784*. Notre Dame, Ind.: University of Notre Dame Press, 2003.

Burney, Frances. *The Witlings and the Woman-Hater*. Ed. Peter Sabor and Geoffrey Sill. Peterborough Ontario: Broadview, 2002.

———. *Evelina: Or, the History of a Young Lady's Entrance into the World* (1778). Ed. Edward Alan Bloom. Oxford: Oxford University Press, 2002.

Burnim, Kalman A., and Philip H. Highfill, Jr. *John Bell, Patron of British Theatrical Por-*

traiture: A Catalog of the Theatrical Portraits in His Editions of Bell's Shakespeare and Bell's British Theatre. Carbondale: Southern Illinois University Press, 1998.

Bush-Bailey, Gilli. "Revolution, Legislation and Autonomy." In *The Cambridge Companion to the Actress*, ed. Maggie B. Gale and John Stokes. Cambridge: Cambridge University Press, 2007. 15–32.

———. *Treading the Bawds: Actresses and Playwrights on the Late-Stuart Stage*. Manchester: Manchester University Press, 2007.

Butler, Judith. *Gender Trouble: Feminism and the Subversion of Identity*. London: Routledge, 1990.

———. "Performative Acts and Gender Constitution: An Essay in Phenomenology and Feminist Theory." In *Performing Feminisms: Feminist Critical Theory and Theatre*, ed. Sue-Ellen Case. Baltimore: Johns Hopkins University Press, 1990. 270–82.

———. *Bodies That Matter: On the Discursive Limits of Sex*. London: Routledge, 1993.

Byrne, Paula. *Perdita: The Life of Mary Robinson*. London: HarperCollins, 2004.

Campbell-Orr, Clarissa. "Countesses and Courtesans." *History Workshop Journal* 62, 1 (2006): 278–92.

Canfield, J. Douglas, and Deborah Payne Fisk, eds. *Cultural Readings of Restoration and Eighteenth-Century English Theater*. Athens: University of Georgia Press, 1995.

Carlson, Julie. *The Theatre of Romanticism: Coleridge, Nationalism, Women*. Cambridge: Cambridge University Press, 1994.

Carlson, Marvin A. *The Haunted Stage: The Theatre as Memory Machine*. Ann Arbor: University of Michigan Press, 2001.

———. *Theories of the Theatre: A Historical and Critical Survey from the Greeks to the Present*. Ithaca, N.Y.: Cornell University Press, 1984.

Case, Sue-Ellen. "Feminism and Performance: A Post-Disciplinary Couple." *Theatre Research International* 26, 2 (2001): 145–52.

———. *The Domain-Matrix: Performing Lesbian at the End of Print Culture*. Bloomington: Indiana University Press, 1996.

———. "Toward a Butch-Femme Aesthetic." In *Making a Spectacle: Feminist Essays on Contemporary Women's Theatre*, ed. Lynda Hart. Ann Arbor: University of Michigan Press, 1989. 282–99.

Castle, Terry. "The Gothic Novel." In *The Cambridge History of English Literature, 1660–1780*, ed. John J. Richetti. Cambridge: Cambridge University Press, 2005, 673–706.

———. *Masquerade and Civilization: The Carnivalesque in Eighteenth-Century English Culture and Fiction*. Stanford, Calif.: Stanford University Press, 1986.

Centlivre, Susanna. *The Wonder: A Woman Keeps a Secret* (1714). Ed. John O'Brien. Peterborough, Ont.: Broadview Press, 2004.

de Certeau, Michel. *The Writing of History*. Trans. Tom Conley. New York: Columbia University Press, 1988

Charke, Charlotte. *A Narrative of the Life of Mrs. Charlotte Charke* (1755). Ed. Robert Rehder. London: Pickering and Chatto, 1999.

———. *A Narrative of the Life of Mrs. Charlotte Charke (Youngest Daughter of Colley Cibber, Esq.)*. Gainesville, Fla.: Scholars' Facsimiles and Reprints, 1969.

———. *An Apology for the Life of Colley Cibber, Written by Himself* (1740). Ed. Robert W. Lowe. 2 vols. London: John C. Nimmo, 1889.

———. *The Careless Husband*. Ed. William Worthen Appleton. Lincoln: University of Nebraska Press, 1966.

———. *The Plays of Colley Cibber*. Ed. Timothy J. Viator and William J. Burling. Madison, N.J.: Fairleigh Dickinson University Press, 2001.

———. *The Provoked Husband* (1728). Ed. Peter Dixon. Lincoln: University of Nebraska Press, 1973.

———. *The Rival Queans, with the Humours of Alexander the Great*. Ed. William Moore Peterson. Lake Erie College Studies 5. Painesville, Ohio: Lake Erie College Press, 1965.

Clark, Peter. *British Clubs and Societies: The Origins of an Associational World*. Oxford: Oxford University Press, 2000.

Clery, E. J. "Bluestocking 'Feminism' and the Fame Game." *British Journal for Eighteenth-Century Studies* 28 (2005): 273–82.

———. *The Feminization Debate in Eighteenth-Century England: Literature, Commerce and Luxury*. New York: Palgrave Macmillan, 2004.

Clive, Catherine. *The Case of Mrs. Clive* (1744). Ed. Richard Frushell. Augustan Reprint Society 159. Los Angeles: William Andrews Clark Memorial Library, UCLA, 1973.

Cohen, Ralph. "Transformation in the *Rape of the Lock*." *Eighteenth-Century Studies* 2, 3 (1989): 205–24.

Cole, Lucinda. "*The London Merchant* and the Institution of Apprenticeship." *Criticism* 37, 1 (Winter 1995): 57–84.

Colley, Linda. *Britons: Forging the Nation 1707–1837*. New Haven, Conn.: Yale University Press, 1992.

Cooke, William. *Memoirs of Charles Macklin, Comedian, with the Dramatic Characters, Manners, Anecdotes, &c., of the Age in Which He Lived; Forming an History of the Stage During Almost the Whole of the Last Century, and a Chronological List of All the Parts Played by Him*. [London: James Asperne; 1804]. New York: B. Blom, 1972.

Copeland, Edward. *Women Writing About Money: Women's Fiction in England, 1790–1820*. Cambridge: Cambridge University Press, 1995.

Cotton, Nancy. *Women Playwrights in England, c. 1363 to 1750*. Lewisburg, Pa.: Bucknell University Press, 1980.

Crean, Patrick J. "The London 'Prentice." *Notes and Queries* 163, 20 (12 November 1932): 346–47.

———. "The Life and Times of Kitty Clive." Dissertation, University of London, 1933.

Crouch, Kimberly. "Public Life of Actresses: Prostitutes or Ladies?" In *Gender in Eighteenth-Century England Roles, Representations, and Responsibilities*, ed. Hannah Barker and Elaine Chalus. London: Longman, 1997. 58–78.

Daly, Augustin. *Woffington: A Tribute to the Actress and the Woman*. 2nd ed. Troy, N.Y.: Nims and Knight, 1891.
Danchin, Pierre, ed. *The Prologues and Epilogues of the Restoration 1660–1700: A Complete Edition*. 4 vols. in 7. Nancy: Presses Université de Nancy II, 1981, pt.. 1. *1660–1676* (2 v.); pt. 2. *1677–1690* (2 v.); pt. 3. *1691–1700* (2 v.); pt. 4. Indexes, with addenda and corrigenda.
———, ed. *The Prologues and Epilogues of the Eighteenth Century: A Complete Edition*. 6 vols. Nancy: Presses Universitaires de Nancy, 1990– , pt. 1. *1701–1720* (2 v.); pt 2, *1721–1737* (2 v.); pt. 3, *1737–1760* (2 v.)
David, Deirdre. *Fanny Kemble: A Performed Life*. Philadelphia: University of Pennsylvania Press, 2007.
Davies, Kate. *Catherine Macaulay and Mercy Otis Warren: The Revolutionary Atlantic and the Politics of Gender*. Oxford: Oxford University Press, 2005.
Davis, Tracy C., *Actresses as Working Women: Their Social Identity in Victorian Culture*. London: Routledge, 1991.
Davis, Tracy C., and Thomas Postlewait, eds. *Theatricality*. Cambridge: Cambridge University Press, 2003.
Davis, Vivian. "Colley Cibber and the Laughter of Tragedy." Unpublished paper.
Diamond, Elin. "Brechtian Theory/Feminist Theory: Toward a Gestic Feminist Criticism." *Drama Review* 32, 1 (1988): 82–94.
———. *Unmaking Mimesis: Essays on Feminism and Theatre*. New York: Routledge, 1997.
Dibdin, Charles. *A Complete History of the English Stage*. 5 vols. London, 1800.
Dimock, Wai Chee, "Introduction: Genres as Fields of Knowledge." *Special Topic: Remapping Genre. PMLA* 122, 5 (2007): 1377–88.
Dircks, Phyllis T. "Garrick's Fail-Safe Musical Venture, *A Peep Behind the Curtain*, an English Burletta, " In *The Stage and the Page: London's "Whole Show" in the Eighteenth-Century Theatre*, ed. George Winchester Stone, Jr. Berkeley: University of California Press, 1981, 136–47.
Dobson, Michael. *The Making of the National Poet: Shakespeare, Adaptation and Authorship, 1660–1769*. Oxford: Clarendon Press, 1992.
Dolan, Jill Susan. *The Feminist Spectator as Critic*. Ann Arbor, Mich.: UMI Research Press, 1988.
Donkin, Ellen. "Mrs. Siddons Looks Back in Anger: Feminist Historiography for Eighteenth-Century British Theater." In *Critical Theory and Performance*, ed. Janelle G. Reinelt and Joseph R. Roach, Ann Arbor: University of Michigan Press, 1992. 276–90.
———. *Getting into the Act: Women Playwrights in London, 1776–1829*. New York: Routledge, 1995.
———. "The Paper War of Hannah Cowley and Hannah More. In *Curtain Calls: British and American Women and the Theater, 1660–1820*, ed. Mary Anne Schofield and Cecilia Macheski. Athens: Ohio University Press, 1991. 143–62.
Downie, J. A. "Public and Private: The Myth of the Bourgeois Public Sphere." In *A Con-

cise Companion to the Restoration and Eighteenth Century, ed. Cynthia Wall. Malden, Mass.: Blackwell, 2005. 58–79.

Dugaw, Dianne, ed. *The Female Soldier; or, the Surprising Life and Adventures of Hannah Snell (1750)*. Augustan Reprint Society No. 257. Los Angeles: Williams Andrews Clark Library, 1989.

———. *Warrior Women and Popular Balladry, 1650–1850*. Cambridge: Cambridge University Press, 1989.

Dunbar, Janet. *Peg Woffington and Her World*. London: Heinemann, 1968.

Eger, Elizabeth. "Representing Culture: 'The Nine Living Muses of Great Britain' (1779)." In *Women, Writing and the Public Sphere, 1700–1830*, ed. Elizabeth Eger, Charlotte Grant, Cliona Gallchoir, and Penny Warburton. Cambridge: Cambridge University Press, 2001, 104–3.

Erickson, Amy Louise. *Women and Property in Early Modern England*. London: Routledge, 1993.

———. "Coverture and Capitalism." *History Workshop Journal* 59, 1 (2005): 1–16.

Ezell, Margaret J. M. *Social Authorship and the Advent of Print*. Baltimore: Johns Hopkins University Press, 1999.

Farquhar, George. *The Complete Works of George Farquhar*. Ed. Charles Stonehill. 2 vols. London: Nonesuch Press, 1930.

———. *The Recruiting Officer*. Ed Peter Dixon. Manchester: University of Manchester Press, 1986.

———. *The Works of George Farquhar*. Ed. Shirley Strum Kenny. 2 vols. Oxford: Clarendon Press, 1988.

The Female Tatler. Ed. Fidelis Morgan. London: J.M. Dent, 1992.

Féral, Josette. "Foreword." *SubStance* 31, 2/3 (2002): 3–13.

Festa, Lynn. "Cosmetic Differences, or the Changing Faces of England and France." *Studies in Eighteenth-Century Culture* 34 (Spring 2005): 25–54.

The Female Tatler. Ed. Fidelis Morgan. London: J.M. Dent, 1992.

Fielding, Henry. *The Complete Works of Henry Fielding, Esq*. Ed. William Ernest Henley. 16 vols. New York: Croscup and Sterling, 1902.

Fineman, Joel. "The History of the Anecdote." In *The New Historicism*, ed. H. Aram Veeser. New York: Routledge, 1989. 49–76.

Fisher, Judith. "'The Quality of Mercy' in the Eighteenth Century; or, Kitty Clive's Portia." *Restoration and Eighteenth-Century Theatre Research* 2nd ser. 14, 1 (Summer 1999): 19–42.

Fitzgerald, Percy. *The Life of Mrs. Catherine Clive, with an Account of Her Adventures On and Off the Stage, a Round of Her Characters, Together with Her Correspondence*. (1888). New York: B. Blom, 1971.

———. *A New History of the English Stage, from the Restoration to the Liberty of the Theatres, in Connection with the Patent Houses*. 2 vols. London: Tinsley Brothers, 1882.

Fone, Bryne R. S. "Preface." *Bell's British Theatre, 1776–1781*. Ed. John Bell. 21 vols. New York: AMS Press, 1977.

Freeburn, Robert D. "Charles II, The Theatre Patentees and the Actor's Nursery." *Theatre Notebook* 48, 3 (1994): 148–56.
Freeman, Lisa. "Introduction" to *Sarah Siddons*. Ed. Lisa Freeman, vol. 2 in *Lives of Shakespearian Actors: Edmund Kean, Sarah Siddons, and Harriet Smithson by their Contemporaries*. 3 vols. London: Pickering and Chatto, 2009, vii–xxii.
———. *Character's Theater: Genre and Identity on the Eighteenth-Century English Stage* Philadelphia: University of Pennsylvania Press, 2002.
———. "The Cultural Politics of Anti-Theatricality: The Case of John Home's *Douglas*." *ECTI* 43 (2002): 210–35.
———. "Introduction." *Lives of Shakespearean Actors II*, vol. 2, *Sarah Siddons*, ed. Lisa Freeman. London: Pickering and Chatto, 2009.
Friedman-Romell, Beth H. "Breaking the Code: Toward a Reception Theory of Theatrical Cross-Dressing in Eighteenth-Century London." *Theatre Journal* 47 (1995): 459–79.
Frushell, Richard. "An Edition of the Afterpieces of Kitty Clive." Dissertation, Duquesne University, 1968.
———. "Kitty Clive as Dramatist." *Durham University Journal* 63, 2 n.s.32.2 (March 1971): 125–32.
———. "The Textual Relationship and Biographical Significance of Two Petite Pieces by Mrs. Catherine (Kitty) Clive." *Restoration and Eighteenth-Century Theatre Research* 9, 1 (May 1970): 51–58.
Fumerton, Patricia. "Introduction: A New New Historicism." In *Renaissance Culture and the Everyday*, ed. Patricia Fumerton and Simon Hunt. Philadelphia: University of Pennsylvania Press, 1999, 1–17.
Fyvie, John. *Comedy Queens of the Georgian Era*. London: Archibald Constable, 1906.
Gale, Maggie B., and John Stokes, eds. *The Cambridge Companion to the Actress*. Cambridge: Cambridge University Press, 2007.
Gallagher, Catherine. *Nobody's Story: The Vanishing Acts of Women Writers in the Marketplace, 1670–1820*. Berkeley: University of California Press, 1995.
———. "Who Was That Masked Woman? The Prostitute and the Playwright in the Comedies of Aphra Behn." *Women's Studies* 15 (1988): 23–42.
Garber, Marjorie. *Vested Interests: Cross-Dressing and Cultural Anxiety*. New York: Routledge, 1992.
Garrick, David. *The Letters of David Garrick*. Ed. David M. Little and George M. Kahrl. 3 vols. Cambridge, Mass.: Belknp Press of Harvard University Press, 1963.
———. *The Plays of David Garrick*. Ed. Harry William Pedicord and Fredrick Louis Bergmann. 7 vols. Carbondale: Southern Illinois University Press, 1980.
Gilder, Rosamond. *Enter the Actress: The First Women in the Theater*. Boston: Houghton Mifflin, 1931.
Greenblatt, Stephen. *Shakespearean Negotiations: The Circulation of Social Energy in Renaissance England*. Berkeley: University of California Press, 1988.
Greene, Jody. *The Trouble with Ownership: Literary Property and Authorial Liability in England, 1660–1730*. Philadelphia: University of Pennsylvania Press, 2005.

Greene, John C., and Gladys L. H. Clark. *The Dublin Stage, 1720–1745: A Calendar of Plays, Entertainments, and Afterpieces*. Bethlehem, Pa.: Lehigh University Press, 1993.

Griffin, Dustin H. *Literary Patronage in England, 1650–1800*. Cambridge: Cambridge University Press, 1996.

Griffith, Elizabeth. *The Delicate Distress, a Novel in Letters*. 1769. Ed. Cynthia Booth Ricciardi and Susan Staves. Lexington: University Press of Kentucky, 1997.

Guest, Harriet. "Bluestocking Feminism." In *Reconsidering the Bluestockings*, ed. Nicole Pohl and Betty A. Schellenberg. San Marino, Calif.: Huntington Library, 2003, 59–80.

———. *Small Change: Women, Learning, Patriotism, 1750–1810*. Chicago: University of Chicago Press, 2000.

Habermas, Jürgen. *The Structural Transformation of the Public Sphere: An Inquiry into a Category of Bourgeois Society*. 1962. Trans. Thomas Burger. Cambridge: Polity Press, 1989.

Hall, Stuart. "Thinking the Diaspora: Home-thoughts from Abroad." In *Postcolonialisms: An Anthology of Cultural Theory*. Ed. Gaurav Desai and Supriya Nair. New Brunswick, N.J.: Rutgers University Press, 2005, 543–60.

Hampshire, Gwen, ed. *Elizabeth Carter, 1717–1806: An Edition of Some Unpublished Letters*. Newark: University of Delaware Press, 2005.

Harley, John. *Music in Purcell's London: The Social Background*. London: Dobson, 1968.

Harris, Jocelyn. "Introduction." In *Samuel Richardson's Published Commentary on Clarissa, 1747–1765*, ed. Thomas Keymer. 3 vols. London: Pickering and Chatto, 1998, 1: lxxii-lxxvi.

Harris, Jonathan Gil. "The New New Historicism's *Wunderkammer* of Objects." *European Journal of English Studies* 4, 2 (2000): 111–24.

Harris, Jonathan Gil, and Natasha Korda, eds. *Staged Properties in Early Modern English Drama*. Ithaca, N.Y.: Cornell University Press, 2002.

Harris, Susan Cannon. "Mixed Marriage: Sheridan, Macklin, and the Hybrid Audience." In *Players, Playwrights, Playhouses: Investigating Performance, 1660–1800*, ed. Michael Cordner and Peter Holland. Basingstoke: Palgrave Macmillan, 2007, 189–212.

———. "Outside the Box: The Female Spectator, *The Fair Penitent*, and the Kelly Riots of 1747." *Theatre Journal* 57, 1 (2005): 33–55.

———. "The Tender Mother and the Faithful Wife: Theater, Charity, and Female Subjectivity in Eighteenth-Century Ireland." *Eire-Ireland: A Journal of Irish Studies* 37, 3–4 (Fall–Winter 2002): 207–30.

Heller, Deborah. "Subjectivity Unbound: Elizabeth Vesey as the Sylph in Bluestocking Correspondence." In *Reconsidering the Bluestockings*, ed. Nicole Pohl and Betty A. Schellenberg. San Marino, Calif.: Huntington Library, 2003. 215–34.

Hesse, Carla. *The Other Enlightenment: How French Women Became Modern*. Princeton, N.J.: Princeton University Press, 2001.

Highfill, Philip H., Jr., Kalman A. Burnim, and Edward A. Langhans. *A Biographical Dictionary of Actors, Actresses, Musicians, Dancers, Managers, and Other Stage Personnel in London, 1660–1800*. 16 vols. Carbondale: Southern Illinois University Press, 1973–93.

Hill, Aaron, and William Popple. *The Prompter: A Theatrical Paper (1734–1736)*. Selected and ed. William W. Appleton and Kalman A. Burnim. New York: B. Blom, 1966.

Holland, Peter. *The Ornament of Action: Text and Performance in Restoration Comedy*. Cambridge: Cambridge University Press, 1979.

Holland, Peter, and Michael Cordner, eds. *Players, Playwrights, Playhouses: Investigating Performance 1660–1800*. Basingstoke: Palgrave Macmillan, 2007.

Hook, Lucyle, ed. *The Female Wits*. Augustan Reprint Society no. 124. Los Angeles: William Andrews Clark Memorial Library, University of California, 1967.

Howe, Elizabeth. *The First English Actresses: Women and Drama, 1660–1700*. Cambridge: Cambridge University Press, 1992.

Hughes, Leo. *Drama's Patrons; A Study of the Eighteenth-Century London Audience*. Austin: University of Texas Press, 1971.

Hume, Robert. *The Development of English Drama in the Late Seventeenth Century*. Oxford: Clarendon Press, 1976.

———. "Drama and Theatre in the Mid and Later Eighteenth Century." In *The Cambridge History of English Literature, 1660–1780*, ed. John J. Richetti. Cambridge: Cambridge University Press, 2005. 316–39.

———. "The Economics of Culture in London, 1660–1740." *Huntington Library Quarterly* 69, 4 (2006): 487–533.

———. *Henry Fielding and the London Theatre, 1728–1737*. Oxford: Clarendon Press, 1988.

———. "The Origins of the Actor Benefit in London." *Theatre Research International* 9, 2 (1984): 99–111.

———. *The Rakish Stage: Studies in English Drama 1660–1800*. Carbondale: Southern Illinois University Press, 1983.

Hume, Robert, and Judith Milhous. "John Rich's Covent Garden Account Books for 1735–36. *Theatre Survey* 31 (Nov 1990): 200–241.

Inchbald, Elizabeth. *The Diaries of Elizabeth Inchbald*. Ed. Ben P. Robertson. 3 vols. London: Pickering and Chatto, 2007.

Ingrassia, Catherine. *Authorship, Commerce, and Gender in Early Eighteenth-Century England: A Culture of Paper Credit*. Cambridge: Cambridge University Press, 1998.

Jackson, Shannon. "Theatricality's Proper Objects: Genealogies of Performance and Gender Theory." In *Theatricality*, ed. Tracy D. Davis and Thomas Postlewait. Cambridge: Cambridge University Press, 2003. 186–213.

Jankowski, Theodora. "The Development of Middle-Class Identity and the 'Problem' of the 'Gentle' Apprentice." In *Proceedings of the Eleventh Annual Northern Plains Conference on Early British Literature*, ed. Michelle M. Sauer. Minot, N.D: Minot State University Printing Services, 2003.

Johnson, Claudia. *Equivocal Beings: Politics, Gender and Sentimentality in the 1790s*. Chicago: University of Chicago Press, 1995.

Johnson, Samuel. "The Life of Rowe." *The Lives of the Most Eminent English Poets*. Ed. Roger Lonsdale. 4 vols. Oxford: Clarendon Press, 2006.

Joncus, Berta. "Handel at Drury Lane: Ballad Opera and the Production of Kitty Clive." *Journal of the Royal Musical Association* 131, 2 (2006): 179–226.

———. "'His Spirit is in Action Seen': Milton, Mrs. Clive and the Simulacra of the Pastoral in *Comus*." *Eighteenth-Century Music* 2, 1 (2005): 7–40.

Joseph, Betty. "Gendering Time in Globalization: The Belatedness of the Other Woman and Jamaica Kincaid's *Lucy*." *Tulsa Studies in Women's Literature* 21, 1 (2002): 67–83.

Kavenik, Frances M. "Aphra Behn: The Playwright as 'Breeches Part'." In *Curtain Calls: British and American Women and the Theater, 1660–1820*, ed. Mary Anne Schofield and Cecilia Macheski. Athens: Ohio University Press, 1991. 177–92.

Kelly, John Alexander. *German Visitors to English Theaters of the Eighteenth Century*. Princeton, N.J.: Princeton University Press, 1936.

Kennard, Nina A. *Mrs. Siddons*. Boston: Robert Brothers, 1887.

King, Thomas. "'As If (She) Were Made on Purpose to Put the Whole World into Good Humour': Reconstructing the First English Actresses." *Drama Review* 36, 3 (Fall 1992): 78–102.

Kinservik, Matthew J. "Benefit Play Selection at Drury Lane 1729–1769; the Cases of Mrs Cibber, Mrs Clive, and Mrs Pritchard." *Theatre Notebook* 50, 1 (1996): 15–28.

———. "Garrick's Unpublished Epilogue for Catherine Clive's *The Rehearsal: Or, Bays in Petticoats* (1750)." *Études Anglaises* 49, 3 (1996): 320–26.

Klein, Lawrence E. "Gender and the Public/Private Distinction in the Eighteenth Century: Some Questions About Evidence and Analytic Procedure." *Eighteenth-Century Studies* 29, 1 (1996): 97–109.

Knapp, Mary E. *Prologues and Epilogues of the Eighteenth Century*. New Haven, Conn.: Yale University Press, 1961.

Korda, Natasha. "Labours Lost: Women's Work and Early Modern Theatrical Commerce." In *From Script to Stage in Early Modern England*, ed. Peter Holland and Stephen Orgel. Basingstoke: Palgrave Macmillan, 2004. 195–230.

Lafler, Joanne. *The Celebrated Mrs. Oldfield: The Life and Art of an Augustan Actress*. Carbondale: Southern Illinois University Press, 1989.

———. "Theatre and the Female Presence." In *The Cambridge History of British Theatre, 1660–1895*, ed. Joseph Donohue. 3 vols. Cambridge: Cambridge University Press, 2004, 2: 71–89.

Langford, Paul. *A Polite and Commercial People: England 1727–1783*. Oxford: Oxford University Press, 1998.

Langhans, Edward A. "Tough Actresses to Follow." In *Curtain Calls: British and American Women and the Theater, 1660–1820*, ed. Mary Anne Schofield and Cecilia Macheski. Athens: Ohio University Press, 1991, 3–17.

Lee, Nathaniel. *The Rival Queens* (1677). Ed. P. F. Vernon. Lincoln: University of Nebraska Press, 1970.

Lerenbaum, Miriam. "The Nine Living Muses of Great Britain." In *Proceedings of the American Society for Eighteenth-Century Studies*. Carbondale: Southern Illinois University Press, 1979.

Lewis, Nancy Eloise. "Nathaniel Lee's *The Rival Queens*: A Study of Dramatic Taste and Technique in the Restoration." Dissertation, Ohio State University, 1957.

The Life of Miss Anne Catley, Celebrated Singing Performer of the Last Century. London, 1888.

The Life of Mrs. Abington (Formerly Miss Barton) Celebrated Comic Actress, by the Editor of the "Life of Quinn." London: Reader, 1888.

Little, David, and George Kahrl, eds. *Letters of David Garrick.* 3 vols. Cambridge, Mass.: Belknap Press of Harvard University Press, 1963.

Lloyd, David. *Ireland After History.* Cork: Cork University Press with Field Day, 1999.

Locke, John. *Two Treatises of Government.* Ed. Peter Laslett. Cambridge: Cambridge University Press, 1988.

Lonsdale, Roger, ed. *The Lives of the Most Eminent English Poets.* 4 vols. Oxford: Clarendon Press, 2006.

Lowenthal, Cynthia. *Performing Identities on the Restoration Stage.* Carbondale: Southern Illinois University Press, 2003.

Lynch, Deirdre Shauna. *The Economy of Character: Novels, Market Culture, and the Business of Inner Meaning.* Chicago: University of Chicago Press, 1998.

Mackintosh, Iain, and Geoffrey Ashton. *The Georgian Playhouse: Actors, Artists, Audiences, and Architecture, 1730–1830.* London: Arts Council of Great Britain, 1975.

Macpherson. C. B. *The Political Theory of Possessive Individualism: Hobbes to Locke.* Oxford: Oxford University Press, 1988.

Mandell, Laura. *Misogynous Economies: The Business of Literature in Eighteenth-Century Britain.* Lexington: University Press of Kentucky, 1999.

Mann, David and Susan Garland Mann. *Women Playwrights in England, Ireland, and Scotland, 1660–1823.* Bloomington: Indiana University Press, 1996.

Marsden, Jean I. *Fatal Desire: Women, Sexuality, and the English Stage, 1660–1720.* Ithaca, N.Y.: Cornell University Press, 2006.

Marshall, David. *The Figure of Theater: Shaftesbury, Defoe, Adam Smith and George Eliot.* New York: Columbia University Press, 1986.

Marshall, P. David. *Celebrity and Power: Fame in Contemporary Culture.* Minneapolis: University of Minnesota Press, 1997.

Marx, Karl. *Capital: A Critical Analysis of Capitalist Production.* 1887. Ed. Frederick Engels. New York: International Publishers, 1967.

Maus, Katherine E. "'Playhouse Flesh and Blood': Sexual Ideology and the Restoration Actress." *ELH* 46, 4 (Winter 1979): 597–617.

McClintock, Anne. *Imperial Leather: Race, Gender and Sexuality in the Colonial Context.* London: Routledge, 1995.

McCollum, John I. *The Restoration Stage.* Boston: Houghton Mifflin, 1961.

McCreery, Cindy. *The Satirical Gaze: Prints of Women in Late Eighteenth-Century England.* Oxford: Clarendon Press, 2004.

McDowell, Paula. *Women of Grub Street: Press, Politics, and Gender in the London Literary Marketplace, 1678–1730.* Oxford: Clarendon Press, 1998.

McKenty, David Edward. "The Benefit System in Augustan Drama." Dissertation, University of Pennsylvania, 1966.
McMillin, Scott. "The Sharer and His Boy: Rehearsing Shakespeare's Women." In *From Script to Stage in Early Modern England*, ed. Peter Holland and Stephen Orgel. Basingstoke: Palgrave Macmillan, 2004. 231–45.
Milhous, Judith. *Thomas Betterton and the Management of Lincoln's Inn Fields, 1695–1708*. Carbondale: Southern Illinois University Press, 1979.
———. "United Company Finances, 1682–1692." *Theatre Research International* 7, 1 (Winter 1981/82): 37–53.
———. "Reading Theatre History for Account Books." In *Players, Playwrights, Playhouses: Investigating Performance 1660–1800*, ed. Peter Holland and Michael Cordner. Basingstoke: Palgrave Macmillan, 2007. 101–31.
Milhous, Judith, and Robert D. Hume. "Theatrical Politics at Drury Lane: New Light on Letitia Cross, Jane Rogers, and Anne Oldfield." *Bulletin of Research in the Humanities* 85 (Winter 1982): 412–29.
———. "John Rich's Covent Garden Account Books for 1735–36." *Theatre Survey* 31 (1990): 200–241.
———. "Playwrights' Remuneration in Eighteenth-Century London." *Harvard Library Bulletin* 10, 2–3 (1999): 3–90.
Moody, Jane, and Daniel O'Quinn, eds. *Cambridge Companion to British Theatre, 1730–1830*. Cambridge: Cambridge University Press, 2007.
Morash, Christopher. *A History of Irish Theatre 1601–2000*. Cambridge: Cambridge University Press, 2002.
Morgan, Fidelis, ed. *The Female Tatler.* (1709–10). London: J.M. Dent, 1992.
Munns, Jessica, and Penny Richards, eds. *The Clothes That Wear Us: Essays on Dressing and Transgressing in Eighteenth-Century Culture*. Newark: University of Delaware Press, 1999.
Nash, Mary. *The Provoked Wife: The Life and Times of Susannah Cibber*. Boston: Little, Brown, 1977.
Nettleton, George H., and Arthur E. Case, eds. *British Dramatists from Dryden to Sheridan*, rev. George Winchester Stone, Jr. 2nd ed. Boston: Houghton Miflin, 1969.
Nicholson, Colin. *Writing and the Rise of Finance: Capital Satires of the Early Eighteenth Century*. Cambridge: Cambridge University Press, 1994.
Nicoll, Allardyce. *A History of Early Eighteenth Century Drama 1700–1750*. Cambridge: Cambridge University Press, 1929.
———. *A History of English Drama, 1660–1900*. 6 vols. Cambridge: Cambridge University Press, 1952–59.
———. *A History of Restoration Drama, 1660–1700*. 4th ed. Cambridge: Cambridge University Press, 1952.
Nussbaum, Felicity. "Actresses and the Economics of Celebrity, 1700–1800." In *Theatre and Celebrity in Britain, 1660–2000*, ed. Mary Luckhurst and Jane Moody. New York: Palgrave Macmillan, 2005. 146–68.

———. *The Autobiographical Subject: Gender and Ideology in Eighteenth-Century England.* Baltimore: Johns Hopkins University Press, 1989.

———. *The Limits of the Human: Fictions of Anomaly, Race, and Gender in the Long Eighteenth Century.* Cambridge: Cambridge University Press, 2003.

———. *Torrid Zones: Maternity, Sexuality and Empire in Eighteenth-Century English Narrative.* Baltimore: Johns Hopkins University Press, 1995, repr. 2005.

O'Quinn, Daniel. "Introduction to Wallace's 'The Ton': The Sport of a Theatrical Damnation." http://www.etang.umontreal.ca/bwp1800/essays/oquinn_ton_intro.html, accessed June 14, 2004.

Orgel, Stephen. *Impersonations: The Performance of Gender in Shakespeare's England.* Cambridge: Cambridge University Press, 1996.

Orr, Bridget. *Empire on the English Stage, 1660–1714.* Cambridge: Cambridge University Press, 2001.

Oxford Dictionary of National Biography. Ed. Colin Matthew et al. 60 vols. Oxford: Oxford University Press, 2004.

Pateman, Carole. *The Sexual Contract.* Stanford, Calif.: Stanford University Press, 1988.

Payne, Deborah C. "Reified Object or Emergent Professional? Retheorizing the Restoration Actress." In *Cultural Readings of Restoration and Eighteenth-Century Theater*, ed. J. Douglas Canfield and Deborah Payne. Athens: University of Georgia Press, 1995. 13–38.

Pearce, Charles E. *Polly Peachum: Being the Story of Lavinia Fenton (Duchess of Bolton) and "The Beggar's Opera".* New York: Brentano's, 1913.

Pedicord, Harry William. *The Theatrical Public in the Time of Garrick.* Carbondale: Southern Illinois University Press, 1966.

Perry, Gill. *Spectacular Flirtations: Viewing the Actress in British Art and Theatre, 1768–1820.* New Haven, Conn.: Yale University Press, 2007.

Perry, Ruth. *Novel Relations: The Transformation of Kinship in English Literature and Culture, 1748–1818.* Cambridge: Cambridge University Press, 2004.

Phelan, Peggy. *Unmarked: The Politics of Performance.* London: Routledge, 1993.

Phillips, Nicola. *Women in Business, 1700–1850.* Woodbridge: Boydell Press, 2006.

Pocock, J. G. A. *The Machiavellian Moment: Florentine Political Thought and the Atlantic Republican Tradition.* Princeton, N.J.: Princeton University Press, 1975.

———. *Virtue, Commerce, and History: Essays on Political Thought, Chiefly in the Eighteenth Century.* New York: Cambridge University Press, 1985.

Pointon, Marcia R. *Hanging the Head: Portraiture and Social Formation in Eighteenth-Century England.* New Haven, Conn.: Yale University Press, 1993.

Pope, Alexander. *The Rape of the Lock and Other Poems.* Ed. Geoffrey Tillotson. *Twickenham Edition of the Poems of Alexander Pope.* Gen. ed. John Butt. 11 vols. London: Routledge, 1993.

———. *The Works of Alexander Pope.* Ed. Whitwell Elwin and William John Courthope. 10 vols. New York: Gordian Press, 1967.

Postlewait, Thomas, and Bruce A. McConachie, eds. *Interpreting the Theatrical Past: Essays in the Historiography of Performance.* Iowa City: University of Iowa Press, 1989.

Pratt, Mary Louise. *Imperial Eyes: Studies in Travel Writing and Transculturation.* London: Routledge, 1992.

Prescott, Sarah. *Women, Authorship and Literary Culture, 1690–1740.* Basingstoke: Palgrave Macmillan, 2003.

Pullen, Kirsten. *Actresses and Whores: On Stage and in Society.* Cambridge: Cambridge University Press, 2005.

Ragussis, Michael. "Jews and Other 'Outlandish Englishmen': Ethnic Performance and the Invention of British Identity Under the Georges." *Critical Inquiry* 26 (Summer 2000): 773–97.

Ribeiro, Aileen. "Costuming the Part: A Discourse of Fashion and Fiction in the Image of the Actress in England, 1776–1812." In *Notorious Muse: The Actress in British Art and Culture, 1776–1812*, ed. Robyn Asleson. New Haven, Conn.: Yale University Press, 2003. 104–27.

Richards, Sandra. *The Rise of the English Actress.* London: St. Martin's Press, 1993.

Richardson, Samuel. *The Apprentice's Vade Mecum* (1734) and *A Seasonable Examination* (1735). Intro. Alan D. McKillop. Augustan Reprint Society nos. 169–70. Los Angeles: William Andrews Clark Memorial Library, University of California, 1975.

———. *Pamela, or, Virtue Rewarded.* Ed. Thomas Keymer and Alice Wakely. Oxford: Oxford University Press, 2001.

Ritchie, Fiona. "The Influence of the Female Audience on the Shakespeare Revival of 1736–1738: The Case of the Shakespeare Ladies Club." In *Shakespeare and the Eighteenth Century*, ed. Peter Sabor and Paul Yachnin. Aldershot: Ashgate, 2008. 57–69.

Roach, Joseph. "Celebrity Erotics: Pepys, Performance, and Painted Ladies." *Yale Journal of Criticism* 16, 1 (2003): 211–30.

———. *Cities of the Dead: Circum-Atlantic Performance.* New York: Columbia University Press, 1996.

———. *It.* Ann Arbor: University of Michigan Press, 2007.

———. *The Player's Passion: Studies in the Science of Acting.* Newark: University of Delaware Press, 1985.

Roberts, David. *The Ladies: Female Patronage of Restoration Drama 1660–1700.* Oxford: Clarendon Press, 1989.

Robinson, Mary. *Walsingham, or, The Pupil of Nature* (1797). Ed. Julie Shaffer. Toronto: Broadview, 2003.

Rogers, Pat. "The Breeches Part." In *Sexuality in Eighteenth-Century Britain*, ed. Paul-Gabriel Boucé. Manchester: Manchester University Press, 1982. 244–58.

———. "'Towering Beyond Her Sex': Stature and Sublimity in the Achievement of Sarah Siddons." In *Curtain Calls: British and American Women and the Theater, 1660–1820*, ed. Mary Anne Schofield and Cecilia Macheski. Athens: Ohio University Press, 1991.

Rojek, Chris. *Celebrity.* London: Reaktion Books, 2001.

Romack, Katherine. "Striking the Posture of a Whore: The Bawdy House Riots and the 'Antitheatrical Prejudice'." Unpublished essay.

———. "Women and Representational Practice, 1642–1660." Dissertation, Syracuse University, 2000.

Rose, Mark. *Authors and Owners: The Invention of Copyright*. Cambridge, Mass.: Harvard University Press, 1993.

Rose, Mary Beth. *The Expense of Spirit : Love and Sexuality in English Renaissance Drama*. Ithaca, N.Y.: Cornell University Press, 1988.

Rosenthal, Angela. "Unfolding Gender: Women and the 'Secret' Sign Language of Fans in Hogarth's Work." In *The Other Hogarth: Aesthetics of Difference*, ed. Bernadette Fort and Angela Rosenthal. Princeton, N.J.: Princeton University Press, 2001. 120–41.

———. *Angelica Kauffmann: Art and Sensibility*. Paul Mellon Centre for Studies in British Art. New Haven, Conn.: Yale University Press, 2006.

Rosenthal, Laura. "'Counterfeit Scrubbado': Women Actors in the Restoration." *The Eighteenth Century: Theory and Interpretation* 34 (1993): 3–22.

———. "Entertaining Women: The Actress in the Eighteenth-Century British Theatre and Culture." In *The Cambridge Companion to British Theatre, 1730–1830*, ed. Jane Moody and Daniel O'Quinn. Cambridge: Cambridge University Press, 2007, 159–74.

———. *Infamous Commerce: Prostitution in Eighteenth-Century British Literature and Culture*. Ithaca, N.Y.: Cornell University Press, 2006.

———. *Playwrights and Plagiarists in Early Modern England Gender, Authorship, Literary Property*. Ithaca, N.Y.: Cornell University Press, 1996.

———. "The Sublime, the Beautiful, 'The Siddons'." In *The Clothes That Wear Us: Essays on Dressing and Transgressing in Eighteenth-Century Culture*, ed. Jessica Munns and Penny Richards. Newark: University of Delaware Press, 1999. 56–79.

Rothstein, Eric. *George Farquhar*. New York: Twayne, 1967.

———. *Restoration Tragedy: Form and the Process of Change*. Madison: University of Wisconsin Press, 1967.

Rowe, Nicholas. *The Fair Penitent*. Ed. Malcolm Goldstein. Lincoln: University of Nebraska Press, 1969.

Russell, Gillian. *Women, Sociability, and the Theatre in Georgian London*. Cambridge: Cambridge University Press, 2007.

Sauter, Willmar. *The Theatrical Event: Dynamics of Performance and Perception*. Iowa City: University of Iowa Press, 2000.

Schechner, Richard. *Between Theater and Anthropology*. Philadelphia: University of Pennsylvania Press, 1985.

———. *Performance Theory*, rev. ed. London: Routledge, 2003.

Schellenberg, Betty A. *The Professionalization of Women Writers in Eighteenth-Century Britain*. Cambridge: Cambridge University Press, 2005.

Sennett, Richard. *Authority*. New York: Knopf, 1980.

Schofield, Mary Anne, and Cecilia Macheski, eds. *Curtain Calls: British and American Women and the Theater, 1660–1820*. Athens: Ohio University Press, 1991.

Shaaber, M. A. "A Letter from Mrs. Barry." *Library Chronicle* 16, 2 (Summer 1950): 46–49.
Shapiro, Michael. "The Introduction of Actresses in England: Delay or Defensiveness?" In *Enacting Gender on the English Renaissance Stage*, ed. Viviana Comensoli and Anne Russell. Urbana: University of Illinois Press, 1999. 177–200.
Sheldon, Esther K. *Thomas Sheridan of Smock-Alley; Recording His Life as Actor and Theater Manager in Both Dublin and London, and Including a Smock-Alley Calendar for the Years of His Management.* Princeton, N.J.: Princeton University Press, 1967.
Sheridan, Frances. *The Plays of Frances Sheridan.* Ed. Robert Hogan and Jerry C. Beasley. Newark: University of Delaware Press, 1984.
Shevelow, Kathryn. *Charlotte: Being a True Account of an Actress's Flamboyant Adventures in Eighteenth-Century London's Wild and Wicked Theatrical World.* New York: Henry Holt, 2005.
Slowey, Desmond. *The Radicalization of Irish Drama, 1600–1900: The Rise and Fall of the Ascendancy Theatre.* Dublin: Irish Academic Press, 2008.
Smallwood, Angela. "Women and the Theatre." In *Women and Literature in Britain, 1700–1800*, ed. Vivien Jones. Cambridge: Cambridge University Press, 2000. 238–62.
Smith, John Harrington. "Shadwell, the Ladies, and the Change in Comedy." *Modern Philology* 46 (1948): 22–33.
Snell, K. D. M. *Annals of the Labouring Poor: Social Change and Agrarian England, 1660–1900.* Cambridge: Cambridge University Press, 1985.
Sofer, Andrew. *The Stage Life of Props.* Ann Arbor: University of Michigan Press, 2003.
Solomon, Diana. "Tragic Play, Bawdy Epilogue? In *Prologues, Epilogues, Curtain-Raisers, and Afterpieces: The Rest of the Eighteenth-Century London Stage*, ed. Daniel J. Ennis and Judith B. Slagle. Newark: University of Delaware Press, 2007. 155–78.
The Spectator. Ed. Donald F. Bond. 5 vols. Oxford: Clarendon Press, 1965.
Stallybrass, Peter. "Travestism and the 'Body Beneath': Speculating on the Boy Actor." In *Erotic Politics: Desire on the Renaissance Stage*, ed. Susan Zimmerman. New York: Routledge, 1992. 64–83.
Stanton, Judith Phillips. "'This New-Found Path Attempting': Women Dramatists in England, 1660–1800." In *Curtain Calls: British and American Women and the Theater, 1660–1820*, ed. Mary Anne Schofield and Cecilia Macheski. Athens: Ohio University Press, 1991, 325–54.
Staves, Susan. *Married Women's Separate Property in England, 1660–1833.* Cambridge, Mass.: Harvard University Press, 1990.
———. "Tragedy." In *The Cambridge Companion to British Theatre, 1730–1830*, ed. Jane Moody and Daniel O'Quinn. Cambridge: Cambridge University Press, 2007, 87–102.
Steele, Richard. *The Theatre.* Ed. John Loftis. Oxford: Clarendon Press, 1962.
Stern, Tiffany. *Rehearsal from Shakespeare to Sheridan.* Oxford: Clarendon Press, 2000.
Stockwell, La Tourette. *Dublin Theatres and Theatre Customs, 1637–1820.* Kingsport, Tenn.: Kingsport Press, 1938.
Stone, George Winchester, Jr., and George M. Kahrl. *David Garrick: A Critical Biography.* Carbondale: Southern Illinois University Press, 1979.

Straub, Kristina. *Sexual Suspects: Eighteenth-Century Players and Sexual Ideology*. Princeton, N.J.: Princeton University Press, 1992.
Swift, Jonathan. *Jonathan Swift: The Complete Poems*. Ed. Pat Rogers. London: Penguin, 1983.
Taylor, Diana. *The Archive and the Repertoire: Performing Cultural Memory in the Americas*. Durham, N.C.: Duke University Press, 2003.
———. "Remapping Genre through Performance: From 'American' to 'Hemispheric' Studies." *Special Topic: Remapping Genre*, PMLA 122, 5 (October 2007): 1416–30.
Taylor, Thomas. *The Great Actors of 1775*. s.l., 1863.
Thomson, Peter. "Acting and Actors from Garrick to Kean." In *The Cambridge Companion to British Theatre, 1730–1830*, ed. Jane Moody and Danny O'Quinn. Cambridge: Cambridge University Press, 2007, 3–19.
Thompson, James. *Models of Value: Eighteenth-Century Political Economy and the Novel*. Durham, N.C.: Duke University Press, 1996.
Tillyard, Stella. "Celebrity in 18th-Century London," *History Today* 55 (June 2005): 20–27.
Todd, Janet. *The Secret Life of Aphra Behn*. New Brunswick, N.J.: Rutgers University Press, 1997.
Tomalin, Claire. *Mrs Jordan's Profession: The Story of a Great Actress and a Future King*. London: Viking, 1994.
Tomlinson, Sophie. *Women on Stage in Stuart Drama*. Cambridge: Cambridge University Press, 2005.
Troubridge, St Vincent. *The Benefit System in the British Theatre*. London: Society for Theatre Research, 1967.
Turner, Cheryl. *Living by the Pen: Women Writers in the Eighteenth Century*. London: Routledge, 1992.
Turner, Victor Witter. *The Forest of Symbols; Aspects of Ndembu Ritual*. Ithaca, N.Y..: Cornell University Press, 1967.
Utter, Robert Palfrey and Gwendolyn Bridges Needham. *Pamela's Daughters*. New York: Macmillan, 1936.
Van Lennep, William. "The Life and Works of Nathaniel Lee . . a Study of the Sources." Dissertation, Harvard University, 1933.
Van Lennep, William, Emmett L. Avery, Arthur H. Scouten, George Winchester Stone, Jr., and Charles Beecher Hogan, eds. *The London Stage 1660–1800: A Calendar of Plays, Entertainments and Afterpieces*. 5 pts. in 11 vols. Carbondale: Southern Illinois University Press, 1960–68.
Vernon, P. F. See Lee, Nathaniel.
Viator, Timothy J. and William J. Burling. See Cibber, Colley.
Vickery, Amanda. "Golden Age to Separate Spheres? A Review of the Categories and Chronology of English Women's History." *Historical Journal* 36, 2 (1993): 383–414.
Voskuil, Lynn M. *Acting Naturally: Victorian Theatricality and Authenticity*. Charlottesville: University of Virginia Press, 2004.
Wahrman, Dror. *The Making of the Modern Self: Identity and Culture in Eighteenth-Century England*. New Haven, Conn.: Yale University Press, 2004.

Walpole, Horace. *The Yale Edition of Horace Walpole's Correspondence*. Ed. W. S. Lewis. 48 vols. in 49. New Haven, Conn.: Yale University Press, 1937–83.
Wanko, Cheryl. "Colley Cibber's *The Rival Queans*: A New Consideration." *Restoration and Eighteenth-Century Theatre Research*, 2nd ser. 3, 2 (1988): 38–52.
———. "Contracts for Two Drury Lane Actresses in 1822." *Harvard Library Bulletin* ser. 2, 5 (1994): 53–67.
———. *Roles of Authority: Thespian Biography and Celebrity in Eighteenth-Century Britain*. Lubbock: Texas Tech University Press, 2003.
Weimann, Robert. *Author's Pen and Actor's Voice: Playing and Writing in Shakespeare's Theatre*. Ed. Helen Higbee and William West. Cambridge: Cambridge University Press, 2000.
———. *Shakespeare and the Popular Tradition in the Theater: Studies in the Social Dimension of Dramatic Form and Function*. Baltimore: Johns Hopkins University Press, 1987.
West, Shearer. "The Public and Private Roles of Sarah Siddons." In *A Passion for Performance: Sarah Siddons and Her Portraitists*, ed. Robyn Asleson. Los Angeles: J. Paul Getty Museum, 1999. 1–39.
Wilson, John Harold. *All the King's Ladies: Actresses of the Restoration*. Chicago: University of Chicago Press, 1958.
Wilson, Kathleen. "Rowe's *Fair Penitent* as Global History: Or, A Diversionary Voyage to New South Wales." *Eighteenth-Century Studies* 41, 2 (2008): 231–51.
———. *The Sense of the People: Politics, Culture and Imperialism in England, 1715–1785*. New York: Cambridge University Press, 1998.
Wilson, Michael S. "The 'Incomparable' Siddons as Reynolds's Muse: Art and Ideology on the British Stage." In *So Rich a Tapestry: The Sister Arts and Cultural Studies*, ed. Ann Hurley and Kate Greenspan. Lewisburg, Pa.: Bucknell University Press, 1995.
Young, Edward. *Love of Fame, the Universal Passion: In Seven Characteristical Satires*. In *Poetical Works of Edward Young*. 1844. Westport, Conn.: Greenwood Press, 1970.
Zarrilli, Phillip B. "Toward a Phenomenological Model of the Actor's Embodied Modes of Experience." *Theatre Journal* 56, 4 (2004): 653–66.

Index

Page numbers in *italics* represent illustrations.

Abington, Frances, 9, 226–64; as Aurelia in *The Twin Rivals*, 242, *243*; as Belinda in *Rape of the Lock*, 240–41; benefit performances, 53–54; and Bluestockings, 227–28, 274; card-playing, 248, 332–33n61; and consumerism, 252; Dublin career, 226–27, 231; epilogues and significant roles, 45, *232*, 236–58, *243*, *251*, *256*; as Estifania in *Rule a Wife and Have a Wife*, 250–52, *251*; and family income, 48; and Garrick, 53–54, 228, 236–37, 248, 250, 258–64, 329n9; as Lady Bab in *Maid of the Oaks*, 231, *232*, 246–49, 252–57, 261; material femininity, 230–31, 246–49, 264, 329n5; and millinery, 228–29, 237–38; nickname "Nosegay Fan," *232*, 248, 330n26; and ornamental pins, 237–41; portraits, *262*, *266*, 333n69; and prostitution rumors, 228; self-styled interiority, 230–31, 236–37, 244, 264; social mobility, 227–28; and stage accessories, 57–58, 231, 237–42, *243*, 250–52, *251*; and stage costuming, 57–58, 228–36, 252; in *The Sultan*, 248–49, 252–58, 333n70; trademark "Abington cap," 231; as Widow Bellmour in *The Way to Keep Him*, 231, 244–46; and women's rights, 248–50, 257–58
Abington, James, 226
The Adventures of a Rupee, 234
Aesop, 167
afterpieces, 11, 41, 178–82, 184–88
Agnew, Jean-Christophe, 62–63, 134, 311n52
Alexander the Great, A Tragedy; with Alterations, 74
Alexander the Great (opera), 70
Alfred, A Masque, 177
Alleyn, Edward, 7
All for Love, 62, 73, 83, 218, 235
Alzira, 55
The Ambitious Step-Mother, 266, 269
Ambross, Miss E., 282
The Amorous Widow; or, The Wanton Wife, 58
Amory, Thomas, 113
Andreini, Isabella, 33
Andrews, Miles Peter, 252
The Anecdotes of the Late Samuel Johnson (Piozzi), 279
Anne, Queen, 140, 156
An Apology for the Life of Colley Cibber, 82, 86, 101, 132, 304n60
An Apology for the Life of George Anne Bellamy, 61, 92, 94, 114–18, 121
The Apprentice, 40–41, 293n37
The Apprentice's Vade Mecum (Richardson), 38
apprentice system, 34–42, 291nn11, 13–14
Archenholz, William, 134
Argyll Rooms, 228
aristocracy: lessening power of, 13; and patronage, 46–47, 54–56, 117–18, 135–37, 140; and scandalous behavior/social decorum, 329n8. *See also* patronage system
Arminius, 177
Armstrong, Nancy, 63, 288n40
Art and Nature, 176

366 INDEX

The Astrologer, 205, 207
audiences, 45, 122–50, 130–34; competition with actresses, 124–26; and cross-dressed performances, 196–98, 214, 218, 220, 223–25, 327n75; and earthy allusions, 136, 138–39; engaging with, 45, 126–27; and epilogues, 20–21, 127, 236; and freedom of expression, 131–33; and full collaborative assembly, 123–34, 309nn28–29; and moral reform, 135–36, 138–39, 310nn43–44; and "public intimacy" of actresses, 16–17, 45, 59–60, 64, 288n34; and relationship to time, 62, 299n5; revising of plays, 127; and she-tragedies, 139–40; and stage as visual spectacle, 130–31, 309nn26–27; and stage costuming, 235–36, 242–44; and theater seating, 20–21, 128–30, 133, 289n43; unruliness, 124, 127–28, 130–34; and women's taste, 138. *See also* patronage system
Aungier Street Theatre (Dublin), 147
Authentick Memoirs of the Life of that celebrated Actress Mrs. Ann Oldfield, 101–4, 111
The Author's Farce, 177
"The Author Written by a Lady Spoken by Mrs. Clive," 128
Aylesbury, Lady, 56

Backscheider, Paula, 15
Baddeley, Sophia, 144, 246, 272–73, 281
Baillie, Joanna, 277
Balibar, Etienne, 160
Ballard, George, 113
Banks, John, 71, 301n27
Barbauld, Anna Laetitia (Aikin), 274
Barker, Jane, 101
Barrell, John, 14
Barrie, Robert, 291n11
Barry, Ann Spranger, 210, *211*, 260–61, 266
Barry, Elizabeth, 49, 151; as apprentice, 35, 37; and celebrity, 31; earnings, 44, 48, 53, 55, 297n79; and patronage, 46, 147; as Roxana in *The Rival Queens*, 76–80; and she-tragedies, 71–72, 222; stage clothing, 58
Barry, Spranger, 6, 70–71
Batchelor, Jennie, 238, 331n38
Battle of the Boyne (1690), 156
The Beaux Stratagem, 99, 103, 130, 142, 226
Beefsteak Club, 34, 154–56, 201, 204
The Beggar's Opera, 15, 67; Abington's role, 231; Clive's role, 58–59, 156, 162, 181, 186–87; Fenton's role, 98; requests for, 142; Woffington's role, 191, 202
The Beggar's Pantomime; or, the Contending Columbine, 59, 163
Behn, Aphra, 10, 18, 98, 136
Bell, John, 265
Bellamy, George Anne, 9; benefit performances, 53–56; and Garrick, 3; and interiority effect, 116; mentoring of other actresses, 38; patronage by ladies of quality, 46–47, 56, 117–18, 144–45, 148–50, 235–36; political activities, 117; popularity in grading scales, 6; possession of roles, 161, 315n26; pregnancy and childbirth, 49; and *The Rival Queens*, 70, 80–81, 303n50; and rivalries, 58, 70, 80–81, 303n50; stage costuming, 80–81, 229–30, 235–36; theatrical memoir, 61, 92, 94, 114–18, 121; and victimization, 114–18; and virtue, 118
Bell's British Theatre, 265–66, 267–70, 334n3
Bell Tavern, 34, 156
benefit performances, 52–56, 297n81; competition over, 53–54; earnings from, 50, 52–56; and patronage, 54–56; and stage seating, 53, 130, 133–34; and ticket sales, 52–55
Benjamin, Walter, 239
Betterton, Mary, 38
Betterton, Thomas, 6, 37, 44, 58, 68, 79, 95
Bhabha, Homi, 206
Bickerstaff, Isaac, 11, 89, 182, 257
Bicknell, Alexander, 115
Biographium Faemineum: The Female Worthies (Amory), 113
Blau, Herbert, 79–80
Bluestockings: and celebrity actresses, 227–28, 272–77; and exemplary virtue, 116–17, 273–78, 335n12; and *The Nine Living Muses*, 274–76, *275*
Boaden, James, 3–4, 52, 119–20, 159, 242, 244, 279–80, 283
bodkins, 240
A Bold Stroke for a Wife, 143
Bonduca, 154
bonesetting trade, 124–26
Booth, Barton, 101
Bordoni, Faustina, 86–88
Boswell, James, 22, 201
Boutell, Elizabeth, 79
boy actors: and apprentice system, 34–36, 291n11; and Cibber's *The Rival Queans*, 75–76; skirts roles, 33–36, 196

Bracegirdle, Anne, 45, 101, 151; as apprentice, 35, 37; charitable acts, 56; earnings, 48, 51; and rivalries, 58; and she-tragedies, 71–72, 222
Bratton, Jacky, 285n12
The Brave Irishman; or Captain O'Blunder, 183–84
breeches roles, 75–76, 193, 195–98, 205–13, 323n20, 326n57; *The Rival Queens* and gender ambiguity, 75–76; Woffington's, 195–98, 205–13, 323n20. *See also* cross-dressing
Brewer, John, 13
British empire: *The Contre Temps* and metaphor of imperial rivalry, 86–88; and Orientalism, 85–86, 304n57; and *The Rival Queens*, 85–90
The British Theatre (1808), 265
Brooke, Frances, 277–78
Brown, John, 205
Brown, Laura, 72, 301n29
Brown, Wendy, 299n5
Buck, Anne, 326n57
Burbage, Richard, 7
Burgoyne, John, 261
Burke, Helen, 320n98
burlettas, 171, 317n56
Burney, Frances, 33, 49, 64, 274, 277
Burnim, Kalman A., 334n3
Bush-Bailey, Gilli, 10
The Busy Body, 50, 142, 156
Butler, Judith, 24–25, 290n59

Calcraft, Thomas, 115
Calisto, 123
La Calprenède, 66
Campbell, Dr., 274
Campbell, Thomas, 32
Campbell-Orr, Clarissa, 329n8
Campion, Mary Anne, 104
Capital (Marx), 234–35
The Capricious Lady, 249–50, 333n64
The Careless Husband, 45, 109–11, 142–43, 156, 166
Carroll, Susannah, 76
Carter, Elizabeth, 144, 274, 275–76
Case, Sue-Ellen, 193, 290n59
The Case of Mrs. Clive submitted to the Publick, 160, 162, 164–66, 182
Castle, Terry, 300n19
Castlemaine, Lady, 75
Catholicism: Irish, 200–204, 207, 325n43, 326n62; Papal Jubilee, 219, 327n79; and Woffington, 203–4, 207, 213, 219, 223
Catley, Ann, 36, 52, 57, 233, 282
Cavendish sisters, 136
Cecilia (Burney), 49
celebrity: and actresses' earning power, 44, 47–60, 296nn64–66, 297n79; cult of celebrity, 12–15; economics of, 31–60; and gossip, 16–17; and interiority effect, 19–22; negative effects, 44–45; and performative property, 23, 159–63; and print culture, 13, 14–15, 22; and public/private sphere, 13–15; and social class instability, 42–43, 47–49, 111, 156–58, 295n56. *See also* celebrity actresses
celebrity actresses: and agency, 17–18, 24–25; and *Bell's British Theatre*, 265–66, 267–70; and Bluestockings, 227–28, 272–77; charitable acts, 56–57; competition between, 58–59, 61–62, 70, 80–81, 86–88; and cult of celebrity, 12–15; early paths into theater, 34; earning power, 44, 47–60, 295n58, 296nn64–66, 297n79; economic power and influence, 17–18, 23, 51–52, 297nn79–80; and exceptional virtue, 100, 104–6, 112, 116–18, 271–84; fetishized as commodities, 45, 57–58, 230–31, 234–35, 244, 330n31; fictional actress characters, 64–65; and "interiority effect," 19–22, 45, 244, 264, 271, 288n41; and performative identity, 18–23, 45, 63–64, 152, 171–72, 244, 264, 271, 288n41; and political consciousness, 117, 156, 248–49, 257–58, 271–72, 313n11, 335n6, 335n8; and possession of roles, 152, 161–63; and property ownership, 22–23, 159–63, 294n54, 314n22, 315nn28–30; prostitution rumors, 16–17, 36, 42–43, 46, 63–64, 98–99, 218, 228, 282, 293n43; and proto-feminism, 117, 175–76, 248–50, 257–58, 271–72; and "public intimacy," 16–17, 45, 59–60, 64, 288n34; and public/private spheres, 13–18, 44–49, 59–60, 64, 271, 280–81, 283–84, 335n9; and social mobility, 42–43, 47–49, 111, 156–58, 295n56; stage alter egos, 44; and theater reforms, 12–15; training and apprenticeships, 34–42; and victimhood, 72–73, 114–18; and virtue, 92–95, 100–101, 104–6, 108–21, 271–84, 305n11. *See also* audiences; celebrity

Centlivre, Susanna, 10–11, 33, 50, 76, 101, 141–42, 295n61
de Certeau, Michel, 194
Charke, Charlotte, 11, 42, 51–52, 94, 100, 113–14, 195, 196
Charles II, 8, 75, 85, 90, 97, 137, 202–3
Charlotte, Queen, 233
Chetwood, William, 34, 56, 108, 116, 156, 200, 218
Churchill, Charles, 46, 107, 183
Churchill, Lady Mary (Duchess of Montagu), 118, 143
Cibber, Colley, 11, 34; and actresses as commodities, 57; and actresses' rivalries, 70; *Apology*, 82, 86, 101, 132, 304n60; and audience-actor interactions, 127, 132; and earliest actresses, 38, 53, 61; and Oldfield, 11, 45–46; and *The Rival Queens*, 66–67, 79, 82–85, 90; and spoof *The Rival Queans*, 70, 75, 82–85, 86, 302n37, 304n55; stage alter ego, 44
Cibber, Jane, 38
Cibber, Susannah, 9; benefit performances, 55; and Clive, 37–38, 162, 292n25, 315n31; as commodity, 57; interactions with audience members, 126–27, 147–48; popularity in grading scales, 3; pregnancy, 49; and rivalries, 4, 37–38, 58–59, 70, 162; salary/earnings, 37–38, 48, 55, 292n25, 295n58; stage props and accessories, 234; writing for stage, 33
Cibber, Theophilus, 34, 41–42, 48, 57, 132, 147–48, 162–63, 199
The Clandestine Marriage, 169–70
Clarissa, 19, 162, 222, 315n27
Clark, Peter, 227
Clive, Catherine Raftor (Kitty), 9, 51, 151–88; addressing audiences, 45, 127–28; aristocratic patrons, 46; benefit performances, 55; career as second generation actress, 151–58, 177–78; chambermaid roles, 156–58, 172–73; charitable, 56–57; and Susannah Cibber, 37–38, 162, 292n25, 315n31; comic roles, 156, 158; and commodity culture, 57, 170; cross-dressed roles, 76, 172–74; discovery as actor, 34, 154–56; and disputes regarding actors' remuneration, 57, 163–66, 316nn38–39; and Dublin stage, 183–84; earnings, 37–38, 55, 292n25; economic independence, 153; epilogues, 40–41, 128, 167–68, 172–78, 289n45;

feminist commentaries by, 175–76, 318n72; fine lady roles, 156–58, *157*, 166–72, 181; and Garrick, 1, 37–38, 152–53, 158, 166, 171, 175–76, 179, 182, 188, 319n92; and interiority effect, 152; Irish-English characters, 182–88; as Lady Fuz in *A Peep Behind the Curtain*, 170–72; and *Lethe*, 57, *157*, 166–68, 181; marriage, 153; parodic feminist afterpieces, 11, 41, 178–82, 184–88; Patriot political sympathies, 156, 313n11; performative identity, 152, 171–72; and performative property, 23, 152, 158, 160–66, 182–88; popularity, 6; as Portia in *The Merchant of Venice*, 172–74; portraits, *155*, *157*; and rehearsal plays, 170–71, 179–80; residence, 154, *154*; retirement, 177–78; and *The Rival Queens*, 76; and rivalries, 37–38, 58–59, 70, 162, 298n101
Clive, George, 153, 187
Coffey, Charles, 156
Cohen, Ralph, 240
A Collection of . . . Prologues and Epilogues (1779), 252
Collection of the Dresses of Different Nations Ancient and Modern, 329n10
Colley, Linda, 205
Collier, Jeremy, 124, 135, 196
Colman, George, 249–50, 261
The Comedian, 156
commedia dell'arte, 33
Commentaries on the Laws of England (Blackstone), 159
The Committee, 142
The Conduct of the Stage Consider'd, 196
Congreve, William, 51, 246, 261
The Conscious Lovers, 123, 142–43, 156
The Constant Couple; or a Trip to the Jubilee: and actresses' rivalries, 58; and addresses to ladies of quality, 136, 138; and anti-Catholic sentiments, 219, 327–28n80; and apprentice system, 35–36; Barry as Wildair, 210, *211*; and Catholic Papal Jubilee, 219; and concept of women, 219–21; Dublin/London performances, 217; and paradox of misogyny, 221; requests for, 142–43; Woffington as Wildair, 45, 191, 202, 205, 208, 212, 217–22, 281, 326n56; Woffington's epilogue, 221–22
The Contre Temps; or, Rival Queans: A Small Farce, 86–88

Conway, Henry Seymour, 207
Cooke, Thomas, 200
Cooke, William, 47, 249
Cooper, Elizabeth, 11
Cooper, Susannah Ashley (Countess of Shaftesbury), 143, 271–72
Coriolanus, 206
costumes. *See* stage costuming
Countess of Kildare (Duchess of Leinster), 118
The Country Wife, 136
The Court of Alexander, 82, 88–90
Covent Garden: Abington's stage costuming, 229, 233; and actors' training, 42; and Clive, 165, 169; seating, 53; and 1737 Licensing Act, 12; and Woffington in *The Constant Couple*, 217; and women playwrights, 277
Covent Garden Tragedy, 176
Coventry, Lady (Maria Gunning), 148
Cowley, Hannah, 11, 33, 50, 277
Cowper, Mary, 143
Cowper, William, 143
craft guilds, 33
Craven, Elizabeth, 258
Crawford, Anne, 315n28
credit economy, 94–95, 305n6
A Critical Balance of the Performers at Drury-Lane Theatre (1765), 1, 2
Critical Review, 92
Cross, Letitia, 59
cross-dressing: breeches roles/skirts roles, 75–76, 83, 193, 195–98, 205–13, 323n20, 326n57; Charke's parts, 195, 196; Clive's Portia in *The Merchant of Venice*, 172–74; critical responses, 197–98; and early actresses, 33; and epilogues, 191, 204–13, 324n30; and interiority effects, 195, 225; and Jacobite crisis, 196, 214–16; and modernity, 194, 225; and moral conservatives, 196–97, 323n20; and national identity, 196, 205, 214–16; and performance of gender, 83–84, 193–98, 323n20; and plot consequences, 195; and private/public, 195; and prostitution, 218; *The Rival Queens* and role of Alexander, 75–76; and sexual ambiguity, 193–94, 196–98, 214, 218, 220, 223–25, 327n75; and she-tragedies/she-comedies, 225; as signifier of political/sexual liberty, 195; and transvestite drama, 83–84, 193–94; and

Wildair in *The Constant Couple*, 45, 191, 202, 205, 208, 210, *211*, 212, 217–22, 281, 326n56; Woffington's patriotic epilogues, 191, 205–13; Woffington's roles, 191–98, 202, 204–13, *209*, 217–25, 281
Crouch, Kimberly, 294n54
Crowne, John, 123
Crow Street Theater (Dublin), 148, 226–27, 231
Cumberland, Richard, 182, 250
A Cure for a Scold, 175
Curll, Edmund, 77, 79, 100, 101, 106
Cuzzoni, Francesca, 86–88

The Daily Advertiser, 76, 196
Danchin, Pierre, 73
Davenant, Alexander, 297n79
Davenant, Lady, 35–37
Davenant, Sir William, 8, 35, 71
Davenport, Hester, 45
Davies, Kate, 275
Davies, Thomas, 80, 81, 109, 151, 158, 160, 168, 197, 223
Davis, Tracy, 135
Davis, Vivian, 302n37
de Bolla, Peter, 172
Deborah (Handel oratorio), 156
Defoe, Daniel, 98
D'Egville, James Harvey, 71
The Delicate Distress, 118–19
de Moissy, Alexandre-Guillaume, 245
Dennis, John, 139
de Vere, Aubrey, earl of Oxford, 79
The Devil to Pay, or the Wives Metamorphosed, 142, 156
Diamond, Elin, 24, 195–96
Dibdin, Charles, 231
Dictionary of the English Language (Johnson), 238
Diderot, Denis, 22
Digges, West, 115
Dircks, Phyllis T., 171
The Discovery, 242
The Disputes Between the Director of D--y, and the Pit Potentates, 160–61
Dissipation, 252
The Distress'd Mother, 105–7, 142–44, 148, 266, 267, 281
Dodsley, Robert, 177
Dolan, Jill Susan, 321n4
The Double Dealer, 143, 226

The Double Gallant; or, The Sick Lady's Cure, 103
The Double Mistake, 277
Douglas, Duchesses of, 149
Downes, John, 62, 299n2
Downie, J. A., 14–15, 287n29
The Dramatic Censor, 173
Dramatic Miscellanies (Davies), 109
The Dramatic Works of Thomas Shadwell, 137
Drury Lane: and actors' revolts, 57, 163–66, 316nn38–39; and Cibber's *The Rival Queans*, 85, 304n55; Clive's performances, 169, 178–79; Garrick's management, 1, 6, 158, 163; seating, 53, 133; and 1737 Licensing Act, 12; and women playwrights, 277
Dryden, John, 97
Dublin Gazette, 129, 233
Dublin Journal, 199–200
Dublin theater: Abington and, 226–27, 231; audiences and stage-seating, 129; Beefsteak Club, 201, 204; Clive and, 183–84; *The Fair Penitent* and Woffington's Catholicism, 223; and patronage system, 143–44, 147
Duchess of Kingston, bigamy trial of, 75
Dugaw, Dianne, 325n55
Duke of Bolton, 100
The Dupe, 175
D'Urfey, Thomas, 32

The Earl of Warwick, 252, 255
earnings, actresses', 7, 44, 47–60, 295n58, 296nn64–67, 297nn79–80; and actresses' memoirs, 99; and benefit performances, 50, 52–56; and charitable acts, 56–57; discretionary income, 51–52; and Drury Lane revolts, 57, 163–66, 316nn38–39; French actresses, 7–8, 285n8; and profit-sharing, 48, 163, 295n61; public complaints, 48–49, 56; Restoration stage, 34
Eger, Elizabeth, 15
Egerton, William [Edmund Curll], 101, 104–6
Elizabeth I, reign of, 135
English Civil War, 8, 97
English common law, 158–66
epilogues, 205–6, 236; Abington's, 45, *232*, 236–58, *243*, *251*, *256*; and actress-audience interactions, 20–21, 127, 236; and actresses as intermediaries between theater and world, 21, 106–7, 236;

Clive's, 40–41, 128, 167–68, 172–78, 289n45; and cross-dressing, 191, 204–13, 324n30; Woffington in *The Constant Couple*, 221–22; Woffington's patriotic epilogues, 191, 200, 203–13
Epistle to a Lady, 46, 245
Erickson, Amy, 15, 161, 314n25
Estimate of the Manners and Principles of the Time (Brown), 205
Evelina (Burney), 49, 64
Every Woman in Her Humour, 178–79
The Excursion (Brooke), 277
Ezell, Margaret, 145

The Fair Penitent: Calista and actresses' virtue, 108–9, 114, 120, 222–55, 266, *268*, 328n84; Dublin performances and Woffington's Catholicism, 223; and female patrons, 129; Oldfield's role, 108; requests for, 142; as she-tragedy, 108, 222; Siddons's role in, 120; stage history, 222–23, 328n84; Woffington's travesty role as Lothario, 191–93, 217, 222–25
The Faithful Irish Woman, 178, 184–88, 321n106
Faithful Memoirs of the Life, Amours, and Performances of That Justly Celebrated, and Most Eminent Actress of her Time, Mrs. Anne Oldfield (Egerton), 101, 104–6, 109
The Fall of Phaeton, 127–28
fans (stage accessories), 241–42, *243*, 332n52
Farquhar, George, 11, 34, 215, 326n56, 327n68. See also *The Constant Couple*; *The Recruiting Officer*
Farren, Elizabeth, 47
The Fatal Discovery, 237, 239
Fatal Dowry, 222
The Fatal Falsehood, 277
The Fatal Marriage, 142
The Fatal Retirement, 177
Faulkner, George, 199–200
The Female Officer, or the Humours of the Army, 208, 213
Female Quixote (Lennox), 64–65, 276
"The Female Volunteer," 205, 207–12, *209*, 325n48
The Female Wits; or the Triumvirate of Poets at Rehearsal, 179–80, 319n89
femes soles, 162
feminism: and Abington, 248–50, 257, 258;

and celebrity actresses, 117, 248–50, 257–58, 271–72; and Clive's commentary and afterpieces, 41, 175–76, 178–82, 184–88, 318n72; and *The Sultan*, 257
Fenton, Lavinia, 45, 47, 97–100; and benefit performance seating, 130; charitable acts, 56; memoir and public virtue, 94, 97–100, 112, 305n9
Féral, Josette, 146
Fielding, Henry, 56–57, 82, 93, 163, 174, 296n64
Filmer, Robert, 67
Fineman, Joel, 303n44
Fitzgerald, Percy, 296n65
Fleetwood, Charles, 12, 48, 58, 163, 165
Foote, Samuel, 168, 234, 276
Foucault, Michel, 130–31
Fountain, Peter, 259
Fox, Charles James, 54, 117, 281
Fraizer, Carey, 137
Freeman, Lisa, 11, 19–20, 72, 281, 288n41, 291–92n14, 309n28, 322n7
French actresses, 7–8, 202–3, 285n8
Fretcheville, Lady, 137
Frushell, Richard C., 178, 321n106
The Funeral, 142
Furnival, Elizabeth, 235

Gallagher, Catherine, 17–18, 288n40
Garber, Marjorie, 193
Garrick, David, 11; and Abington, 53–54, 228, 236–37, 248, 250, 258–64, 329n9; and actors in disguise in audience, 127; and Bluestockings, 276; and Clive, 1, 6, 37–38, 152–53, 158, 166, 171, 175–76, 179, 182, 188, 319n92; Drury Lane management, 1, 6, 158, 163; epilogues written for actresses, 174–76, 236–37, 248, 250, 334n82; portraits, *7*, 261, *263*, 266; rivalries with actresses, 1, 3–6, 158, 179, 182, 188, 228, 258–64, 319n92; and rowdy audiences, 133; and Shakespearean revival, 283, 311n61; and Woffington, 197, 199, 218, 323n27; and women playwrights, 258–59, 277–78, 336n22
Gay, John, 15, 142, 148, 239. See also *The Beggar's Opera*
gender theory, 23–25, 290n59
Gentleman, Francis, 197
George Jolly Hatton Garden Nursery, 36
Godolphin, Elizabeth, 137

Goldsmith, Oliver, 158, 182
"gold tickets" ("guineas"), 54
Gothic novels, 300n19
grading scale systems rating performers, 1–6, *2*, *4*, *5*
Gray's Inn Journal, 124, 204
Greene, Jody, 315n30
Griffin, Dustin, 145–46
Griffith, Elizabeth, 11, 33, 50, 118–19, 182, 274, 277
Grub-Street Journal, 58, 124–26, 141
Guest, Harriet, 15, 287n22, 288n40, 335n6
A Guide to the Stage (1751), 212, 234
Gunning sisters, 199
Gwyn, Nell (Eleanor), 47, 90, 94, 95–97, *96*, 107

Habermas, Jürgen, 13–14
Hamilton, Esther, 70
Hamilton, Mary, 195
Hamlet, 126, 142–43
Handel, George Frideric, 156, 313nn8, 11
Harris, Jocelyn, 92–93
Harris, Jonathan Gil, 239, 331n43
Harris, Susan Cannon, 129, 223, 328n84
Harry the Fifth, 205
Hart, Charles, 32, 68, 75, 291n4
Havard, William, 205
Haymarket Theater and Drury Lane actors' revolt, 57, 163
Haywood, Eliza, 11, 64, 98
Hedelin, Abbé, 33–34
Heidegger, John James, 87
Heller, Deborah, 271
Henry IV, 143
Henry V, 143
Henry VIII, 283
heroic tragedy, 68, 82–84
Hesse, Carla, 17
Hickey, Thomas, 231, *232*
Highfill, Philip H., Jr., 334n3
High Life below Stairs, 231
Highmore, John, 163
Hill, Aaron, 174
History of the English Stage, from the Restauration to the Present Time (Betterton), 101, 106, 111–12
History of the Stage (Chetwood), 116
Hitchcock, Robert, 197, 199
The Hob; or The Country Wake, 142
Holland, Peter, 288n33

Home, John, 237
An Hospital for Fools, 167, 177
Howard, Anne, 137
Howard, Dorothy, 137
Howard, Robert, 97
Howe, Elizabeth, 11, 37, 70
Hughes, Margaret, 8
Hume, Robert, 50, 68, 297n81, 300n12
The Humours of Falstaff, 143
The Husband's Relief, 124–25, 307n7
The Hypocrite, 249

An Impartial Examen of the Present Contests between the Town and the Manager, 164
Inchbald, Elizabeth, 33, 49–50, 56, 238, 265, 277
The Inconstant or The Way to Win Him, 266, 270
The Indian Emperor, 62, 142
"interiority effect," 18–22; and Abington, 236, 237, 244, 264; and Bellamy, 116; and Clive, 152; and cross-dressing, 195, 225; and private/public identities, 18–22, 45, 271, 288n41; and *The Rival Queens*, 90–91; and Woffington's travesty roles, 225
The Intriguing Chambermaid, 156, 176
The Irish Fine Lady, 183, 186
Irish Protestants, 200–204, 207, 324n33, 325n43, 326n62
Irish theater: Clive's Irish-English characters, 182–88; Irish language and Irish-English identity, 185–86; relationship to English theater, 182–83, 320nn94, 98; and Woffington, 199–200

Jackson, Shannon, 23–24
Jacobites: and Farquhar's *The Constant Couple*, 219, 327–28n80; and Farquhar's *The Recruiting Officer*, 214–16; and Lee's *The Rival Queens*, 67; and Woffington's patriotic epilogues, 196, 203–13
James II, 137–38, 156
Jane Shore, 62, 108–9, 142–43
Jekyll, Joseph, 258
Jennings, Sarah (duchess of Marlborough), 137
Johnson, Samuel: biographies, 113; and Calista in Rowe's *The Fair Penitent*, 222; and Clive, 151, 158; definition of "appendix," 216; definition of "pin," 238; and Thrale, 274; and Woffington as Lothario, 225

Joncus, Berta, 313nn11, 8–9
Jonson, Ben, 32
Jordan, Dorothy, 48, 51–52, 281, 282–83
Joseph Andrews (Fielding), 82
Julius Caesar, 142–43

Kauffman, Angelica, 261, *263*
Kelly, Frances Maria (Fanny), 316n45
Kelly, Hugh, 182, 184, 227, 261
Kelly Riots (1747), 133, 328n84
Kemble, John Philip, 51, 71, 266
Kemp, Will, 6–7
Kenny, Shirley Strum, 327n79
Killigrew, Anne, 137
Killigrew, Thomas, 36–37
King, Thomas, 119
King Henry the VII; or The Popish Imposter, 205–7
King John, 283
King Lear, 142–43
King's Theatre (Haymarket Opera House), 278
Kinservik, Matthew J., 318n72
Knapp, Mary, 174, 259
Knowles, Eleanor, 154
Know Your own Mind, 260–61
Korda, Natasha, 62–63
Kynaston, Charles, 32, 291n4
Kynaston, Edward, 75–76, 197

Lacy, James, 184, 327n67
Ladies Club, 272, 335n7
ladies of quality. *See* patronage system
The Lady's Last Stake, 207
Lafler, Joanne, 297n80, 306n21, 318n76
Langford, Paul, 227, 291n13
Lee, Nathaniel. *See The Rival Queens*
Lee, Sophia, 277
Leigh, James, 265
Lennox, Charlotte, 64, 274, 276
Lethe; or, Aesop in the Shades, 57, 157, 166–68, 181
Licensing Act of 1695, 13, 14
Licensing Act of 1737, 12–15, 143, 163
Life of Lavinia Beswick, alias Fenton, alias Polly Peachum, 97–100, 305n9
The Life of Mr. James Quin, Comedian, 153
Life of Savage (Johnson), 113
The Life of that Eminent Comedian Robert Wilks, 234
Lillo, George, 15, 35, 171

Lincoln's Inn Fields, 70, 83, 124, 307n7
Linley, Elizabeth, 274, 276
Lloyd, David, 321n109
Locke, John, 22–23, 159–60
London Daily Post, 127, 162
The London Merchant, 15, 35–36, 39, 171
The London 'Prentice, 178
The London Tradesman, 228–29
The Lost Lover, 180
The Lottery, 174
Love à la Mode, 183
Love for Love, 103, 142–43, 208, 261
Love in a Riddle, 156
Love Makes a Man, 84, 154
Love of Fame, 31
Love's Last Shift, 138
The Luckey Chance, 136
Lynch, Deirdre Shauna, 18–19

Macaulay, Catherine, 116–17, 274
Macbeth, 142–43
Macklin, Charles, 38; and actors' training, 42; and Clive, 51, 163, 173, 183; and Drury Lane actors' revolt, 163; and Oldfield, 111; and rowdy audiences, 133–34; stage alter ego, 44; and Woffington, 201, 206–7, 324n34
Macky, John, 137, 308n9
Macpherson, C. B., 16
MacSwinny, Owen, 204
Magdalen House, 238–39
The Maid of Bath, 276
Maid of the Oaks, 332nn59–60; Abington as Lady Bab, 231, 232, 246–49, 252–57, 261; and English rural values, 246–47
managers: and celebrity actresses, 44, 159, 329n9; and disruptive audiences, 133–34; and Drury Lane actors' revolt, 163–66, 316nn38–39
Manley, Delarivier, 10, 98, 180
The Man of Mode, 37, 142
Mapp, Mrs. (née Sarah Willon), 124–26, 308n9
Maria, Henrietta, 136
Maria Beatrice of Modena, 58
Marsden, Jean I., 300n13, 309n26
Marshall, David, 62
Marshall, P. David, 131, 309n28
Marshall, Rebecca, 47, 79–80
Marx, Karl, 234–35
Massinger, Phillip, 222

Maus, Katherine E., 10
Maynwaring, Arthur, 46, 106, 107–8
McClintock, Anne, 194, 322n11
memoirs and biographies, 92–121; and actresses' virtue, 92–95, 100–101, 104–6, 112–21, 281–83, 305n11; Bellamy's *Apology*, 61, 92, 94, 114–18, 121; burgeoning public interest in, 113; Charke's *Narrative*, 113–14; Fenton, 94, 97–100, 112; Gwyn, 94–97; and interiority, 116, 121; Oldfield, 94, 100–112; and public/private tensions, 44–45, 117; Siddons, 94, 119–20, 279–80; and social class, 111; and victimization, 114–17; and wages, 99; Woffington, 94, 203–4, 218, 223–24
Memoirs of Mrs. Anne Oldfield, 106
Memoirs of Several Ladies of Great Britain (Amory), 113
Memoirs of Several Ladies of Great Britain (Ballard), 113
Memoirs of the Celebrated Mrs. Woffington, 203–4, 218, 223–24
Memoirs of the Life of Eleanor Gwinn (Seymour), 95–97
The Merchant of Venice, 143, 172–74, 207
The Merry Wives of Windsor, 142–43
Metham, George, 115
Milhous, Judith, 296n66, 311n56
Miller, James, 167, 176, 177
millinery/dressmaking trades, 228–29, 237–38
Miniature Picture, 258
The Miser, 156
Mithradates, King of Pontus, 142, 154
Mohun, Charles Lord, 79
Montagu, Elizabeth, 116–17, 258, 273–76
Montagu, Lady Mary Wortley, 85–86, 257
Morash, Christopher, 320n94, 326n62, 327–28n80
More, Hannah, 116–17, 258, 274, 276–77
Morning Chronicle and London Advertiser, 144
Mossup, Henry, 6
Mountfort, William, 79
The Mourning Bride, 62, 73, 142
Murphy, Arthur, 1, 11, 182; and Abington, 244–46, 260–61; and Clive in *The Apprentice*, 40–41, 293n37

A Narrative of the Life of Mrs. Charlotte Charke, Written by Herself, 113–14
Nash, Mary, 147

374 INDEX

national identity: cross-dressing and patriotism, 205; Irish Catholicism and Anglo-Irish Protestants, 200–204, 207, 324n33, 325n43, 326n62; and Jacobite crisis, 67, 196, 203–16, 219; and sexual difference, 198; and tragedies, 194, 322n7; and Woffington's patriotic epilogues, 191, 200, 203–13, 327–28n80; women and patriotic nationhood, 194
Needham, Mr., 227
New Theatre (Glasgow), 235
Nicoll, Allardyce, 6
Nicolson, Colin, 305n6
The Nine Living Muses of Great Britain (Samuel), 274–78, 275
The Nobody, 145
Nokes, James, 32, 291n4
The Non-Juror, 205, 212–13
Nonsense Club, 117
Nossiter, Maria, 70
Nouvelle école des femmes (de Moissy), 245
novels, eighteenth-century, 18–20, 288nn40–41; Gothic, 300n19; women novelists' incomes, 49–50

Observations on Mr. Fielding's Plan, 238, 331n38
Odell, Thomas, 39
O'Keeffe, John, 202, 237
Old City Manners, 276
Oldfield, Anne, 9, 34, 151; acting abilities, 103, 106; and audience disruptions, 127; benefit performances, 50–51; as Calista in *Fair Penitent*, 108–9; charitable acts, 56; as commodity, 57; epilogues, 106–7; and fashion, 110–12, 333n64; as intermediary/example for other women, 106–7; as Lady Modish in *The Careless Husband*, 45, 109–11; maternal generosity, 108; portrait, *102*; pregnancy, 49; private/public personas, 45–46; and prostitution, 46; and rivalries, 58; salary/earnings, 50–51, 297n79; sexuality and virtue, 101, 104–6, 112; she-tragedy heroines, 108–11; and social class, 111, 306n21; theatrical memoirs, 94, 100–112; and Woffington, 199
Oldys, William, 106
"On the Profession of a Player" (Boswell), 22
O'Quinn, Daniel, 312n69
Orgel, Stephen, 196
Orientalism: and epilogue to *Miniature Picture*, 258; and *The Rival Queens*, 71, 85–86, 89–90, 304nn57–58; Stevens's *The Court of Alexander* and racial hybridity, 89–90; and *The Sultan*, 257–58
Original Letters, Familiar, Moral and Critical (Dennis), 139
Oroonoko, 40, 45, 293n37
The Orphan, 71, 142, 234
Orr, Bridget, 11, 85, 304n57
Othello, 154
Otway, Thomas, 31, 71

The Padlock, 89
Pamela (Richardson), 19, 92–94, 106–7
Pantheon, 272
Papal Jubilee, 219, 327n79
Papal Tyranny in the Reign of King John, 174
Paradoxe sur le comédien (Diderot), 22
parodies: Cibber's *The Rival Queens*, 70, 75, 82–85, 86, 302n37, 304n55; Clive's feminist afterpieces, 41, 178–82, 184–88; and gender ambiguity, 76, 82–84; and Lee's *The Rival Queens*, 70, 75–76, 81–90; and scatological humor, 84; and symbols of royalty, 84
Pasquin, 143
Pasquin, Anthony, 326n56
Pateman, Carole, 23, 159
patent theaters, 12, 15, 33
Paterson, William, 177
Patriarcha, 67
patronage system, 45–47, 122–50; and actresses' reputations, 117–18; actresses' testimony on importance of, 144–45; aristocratic and courtly women, 46–47, 54–56, 117–18, 135–37, 140; and benefit performances, 54–56; and commercial marketplace, 140, 145–47; Dublin stage, 143–44, 147; exchanges of clothing, 58, 147, 150, 235–36; and influence of female patrons, 134–45, 310n49; literary patronage, 145–46; and objects of dedication, 137; and privately staged plays, 144; and profits, 141, 311n56; relationships of actresses and ladies of quality, 46–47, 126, 128–29, 134–50; requests for certain plays, 140–44; rivalries of patronesses and actresses, 148–50; and "theatrical contact," 134. *See also* audiences
Payne, Deborah C., 293n43

A Peep Behind the Curtain; or, The New Rehearsal, 170–72
Pepys, Elizabeth, 137
Pepys, Samuel, 32, 47, 249, 291n4
Percy, 276–77
performance studies: and the archive and the repertoire, 10, 286n14; and eighteenth-century novels, 18–20; and eighteenth-century women actresses/playwrights, 10–11; and femininity on the stage, 11–12; and gender theory, 24–25; redefining performance as quotidian activities, 23, 289n54
performative identity, 18–23, 45, 63–64, 152, 171–72, 244, 264, 271, 288n41
performative property, 23, 159–63; and Abington's role as Widow Bellmour in *The Way to Keep Him*, 245; and actor-manager relationships, 164; and actresses' possession of roles, 152, 161–63; and celebrity, 23, 159–63; Clive and, 23, 152, 158, 160–66, 182–88; and English common law, 158–66, 314n22; and self-possession, 159–60
Perry, Ruth, 15, 315n27
Perry, William, 227
Perseus and Andromeda, 154
Phaedra and Hippolitus, 107
Phelan, Peggy, 64
Philips, Ambrose, 106, 266
Pilkington, Laetitia, 178
The Pin and the Needle, 239
"pin money," 238–39
pins (stage accessories), 237–41
Piozzi, Gabriel, 274, 278–79
Pix, Mary, 10, 180, 319n89
The Platonic Wife, 277
The Playhouse Pocket-Companion, or Theatrical Vade Medum, 8
playwrights, female, 10–11, 33, 50, 101, 277–78, 318n76; Clive's writing for stage, 41, 178–82, 184–88; and commercial markets, 22; and Garrick, 258–59, 277–78, 336n22; incomes, 50
Pocock, J. G. A., 159
"A Poem to the Memory of Mrs. Oldfield," 104–5
Pohl, Nicole, 15
politics: actresses and political consciousness, 117, 156, 248–49, 257–58, 271–72, 313n11, 335nn6, 8; Clive's Patriot sympathies,

156, 313n11; and national identity, 200–204, 207, 324n33, 325n43, 326n62; *The Rival Queens* and issues of political patriarchy, 67–68, 69, 300n17. *See also* national identity
Polly Honeycombe, 252, 254
Pope, Alexander, 113, 240–41, 245
Pope, Elizabeth, 266
Pope, Jane, 259
Porter, Edward, 51
Porter, Mary, 37
Portraits in the Characters of the Muses in the Temple of Apollo (The Nine Living Muses of Great Britain) (Samuel), 274–78, 275
Postlewait, Thomas, 113, 135
pregnancies of actresses, 49
Price, Henrietta, 137
Price, Mary, 195
Pritchard, Hannah: benefit performances, 55, 133, 141; and Drury Lane actors' revolts, 163; earnings, 51, 55; and fashion, 233; patrons, 141; popularity in grading scales, 6; portrait, 7; rivalry with Garrick, 1, 3, 258–59
private sphere. *See* public/private spheres
"A Prologue upon Epilogues, Spoken at a Private Benefit," 173–74
The Prompter, 53, 67–68, 76
property ownership, 22–23, 159–63, 294n54, 314n22, 315nn28–30. *See also* performative property
prostitution: actresses and rumors of, 16–17, 36, 42–43, 46, 63–64, 98–99, 218, 228, 282, 293n43; and cross-dressing, 218; and female apprentices, 36
Protestants, Anglo-Irish, 200–204, 207, 324n33, 325n43, 326n62
The Provok'd Husband, 111, 127, 142
The Provok'd Wife, 142, 143, 156
public/private spheres, 13–22, 44–49, 283–84, 335n9; and actresses' memoirs, 44–45, 117; audiences and "public intimacy," 16–17, 59–60, 64, 288n34; and bourgeois revolution, 13–15; and cult of celebrity, 13–15; and interiority effects, 18–22, 45, 271, 288n41; and reading/novels, 18–20; and Siddons, 119–20, 279–81, 283–84; and virtue, 9, 44–45, 60, 94, 119–20, 271, 279–80, 287n30

Queensberry, Duchess of, 56, 118, 148–50
Quin, James, 6, 153, 197, 199, 313n3

Radnor, earl of, 169
Raftor, James, 167, 178
Raftor, William, 156
Ragussis, Michael, 321n108
Ralph, James, 133, 205
The Rape of the Lock (Pope), 240–41
The Recruiting Officer, 103, 143, 214–16, 327n70; and anatomy/body parts, 215–16; Woffington's cross-dressed role as Silvia, 191, 202, 208, 214–16, 217
Regulus, 205, 206
The Rehearsal; or, Bays in Petticoats, 171, 175, 178–82, 319n82; as Clive's feminist parodic afterpiece, 41, 178–82; epilogue, 175–76, 179, 318n72
The Rehearsal (Buckingham), 179–82
rehearsal plays, 170–71, 179–80
The Relapse, 142, 143
Restoration stage, 7–9, 32–33, 61–64; and actresses' virtue, 8–9; apprenticeships and training, 34–42; audience attitudes, 135–36, 138–40, 310nn43–44; and audiences' relationship to time, 62, 299n5; breeches roles, 193; craft guilds, 33; financial motivations for acting, 34; and patronage system, 134–39; performances of older dramas, 62; salaries, 34; seduction plots and sexual references, 138–39; skirts roles, 32–36, 29n4; and social class instability, 42–43; stage costuming, 43, 230; stage seating, 39–40; and theater economy, 62–63
Reynolds, Sir Joshua, 191, 227, 257, 261, *262*, 266, 333n69, 334n4
Ribeiro, Aileen, 238, 329n10
Rich, John, 6, 12, 15, 201; and Drury Lane actors' revolt, 163, 166; and rowdy audiences at Drury Lane, 133; and Woffington, 80, 189–91, *190*
Richards, Sandra, 11, 315n28, 334n4
Richardson, Samuel, 19, 38, 92–94, 106–7, 162, 222
The Rise of the English Actress (Richards), 11
The Rival Queans, 70, 75, 82–85, 86, 302n37, 304n55
The Rival Queens, 1, 61–62, 66–91, *69*, *77*; and actresses in role of Roxana, 70, 73–81; and actresses' rivalries, 68–70, 79–81, 86–88; and Alexander's tragic heroism, 82–84; anecdotes evoked by, 78–81, 303n44; benefit performances, 68; breeches roles, 75–76; and British empire, 85–90; and Cibber's *The Rival Queans*, 70, 75, 82–85, 86, 302n37, 304n55; class-diverse audiences, 68; comic epilogue, 73–75, 302n31; and gender ambiguity, 75–76, 82–84; and interiority effects, 90–91; and Jacobite monarchy, 67; and male admirers of actress queens, 78–79; and modernity, 71–78; and Orientalism, 71, 85–86, 89–90, 304n57–58; parodic reinterpretations, 70, 76, 81–90; performance history, 66–71, 81, 90, 303n43; and political patriarchy, 67–68, 300n17; prologue, 124; revivals, 70–71; sexual chemistry between actresses, 76–78; as she-tragedy, 71–72; stage properties, 79–81, 88; women's bodies and Christian/Oriental values, 85–86, 304n58; and women's power, 72–73, 90–91
rivalries and public quarrels: between actresses, 58–59, 61–62, 70, 80–81, 86–88; *The Contre Temps* and metaphor of imperial rivalry, 86–88; and Garrick, 1, 3–4, 158, 179, 182, 188, 228, 258–64, 319n92; and grading scales, 1–6; between patronesses and actresses, 148–50; and *The Rival Queens*, 68–81, 88, 303n50; stage reenactments, 61–62
The Rivals, 167
Roach, Joseph, 16–17, 67, 288n33, 294nn46, 48
Roberts, David, 137, 138, 295n61
Robinson, Frederick, 330n17
Robinson, Mary, 45, 145, 265, 281–82, 304n58
Rogers, Jane, 45, 51, 58, 100, 113
Rogers, Pat, 280
Rojek, Chris, 230, 330n31
Romack, Katherine, 36
Romeo and Juliet, 127, 129–30, 148
The Rosciad, 183–84
Rose, Mary Beth, 75
Rosenthal, Angela, 326n58, 333n69
Rosenthal, Laura, 42–43, 283, 293n43, 305n11, 326n57, 327n76, 337n30
Rothstein, Eric, 327n80
Rowe, Nicholas, 11. See also *The Fair Penitent*
The Royal Convert, 144
The Royal Merchant, 142
Rule a Wife and Have a Wife, 142, 249–52, *251*
The Runaway, 252, 253
Russell, Gillian, 23, 227, 335n9

Sackville, Lionel, Duke of Dorset, 201
salaries. *See* earnings, actresses'
Samson, 313n11
Samuel, Richard, 274–78
Sandoni, Pietro Giuseppe, 88
Saunderson, Mary, 37
Sauter, Willmar, 131
Savage, Richard, 297n79
Scarsdale, earl of, 51
Schechner, Richard, 67, 289n54
Schellenberg, Betty, 15
The School for Rakes, 182, 277
The School for Scandal, 248
School for Wives, 227, 261, 334n82
The Scornful Lady, 142–43, 207, 249
Sedley, Charles, 97
Senese, Lucrezia, 33
Sennett, Richard, 62
The Servants Calling, 43
Seven Years' War, 12–13
Seymour, John, 95, 96
Shakespearean plays, 142–43, 283–84, 311n61
Shakespeare Ladies Club, 142–43, 271–72, 311n61
Shapiro, Michael, 35
Sheldon, Frances, 137
Sheridan, Elizabeth Linley, 274
Sheridan, Frances, 6, 11, 50, 175, 242
Sheridan, Richard, 6, 11, 133, 276
Sheridan, Thomas, 172, 183; and Anglo-Irish politics, 200–201, 324n33; and Smock Alley affair, 191; and training of early actors, 42; and Woffington, 200–201, 204, 324nn33, 35
she-tragedies, 300n13, 301n27; audiences' reactions to, 139–40; disappearance of, 71–72; female heroism in, 71–72; Lee's *The Rival Queens*, 71; Oldfield's heroines combining virtue and chastity, 108–11; Rowe's *The Fair Penitent*, 108, 222
Shevelow, Kathryn, 317n56
A Short View of the Immorality and Profaneness of the English Stage (Collier), 124
Siddons, Sarah, 32, 278–84, 336n24; and aristocratic patronage, 56, 145; benefit performances and ticket sales, 55, 56; and Bluestockings, 228, 278; as commodity, 57; and contracted virtue, 278–84; dignified stage presence, 279–81, 283; earnings, 51, 56, 284; and gender ambiguity, 279–81, 337n30; mentoring, 38; and performative realism, 281; portraits, 266, 334n4; private/public persona and virtue, 94, 119–20, 279–81, 283–84; stage costumes, 58; theatrical memoir, 94, 119–20, 279, 280; and Thrale, 278–79
The Silent Woman, 32
Sir John Cockle at Court, 177
The Sister, 276
The Sketch of a Fine Lady's Return from a Rout, 178–79, 184, 320n103
skirts roles, 32–36, 83, 291n4; boy actors, 33, 34–36, 196; Cibber's *The Rival Queens*, 83–84; Woffington's cross-dressed roles, 193–98, 323n20
Sloper, William, 48
Slowey, Desmond, 325n43
Smallwood, Angela, 329n5, 336n18
Smart, Christopher, 40
Smith, Adam, 238
Smith, Charlotte, 49
Smith, J. H., 135
Smock Alley Theater (Dublin), 51, 148, 191, 217, 226
Snell, Hannah, 195
Sofer, Andrew, 242, 332n52
A Soldier's Letter to the Female Volunteer, 210–12
The Spanish Fryar, 142
The Spectator, 242, 306n17
Spencer, Georgiana, 56, 258
St. James Street playhouse, 52
The Stage Coach, 142
stage costuming: and Abington's fashion expertise, 57–58, 228–36; audience demands for accuracy, 228, 329n10; Bellamy's, 80–81, 229–30, 235–36; costume allowances, 229; and everyday dress, 230, 330n17; fans, 241–42, 243, 332n52; and fetishization of actresses, 57–58, 230–31, 234–35, 244, 330n31; hoop skirts, 241; and Lady Modish in *The Careless Husband*, 109–10; material femininity and interiority, 230–31, 237, 246–49, 264; and millinery, 228–29, 237–38; pins, 237–41; pistols, 250–52, 251; and relations between actresses and female audiences, 235–36, 242–44; Restoration stage, 43, 230; *The Rival Queens* and actresses' rivalries over, 79–81, 88, 303n50; and semiotic agency of clothing, 57–58, 233–35; and stage accessories, 57–58, 231, 237–44,

stage costuming (*continued*)
    243, 250–52, *251*; veils, 79–80; and weaponry, 241–44, 250–52, *251*; Woffington's waistcoat, 208–10, *209*
stage seating, 20–21, 39–40, 53, 128–30, 133–34, 289n43, 308n9
Stallybrass, Peter, 83
Statute of Anne (1710), 152
Staves, Susan, 15, 62, 162, 238–39, 315n29
Steele, Sir Richard, 122–24, 126, 129, 132, 140
Stern, Tiffany, 289nn43, 45
Stevens, George Alexander, 82, 88–90
Straub, Kristina, 11, 114–15, 130–31, 196–97, 309n27
Strephon and Chloe (Swift), 245
The Sultan, 248–49, 252–58, 333n70
sumptuary laws, 39
The Suspicious Husband (Hoadley), 7
Swift, Jonathan, 139, 245

Tamerlane, 142
Tarleton, Banastre, 281
Taylor, Charles, 34
Taylor, Diana, 10, 23, 81, 198, 286n14, 321n3
Taylor, John, 182, 319n92
Temple, Phillipa, 137
The Tender Husband, 142
The Theatre (Steele's periodical), 122–24, 126, 129, 140
The Theatrical Bouquet, 128
Theatrical Correspondence in Death (1743), 48–49
theatrical interactions: and full collaborative assembly, 123–34, 309nn28–29; mutual exchange, 124, 134; and social hierarchies, 132–33; and stage as visual spectacle, 130–31, 309nn26–27. *See also* audiences
The Theatrical Review, 3–6, *4*, *5*
Thespis, 184
Thomas, Elizabeth, 101
Thomson, James, 206
Thomson, Peter, 335n8
Thrale, Hester, 3, 273–74, 278–79, 335n12
Thraliana, 273, 278
Tillyard, Stella, 12–13, 287nn21, 30
The Times, 277
Todd, Janet, 136
Tomlinson, Sophie, 8, 10, 71, 135
The Ton, 145, 312n69
Town and Country Magazine, 237
Townley, James, 231

Tragedy of Zara, 174
Tragedy of Zingis, 252, 256
transvestite drama, 83–84, 193–94
travesty roles: and interiority effects, 225; and prostitution/loose sexuality, 218; and she-tragedies/she-comedies, 225; Woffington's, 191–94, 198, 202, 204–13, 217–25, 281
Trotter, Catherine, 10, 180
The True-Born Irishman, 183
Turkish Letters (Montagu), 85
Turner, Victor, 146
Twelfth Night, 143
The Twin Rivals, 242, *243*
Tyrannick Love, 97

United Company, 52–53, 297n79
The Universal Passion, 176

veils (stage costuming), 79–80
Venice Preserved, 142, 177
Verbruggen, Susannah, 217
Vernon, P. F., 68, 303n43
Vesey, Elizabeth, 273
victimhood, 72–73, 114–18
Victor, Benjamin, 101, 201, 212
Villiers, George, Duke of Buckingham, 170
Violante, Mademoiselle, 34, 202
Violette, Eva Maria, 195
virtue, 92–121, 271–84; and Bluestockings, 116–17, 273–78, 335n12; and chastity, 92–95, 100–101, 104–6, 108–21, 281–83, 305n11; contracted, 278–84; exceptional, 100, 104–6, 112, 116–18, 271–84; Oldfield and, 94, 100–112; public/private, 9, 44–45, 60, 94, 119–20, 271, 279–80, 287n30; and Restoration stage, 8–9; Siddons and, 94, 119–20, 279–81, 283–84; and victimization, 114–17. *See also* memoirs and biographies
The Virtuous Wife, 32
Visits from the Shades: or, Dialogues Serious, Comical, and Political, 84–85
Volunteer Manager, 126
Voskuil, Lynn M., 234

Wahrman, Dror, 196–97, 323n20
Walker, Ann, 137
Wallace, Lady, 145, 312n69
Walmesly, Gilbert, 182
Walpole, Horace, 1, 154, 174, 176, 226, 244, 272

Walpole, Robert, 156
Walsingham (Robinson), 145
Wanko, Cheryl, 300n12, 304n55, 305n9
Ward, Sarah (Mrs. West Digges), 70
War of Spanish Succession, 215, 327n70
The Way of the World, 142, 246
The Way to Keep Him, 231, 244–46, 249, 335n8
The Wealth of Nations (Smith), 238
Weekly Miscellany, 39
Weimann, Robert, 21, 131, 236, 309n29
The West Indian, 250, 259
The What D'ye Call It, 142
Whig and Tory, 154
The Whole Life of Polly Peachum; Containing an Account of her Birth, Parentage and Education, 98
The Wife in the Right, 277
The Wife's Relief; or, the Husband's Cure, 307n7
Wilkes, Thomas [Samuel Derrick], 329n10
Wilkinson, Tate, 39–40, 43, 54, 129–30, 153, 241, 323n27
Wilks, Robert, 45, 58, 100, 101, 103, 109, 154, 217
Wilson, John Harold, 7–8, 35, 193
Wilson, Kathleen, 194, 322n9
Wilson, Sarah, 252, *254*
Wit Without Money, 142
The Wives Excuse, 138
Woffington, Margaret (Peg), 9, 189–225; apprenticeship, 34, 202; and audiences, 45, 197–98; and Beefsteak Club, 201, 204; and Catholicism, 203–4, 207, 213, 219, 223; charitable acts, 43, 56; as commodity, 57; and cross-dressed/travesty roles, 191–98, 202, 204–13, 217–25, 281; economic success, 48, 51, 323n25; elevated manners, 199–200; as

"The Female Volunteer," 205, 207–12, *209*, 325n48; and Garrick, 197, 199, 218, 323n27, 324n34; gendered identity, 195, 197–98, 221–22; and interiority effect, 225; Irish accent, 199–200; as Lothario in *The Fair Penitent*, 191–93, 217, 222–25; as Macheath in *Beggar's Opera*, 191, 202; memoirs, 94, 203–4, 218, 223–24; and national identity/Jacobite crisis, 196, 203, 204–16; patriotic epilogues, 191, 200, 203–13; popularity in grading scales, 6; portrait, *192*; and prostitution rumors, 218; and Rich, 189–91, *190*; and rivalries, 58, 70, 80–81, 298n101, 303n50; as Roxana in *The Rival Queens*, 70, 74, 80–81, 303n50; sartorial influence, 233; and Sheridan, 200–201, 204, 324nn33, 35; as Silvia in *The Recruiting Officer*, 191, 202, 208, 214–16, 217; as Wildair in *The Constant Couple*, 45, 191, 202, 205, 208, 212, 217–22, 281, 326n56
Woffington's Ghost: A Poem, in answer to the Meretriciad, 218
Wollstonecraft, Mary, 228, 246
The Wonder: A Woman Keeps a Secret (Centlivre), 141–42
Woodward, Henry, 163
Worsdale, James, 175
Wycherley, William, 104

Yates, Mary Anne, 51, 57, 252, *255*, 266, *268*, 278
Young, Edward, 31

Zarilli, Philip B., 323n24
Zenobia, 236–37

ACKNOWLEDGMENTS

In the course of writing this book I have recognized anew the extraordinary generosity of the scholarly community, and the debts incurred over the past several years as *Rival Queens* moved toward completion are indeed profound. For reading various parts of the manuscript, I am most grateful to Joseph Roach and to Lisa Freeman, each of whom generously shared their helpful, and sometimes provocative, suggestions. Every scholar interested in Restoration and eighteenth-century theater recognizes the extraordinary contribution of Robert D. Hume, and I am very appreciative for the warm encouragement he has offered for this project from its inception.

The kindness, sagacity, and good humor of colleagues has buoyed my spirits throughout the writing of this book, including most especially Jean Howard, Harriet Guest, Donna Guy, and Paula Freedman, whose very special friendships extend over decades. It is a great pleasure to acknowledge those at UCLA who offered illuminating ideas and enthusiastic support, including Joseph Bristow, Helen Deutsch, Jonathan Grossman, Anne Mellor, Sue-Ellen Case, and Kathleen McHugh. Emily Anderson cheerfully took on more than her share of responsibilities for the Huntington Library Seminar. Other intellectual and personal debts extend to a very long list of valued colleagues, and I can mention only a few: Ilias Chrissochoidis generously allowed me to benefit from his extensive research in eighteenth-century periodicals and shared his rich knowledge of Handel and the English opera. Angela Rosenthal offered expert assistance in helping me make sense of several images. Paula Backscheider more than once offered the fruits of her own research. Others who helped this book become a better one include John Bender, Laura Brown, Dympna Callaghan, Carole Fabricant, Jocelyn Harris, Susan Cannon Harris, Berta Joncus, Betty Joseph, Sarah Kareem, Isabel Karremann, Dian Kriz, Jayne Lewis, Judith Meyer, Judith Milhous, Jane Moody, Max Novak, Bridget Orr, Ruth Perry,

Shef Rogers, Norbert Schürer, Stuart Sherman, Kathryn Shevelow, Cedric D. Reverand II, Vanessa Rogers, Alice Wexler, and Roxann Wheeler.

I dedicate this book to the many UCLA graduate students who asked tough questions, shared insights, and allowed me to test my ideas, even when they were still in embryonic form. The list is too long to provide in full, but Wendy Belcher, Noelle Chao, Vivian Davis, Jenna Gibbs, Elizabeth Goodhue, Alex Hernandez, Nicole Horejsi, Chris Loar, Nush Powell, Sean Silver, Melissa Sodeman, and Matthew Wickman deserve special mention and, most especially, Reggie Allen for her remarkable research skills. Michelle Lee and Tara Fickle provided skilled assistance in the final preparations of the manuscript for the press, and Ian Newman and Nandeep Chan tracked down elusive references. In addition, Lynda Tolly, English Reading Room Librarian, remained remarkably good-natured when faced with yet another of my requests.

The research for this book has been conducted at many libraries, including the British Library, the Harvard Theatre Collection (Houghton Library), the Folger Library, and the Henry E. Huntington Library. I am especially grateful to Roy Ritchie, W.M. Keck Foundation Director of Research, for a National Endowment for the Humanities Fellowship (2004–2005), awarded when this book was just getting off the ground, and to the Huntington Library intellectual community for ongoing encouragement. My heartfelt thanks go to Peter Reill, Director of the UCLA Seventeenth- and Eighteenth-Century Studies Center, for unstinting research assistance and kind support. Rafael Pérez-Torres, Chair of the UCLA English Department, and the Academic Senate provided significant research grants. Portions of chapters were presented at the Henry E. Huntington Library, the David Nichol Smith Seminar (University of Otago, New Zealand), the American Society for Eighteenth-Century Studies (Atlanta and Portland), the National Portrait Gallery (UK), the Royal College of Surgeons (UK), the University of Bamberg (Bavaria); and the Stanford Humanities Center, as well as other venues. I am very appreciative to these audiences for their perceptive responses. Jerome Singerman, Senior Editor at the University of Pennsylvania Press, has been an unfailing source of excellent advice, and I want to thank him for his help at every stage of the publication process.

Versions of several chapters in earlier incarnations have been previously published. These include sections of Chapter 2 as " 'Real, Beautiful Women': Actresses and *The Rival Queens*," *Eighteenth-Century Life* 32, 2 (Spring 2008): 138–58, reprinted by permission of Duke University Press; a portion of Chapter 3 as "Actresses and the Economics of Celebrity, 1700–1800" in *Celebrity and*

British Theatre, 1660–2000, ed. Mary Luckhurst and Jane Moody (London: Palgrave Macmillan, 2005), 148–68; and a section from Chapter 5 in " 'More Than a Woman': Early Eighteenth-Century Memoirs of Actresses" in *New Windows on a Woman's World*, ed. Lisa Marr (Dunedin, N.Z.: University of Otago Press, 2005), 225–42. I am most grateful for permission to include these essays.

Alexandria Currin, Chris Contreras, Tyrell McGlothen, Jennifer Arias, Emily Hart, Meme Chow, and LeNisha Love freed me from responsibilities and allowed me to pursue my work without worry. Most important, my family near and far sustain me—my father, sister, brother, and their families. My mother, who died as this book was being completed, provided an inspiring model as a creative, sharp-minded woman not unlike the actresses in this book, and my daughter Nicole happily follows in her footsteps. She and my son Marc enliven each day and offer welcome distraction from the demands of a scholar's life. This book could not have been written without their support, or without the steadfast encouragement of John Agnew who enriched with wit and wisdom the years during which this book came to fruition.

www.ingramcontent.com/pod-product-compliance
Lightning Source LLC
Chambersburg PA
CBHW030104010526
44116CB00005B/93